DATE DUE

NOV 2 9 2004	

BRODART   Cat. No. 23-221

Treating and Preventing Obesity

Edited by
J. Östman, M. Britton, E. Jonsson

Related Titles

Treating and Preventing Obesity

Edited by
J. Östman, M. Britton, E. Jonsson

WILEY-VCH Verlag GmbH & Co. KGaA

Edited by

Jan Östman, M.D., Ph.D.
Associate Professor, Karolinska Institute
SBU

Mona Britton, M.D., Ph.D.
Professor, Karolinska Institute
SBU

Egon Jonsson, Ph.D.
Professor, Karolinska Institute
WHO Health Evidence Network

SBU – The Swedish Council on Technology
Assessment in Health Care
Box 5650
SE-11486 Stockholm
Sweden

Library of Congress Card No.: applied for
British Library Cataloguing-in-Publication Data
A catalogue record for this book is available
from the British Library.

Bibliographic information published by
Die Deutsche Bibliothek
Die Deutsche Bibliothek lists this publication
in the Deutsche Nationalbibliografie;
detailed bibliographic data is available in the
Internet at http://dnb.ddb.de.

Printed in the Federal Republic of Germany.
Printed on acid-free paper.

Typesetting   Hagedorn Kommunikation,
Viernheim
Printing   betz-druck GmbH, Darmstadt
Bookbinding   Großbuchbinderei J. Schäffer
GmbH & Co. KG, Grünstadt

ISBN   3-527-30818-0

Preface

Evidence-Based Medicine and The Swedish Council on Technology Assessment in Health Care

Like many governments in the early 1980s, the government of Sweden faced an accelerating number of emerging technologies and medical innovations that were being rapidly diffused into the health care system. The related, and alarming, increase in the cost of health care became an urgent concern. This situation led in 1987 to the founding of the Swedish Council on Technology Assessment in Health Care (the official acronym is SBU).

As its name implies, the SBU assesses the technologies and methods used in providing health services. In these assessments, the medical and scientific literature from around the world is systematically evaluated and summarized. Leading experts, mostly from Sweden but also from other countries, are involved in conducting and reviewing the SBU assessment projects.

Striving to keep the needs of the patient – the whole patient – at the center of health care planning, each assessment project investigates not only the medical aspects of a treatment option, but also its economic, social, and ethical aspects.

Assessment projects aim to identify the most effective and, if possible, the most cost-effective interventions. They also aim to identify the technologies already in use that are not adequately supported by scientific evidence. Assessment findings can be used by clinicians, administrators, and policy makers to ensure that the limited resources available to health care are allocated in the most appropriate manner.

A Project Group composed of twelve investigators was selected to assess the wealth of scientific literature on the prevention and treatment of obesity. Eight additional contributors and three manuscript reviewers complemented the work of the Group. The Project Group performed the initial, integrated literature search, with guidance from a specially trained librarian. A checklist for rating quality was developed, based on already available methods.

Based on the completed reviews and guided by comments from several external reviewers, members of the Project Group and SBU staff wrote an Executive Summary. The SBU Board of Directors and the SBU Scientific Advisory Committee approved the Summary and Conclusions.

The scope of the SBU review was extremely comprehensive, covering all clinically relevant controlled trials on the prevention and treatment of obesity.

Treating and Preventing Obesity. Edited by J. Östman, M. Britton, E. Jonsson
Copyright © 2004 WILEY-VCH Verlag GmbH & Co. KgaA, Weinheim
ISBN 3-527-30818-0

Quality Assessment

Many methods for assessing the quality of studies have been described, ranging from a few basic aspects to elaborate scales with weighting of the individual items.

The purpose of quality rating is to identify sources of bias, which could endanger the results of the study. In many cases, aspects of external validity or generalizability are also included in the quality assessment.

The studies included in our review were rated based on study design, the number of subjects included, followup time, and dropout. Conclusions were graded according to a three-level scale reflecting strong scientific evidence, moderate scientific evidence, and limited scientific evidence. Strong evidence was considered to be present when there were at least two high-quality, independent studies supporting the conclusion and nothing pointing in another direction. For limited scientific evidence at least two studies of medium quality were required. With less scientific evidence, no conclusions were drawn. A detailed description of the methodology used in the systematic literature review is presented in Chapter 2.

Jan Östman, Mona Britton, Egon Jonsson, September 2003

Foreword

"No one wants to be obese". This statement appears near the end of the summary of this important report, and catches many features of the problem. It appears in the section on "prejudice" against the obese. The search for remedies from obesity and the anguish it causes underlies the effort of this report. In addition to its relevance to the social issues posed by obesity, the statement "no one wants to be obese" also encompasses the entire range of health care issues that are caused or worsened by obesity. This valuable report provides a timely new analysis of a growing problem.

Assessment of risk, benefit and response to intervention is the heart of decision making related to prevention and treatment of obesity. Obesity poses a challenge to governments and health professionals alike as they confront the rising tide of obesity that now constitutes an epidemic. The publication "Treating and Preventing Obesity – An Evidence Based Review" provides a careful and thoughtful assessment of this disease and the options for its control and treatment. It started with the medical model where cure is the outcome. The authors, eminent Swedish physicians and scientists involved with obesity research, bring their perspective and experience to bear in evaluating the data.

They properly adopt the body mass index, which might be referred to as the Quetelet index after the man who first described it, as the first line for assessing the risk from obesity. They then recommend measurement of central fatness and correlated risks. Next they outline the causes of obesity, including the role of genetic and environmental factors, i. e. high energy intake and decreased physical activity. Health risks of obesity are an important medical reason for concern about obesity, and they are dealt with next, along with the economic impact and detrimental influence of obesity on the quality of life. Before beginning the review of prevention and the types of treatments that are available, they provide us with an assessment of the relative quality of the data and how they rated this data. Following this is a set of conclusions. Although many of these conclusions follow from the earlier discussion there are a few that merit comment.

Although prevention is obviously the heart of the challenge to prevent the onslaught of obesity, the report points out the limited success in this area. Prevention has been difficult for both adults and for children, but there are examples, especially among the young, that have been successful. It is the epidemic in children

Treating and Preventing Obesity. Edited by J. Östman, M. Britton, E. Jonsson
Copyright © 2004 WILEY-VCH Verlag GmbH & Co. KgaA, Weinheim
ISBN 3-527-30818-0

with increased risk for early onset of type 2 diabetes that poses one of the most serious problems associated with the rising prevalence of obesity. New strategies need to be worked out, applied and evaluated.

For those already obese treatment is the only alternative. Evidence for various types of dietary treatment, including very low calorie diets is given a critical discussion. Evidence for the effectiveness of behavior therapy and physical exercise, the other two components of "lifestyle" are also reviewed. Even though there are only two medications approved by most health authorities for treatment of obesity, the evidence supporting use of these medications is reviewed in detail. The book includes a detailed section on surgery and includes the SOS (Swedish Obese Subjects) study that aims at answering the important question of whether or not weight loss will reduce mortality in obese subjects. Evaluation of alternative medicines such as acupuncture, aroma therapy, caffeine, hypnosis, chromium and vinegar are also included in the discussion. Finally, the book reviews the beneficial effects of modest weight loss on obesity-related disorders, presents limited information about the economic impact that might be expected if treatments are successful and addresses ethical aspects.

The conclusions state that one-fifth of those participating with successful results in a commercial program achieve "permanent" weight loss. This implies that obesity can be "cured" by commercial programs. This conclusion does not fit the usual paradigm of obesity. Rather it could be argued that obesity is a chronic relapsing neurochemical disease that is rarely cured. From this perspective, it would be unexpected to have any but a very few individuals maintain long term weight loss with any technique other than surgery. If obesity is not cured, then we should not be surprised over the observation that "weight loss is usually not maintained". In their conclusion the authors say, "Therefore, it is particularly important to develop and assess long-term treatment aimed at permanent weight reduction". For any method except surgery, permanent weight reduction seems out of line with the evidence and contrary to the chronic, relapsing nature of this disease. To conquer the problem posed by obesity, we need to utilize a broader array of preventive strategies. Here we might take a lesson from dental science where fluoride was found to be much more effective in combating dental disease than the usual "tooth brush" strategies. We need to identify the "fluorides" that can act to prevent obesity.

George A. Bray, M. D.
Boyd Professor, Pennington Center
Louisiana State University
Baton Rouge, LA 70808
USA

Contents

Treating and Preventing Obesity. Edited by J. Östman, M. Britton, E. Jonsson
Copyright © 2004 WILEY-VCH Verlag GmbH & Co. KgaA, Weinheim
ISBN 3-527-30818-0

List of Contributors

Editors

Jan Östman
Associate Professor
Center of Metabolism and Endocrinology,
Huddinge University Hospital,
Karolinska Institute
Stockholm, Sweden

Mona Britton
Professor, Internal Medicine,
Senior Medical Adviser
Swedish Council on Technology
Assessment in Health Care
Stockholm

Egon Jonsson
Professor, Karolinska Institute,
Department of Medicine, Stockholm.
Leader of the WHO Health
Evidence Network.
Copenhagen

**Authors, Primary Contributors
(Project Group)**

Nils-Georg Asp
Professor, Industrial Nutritional
Sciences and Food Chemistry
Center for Chemistry, Lund University
Lund

Per Björntorp*
Professor Emeritus, Cardiovascular
Section Gothenburg University
Göteborg

Mona Britton (Project Coordinator)
Professor, Internal Medicine,
Senior Medical Expert
SBU
Stockholm

Per Carlsson
Professor, Health Economics
Linköping University
SBU
Stockholm

Thomas Kjellström (Project Group Chair)
Associate Professor, Internal Medicine
Helsingborg Hospital
Helsingborg

Claude Marcus
Professor, Department of Pediatrics
Huddinge University Hospital
Huddinge

Christina Nerbrand, MD
Director of Research, Development,
and Education
Primary Care
Lund

*Deceased

Treating and Preventing Obesity. Edited by J. Östman, M. Britton, E. Jonsson
Copyright © 2004 WILEY-VCH Verlag GmbH & Co. KgaA, Weinheim
ISBN 3-527-30818-0

Ingmar Näslund, Associate Professor
Department of Surgery
Örebro Medical Center Hospital
Örebro

Ewalotte Ränzlöv (Project Assistant)
SBU
Stockholm

Stephan Rössner
Professor, Obesity Unit
Huddinge University Hospital
Huddinge

Lars Sjöström
Professor, Department of Medicine
Sahlgrenska Hospital
Göteborg

Jan Östman
Associate Professor
SBU
Stockholm

Other Contributors

Alternative Medicine
Daniel Richter, MD
Xianrong Zeng, MD (China)

Health Economics
Martin Henriksson
Health Economist
Center for Assessment
of Medical Technology
Linköping

Ethics
Sven Ove Hansson
Professor (Philosophy)
Royal Institute of Technology
Stockholm

Quality of Life
Marianne Sullivan
Professor (Care Research)
Sahlgrenska Hospital
Göteborg

Jan Karlsson
Psychologist (Care Research)
Sahlgrenska Hospital
Göteborg

Primary Care
Rolf Wahlström, MD
Institute for Public Health,
Karolinska Institute
Stockholm

Manuscript Review

Göran Berglund
Professor, Department of Medicine,
University Hospital
Malmö

Staffan Lindeberg, MD
District GP
Sjöbo

Birgitta Strandvik
Professor, Department of Maternal
and Child Health
HM Queen Sylvia Hospital
Göteborg

English Translation

Ron Gustafson
SBU Publisher Liaison
Hörby

Treating and Preventing Obesity
A Systematic Review of the Evidence

Summary

Background

In recent decades, the percentage of people with obesity has increased markedly in many countries. This trend is observed in most European countries, North America, and several South American and Asian countries.

The prevalence of obesity varies by country. In the United States, for example, the total percentage of the population with obesity is somewhat over 20%. The rates in England, Germany, and Poland exceed 15%, and the rates in Sweden are 8% for adults and approximately 4% for children and adolescents.

Definition of Obesity

The cutoff points for overweight and obesity are presented in the "Facts" box (p. 2). The definition of obesity most often used in a research context is based on body mass index (BMI), obesity being defined as BMI 30 or more. The measure is based on the combination of height and body weight. In general, men have a higher BMI than women, and in Western nations BMI increases with increasing age in both males and females.

The BMI measure has some deficiencies, particularly as regards obesity in children. It underestimates the degree of overweight in short children and overestimates overweight in tall children. Furthermore, BMI does not consider the relative percentage of fat and muscle; nor does it reflect the distribution of fat in the body. Clearly, this is a weakness, particularly since research in recent years has shown that the risks from obesity-related diseases are substantially higher when there is a high accumulation of abdominal adipose tissue, especially visceral (intraabdominal) adipose tissue. Waist circumference is a simple and informative measure that reflects total abdominal fat. Another common method is to determine waist circumference in relation to hip circumference, i. e., the waist-to-hip ratio. Both methods are beginning to appear in clinical practice. The measures used most often in the studies reviewed in this report are BMI, weight reduction in kilograms, and weight reduction as a percent of original weight.

Treating and Preventing Obesity. Edited by J. Östman, M. Britton, E. Jonsson
Copyright © 2004 WILEY-VCH Verlag GmbH & Co. KGaA, Weinheim
ISBN 3-527-30818-0

Facts   Defining Obesity
BMI (Body Mass Index) = body weight in kilograms divided by height in meters squared.
For example:

$$\frac{90\ kg}{1.70\ m \times 1.70\ m} = 31\ kg/m^2 = BMI = 31$$

Overweight = BMI 25–29.9
Obesity = BMI $\geq$ 30

At the following heights, the lowest weights for obesity are:
160 cm $\rightarrow$ 77 kg
170 cm $\rightarrow$ 87 kg
180 cm $\rightarrow$ 97 kg

Age-adjusted BMI limits are used in children. For example, for a 10-year-old girl the BMI cutoff points would be 20 for overweight and 24 for obesity.

The report defines obesity as BMI 30 or higher. Severe obesity is defined here as BMI 35 or higher.

The definition of obesity is based on studies of risks of getting different obesity-related diseases. The risks of serious complications increase markedly at a BMI around 30. There are arguments for and against considering obesity as a disease, and this is debated in scientific journals. The project group that worked on the SBU report defines obesity as a disease. However, obesity can exist even without serious complications or disabling conditions. A risk factor does not necessarily lead to disease in any individual case. The SBU Board of Directors, responsible for the introductory summary, has elected to regard obesity as a risk factor and not a disease. This, however, is not intended to tone down the threat that obesity presents to public health.

Causes of Obesity

Research in this field suggests that many different factors, e. g., genetic, social, behavioral, and cultural, are involved in the development of obesity and that these factors influence each other in different ways.

Obesity can develop through a combination of genetic, lifestyle, and environmental factors. The strong role played by genetic factors in this context has been demonstrated in studies of twins and adopted children. Regardless of whether monozygotic twins grow up in the same home or in different environments, as adults their body weights and fat deposits are similar. Adopted children develop obesity in the same way as their biological parents rather than their adoptive parents. The genes that regulate this are basically unknown. Various genetic conditions can, however, help to explain why some individuals become obese, while others who live under the same conditions do not.

The increase in the prevalence of obesity in recent decades cannot, however, be fully explained by genetic factors, but can be attributed to changes in lifestyle, dietary habits, and physical activity. The risk of becoming obese is greater in societies where there is ample, 24-hour access to fat- and energy-rich foods and where the demand for physical activity is low.

Social factors can also influence the development of obesity. Obesity is substantially more common among children and adults who live under disadvantaged socioeconomic conditions.

evirmentent

Health Risks of Obesity

Being slightly overweight does not necessarily cause health problems. Obesity, at least before the age of 64 years, clearly increases the risk of disease and premature death. The risk increases with increasing levels of obesity, particularly abdominal obesity. The most common obesity-related complications are type 2 diabetes, high blood pressure, myocardial infarction, gallstones, sleep apnea, joint problems, some cancers, and infertility.

Impact on Quality of Life

Obesity, particularly severe obesity, often has a negative impact on quality of life in both a physical and psychological context. Studies of people with obesity have shown that the health-related quality of life can be very low.

The general stigma associated with obesity, which can lead to negative and prejudicial attitudes toward obese people, often results in major personal suffering and a burden of guilt. No one wants to be obese. The condition is largely genetically driven and triggered by a combination of social, cultural, and community factors, which the individual, particularly at a young age, finds difficult to combat.

Economic Aspects

A comprehensive review of international studies addressing the costs of obesity and related complications suggests that the direct healthcare costs may be approximately 2 % of the total expenditure for health and medical services. In addition, there are the indirect costs due to absence from work and early retirement, which are at least as high as the direct healthcare costs.

Report Design and Content

This report reviews the scientific evidence concerning mainly the medical interventions against obesity. The report presents the results found in studies of various strategies for preventing and treating obesity. The evidence presented in the report was obtained through a systematic review of the international scientific literature on the subject. The introductory chapter on the background of obesity as a health problem and the chapter on ethics, however, are not based on a systematic literature review but on a synthesis of other reviews and studies, information from textbooks, questionnaires, and statistical data.

By searching various databases of scientific literature published from 1966 to 2002, the project group identified 2600 publications that addressed some aspect of interventions against obesity. The systematic review process found that most of these publications were either irrelevant or did not meet the standards established for definition, scientific rigor, and reliability. Some studies used definitions of obesity other than BMI $\geq$ 30. Nevertheless, these were included in cases where it was obvious that many of the study subjects would meet the BMI criteria used to define obesity in the report.

Ultimately, around 300 studies were used to form the conclusions of the report. However, not all are equal in scientific quality. The conclusions were graded (i.e., given as Evidence Grade of 1, 2, or 3) based on the quality presented by the study, i.e., depending on study design, the number of subjects included, followup time, and dropout.

The evidence grades are defined as follows:

Evidence Grade 1: Strong scientific evidence. When at least two studies present high quality.

Evidence Grade 2: Moderate scientific evidence. When one study presents high quality and at least two studies present medium quality.

Evidence Grade 3: Limited scientific evidence. When at least two studies present medium quality.

Preventive Interventions against Obesity

Studies that have investigated the possible methods of influencing body weight in a population have included relatively limited interventions. Often, the studies have been part of a campaign to reduce high blood pressure, smoking, blood cholesterol levels, and other cardiovascular risk factors. The programs are based on information concerning the importance of suitable diets and increased exercise and other health information directed at a particular group or region. Concurrently, changes in the variables are measured and assessed in a control group or a reference area that did not receive the information. Often, mass media are used for campaigns, and newsletters are used for reminders. In some instances, the programs involve professional organizations, voluntary associations, and workplaces. Those recruited for the intervention groups and the control groups are usually examined at the outset of the study and later at specific followup intervals for several years.

Studies on the effects of preventive interventions on children and adolescents are often designed to involve certain schools in providing education, advice, and encouragement toward good dietary habits and physical exercise, while other schools are used as control groups.

Preventing Obesity in Adults

Twelve studies met the quality standards outlined in the report. In these studies, the goal was to prevent cardiovascular diseases. Limited attention was given to counteracting the incidence of obesity. The evidence presented in five studies is of low quality, mainly because the observation periods were too short or participation in the intervention program was low. Five of the studies presented medium quality, and only two of the studies presented high quality. A study from Sweden (Norsjö) did not report any favorable effects on the onset of obesity. Similar results were found in five large North American studies. Two of these studies, however, showed that the weight increase that usually occurs in many populations was somewhat less pronounced in cities with the intervention program in contrast to the control cities. In a region in Israel, an ambitious prevention program resulted in a lower prevalence of overweight.

Favorable effects on the prevalence of obesity have not been observed in most population-based prevention programs that have been scientifically assessed.

Preventing Obesity in Children and Adolescents

Fourteen controlled studies were found on this topic. Eight of these provided high or medium quality, and all involved school children aged 5 years or older. Most included programs to promote physical exercise and good dietary habits. Some of the studies also included elements targeted directly at parents. The effects were studied in followup after 2–5 years.

Only two of the studies used the most relevant way to measure outcome, i.e., the percentage of children with overweight and obesity. One of these studies found no difference between the trial group and the control group. In the other study, a reduction was achieved in the percentage of overweight girls, but no change was reported among boys in the trial groups. The other studies monitored the mean BMI. This declined in two of the studies, but was not influenced in the other four studies. These conclusions were based on moderate-grade evidence. Overall, a positive result was achieved in three studies, but no effects were reported in five of the eight best studies concerning preventive interventions in children and adolescents. Hence, reliable conclusions cannot be drawn. Several studies noted improved blood lipid levels and reduced blood pressure in the trial groups.

In summary, most of the studies on preventive interventions against obesity have not reported any favorable effects. However, there are examples of programs in both adults and children where up to several kilograms in mean weight reduction has been achieved in the trial areas. Apparently, moderate success in influencing the mean weight in a population can have a major effect on the prevalence of obesity. Therefore, it is particularly important to use well-executed studies to design and assess new strategies adapted to the population, e. g., through better intervention for establishing good dietary habits in pre-school and school-aged children and by increasing the interest in physical activity in children and adults. Interventions at the national level (e. g., tax and price policies) also need to be tested as a means to reduce the incidence of obesity.

Treating Obesity

The fundamental element in all treatment for obesity in both children and adults is changing to a diet with less energy content, essentially by limiting the fat intake. Dietary counseling is often combined with recommendations to exercise regularly to increase energy expenditure. Drugs can be considered as complementary treatment in adults. Treatment using special protein formulas results in a much greater reduction in energy intake and thereby more pronounced weight reduction in the short term than that achieved by other methods.

Weight reduction achieved in this way can have an important impact on an individual's quality of life, morbidity, and future risks. The problem, however, is that obesity often returns. Studies show that most people have regained their original weight after 5 years. However, in some groups of obese patients, favorable results have been maintained for several years, particularly if the initial weight reduction was substantial.

To be successful, obesity treatment requires a long-term commitment, and patients must be highly motivated and involved. It is a matter of treating a chronic condition that threatens health, and is not about making cosmetic changes. However, no special measures are needed if the risk is insignificantly higher, such as in people over age 65 years. Earlier treatment strategies have assumed that short-term interventions could have permanent effects. A real problem, however, is to maintain the weight loss which has been achieved during shorter periods of time, often through different methods and a great deal of effort. It is uncertain whether long-term treatment and followup yield better and more permanent results than the methods that have been studied up to now. It is essential to apply and assess different types of long-term treatment.

Gastric surgery is a treatment alternative that can be considered in cases of severe obesity, since substantial and permanent weight loss has been achieved in this patient group.

Treating Obesity in Adults

Dietary treatment

Dietary treatment involves counseling on the amounts and proportions of foods eaten, energy restrictions, limiting fat content with or without energy restrictions, or vegetarian diets. Dietary treatment can also focus on meals and their timing or on replacing meals with formula products.

Twenty-five studies that met the established criteria showed that weight reductions of between 3 and 10 kg can be achieved through energy-reduced diets for a 1-year period (Evidence Grade 1). Dietary counseling can be provided to individuals or groups by dieticians or other dietary experts. Replacement of one or more main meals with special products, such as milk or soy-based drinks like those used in

VLCD (Very Low Calorie Diets) or "bars" with high nutrient content, can enhance weight reduction (Evidence Grade 2). The few studies that followed weight trends for a longer period, up to 5 years, reported a return to the original weight in most cases (Evidence Grade 2).

Unlimited carbohydrate-rich diets (i. e., at least 50–55 % of the energy from carbohydrates and a maximum of 30 % of energy from fat, corresponding to 60–75 g fat intake per day) can yield several kilograms weight reduction in 6 months. More pronounced energy restrictions, where fat intake is usually limited to 20–30 g/day, yields more rapid weight reduction, but is more difficult to tolerate for longer periods. Abundant amounts of fruit and vegetables contribute to low fat content and low energy density. A protein-rich diet, with more fish, lean meat, and low-fat milk products, appears to promote weight reduction, probably mainly due to increased satiety. Studies offer no support for the idea that lactovegetarian diets lead to better weight reduction than mixed diets of the same energy content.

Dietary fiber is a constituent element in the diet. Three studies, two providing low and one providing medium quality, assess the effects of special dietary fiber supplements. The difference between the treatment and control groups was, at most, a few kilograms over 6 to 12 months, but the conclusions are uncertain. There are no studies of long-term effects. General dietary advice encourages a high fiber intake because of other health-promoting effects, which also applies to weight reduction.

Very Low Calorie Diets

Low energy diets, Very Low Calorie Diets (VLCDs), are protein-rich formulas manufactured mainly from milk or soy. Dietary recommendations are met by adding essential fatty acids, minerals, and vitamins. A VLCD can be used for several weeks as the only source of energy, or to replace some meals. Common treatment periods using VLCDs are 12 weeks or, in some cases, up to 16 weeks.

Eight randomized studies have been identified. Initially, substantial weight reduction is achieved, often 15–20 kg, which is more than with conventional energy-reduced diets. There is a strong tendency to return to the original weight after the treatment, however. Studies for 1–2 years, where a VLCD has been used intermittently for shorter periods, reported a maintained weight reduction of a few kilograms more than that achieved with conventional dietary treatment (Evidence Grade 3).

Starvation was used during the 1960s and 1970s as a treatment for severe obesity. The method involves one or more weeks of total fasting, except for liquids, minerals, and vitamins. The scientific evidence for starvation treatment is weak, and this method is no longer used, mainly because muscle mass also declines sharply during starvation.

Behavior therapy

Behavior therapy is used as a component of various types of treatment, but it is difficult to isolate its effects. The effects of different types of behavior therapy have been analyzed in four randomized controlled studies. In one study (high quality), various behavior therapies in combination with different forms of dietary counseling/treatment led to weight loss that was moderate but significantly greater than in the control group. In two other studies (medium quality), no significant differences were found between weight loss after 1–2 years and equivalent weight loss in the control groups. Firm conclusions, however, cannot be drawn.

Physical exercise

In the studies reviewed, increased physical activity consisted mainly of walking and, to some extent, jogging in younger individuals. Four studies, two of which provide high quality, highlight the effects of physical exercise as a supplement to traditional dietary treatment. A much greater weight reduction, on average about 4 kg within 1 year, could be achieved in exercise programs compared to that achieved in the control group (Evidence Grade 1).

Increased physical activity as the only intervention against obesity is substantially less effective than normal dietary treatment (Evidence Grade 3).

It cannot be confirmed whether regular physical exercise can counteract the weight increase that usually occurs within 1 to 2 years after successful weight loss.

Pharmacotherapy

Two drugs used in weight reduction therapy are orlistat (Xenical©) and sibutramine (Reductil©). This report reviews nine drug studies. Six of the studies address orlistat treatment and include approximately 2500 patients on active therapy. They are based on medium quality as regards the effects after 1 year of treatment. Two of the four studies, which report results after 2 years, provide low quality due to high dropout. On average, weight reduction after 1 year was 8 kg (6–10 kg) after treatment with orlistat and 5 kg (4–6 kg) in groups treated with placebo – on average 3 kg more with pharmacological treatment after 1 year (Evidence Grade 2).

Three studies of sibutramine (approximately 1400 actively treated) all provide medium quality. After approximately 1 year, two studies with sibutramine show approximately 4 kg greater weight reduction than that in the placebo groups. In the largest study, weight reduction after 2 years was more than 5 kg greater than that in the control group (Evidence Grade 2).

The side effects associated with orlistat are linked to the active mechanisms of the drug. Diarrhea after intake of too much fat is an expression of deficient compliance with dietary advice. Sibutramine lowers blood pressure less than what would be expected from the weight reduction. Other side effects include sleep disorders, mouth dryness, and constipation.

Both orlistat and sibutramine treatment show a weight reduction of 2–5 kg more than that in the control group in treatment up to 2 years. Both drugs yield a weight reduction of at least 10 % in one fourth to one fifth of the patients who started treatment, compared to half as many in the placebo group. None of the published drug studies report a treatment time exceeding 2 years. The effects on obesity-related morbidity and mortality are unknown.

Surgery

Surgical treatment may be appropriate for severely obese individuals, but only after other treatment attempts have failed. BMI >40 is generally accepted as a cutoff point for surgery. In special cases, surgery can be appropriate even at a somewhat lower degree of obesity. Seventeen randomized studies and numerous long-term effects (at least 5 years) were assessed. Fifteen nonrandomized, comparative studies contribute to the conclusions, as do certain findings from an ongoing nonrandomized, but controlled, matched study, i.e., the SOS (Swedish Obese Subjects) study. The SOS study compares 2000 individuals treated by surgery with an equally large control group given routine treatment in primary care.

Over ten different surgical methods are available for treating obesity, and there are several variants of these methods. Of the surgical methods studied, gastric bypass has the strongest scientific documentation and the best effect on weight reduction (Evidence Grade 1).

Surgical treatment of individuals with severe obesity yields greater weight reduction than the nonsurgical methods that have been assessed in this patient group. Up to 5 years following surgery, weight reduction is 50% to 75% of the excess weight prior to surgery, which means 30–40 kg in individuals weighing 125 kg and with a height of 170 cm (Evidence Grade 1). A 10-year followup of the SOS study showed that the retained weight loss was, on average, 16% of the original weight. This corresponds to an average of 20 kg in permanent weight loss 10 years after surgical treatment. No weight loss was reported in the control groups.

Weight loss has a positive effect on health-related quality of life (Evidence Grade 2). With major weight loss following surgery, the number of new diabetes cases falls dramatically, and blood glucose levels are almost completely normalized in individuals with severe obesity and type 2 diabetes (Evidence Grade 1). It is not known whether weight reduction from surgery for severe obesity leads to reduced mortality or less morbidity from myocardial infarction and stroke. In any case, compared to the control groups, surgical treatment for obesity does not increase total mortality over a period of 8 to 10 years. Swedish data suggest that mortality associated with surgery is below 0.5%, and complications during the first episode of care appear in up to 15% of cases. In approximately 2% of new surgery cases, the complications are severe enough to require acute reoperation.

In people with severe obesity, surgical treatment has positive, well-documented long-term effects on weight, quality of life, and morbidity from diabetes.

Alternative medicine

A relatively large number of methods and agents for the treatment of obesity are available outside of the ordinary healthcare system. Examples include acupuncture, aromatherapy, caffeine, hypnosis, chromium, and vinegar.

More than 500 articles on alternative treatment methods were identified. A thorough review was conducted of the 80 (approx.) articles that are based on studies and describe over 20 treatment alternatives. Eleven of the studies met the minimum criteria for scientific documentation. They included acupuncture, hypnosis, aromatherapy, and chromium-enhanced dietary supplements. The overall judgement was that evidence is lacking on the effects of using alternative methods to treat obesity.

Treating Obesity in Children and Adolescents

Twenty studies on treatment with diet, exercise, and behavior modification were found that met the minimum criteria. Three studies compared the treatment groups to control groups that received no treatment.

The treatment groups reported a weight loss of approximately 10%, while the control groups varied in weight between ± 3% for the first study year (Evidence Grade 3). Five studies examined long-term followup 3 to 10 years after treatment. Some of these studies found some, albeit weak, retained weight loss, while this could not be observed in other studies. The evidence is insufficient to draw conclusions.

In extremely overweight adolescents, surgery has shown positive treatment results, but the deficiency of adequate studies makes it impossible to draw reliable conclusions. VLCD treatment can also be applied in children and adolescents, but the value of this treatment for longer than a few months cannot be assessed. Rapid weight loss can influence height growth, at least in a 1-year perspective. Studies have reported elevated self-esteem following successful treatment and lowered self-esteem following treatment failure.

Quality of Life

Probably the most important reason why obese individuals attempt to lose weight is the negative impact of obesity on the quality of life. This refers to how people feel and function in daily life and the effects that weight-loss treatment can have. Quality of life measurements can provide information on this issue, and we found 27 studies on the topic in the scientific literature.

Clearly, obese individuals perceive themselves to have a lower quality of life than that of the population on average, e. g., as regards physical function, general health status, and vitality (Evidence Grade 1). This association is stronger than that found with other concurrent morbidity, and increases as obesity becomes more pronounced and if the individual seeks health care (Evidence Grade 2). In many cases, quality of life is lower in those with severe obesity than in patients with other severe, chronic diseases (Evidence Grade 3).

Quality of life improves with weight loss. The greater the weight loss, the better is the quality of life (Evidence Grade 2). Substantial improvements have been measured in individuals with severe obesity who received surgery and maintained a substantial, long-term weight loss (Evidence Grade 2). Uncertain short-term effects on quality of life for less than 1 year are reported, but the evidence is insufficient to draw conclusions.

Effect of Weight Loss on Obesity-related Diseases and Conditions

Weight loss of 5–10 kg in obese or overweight individuals who also have type 2 diabetes results in improved blood glucose control, usually for 6 months to a maximum of 12 months (Evidence Grade 3). Thereafter, the effects are modest, which is partly attributed to the failure to maintain weight loss, but also to the natural course of diabetes. With the substantial and permanent weight reduction that can be achieved by surgery in individuals with severe obesity, a large percentage of patients have a normal blood glucose level and can discontinue taking medication (Evidence Grade 2).

Using a simple method (glucose tolerance test), it is possible to identify the obese individuals who are particularly at risk of developing type 2 diabetes. Two well-executed studies have shown that moderate weight reduction in combination with physical exercise for 2–3 years can reduce by half the onset of type 2 diabetes (Evidence Grade 1).

In overweight or obese individuals with moderately elevated blood pressure, a weight loss of approximately 5 % is sufficient to achieve a blood pressure reduction for approximately 6 months (Evidence Grade 2). Routine treatment with antihypertensive drugs is, however, more effective during this period and up to one year. Despite permanent weight loss after surgery, there is no difference in blood pressure compared to untreated controls in long-term followup.

Effects on blood lipids are related to the extent of weight reduction. When accompanied by weight loss that can be maintained for more than one year, dietary treatment results in some increase in "good" HDL cholesterol, which helps to diminish the risk of atherosclerosis (Evidence Grade 3). A weight loss of 20–30 kg is required to reduce the blood level of cholesterol (Evidence Grade 2).

A reduction in sleep apnea has been reported following surgery for obesity. This effect has not been reported in studies of non-surgical treatment methods.

Some studies suggest that weight reduction is an effective treatment method for normalizing sex hormones, increasing fertility, and improving pregnancy outcomes in women with obesity and menstrual disorders. However, available studies do not permit reliable conclusions to be drawn.

Cost Effectiveness of Different Treatment Methods

Twelve assessment studies were reviewed. Five studies address dietary treatment, behavior therapy, and VLCD. One of these shows that dietary counseling with a dietician alone or dietician and physician resulted in weight loss at a low cost. The results apply after 1 year of followup. Another study shows that behavior therapy can reduce weight at a low cost. The cost for VLCD, or a combination of behavior therapy and VLCD, appears to be somewhat higher.

Several health economic model analyses show that surgical treatment leads to weight reduction at a relatively low cost. Three studies (Sweden) reported that the total cost of surgery and followup during a 4- to 6-year period after surgery was approximately 7000 USD higher than that in the control group where no weight loss was reported. Related to the percentage of weight loss in the SOS study (16 % after 6 years), the costs exceed 400 USD (1994 monetary value) per percent of weight reduction. No further conclusions can be drawn concerning the cost effectiveness of surgical treatment for obesity.

As regards pharmacotherapy, a health economic assessment has been published on the use of orlistat in treating obesity. This study considered improved life quality from weight reduction. The overall benefit experienced by patients from improved quality of life after 2 years of followup was converted to the number of years of full health, i. e., quality-adjusted life-years. The results show that the direct costs slightly exceed 60 000 USD per quality-adjusted life-year. This would suggest that pharmacological treatment with orlistat has relatively low cost effectiveness. However, because of the weak scientific documentation it is difficult to draw reliable conclusions.

Conclusions by SBU

The incidence and complications of obesity are increasing rapidly.

The number of obese individuals (both adults and children) has increased rapidly during the past 20 years. Obesity – particularly that localized to the abdomen – increases the risk of many serious diseases, e. g., diabetes, cardiovascular diseases, and joint diseases. The association between obesity and some cancers is strong. Obesity – particularly severe obesity – also has a strong negative impact on the quality of life.

The causes of obesity are not fully understood.

The development of obesity depends largely on genetic factors. The inherited predisposition for obesity is widespread in the population.

In genetically predisposed individuals, factors related to lifestyle (diet and exercise) and social, behavioral, cultural, and community factors determine whether or not obesity develops.

It is difficult to prevent obesity.

Most population-based prevention programs that have been scientifically assessed have not shown any favorable effects on the prevalence of obesity. However, examples exist of programs for both adults and children that have been successful, at least in the short term. New strategies to disseminate knowledge about the causes and risks of obesity and to change dietary habits and motivate people to increase physical activity need to be developed and assessed. Concurrently, there is a need for policy interventions at the societal level to reduce the prevalence of obesity.

Scientific assessment of treatment methods for obesity shows that:

- changing dietary habits through successful dietary counseling (mainly reducing energy and fat intake) can lead to weight loss, as a rule 3 kg to 10 kg during the first year (or 10 % of body weight in children). The long-term effects are uncertain.
- regular exercise contributes to weight reduction.
- behavior therapy in conjunction with changes in diet and exercise can yield further effects on weight if the supportive interventions are continued for a longer period.
- approximately one fifth of those treated according to Weight-Watcher methods achieve a permanent weight loss of 10 % or more of their starting weight.
- VLCD for 6–12 weeks yields a greater weight loss than a conventional low energy diet. In studies of VLCD for 1–2 years, where treatment often has been periodic, researchers have noted a maintained weight loss of a few kilograms more than in treatment with a balanced diet alone (VLCD = Very Low Calorie Diets, i. e., protein-rich formula).
- pharmacological treatment with orlistat (Xenical$^©$) or sibutramine (Reductil$^©$) yields an average 2–5 kg weight loss beyond that achieved with diet and exercise counseling alone after 1 year. In clinical trials, one fourth to one fifth of those who started pharmacological treatment lost at least 10 % weight compared to half as many in the group treated with placebo.
- the major problem is that weight loss is usually not maintained. Within a few years, most of those who initially succeeded in losing weight had returned to their original weight. Therefore, it is particularly important to develop and assess long-term treatment aimed at permanent weight reduction.
- treatment with gastric surgery, which can be appropriate for patients with severe obesity, lowers weight on average by more than 25 % (e. g., from 125 kg to 90 kg) up to 5 years after surgery. After 10 years, the retained weight loss is approximately 16 %, or on average somewhat over 20 kg. This represents substantial gains in health and quality of life in these patients. However, surgical intervention carries some risk of complications.
- the scientific evidence for a wide range of alternative medicine methods is too weak to draw any reliable conclusions about the possible effects that these methods may have on obesity.

Risks related to obesity can be reduced.

The risks related to obesity can be reduced through weight reduction, regardless of the methods used. Intervening against other risk factors – even if weight reduction is not successful – can reduce the risks associated with obesity. Examples of such interventions include increased physical activity, smoking cessation, and improved control of diabetes, high blood pressure, and elevated blood lipids.

Information about cost effectiveness is limited.

The costs to society of obesity and the diseases associated with obesity are high. Information about the cost effectiveness of different methods is, however, limited. The cost effectiveness of preventive methods cannot be calculated because of uncertainty concerning their effects. In treating obesity, the costs are relatively low for weight loss achieved through dietary counseling, behavior therapy, dietary replacement formulas with low-energy content, and surgical treatment, but considerably higher for pharmacological treatment. Studies have not calculated cost effectiveness based on the observed reduction in morbidity or mortality or improvements in quality of life.

Prejudice against obesity must be counteracted.

Those affected by obesity should not be treated with negative or prejudicial attitudes – many people are at risk of obesity, but no one wants to be obese. The lower quality of life that people with obesity experience is somewhat related to the attitudes of society. Increased understanding of the reasons for obesity and difficulties in treating it may help to reduce the prejudice against people with obesity that is found both in health services and in society at large.

1
Background

1.1
Obesity as a Health Problem in Adults

1.1.1
What is Obesity?

The body of a middle-aged male normally contains 10–15 kg of fat mass. Since women at corresponding ages have a greater number of fat cells than men, their fat mass is normally about 50 % higher. When fat mass substantially exceeds normal levels, this condition can lead to a range of different health disorders. Common problems include elevated risk of cardiovascular diseases, diabetes, and some types of cancer, and a greater risk of premature death than that for individuals with a normal body weight.

Methods have been developed to directly measure the amount of fat in the body, but these are complicated and available only at special laboratories. Several indirect methods, based on the relationship between weight and height, have been used in clinical and epidemiological studies. The method which best reflects the amount of body fat is the body mass index (BMI), where weight (in kilograms) is divided by height (meters) squared.

An individual who weighs 90 kg and is 170 cm tall has a body mass index of:

$$\frac{90 \text{ kg}}{1.70 \text{ m} \times 1.70 \text{ m}} = 31 \text{ kg/m}^2 = \text{BMI} = 31$$

A serious deficiency with the BMI method is that it does not distinguish between fat mass and muscle mass.

The generally accepted definitions of overweight and obesity have been developed by the World Health Organization, WHO (Facts 1) [4]. Classification is based on the association between BMI and mortality as demonstrated in large North American studies. However, the cutoff points assigned by WHO for normal weight, overweight, and obesity are somewhat arbitrary. They are the same for men and women even though men have a generally higher BMI than

Treating and Preventing Obesity. Edited by J. Östman, M. Britton, E. Jonsson
Copyright © 2004 WILEY-VCH Verlag GmbH & Co. KGaA, Weinheim
ISBN 3-527-30818-0

Facts 1   WHO Definitions of Obesity [4].

	BMI (Body Mass Index) (kg/m²)
Normal weight	18.5 – 24.9
Overweight	25 – 29.9
Obesity, Grade I	30 – 34.9
Obesity, Grade II	35 – 39.9
Obesity, Grade III	40 –

Facts 2   Upper limits for waist-hip ratio and waist circumference.

Upper limits	Male	Female
Waist-hip ratio (WHR):	>1.0	>0.85
Waist circumference (increased risk):	94 cm	80 cm
Waist circumference (greatly increased risk)	102 cm	88 cm

Facts 3   Measurement of obesity.

Method	Measure
Body Mass Index (BMI)	Degree of overweight/obesity – measures body fat and muscle mass
Waist-hip ratio (WHR)	Abdominal fat in relation to body size
Sagittal abdominal diameter	Fat in the abdomen
Waist measurement	Fat in and around the abdomen

Facts 4   Methods to determine abdominal circumference, hip circumference, and sagittal abdominal diameter.

Abdominal circumference is measured after fasting from the previous evening, with the patient standing and breathing normally. The measurement is performed horizontally from the center of the lower costal arch and iliac crest.

The hip circumference is measured over the broadest portion of the buttocks. It is a simple measurement to perform and can be conducted with suitable accuracy by patients themselves after careful instruction.

Sagittal abdominal diameter is measured with the patient in a supine position. It measures the distance between the back and the highest point of abdomen.

women, particularly at ages 35–59 years. As age increases – starting from age 30 years – the mean BMI in the population increases approximately 2–4 units per year.

Recent research has shown that the risk of complications is related not only to BMI but also to the distribution of fat mass in the body [4, 8]. When an increased percentage of body fat is situated in the torso, and mainly in fat depots in the abdomen, the risk of acquiring cardiovascular disease and type 2 diabetes is substantially higher. Excess abdominal fat constitutes a risk factor for myocardial infarction – similar to elevated cholesterol values or elevated blood pressure [3]. The extent of abdominal fat can be accurately determined by magnetic resonance imaging (MRI), but it can also be estimated in several other ways (Facts 2–4) [26, 35]. A common method, used mainly in a research context, is to determine waist circumference in relation to hip circumference, so called waist-hip ratio. Normal values for this ratio have been developed based on population studies from Sweden. Waist circumference alone provides a simple measure of the total abdominal fat mass, both around and within the abdomen. The change in waist circumference, more so than BMI, shows how the amount of abdominal fat varies over time, and has a stronger association with the onset of, e. g., type 2 diabetes [22, 35, 64]. In assessing the risk of obesity, waist measurement or the waist-hip ratio should be used to complement BMI, particularly within the BMI interval of 25–30.

1.1.2
Prevalence of Obesity in Different Population Groups

The prevalence of obesity varies markedly among nations, as reported by a large WHO project (the MONICA project). In this project, different nations report information on, e. g., BMI among individuals aged 35 through 64 years. The information is limited, however, to a sample of people living in a city or a region reported to be representative of the population in the respective nations (Table 1.1) [2, 4, 42, 43]. In this study, obesity (BMI > 30) was found in approximately 10 % of the middle-aged population in Denmark and Sweden, while in Norway the percentage among men was somewhat lower and the percentage among women was somewhat higher [42]. In Finland, prevalence was higher, mainly among women in North Karelia County. The highest prevalence of obesity was reported from the former Soviet republics and Poland, where prevalence was 30–40 % in men. In the United States, the prevalence of obesity was 20 % among men and 25 % among women during the early and mid 1990s [4]. Prevalence among Mexican-Americans and blacks was higher, 40–50 % [4]. Among some Indian tribes in the United States, obesity was prevalent in nearly the entire population, and similar findings have been reported from some islands in the Pacific Ocean.

The prevalence of obesity has been increasing in many countries, e. g., in Norway, Sweden, England, the United States, and the former East German Republic (Table 1.2). In Sweden, for example, the prevalence of obesity has increased in recent decades from 5.2–7.8 % among women and from 4.9–7.9 % among men (Figure 1.1) [5]. Prevalence has also increased in some Asian countries. In China and

Table 1.1 Prevalence of obesity (BMI ≥ 30) in individuals aged 35–64 years in some of the countries participating in the WHO MONICA project [4, 43].

Country	Region and city	Population size	Number of participants	% participating from no. recruited	Time frame (year, month)	Men %	Women %
Sweden	North Sweden	187 700	1501	84	8601–8604	11	11
	Göteborg	153 400	1461	75	8502–8611	9	10
Denmark	Glostrup	132 000	3563	79	8211–8402	11	8
Finland	North Karelia	59 800	3085	80	8201–8204	19	21
	Kuopio	87 900	2397	85	8201–8204	16	20
	Åbo	74 200	3019	85	8201–8204	16	19
Norway	Nord-Tröndelag	127 000	52 437**	–	8401–8512	8	13
Germany	Rhein-Neckar	235 900	2865	86	8309–8707	18	26
	Augsburg (city)	95 300	1866	75	8410–8505	15	15
	Augsburg (region)	109 500	2118	80	8410–8505	18	21
Scotland	Glasgow	135 100	1536	64	8602–8610	11	16*
Northern Ireland	Belfast	157 300	2649	70	8310–8409	11	14*
Poland	Warsaw	180 100	3600	74	8312–8501	17	26*
Russia and Baltic States	Kaunas	138 200	2086	67	8301–8503	21	44*
	Moscow (intervention)	227 600	3548	78	8402–8610	13	34*
	Moscow (control)	88 300	1825	73	8402–8602	12	33*
Hungary	Budapest	94 000	1472	80	8207–8306	15	18*

* Estimated from figure (WHO) [4]
** Estimated for group aged 30–69 years [42]

Percentage (%) of individuals with BMI above 29.9

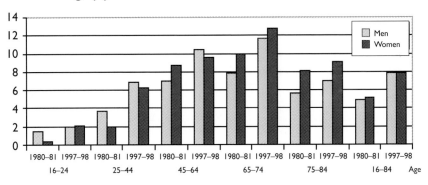

Percentage (%) of individuals with BMI 25.0–29.9

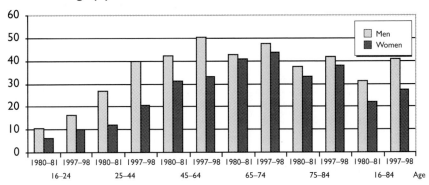

Figure 1.1 Obesity trends (example Sweden). The data on height and weight are self-reported via personal interviews. The net sample in the 1998 study was approximately 7000 individuals aged 16–84 years, and the number of interviews was approximately 5700, i.e., dropout was approximately 23 % [5].

Japan, obesity is uncommon – approximately 1–2 % of the population aged 20 to 45 years [4].

Several countries, including Canada and the United States, have developed guidelines for treating obesity. Action programs from Australia, France, New Zealand, and Norway focus mainly on preventive interventions. The focus in Finland is on improving physical activity as a way to prevent cardiovascular disease (see Section 1.3).

1.1.3
Causes of Obesity

Obesity is the result of an energy intake which is too great or energy utilization which is too little, or a combination of the two.

Table 1.1.2 Trends in prevalence of obesity in different countries, 1970s to 1990s [4, 42].

Country	Year	Age group	Men %	Women %
Finland	1978–1979	20–75	10.0	14.0
	1989–1993		14.0	11.0
Norway	1984–1986	20+	7.5	13.0
	1995–1997		14.0	17.8
England	1980	16–64	6.0	8.0
	1995		15.0	16.5
East Germany	1985	25–65	13.7	22.2
(former)	1992		20.5	26.8
Holland	1987	20–59	6.0	8.5
	1995		8.4	8.3
USA	1960	20–74	10.0	15.0
	1991		19.7	24.7
China	1989	20–45	0.29	0.89
	1991		0.36	0.86
Japan	1976	20+	0.7	2.8
	1993		1.8	2.6

1.1.3.1 Energy Intake

Energy derived from food and beverages comes from fat, carbohydrates, and protein. Both carbohydrates and protein contain less energy per unit weight than fat does, and generate stronger satiety signals per unit energy (calorie) than fat does. The body's regulating mechanisms can maintain the amount of carbohydrates and proteins within relatively narrow limits. However, fat can be stored in the body in large quantities.

In several countries where obesity is common, the percentage of fat in the diet has been high for many years, accounting for approximately 40 % of the energy intake [4]. A reason why humans prefer fatty food is that such food is rich in taste substances. However, in the United States a reduced intake of energy, mainly from fat, has not prevented the prevalence of obesity from increasing [31]. In England, fat intake from food has remained relatively constant in recent years, and intake from carbohydrates has declined. Nevertheless, the prevalence of obesity has increased [48]. This would suggest that reduced physical activity may be the main reason for the higher prevalence of overweight and obesity in these countries.

Alcohol contains less energy than fat but nearly twice as much energy as carbohydrates and protein[1]. Since alcohol can be metabolized quickly in the body, this means that other foods ingested at the same time are stored to a greater extent. High alcohol consumption has been documented as a cause of obesity, e.g.,

---

1) Energy content per gram: carbohydrates =
17 kJ/4 kcal, fat = 38 kJ/9 kcal, and alcohol =
29 kJ/7 kcal

among men in Finland [51]. Furthermore, an association between abdominal obesity and high alcohol intake has been shown [11, 62]. The role of alcohol in obesity among women, however, is not fully understood [20, 47].

Obesity develops over a longer period where there is an imbalance between intake and utilization of energy. This lengthy time dimension is often neglected when analyzing the reasons for, and the treatment of, obesity. An average energy surplus of approximately 50 kilocalories (kcal) per day is sufficient for obesity to develop during a 5-year period – i.e., if this surplus of energy is not used, e.g., through physical activity. The amount of energy is so small that it usually goes unnoticed by the individual. Obesity therefore develops through relatively small, but long-term, changes in the balance between intake and utilization of energy. Likewise, weight reduction requires a long-term and continual change in the energy balance by reducing energy intake or increasing energy utilization, or a combination of both.

1.1.3.2 Energy Utilization

Energy is utilized through heat generated from metabolism and through physical activity. The heat generated is normally greater than that needed to maintain body temperature, i.e., surplus heat is normally utilized through various regulation mechanisms. Basal metabolism does not differ among individuals with normal weight, overweight, and obesity. However, it has been demonstrated that normal weight individuals use more energy through higher spontaneous motor activity (i.e., nonexercise activity thermogenesis), for example, changes in body position and unconscious muscle movement [37]. This is one of many explanations why people have different capacities for adapting to increased energy intake.

Low-grade physical activity, e.g., slow walking, uses approximately 50% more energy than sitting still or resting. High-grade physical activity, e.g., jogging or skiing, uses approximately three to four times as much energy compared to sitting still or resting. In addition, physical activity has the effect of reducing the appetite and creates better conditions for regulating food intake. There is no scientific evidence to support the claim that obese people utilize less energy than others do during a particular physical activity. However, it has been shown that physical activity leads to lower BMI and that physical activity can prevent the incidence of obesity [31, 51, 65].

The lower requirement for physical activity in modern society is accompanied by an increased risk of the incidence of obesity in the adult population [31, 48]. A 10-year followup of over 5000 men and women aged 18–63 years has shown that the risk of a weight gain of 5 kg or more is nearly twice as high if physical activity outside of work is low [29]. A part of daily life which previously demanded relatively great muscular activity has been replaced by effective means of transportation, e.g., automobiles, elevators, escalators, etc. To a great extent, people now spend working hours in front of a computer and nonworking hours in front of a television.

1.1.3.3 Risk Factors for Obesity

Women develop obesity more frequently than men, and the condition is often associated with pregnancy and menopause. Data from Sweden show that more than one half of all Swedish women with high-grade obesity (BMI $\geq$ 40) reported that pregnancy was the determining factor for weight gain [52, 53].

Smoking cessation also leads to some weight gain, on average 2 kg in women and 3 kg in men, but with substantial individual variation [51]. Generally, this weight gain ceases after 6 months. Increased weight following smoking cessation is somewhat associated with an increased consumption of energy-rich products, which are viewed as a compensation mechanism for smoking. Metabolic changes involving greater storage of body fat also occurs when the use of nicotine ceases.

Some drugs that are used for chronic, psychiatric diseases (psychoses) can often lead to weight gain. This can also occur with treatment with high doses of insulin or cortisone.

Obesity is more common in people living under lower socioeconomic conditions [34, 51]. Obesity is also more common among children in families with parents who are overweight or obese, which may be related to both genetic factors and dietary and exercise habits [27, 28].

1.1.3.4 Genetic Factors

The strongest arguments supporting the role of genetic factors in the onset of obesity come from studies of twins [59]. These studies show that monozygotic twins who have been raised in separate families after adoption have close similarities in body weight and body fat mass despite differences in the adoptive parents' dietary habits and level of obesity. The twins have basically the same weight and fat mass as their original siblings and parents [60]. Genetic factors are therefore assumed to play a major role in the development of obesity [27]. Furthermore, obesity is included as a component in over 20 rare, congenital, genetic syndromes [18].

One of the hypotheses in obesity research is that, during evolution, survival required the development of genes that could store energy in the body for periods when access to food was deficient. In such situations, these so-called "thrifty genes" were an advantage [45]. However, in a society with abundant access to food, these genes can instead promote the development of obesity.

Studies have shown that obesity develops in mice when a particular protein (leptin) that sends satiety signals to the brain is absent, or when this signal system is not functioning in the signal receptors (leptin receptors) [16]. In humans, leptin forms mainly in fatty tissues, and the leptins have receptors in the brain. In humans, the regulation system for leptins functions in much the same way as it does in animals [39]. A rare genetic, and usually high-grade, obesity has been related to a deficiency of leptin caused by mutations of these genes [44]. Also, a reduced leptin receptor function attributed to genetic changes has been described in three sisters with extreme obesity [19]. Three other genetic disturbances that cause changes in hunger or satiety have also been described in over 20 cases [18].

Knowledge concerning the role of the brain in regulating appetite and how the body regulates the balance of energy has increased markedly in recent years through animal studies. This has not resulted in any medical solutions to the problem. Research success in this area can increase the understanding of obesity in humans and thereby lead to the development of new drugs [14, 54].

Research on genetic factors is intensive and comprehensive – by 1999 over 40 potential genes had been identified. However, it has not been possible to determine which genes and mutations have the strongest connection to the most common types of obesity and abdominal obesity.

1.1.4
Risks of Obesity

1.1.4.1 Mortality

Since the early 1900s, actuarial tables have suggested a correlation between obesity and premature death [1, 3]. All prospective studies with more than 20 000 participants and nearly all cohort studies with more than 7000 participants have shown a twofold increase in total mortality among individuals with severe obesity [56]. In recent years, over 50 large and representative studies have shown that obesity is associated with increased premature death. One of the studies covers nearly the entire Norwegian population [36, 63]. Another of these studies covers more than one million individuals who were followed for 14 years [15]. A third study includes approximately 32 000 individuals who were followed for 14 years [58]. The last two studies also incorporated smoking, history of illness, and the participants' own attempts at weight reduction. Major similarities are found in the risks for elevated BMI, elevated cholesterol values, or elevated blood pressure [4].

Several studies have shown that the risks increase with both low and high BMI (Figure 1.2). Among the explanations for a high mortality rate among individuals with low BMI are that many diseases, e. g., cancer, involve both low weight and high mortality, and that smokers who are thinner have a higher mortality rate than non-smokers. A Danish dissertation concluded, however, that mortality increases in individuals who lose weight, and this cannot be explained by smoking or hidden severe disease [38]. Two large prospective studies of overweight women and men, aged 40 through 64 years, found that intentional weight loss reduces mortality from diabetes-related diseases, but not mortality from cardiovascular disease or total mortality [66, 67]. The methodological problems with this type of study are that intentional weight reduction cannot be reliably distinguished from unintentional reduction. Two large, longitudinal cohort studies of men provided another explanation of the higher mortality associated with low body weight, where age, smoking, and education were taken into consideration [6]. The findings suggest that the increased mortality is related to reduced muscle mass and not to a lower level of body fat.

Several studies have shown that the relative risk of mortality from cardiovascular diseases is lower in individuals at higher ages compared to younger and middle-aged people. This has been shown by the large North American studies referred

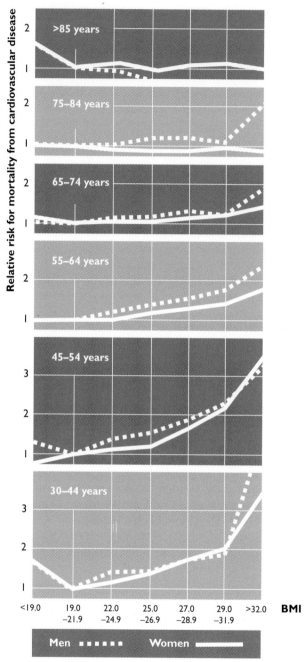

Figure 1.2 Relative risk of mortality from cardiovascular disease at different ages and different BMI. Findings based on men and women who had never smoked [58].

to earlier [15, 58]. One study of approximately 17 000 women, aged 25 through 64 years, shows that mortality was similar for all BMI values [50]. The second cohort study of 85-year-old men and women found that survival was highest for those who had a BMI above 27 when the study started [41]. Recently published studies show that mortality is higher among older individuals with obesity only if it is associated with diabetes and cardiovascular disease, with or without elevated blood pressure [25, 46].

1.1.4.2 Cardiovascular Disease

The main risk factors for myocardial infarction in men at higher ages are elevated cholesterol values, high blood pressure, and smoking. These are followed by obesity as a risk factor in both men and women [15, 24, 40, 58]. According to these studies, when BMI exceeds 32 the relative risk of dying from myocardial infarction at ages 30 through 44 years was more than three times higher in women and more than five times higher in men than in individuals with normal weight BMI (between 19 and 22). A particularly strong correlation was shown between abdominal fat and myocardial infarction in both men and women [13, 56]. Obesity is associated with other diseases of the heart, such as enlargement of the left ventricle and the risk of heart failure [33]. The association between obesity and hypertension has been reported both in cross-sectional studies and in studies that followed obese subjects for a prolonged period [57]. Hypertension is approximately three times more common in overweight individuals than in normal weight individuals, particularly among younger people and in those with a longer duration of obesity [4]. The association between obesity, particularly abdominal obesity, and stroke has also been shown, but the documentation is weaker than that for myocardial infarction [13].

1.1.4.3 Diabetes mellitus (type 2)

Numerous cross-sectional studies and cohort analyses have reported a strong association between obesity and the development of type 2 diabetes mellitus. One study estimated a 40-fold increase in the risk of diabetes among subjects with high-grade obesity [17]. The increase in this type of diabetes has been reported worldwide, particularly in non-industrialized countries, in parallel with the increasing prevalence of obesity [12]. Type 2 diabetes is attributed to a reduced sensitivity to insulin in different body tissues and reduced insulin production. Insulin resistance in obesity can be caused by both genetic and environmental factors, e. g., fatty foods and physical inactivity. Intensive research efforts should be targeted at the mechanisms of origin [34].

Type 2 diabetes, high blood pressure, blood lipid disorders, myocardial infarction, and stroke often appear together in various combinations. This group of diseases and symptoms are reported to have a common background and thereby comprise a syndrome – the so-called "metabolic syndrome". Insulin resistance and increased amount of abdominal fat represent important components of this syn-

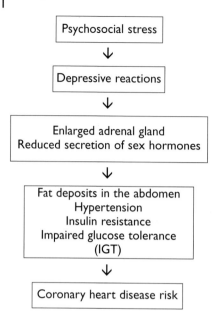

Figure 1.3 Occurence of obesity-related conditions in monkeys – from psychosocial stress via endocrine disturbances [55].

drome [8, 10]. Various stress factors, initiated by, e. g., psychosocial conditions, can be involved in the genesis of the syndrome (see Figure 1.3) [13, 55]. Frequently, the syndrome also includes high alcohol consumption, smoking, depression, and anxiety, i. e., factors that are recognized as activating stress reactions in the brain [13].

1.1.4.4 Cancer

Several cancers are shown to be more common in obesity [4]. These include cancers involving the uterus, breast, ovaries, gall bladder, pancreas, liver, kidneys, and prostate. Hormone-dependent forms of cancer are shown to be more common with abdominal obesity. As regards cancer in the gastrointestinal tract, it has not been established whether it is obesity itself or associated factors such as high intake of saturated fats and/or physical inactivity that are responsible for the statistical association. Based on data from 15 EU countries, a meta-analysis has been performed concerning the association between prevalence and overweight/obesity and six of these forms of cancer [7]. The analysis shows that the risk of cancer in the uterus, gall bladder, and kidneys is higher than for other types of cancer.

1.1.4.5 Gall Bladder and Liver Diseases

Gall stone disease is three to four times more common in both men and women with obesity, irrespective of age [4]. The risk is increased even at moderate overweight and is higher for abdominal obesity. Storage of fat in the liver (liver steatosis) is also common, particularly in abdominal obesity.

1.1.4.6 Musculoskeletal Diseases

Obesity is often accompanied by problems in the back and joints. Load-related, osteoarthritis-type injuries involving cartilage reduction often appear in joints subjected to increased weight, e. g., hips and knees [22, 23]. Gout, i. e., the collection of uric acid in the body leading to acute or chronic joint inflammation, is more common among obese people [4].

1.1.4.7 Production of Sex Hormones

In women, mainly those with abdominal obesity, an increase in male sex hormones (androgens) is often traced in the blood [9]. The reason for the increased production of male sex hormones (which is shown to be associated with insulin resistance) among these women may be stress-related. Some masculine characteristics, including an increase in body hair, frequently appear among women with abdominal obesity. An increased level of androgens in women is an independent risk factor for diabetes, myocardial infarction, hypertension, and some types of cancer [9]. Infertility is not infrequent among women with obesity [4].

1.1.4.8 Diseases of the Respiratory Organs

Respiratory distress is a common symptom of obesity. This disorder is thought to result from increased weight and rigidity in the thoracic wall, making respiratory action more difficult. A horizontal position exacerbates the disorder and can lead to oxygen deficiency in the blood. Periodically recurring cessation of breathing during sleep (sleep apnea) occurs in approximately 10 % of those with obesity, particularly abdominal obesity [4]. This probably results from the higher volume of abdominal fat, which reduces lung capacity, and the increased amount of fat in the neck region, which compresses the airways when the individual is lying down. Common symptoms include snoring, uneasy sleep, and pronounced tiredness during the day. There is some indication of higher mortality and a higher incidence of cardiovascular disease in sleep apnea. However, prospective studies for a longer period are required to determine the strength of this relationship. Different types of studies have reported on the relationship between traffic accidents caused by day tiredness and sleep apnea [30, 32].

1.1.4.9 Health-related Quality of Life

Psychosocial problems are common among patients with obesity [4]. One study shows that self-reported, health-related quality of life in severely obese people is as low as quality of life in patients with spinal cord injury, severe chronic pain, and advanced cancer [68]. Obesity per se often causes fewer problems for the patient than do the psychological problems caused by the reactions and comments of others. Obese people can face discrimination in employment and may have lower incomes than others [61]. Even health services' staff may have a negative attitude toward obese individuals.

1.1.5
Summary

Obesity constitutes a global problem that has been steadily increasing and now also affects populations in some developing countries. Studies show that the rate of obesity is similar in men and women.

Obesity is caused by an imbalance between the intake and the utilization of energy. This imbalance can appear from a relatively small, but long-term, increase in the intake of food and beverages and from insufficient physical activity. It is well documented that genetic factors play a major role in the onset of obesity, but exactly how great a role they play and the mechanisms involved remain to be determined.

A range of disorders accompanies obesity. Obesity is the most important risk factor for type 2 diabetes and a strong contributing factor to the global increase in this type of diabetes. Epidemiological studies have shown obesity to be an important risk factor for cardiovascular disease. The most important risk factor for cardiovascular disease is, however, high age, smoking, high blood pressure, and blood lipid disorders. A range of other diseases are associated with obesity, e. g., certain cancers, gall stone and liver disorders, and muscular and joint disorders. Obesity can cause psychological suffering, not least because of the intolerance and ignorance found in the environment, and may result in negative social consequences leading to a substantially lower quality of life, comparable to that of patients with other severe and life-threatening diseases.

1.1.6
Comments on Facts 1–4

Fat deposits can be accurately measured by computed tomography (CT) or magnetic resonance imaging (MRI), but less sophisticated methods are used in practice and in population studies. A common practice has been to measure the thickness of skin folds at various sites on the body. This type of examination is technically difficult to perform with adequate precision and does not provide information about the size of the fat deposits in the abdomen. The amount of abdominal fat can also be estimated by direct measurement of the circumference of the abdomen or its diameter. The diameter is measured while the patient is in a supine position and is the distance between the back and the highest part of the abdomen (sagittal abdominal diameter) [4]. To adjust for a person's size, abdominal circumference is divided by hip circumference, giving the waist-hip ratio. The waist measurement or the abdominal circumference provides information about the total fat mass in and around the abdomen [35]. The correlation between abdominal fat mass and the risk of disease has been documented mainly in studies where the waist-hip ratio (WHR) has been used to determine fat deposits. In contrast to BMI, the association between the waist-hip ratio and risk factors is more proportional. The upper limit for men has been established at 1.0, i. e., the value where the circumferences of the waist and the hip are equal. Above this value, the risk of disease increases sharply.

Because of broader hips in females, the upper limit for women is 0.85 [4]. The upper limits for the waist measurement alone in middle-aged men and women are 102 cm and 88 cm respectively for a substantial risk increase. These cutoffs add the disease risk of abdominal fat to the disease risk of elevated BMI [4]. The sagittal diameter has not been assessed to the same extent. These measures vary substantially among different groups of people, and therefore caution is advised when comparing data among different populations.

References Section 1.1

1. Medico-Actuarial Mortality Investigation. New York: New York, NY Association of Life Insurance Medical Directors and Actuarial Society of America; 1913.
2. Geographical variation in the major risk factors of coronary heart disease in men and women aged 35–64 years. The WHO MONICA Project. World Health Stat Q 1988;41(3-4):115-40.
3. Build Study 1979: Recording and Statistical Corp, USA; 1989.
4. Obesity. Preventing and managing the global epidemic. Report of WHO Consultation on Obesity, Geneva, 3–5 June 1997, WHO/NUT/NCD/98;1997, 3–5 June.
5. Hälso- och sjukvårdsstatistisk årsbok: Socialstyrelsen; 1999.
6. Allison DB, Zhu SK, Plankey M, Faith MS, Heo M. Differential associations of body mass index and adiposity with allcause mortality among men in the first and second National Health and Nutrition Examination Surveys (NHANES I and NHANES II) follow-up studies. Int J Obes Relat Metab Disord 2002;26(3):410-6.
7. Bergström A, Pisani P, Tenet V, Wolk A, Adami HO. Overweight as an avoidable cause of cancer in Europe. Int J Cancer 2001;91(3):421-30.
8. Björntorp P. Abdominal fat distribution and disease: an overview of epidemiological data. Ann Med 1992;24(1):15-8.
9. Björntorp P. Neuroendocrine perturbations as a cause of insulin resistance. Diabetes Metab Res Rev 1999;15(6):427-41.
10. Björntorp P. Visceral Obesity: A "Civilization Syndrome". Obes Res 1993;1(3):206-21.
11. Björntorp P. The regulation of adipose tissue distribution in humans. Int J Obes Relat Metab Disord 1996;20: 291-302.
12. Björntorp P. Obesity and diabetes. In Alberti KGMM and Krall LP, eds. The Diabetes Annual 1990;5:373-95.
13. Björntorp P. Visceral Obesity: A "Civilization Syndrome". Obes Res 1993;1:206-22.
14. Bray GA, Tartaglia LA. Medicinal strategies in the treatment of obesity. Nature 2000;404(6778):672-7.
15. Calle EE, Thun MJ, Petrelli JM, Rodriguez C, Heath CW, Jr. Body-mass index and mortality in a prospective cohort of U.S. adults. N Engl J Med 1999;341(15):1097-105.
16. Campfield LA, Smith FJ, Guisez Y, Devos R, Burn P. Recombinant mouse OB protein: evidence for a peripheral signal linking adiposity and central neural networks. Science 1995;269(5223):546-9.
17. Carey VJ, Walters EE, Colditz GA, Solomon CG, Willett WC, Rosner BA, et al. Body fat distribution and risk of non-insulin-dependent diabetes mellitus in women. The Nurses' Health Study. Am J Epidemiol 1997;145(7):614-9.
18. Chagnon YC, Perusse L, Weisnagel SJ, Rankinen T, Bouchard C. The human obesity gene map: the 1999 update. Obes Res 2000;8(1):89-117.
19. Clement K, Vaisse C, Lahlou N, Cabrol S, Pelloux V, Cassuto D, et al. A mutation in the human leptin receptor

gene causes obesity and pituitary dysfunction. Nature 1998;392(6674): 398-401.

20. Colditz GA, Giovannucci E, Rimm EB, Stampfer MJ, Rosner B, Speizer FE, et al. Alcohol intake in relation to diet and obesity in women and men. Am J Clin Nutr 1991;54(1):49-55.

21. Davis MA, Neuhaus JM, Ettinger WH, Mueller WH. Body fat distribution and osteoarthritis. Am J Epidemiol 1990; 132(4):701-7.

22. Despres JP, Lemieux I, Prud'homme D. Treatment of obesity: need to focus on high risk abdominally obese patients. BMJ 2001;322(7288):716-20.

23. Felson DT, Zhang Y, Anthony JM, Naimark A, Anderson JJ. Weight loss reduces the risk for symptomatic knee osteoarthritis in women. The Framingham Study. Ann Intern Med 1992; 116(7):535-9.

24. Garrison RJ, Castelli WP. Weight and thirty-year mortality of men in the Framingham Study. Ann Intern Med 1985;103:1006-9.

25. Grabowski DC, Ellis JE. High body mass index does not predict mortality in older people: analysis of the Longitudinal Study of Aging. J Am Geriatr Soc 2001;49(7):968-79.

26. Gray DS, Fujioka K, Colletti PM, Kim H, Devine W, Cuyegkeng T, et al. Magnetic-resonance imaging used for determining fat distribution in obesity and diabetes. Am J Clin Nutr 1991;54(4):623-7.

27. Grilo CM, Pogue-Geile MF. The nature of environmental influences on weight and obesity: a behavior genetic analysis. Psychol Bull 1991;110(3):520-37.

28. Guillaume M, Lapidus L, Beckers F, Lambert A, Björntorp P. Familial trends of obesity through three generations: the Belgian– Luxembourg child study. Int J Obes Relat Metab Disord 1995;19(Suppl 3):S5-9.

29. Haapanen N, Miilunpalo S, Pasanen M, Oja P, Vuori I. Association between leisure time physical activity and 10-year body mass change among working-aged men and women. Int J Obes Relat Metab Disord 1997; 21(4):288-96.

30. Harding SM. Complications and consequences of obstructive sleep apnea. Curr Opin Pulm Med 2000;6(6):485-9.

31. Heini AF, Weinsier RL. Divergent trends in obesity and fat intake patterns: the American paradox. Am J Med 1997;102(3):259-64.

32. Horstmann S, Hess CW, Bassetti C, Gugger M, Mathis J. Sleepiness-related accidents in sleep apnea patients. Sleep 2000;23(3):383-9.

33. Hubert HB, Feinleib M, McNamara PM, Castelli WP. Obesity as an independent risk factor for cardiovascular disease: a 26-year follow-up of participants in the Framingham Heart Study. Circulation 1983;67(5):968-77.

34. Kahn BB, Flier JS. Obesity and insulin resistance. J Clin Invest 2000;106(4):473-81.

35. Lean ME, Han TS, Morrison CE. Waist circumference as a measure for indicating need for weight management. BMJ 1995;311(6998):158-61.

36. Lew EA, Garfinkel L. Variations in mortality by weight among 750,000 men and women. J Chronic Dis 1979;32(8): 563-76.

37. Levine JA, Eberhardt NL, Jensen MD. Role of nonexercise activity thermogenesis in resistance to fat gain in humans. Science 1999;283(5399): 212-4.

38. Lyngby Mikkelsen K. Vaegt, vegtaendringar og dödelighed. Köpenhamn: Center för Epidemiologisk Grundforskning, Institut for Sygdomsforebyggelse, Kommunehospitalet; 1999.

39. Maffei M, Halaas J, Ravussin E, Pratley RE, Lee GH, Zhang Y, et al. Leptin levels in human and rodent: measurement of plasma leptin and ob RNA in obese and weight-reduced subjects. Nat Med 1995;1(11):1155-61.

40. Manson JE, Colditz GA, Stampfer MJ, Willett WC, Rosner B, Monson RR, et al. A prospective study of obesity and risk of coronary heart disease in women. N Engl J Med 1990;322(13): 882-9.

41. Mattila K, Haavisto M, Rajala S. Body mass index and mortality in the elderly. BMJ (Clin Res Ed) 1986;292(6524): 867-8.

42. Midthjell K, Kruger O, Holmen J, Tverdal A, Claudi T, Bjorndal A, et al. Rapid changes in the prevalence of obesity and known diabetes in an adult Norwegian population. The Nord-Trondelag Health Surveys: 1984–1986 and 1995–1997. Diabetes Care 1999;22(11):1813-20.

43. Molarius A, Seidell JC, Sans S, Tuomilehto J, Kuulasmaa K. Varying sensitivity of waist action levels to identify subjects with overweight or obesity in 19 populations of the WHO MONICA Project. J Clin Epidemiol 1999;52(12):1213-24.

44. Montague CT, Farooqi IS, Whitehead JP, Soos MA, Rau H, Wareham NJ, et al. Congenital leptin deficiency is associated with severe early-onset obesity in humans. Nature 1997; 387(6636):903-8.

45. Neel J. Diabetes mellitus: a thrifty genotype rendered detrimental by progress? Am J Hum Genet 1962;14: 353-62.

46. Oldridge NB, Stump TE, Nothwehr FK, Clark DO. Prevalence and outcomes of comorbid metabolic and cardiovascular conditions in middle- and older-age adults. J Clin Epidemiol 2001;54(9):928-34.

47. Prentice AM. Alcohol and obesity. Int J Obes Relat Metab Disord 1995;19(Suppl 5):S44-50.

48. Prentice AM, Jebb SA. Obesity in Britain: gluttony or sloth? BMJ 1995; 311(7002):437-9.

49. Rasmussen F, Johansson M, Hansen HO. Trends in overweight and obesity among 18-year-old males in Sweden between 1971 and 1995. Acta Paediatr 1999;88(4):431-7.

50. Rissanen A, Knekt P, Heliovaara M, Aromaa A, Reunanen A, Maatela J. Weight and mortality in Finnish women. J Clin Epidemiol 1991;44(8):787-95.

51. Rissanen AM, Heliovaara M, Knekt P, Reunanen A, Aromaa A. Determinants of weight gain and overweight in adult Finns. Eur J Clin Nutr 1991;45(9): 419-30.

52. Rössner S. Pregnancy, weight cycling and weight gain in obesity. Int J Obes Relat Metab Disord 1992;16(2):145-7.

53. Rössner S, Ohlin A. Pregnancy as a risk factor for obesity: lessons from the Stockholm Pregnancy and Weight Development Study. Obes Res 1995;3(Suppl 2):267S-75S.

54. Schwartz MW, Woods SC, Porte D, Jr, Seeley RJ, Baskin DG. Central nervous system control of food intake. Nature 2000;404(6778):661-71.

55. Shively CA, Laber-Laird K, Anton RF. Behavior and physiology of social stress and depression in female cynomolgus monkeys. Biol Psychiatry 1997;41(8):871-82.

56. Sjöström LV. Mortality of severely obese subjects. Am J Clin Nutr 1992;55 (Suppl 2):516S-23S.

57. Stamler R, Stamler J, Gosch FC, Civinelli J, Fishman J, McKeever P, et al. Primary prevention of hypertension by nutritional-hygienic means. Final report of a randomized, controlled trial. JAMA 1989;262(13):1801-7.

58. Stevens J, Cai J, Pamuk ER, Williamson DF, Thun MJ, Wood JL. The effect of age on the association between body-mass index and mortality. N Engl J Med 1998;338(1):1-7.

59. Stunkard AJ, Foch TT, Hrubec Z. A twin study of human obesity. JAMA 1986;256(1):51-4.

60. Stunkard AJ, Sorensen TI, Hanis C, Teasdale TW, Chakraborty R, Schull WJ, et al. An adoption study of human obesity. N Engl J Med 1986;314(4): 193-8.

61. Stunkard AJ, Wadden TA. Psychological aspects of human obesity. In: Björntorp P, Brodoff BN, Lippincott. In. Philadelphia; 1992;3522-60.

62. Troisi RJ, Heinold JW, Vokonas PS, Weiss ST. Cigarette smoking, dietary intake, and physical activity: effects on body fat distribution – the Normative Aging Study. Am J Clin Nutr 1991;53(5):1104-11.

63. Waaler HT. Height, weight and mortality. The Norwegian experience. Acta Med Scand Suppl 1984;679:1-56.

64. van der Kooy K, Leenen R, Seidell JC, Deurenberg P, Droop A, Bakker CJ.

Waisthip ratio is a poor predictor of changes in visceral fat. Am J Clin Nutr 1993;57(3): 327-33.

65. Williamson DF, Madans J, Anda RF, Kleinman JC, Kahn HS, Byers T. Recreational physical activity and ten-year weight change in a US national cohort. Int J Obes Relat Metab Disord 1993;17(5):279-86.

66. Williamson DF, Pamuk E, Thun M, Flanders D, Byers T, Heath C. Prospective study of intentional weight loss and mortality in never-smoking overweight US white women aged 40–64 years. Am J Epidemiol 1995;141(12):1128-41.

67. Williamson DF, Pamuk E, Thun M, Flanders D, Byers T, Heath C. Prospective study of intentional weight loss and mortality in overweight white men aged 40–64 years. Am J Epidemiol 1999;149(6):491-503.

68. Sullivan M, Karlsson J, Sjöström L, Backman L, Bengtsson C, Bouchard C, et al. Swedish Obese Subjects (SOS) – an intervention study of obesity. Baseline evaluation of health and psychosocial functioning in the first 1743 subjects examined. Int J Obes 1993;17:503-12.

1.2
Obesity as a Health Problem in Children and Adolescents

1.2.1
Background

Obesity in children and adolescents is a growing problem in all western nations. In most countries there is a tendency for an increasing proportion of children to be overweight and obese, even as early as preschool age [6, 17]. In the United States, the prevalence of obesity in children and adolescents doubled from 1980 to 1999. The percentage of obese children aged 6 to 11 years is estimated to be 15 % [1, 30]. Studies of children in Switzerland showed that approximately 10 % of children aged 6 to 12 years were obese and 22–34 % were overweight [36]. A study from England (1997) showed that 10 % of children at age 6 were obese and 22 % were overweight [23].

Preliminary data from Sweden show that obesity occurs in approximately 3–4 % of children at age 10, and that 18–25 % of the children in this age group are overweight. A comparison shows that the percentage of overweight children at age 10 in Sweden today is 5 to 8 times higher than for a corresponding group of children in France in the early 1980s [25]. The data collected in Sweden for the past 25 years also clearly shows an increase in overweight and obesity among adolescents [24].

1.2.2
Definition

Previously, obesity that required treatment was defined as a weight 20 % above normal weight. In some cases, 40 % above normal weight was also used as the limit defining severe overweight or obesity. Normal weight is calculated for the population of each country as the average weight of a group of individuals having the same age, height, and gender. This means that "normal weight" tends to creep upward in countries where the percentage of overweight children and adolescents is higher. Also, normal variation in weight is higher in certain ages, which means that, e. g., 20 % overweight is a substantially greater deviation for a 6-year-old than for a 16-year-old. For these reasons, this simple definition of overweight is becoming obsolete.

Currently, BMI is used to define obesity, even in children. This method is, however, not without problems – BMI varies with body proportions and thereby also with age and puberty status (Figure 1.4). Therefore, the degree of overweight should be expressed in standard deviations from a mean BMI for a particular age in a population. Mean BMI varies in the same way as normal weight with nutritional status and the frequency of overweight in the population that mean BMI and standard deviations have been calculated for. These relative overweight measures are, however, unsuitable for comparisons among different populations. (For example, a child at +1 SD in BMI based on the conditions in one country probably does not have the same degree of overweight as another child at +1

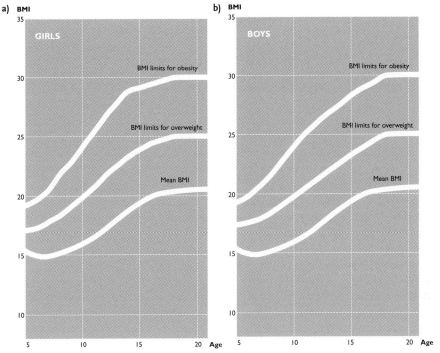

Figure 1.4 BMI curves for children (male and female). The mean BMI is based on information concerning French children and was published in 1982 [25]. The limits for overweight and obesity in children at different ages are estimated to correspond to BMI 25 and 30 in adults, according to Cole [9]. BMI varies widely by age, and therefore the adult limits for obesity and overweight cannot be applied to children.

SD in BMI in another country). To enable better comparisons of the prevalence of overweight and obesity among children and adolescents to be made, a proposal was made recently to define overweight and obesity in these groups in terms of a standard deviation from the mean BMI for a particular age, which corresponds to BMI 25 (overweight) and BMI 30 (obesity) at 18 years of age [9]. As a basis, data on growth in children from ages 2 to 18 years from several countries were analyzed. However, this method cannot be used without reservation, since BMI measurement does not fully compensate for differences in height. It underestimates the degree of overweight in short children and overestimates it in tall children. Hence, BMI should be interpreted with caution in children and adolescents, especially when giving individual advice.

1.2.3
Causes of Obesity

Both genetic and environmental factors play a role in the development of obesity. The question of whether obesity results mainly from genetics or social environment has long been debated. However, several studies show that biological heredity plays a key role. Studies of adopted children have shown that, as adults, their body constitution is much the same as that of their biological parents. The association with the biological mother was stronger than that with the father. This can be because of early influences during fetal life. It has not been possible to find a correlation between the BMI of adoptive parents and that of their adopted children [28]. Studies of twins further support the importance of genetic inheritance in body development. Monozygotic (identical) twins have a very similar body composition, whether or not they were reared in the same home. Dizygotic (fraternal) twins may differ to a much greater extent as regards the development of overweight and obesity. There is substantial covariance in weight trends among dizygotic male twins who have been reared in the same home [27].

The tendency to gain weight from surplus energy intake varies among individuals, which may be partially due to genetic factors [3]. The tendency to carry on, or not carry on, spontaneous physical activity may be an important factor that influences weight regulation when caloric intake is too high [33]. Another important factor may be the ability to offset a large energy intake from one meal with a smaller energy intake from the next meal [2]. Other factors which are probably of importance, although evidence from experimental studies is lacking, concern the ability to compensate for lower physical activity with lower food intake. Different reactions to stress also play a role, which leads some individuals to react by gaining weight while others react by losing weight.

Little is known about the genes that regulate the factors mentioned above. Leptin, a hormone that is released from fat cells and inhibits hunger via receptors in the central nervous system, is an important regulator. Changes in the leptin and leptin receptor genes have been identified, but only in a few families worldwide. Mutations in another gene for the melanocortine-4-receptor, which mediates the effects of leptin in the central nervous system, have been shown to account for as much as 5 % of all severe obesity in children and adolescents [31].

Nevertheless, environmental factors are decisive in the development of obesity. When living conditions limit the intake of food there is no overweight. But with greater access to a varied supply of fat-rich and otherwise energy-dense food, in combination with lowered incentives for physical activity, more individuals become overweight and obese. As unfavorable environmental factors increase, less is required of genetic factors for obesity to develop. Probably, however, certain genetic tendencies must always exist that can explain why, under the same living conditions, some individuals become overweight while others maintain normal weight.

Many studies have shown that social factors influence the onset of obesity. For example, overweight was found to be twice as common in a group of young men whose mothers had less than 9 years of education compared to those whose mothers had a college education [24]. The mechanisms that explain the social differences are not known. Previously, breast-feeding was reported to protect against obesity, but, when social differences are taken into consideration, no studies show that bottle-feeding increases the risk of later development of obesity [7]. A high intake of sugar-sweetened drinks is shown to be associated with obesity [18]. When calories are acquired in liquid form, this may impair one's ability to automatically compensate for this at the next meal [19]. Several studies, e. g., the Framingham Children's Study, have clearly demonstrated the important role that physical inactivity plays in the development of obesity [21].

1.2.4
Morbidity and Obesity

A longitudinal study from the United StatesUSA reported that moderate overweight during teenage years – regardless of weight later in life – results in increased mortality from cardiovascular diseases prior to 66 years of age [22]. A long-term followup of overweight children in Sweden found that the prevalence of obesity during puberty was significantly higher in the group who died before the age of 55 than among those who lived longer [11].

Obesity during childhood leads to changes in hormone balance and growth patterns. The level of growth hormone declines with an increasing level of overweight, but, nevertheless, overweight children usually grow faster than do their peers prior to puberty. Although growth in overweight children is worse during puberty, ultimately it is usually the same for overweight and normal weight children [10]. Overweight in children and adolescents leads to elevated insulin levels and reduced sensitivity to insulin, similar to that which occurs in adults [20]. Elevated blood lipids and elevated blood pressure also occur in obese children and adolescents [20]. However, it is uncommon for these to lead to diseases that require treatment during childhood and adolescence despite substantial overweight. A sharp increase in type 2 diabetes has, however, been noted in the United States [8, 13]. This primarily applies to black and Mexican adolescents, and can be attributed to the higher risk of these ethnic groups developing type 2 diabetes. Even if this risk is lower in some populations, the increased degree of overweight and obesity can result in a higher rate of diabetes in younger adults. Fatty liver, joint damage, and enlargement of the myocardium are also found in obese children, as well as some cases of elevated pressure in the central nervous system that can lead to headache and affect the optic nerve [16].

Many studies have found a strong association between poor psychosocial health and overweight in children. A study from Holland found, e. g., that overweight children aged 9 to 12 years were consistently more dissatisfied with their physical ability and had lower self-esteem than normal weight children of the same age [4, 5]. Many overweight children report that they are teased and sometimes bullied because they are overweight. This agrees with attitudes among children found in a study where they were shown silhouette images. The rounder silhouettes were described as ugly, dirty, lazy, and dumb [34].

Mental illness has been found to be more common among overweight children than among normal weight children, but this could also be attributed to poor psychosocial health being more common among parents of overweight children [12]. Overweight can be an effect of poor psychosocial health in families, rather than a cause of it. A study from the United States showed that overweight teenagers and younger adult women lived under less favorable social and economic conditions than normal weight women of the same age with other chronic disease [15]. The overweight individuals had lower education, lower marriage rates, and lower incomes. The study, however, provided no answer to the question of causes and effects. Some studies have not noted any lower self-esteem among overweight adolescents [14].

1.2.5
Risk of Children becoming Overweight Adults

The risk of permanent overweight is low in children younger than three years of age [35]. In these children, the risk of obesity as adults is the same as in normal weight children [35]. Studies have shown that a high percentage (50–60%) of children who are overweight at seven years of age become normal-weight adults [26, 29, 35]. One study followed weight progression over time in seven-year-old children who had been severely obese, i. e., more than 40% overweight [26]. Approximately one half of these very overweight children developed into normal-weight adults. The tendency for a "spontaneous cure" of overweight appears, however, to decline with an increasing degree of overweight and age. In seven-year-old children, a strong correlation was found between an elevated BMI and the risk of being overweight as an adult [32].

In obese children above 10 years of age the risk of permanent obesity is high. A study from the United States shows that approximately 90% of 12-year-old boys with 50% overweight (BMI > 23) will probably be overweight as adults [32]. Teenagers with severe obesity demonstrated an even worse prognosis. Basically, all 15-year-olds with a BMI above 30 appear to remain obese as adults [32].

The epidemiological studies available in the field were performed before the increase in obesity among children and adolescents became substantial. Therefore, it may be possible that the prognosis for overweight children is even worse than estimated.

Pharmacotherapy for obesity should not be given prior to age three, and should be used very conservatively up to six years of age. Consideration should also be given to the parents' level of overweight, which might play a role in the prognosis [27]. If neither parent is overweight the prognosis is more favorable.

1.2.6
Summary

Overweight and obesity among children and adolescents is increasing rapidly. The risk is small that overweight children below three years of age are destined to become overweight adults. However, this risk increases as early as the preschool years and with increasing overweight, and it may become permanent. The percentage of overweight children who become overweight adults has increased in the past 25 to 35 years. The reasons for the rapid increase in obesity are probably found in the trends in modern society, i.e., lower demands for physical activity combined with unchanged or increased energy intake.

References Section 1.2

1. CDC Update: Prevalence of overweight among children, adolescents and adults in the United States 1988–1994. Morbidity and mortality weekly report 1997;46:199-202.

2. Bellisle F, Rolland-Cachera MF. How sugar-containing drinks might increase adiposity in children. Lancet 2001;357(9255):490-1.

3. Bouchard C, Tremblay A, Despres JP, Nadeau A, Lupien PJ, Theriault G, et al. The response to long-term over-feeding in identical twins. N Engl J Med 1990;322(21):1477-82.

4. Braet C, Mervielde I, Vandereycken W. Psychological aspects of childhood obesity: a controlled study in a clinical and nonclinical sample. Journal of Pediatric Psychology 1997;22(1):59-71.

5. Braet C, Van Strien T. Assessment of emotional, externally induced and restrained eating behaviour in nine to twelve-year-old obese and non-obese children. Behaviour Research & Therapy 1997;35(9):863-73.

6. Bundred P, Kitchiner D, Buchan I. Prevalence of overweight and obese children between 1989 and 1998: population based series of cross sectional studies. BMJ 2001;322(7282):326-8.

7. Butte NF. The role of breastfeeding in obesity. Pediatr Clin North Am 2001;48(1):189-98.

8. Callahan ST, Mansfield MJ. Type 2-diabetes mellitus in adolescents. Curr Opin Pediatr 2000;12(4):310-5.

9. Cole TJ, Bellizzi MC, Flegal KM, Dietz WH. Establishing a standard definition for child overweight and obesity worldwide: international survey. BMJ 2000;320(7244):1240-3.

10. De Simone M, Farello G, Palumbo M, Gentile T, Ciuffreda M, Olioso P, et al. Growth charts, growth velocity and bone development in childhood obesity. Int J Obes Relat Metab Disord 1995;19(12):851-7.

11. DiPietro L, Mossberg HO, Stunkard AJ. A 40-year history of overweight children in Stockholm: life-time over-weight, morbidity, and mortality. Int J Obes Relat Metab Disord 1994;18(9):585-90.

12. Epstein LH, Myers MD, Anderson K. The association of maternal psycho-pathology and family socioeconomic status with psychological problems in obese children. Obesity Research 1996;4(1):65-74.

13. Fagot-Campagna A. Emergence of type 2 diabetes mellitus in children: epidemiological evidence. J Pediatr Endocrinol Metab 2000;13(Suppl 6): 1395-402.

14. French SA, Story M, Perry CL. Self-esteem and obesity in children and adolescents: a literature review. Obes Res 1995;3(5):479-90.

15. Gortmaker SL, Must A, Perrin JM, Sobol AM, Dietz WH. Social and economic consequences of overweight in adolescence and young adulthood. N Engl J Med 1993;329(14):1008-12.

16. Lehman LB. Pseudotumor cerebri: an enigmatic process. Hosp Pract (Off Ed) 1988;23(12):127-8, 30.

17. Lindgren G, Strandell A, Cole T, Healy M, Tanner J. Swedish population reference standards for height, weight and body mass index attained at 6 to 16 years (girls) or 19 years (boys). Acta Paediatrica 1995;84(9):1019-28.

18. Ludwig DS, Peterson KE, Gortmaker SL. Relation between consumption of sugar-sweetened drinks and childhood obesity: a prospective, observational analysis. Lancet 2001;357(9255):505-8.

19. Mattes RD. Dietary compensation by humans for supplemental energy provided as ethanol or carbohydrate in fluids. Physiol Behav 1996;59(1): 179-87.

20. McMurray R, Harrell J, Levine A, Gansky S. Childhood obesity elevates blood pressure and total cholesterol independent of physical activity. Int J Obes 1995;19:881-6.

21. Moore LL, Nguyen U-SDT, Rothman KJ, Cupples AL, Ellison CR. Preschool physical activity level and change in body fatness in young children, The Framingham Children's Study. Am J Epidemiol 1995;142(9)982-8.

22. Must A, Jacques PF, Dallal GE, Bajema CJ, Dietz WH. Long-term morbidity and mortality of overweight adolescents. A followup of the Harvard Growth Study of 1922 to 1935. N Engl J Med 1992;327(19):1350-5.

23. Prescott-Clark P, Primatesta P. Health Survey for England 1995. London: The Stationery Office, 1997.

24. Rasmussen F, Johansson M. Övervikt bland unga män i riket och Stockholms Län. Tidstrender samt sociala och geografiska variationer. Epidemiologiska enheten, Samhällsmedicin, Stockholms Läns Landsting; 1997. Rapport nr 2.

25. Rolland-Cachera MF, Sempe M, Guilloud-Bataille M, Patois E, Pequignot-Guggenbuhl F, Fautrad V. Adiposity indices in children. Am J Clin Nutr 1982;36(1):178-84.

26. Stark O, Atkins E, Wolff O, Douglas J. Longitudinal study of obesity in the National Survey of Health and Development. BMJ 1998;283:13-7.

27. Stunkard AJ, Harris JR, Pedersen NL, McClearn GE. The body-mass index of twins who have been reared apart. N Engl J Med 1990;322(21):1483-7.

28. Stunkard AJ, Sörensen TIA, Hanis C, Teasdale TW, Chakraborty R, Schulli WJ, et al. An adoption study of human obesity. N Engl J Med 1986;314:195-8.

29. Sörensen TIA, Sonne-Holm S. Risk in childhood of development of severe adult obesity: Retrospective, population-based case-cohort study. Am J Epidemiol 1988;127(1):104-13.

30. Troiano RP, Flegal KM, Kuczmarski RJ, Campbell SM, Johnson CL. Overweight prevalence and trends for children and adolescents. The National Health and Nutrition Examination Surveys, 1963 to 1991. Arch Pediatr Adolesc Med 1995;149(10):1085-91.

31. Vaisse C, Clement K, Durand E, Hercberg S, Guy-Grand B, Froguel P. Melanocortin-4 receptor mutations are a frequent and heterogeneous cause of morbid obesity. J Clin Invest 2000; 106(2):253-62.

32. Valdez R, Greenlund K, Wattigney W, Bao W, Berenson G. Use of weight-for-height indices in children to predict adult overweight: the bogalusa heart study. Int J Obes 1996;20:715-21.

33. Vanltallie TB. Resistance to weight gain during overfeeding: a NEAT explanation. Nutr Rev 2001;59(2):48-51.

34. Wardle J, Volz C, Golding C. Social variation in attitudes to obesity in children. Int J Obes Relat Metab Disord 1995;19(8):562-9.

35. Whitaker RC, Wright JA, Pepe MS, Seidel KD, Dietz WH. Predicting obesity in young adulthood from childhood and parental obesity. N Engl J Med 1997;337(13):869-73.

36. Zimmermann MB, Hess SY, Hurrell RF. A national study of the prevalence of overweight and obesity in 6–12 y-old Swiss children: body mass index, body-weight perceptions and goals. Eur J Clin Nutr 2000;54(7):568-72.

1.3
International Overview of Obesity Intervention Programs

Several nations have developed strategies to treat or prevent obesity. The recommendations are based on systematic reviews of the scientific literature. Although the approaches and guidelines are largely in agreement, there are also certain differences among nations.

1.3.1
Australia

A report from 1995, "Healthy Weight Australia", presented a national strategy to prevent and treat obesity, a major public health problem in Australia. The report showed that the prevalence of overweight and obesity had reached 25 % in younger men and 60 % in men aged 60 through 64 years. The corresponding figures for women were 18 % and 52 % respectively. Obesity is highest among the indigenous population, mainly the aborigines and some other ethnic groups, and in special regions with lower socioeconomic conditions. Previous preventive interventions aimed at diet and physical activity that focused on cardiovascular disease had not been successful.

The goal of the prevention program was to increase access to, and demand for, low energy diets, both at home and in restaurants. The strategy involved enlisting the joint cooperation of researchers, consumers, and representatives of the food industry. Public information should consider gender, age, and socioeconomic conditions. The report showed that TV commercials for food and beverages during children's programming were dominated by inappropriate products with high fat content and high energy density. The report also emphasized that the advertising cost of sweets and soft drinks was 1 million dollars per day, while the amount spent on information about nutritious food was only 1 million dollars per year. Greater input from primary care physicians to identify patients at risk and participate actively in nutritional information was part of the strategic plan, as was engaging dieticians to participate in population-based dietary information.

Physical activity was estimated to be minimal or low in two thirds of the population, which suggested that there had been little effect from earlier interventions to reduce this public health problem. The action plan therefore included the development of new and more attractive exercise programs more specifically adapted to different ages, genders, and cultures. A second main goal of the public health program was to reduce the percentage of overweight or obese individuals. The program placed greater responsibility on dietary experts, primary care physicians, and dieticians, who were given the responsibility to develop guidelines for various interventions, identify people at risk, include behavior modification in treatment, and establish realistic individual treatment goals. This requires more extensive knowledge in the field among caregivers of various types. The research directive included, e. g., overweight and obesity in children, adolescents, and aborigines. The directive also included an assessment of medications and the psychological consequences that the preventive interventions can lead to.

1.3.2
France

Recommendations have been developed in France on the prevention, diagnosis, and treatment of obesity, emphasizing preventive interventions[1]. The population-based interventions include programs to promote physical activity in daily life, recreation, and information on the importance of reducing energy intake by limiting fat, alcohol, and certain types of snack foods. The preventive interventions are targeted mainly at schools, groups, or regions with a particularly high prevalence of obesity. The recommendations also include interventions targeted at certain individuals, e. g., close relatives of obese people. The recommendations particularly address certain risk periods, for example, those related to smoking cessation, pregnancy, or post-menopause. Also, the increased vulnerability associated with psychosocial problems is emphasized. The treatment section suggests that the goals in weight reduction should be realistic, but are often 5–15 % of present weight. The value of physical activity is emphasized. The cutoff point for pharmacotherapy was set at BMI $\geq$ 25 in patients with a comorbidity related to obesity and at BMI $\geq$ 30 without a comorbidity. In high-grade obesity, where surgical treatment is an option, treatment is recommended at special units in collaboration with primary care.

1.3.3
Norway

A State Council for Diet and Physical Activity (SEF) was initiated in Norway in March 1999. The Council has the responsibility to improve health in the population by promoting more physical activity and healthier dietary habits. The three specific goals are

1. At least 30 min physical activity every day
2. Higher consumption of fruit and vegetables
3. Lower fat intake by greater consumption of fish as well as milk and meat with low fat content.

The Council has been assigned to conduct a critical review of the scientific literature and develop guidelines, to collect data on dietary and exercise habits in relation to the population's health, and to monitor trends. Particular emphasis is placed on determining which factors in society (social, economic, cultural) have an unfavorable effect on diet and exercise habits. Other factors to be studied are the possible negative effects of greater internationalization of food products and the limitations placed on public agencies in regulating the supply of food products

---

1) Recommendations for the diagnosis, prevention, and treatment of obesity, July 1999

under current EU agreements. Interventions to prevent overweight and obesity include more physical activity in daily life and improved dietary habits, mainly in schools and at workplaces, but also in the home. Broad-based collaboration is planned and engages the mass media (newspapers, radio, TV, IT), sports, food industry, national and international institutions, and public authorities. Interventions by the council focus on children, pregnant women, parents of babies and small children, and immigrants.

1.3.4
New Zealand

In New Zealand, the NZHTA Report 2001 presents a critical review of the scientific literature addressing environmentally based methods of preventing obesity. The background is that approximately half of the adult population is overweight or obese. The search covered the years 1980 to 2000 and identified 1165 English-language articles. Only 13 studies met all of the inclusion criteria. The report also includes 63 studies which were methodologically weak in one area or another, but which nevertheless contained valuable information. The report does not address ethical, legal, or economic aspects. Studies that are included in the report and which address possible effects of improving dietary habits, mainly through limited fat intake, have been conducted in the following environments: schools, restaurants, workplaces, supermarkets, and society in general. Some of these are mentioned below.

Most of the school-based studies were conducted at the primary school level. In the only study with high quality, the intervention program was based on comprehensive information to school kitchen staff and was aimed at reducing the total content of fat and saturated fat in school food. In followup after 2.5 years, the treatment goal had not only been achieved in the intervention schools but even in the control schools. The authors assume that this is explained by the concurrent mass media coverage of dietary information and awareness about national guidelines. None of the studies in the restaurant environment met the inclusion criteria, since they were small and not controlled. Posters with information about healthy diets and menus with information about low-energy and low-fat alternatives were usually included. Of 16 workplace-based studies, 7 were randomized, but most had low quality for other reasons. The effects of low intensity, three-month educational programs focusing on low fat intake were studied in four factories in Belgium. The participation rate was somewhat over 50 %. Knowledge about healthy diets increased in the intervention group, while the blood lipid levels dropped concurrently, but the mean BMI increased.

Three large workplace-based intervention programs with a primary focus on reducing smoking and fat intake and increasing fiber intake were conducted in the United States. The programs were somewhat different, but all were ambitious, e.g., one program included both theoretical and practical dietary instruction. None of the studies achieved the established treatment goals regarding fat intake and blood cholesterol.

Two studies in supermarket environments were randomized, one of which registered the purchase of food products with low fat and fiber content. The studies included computer-based registration of planned purchases, education through video films, and confirmation of purchases based on cash register receipts. During the trial period of 8 weeks, the intake of all types of fat declined somewhat in the intervention groups. At later followup, a corresponding decline had occurred in the control groups. The participants were few and generally well educated.

1.3.5
Finland

In 1999, an action plan by the Ministry of Health in Helsinki to prevent cardiovascular disorders among people in Finland presented the public health program that was subsequently initiated in 2001. The goal of the program has been to increase physical activity among the population. For children and adolescents this implies a higher level of activity during recreation, and for adults it implies a higher level of activity in daily life. Interventions include efforts to promote using bicycles and taking longer walks. A change in infrastructure and improvement in traffic safety are among the means used.

1.3.6
Canada

Nearly a decade ago, two reports were released in Canada that presented guidelines for interventions against obesity[1]. Revised guidelines were later released (1994)[2] supported by results from studies identified in the MEDLINE database for the period 1966 to June 1993. They found that in studies presenting medium to high quality, the prevention programs had been ineffective. Hence, routine examinations to determine BMI in the adult population were not viewed as meaningful. Furthermore, some studies showed increased mortality and morbidity in conjunction with weight loss and widely varying body weight. In high-risk patients with type 2 diabetes, hypertension, and blood lipid disorders, active interventions were recommended aimed at weight reduction, which was found to have a favorable effect in the short term. It was reported that reduced morbidity and mortality from stroke and cardiovascular disease had not been documented. Further research was called for, focusing on the causes of obesity and better studies of obesity treatment and its effect on obesity-related morbidity and mortality.

1) Canadian Guidelines for Healthy Weights, 1988; Report of the Task Force on the Treatment of Obesity, 1990

2) Prevention of Obesity in Adults, 1994

1.3.7
Sweden

In 2000, the Swedish Council on Technology Assessment in Health Care (SBU) surveyed 8 university hospitals, 68 hospital pediatric departments and a large number of primary care pediatric clinics, and 140 randomly selected district physicians. The survey showed that a very small percentage of obese children receive medical treatment for this problem in Sweden. The treatment usually offered consists of general advice concerning behavior modification in combination with specific dietary and exercise counseling. Treatment usually lasts 1 to 2 years with visits to outpatient clinics every third month. Treatment can be discontinued because of the patient/parent wishes or because the patient fails to appear. Medication is used to a limited extent.

1.3.8
United States

The following treatment strategies were presented in a report from the National Institutes of Health in the United States[1]:

- Various types of dietary treatment (although not dietary fiber)
- Energy-reduced diet formulas
- Physical activity
- Behavior modification
- Pharmacotherapy
- Surgery.

The report is based on a review of risk, mortality and genetic aspects of obesity, and a review of randomized controlled studies on obesity-related diseases. The report generally addresses the effects of weight reduction on blood pressure, blood lipids, type 2 diabetes, and abdominal obesity. The general treatment recommendations originate from definitions and classifications of overweight and obesity with consideration to risk determination, exclusion criteria, and factors for successful treatment results over a longer period.

1) Clinical Guidelines on the Identification, Evaluation, and Treatment of Overweight and Obesity in Adults – The Evidence Report, National Institutes of Health and National Heart, Lung and Blood Institute, Obesity Research supplement 2, September 1998.

1.4
Cost of Obesity and Obesity-Related Diseases

1.4.1
Methods of Estimating the Cost to Society

Two fundamentally different approaches to analyzing health care from an economic perspective are usually taken. One involves estimating the cost of illness. This type of cost estimate generally focuses only on describing the scope of a particular health problem in economic terms. The second approach involves various economic assessments, such as assessing the cost effectiveness of different ways of preventing or treating a disease. This Section addresses the cost of obesity and obesity-related disorders.

The cost of disease is usually divided into direct and indirect costs. The direct costs comprise the cost of treatment and care of a particular disease, regardless of who is responsible for treatment (public health, private health, insurance companies, self care, etc). This category also includes expenses for travel to and from the caregiver. Indirect costs are those incurred as a consequence of disease and treatment. Indirect costs include the productivity lost because of absenteeism from illness or death prior to pension age as well as non-working time lost.

The cost to society from disease can be calculated using either a prevalence or incidence method. The most common is the prevalence method, which includes the direct and indirect costs in a given year for everyone who, during that year, already has a particular disease and everyone who will incur the disease. The prevalence method also includes the cost of complications from the disease. The incidence method, on the other hand, includes the direct and indirect costs of a given disease and its complications in only those who contract the disease during a particular year, but the costs are compiled for the entire time the disease persists. Many diseases are chronic, which means that the incidence method must calculate the costs until the end of life. This is often difficult. No studies have been found in the literature which use the incidence method for obesity and obesity-related diseases. Rather, all studies that have been identified are based on the prevalence method.

1.4.2
Methods of Searching the Literature

The following databases were used to search for economic studies: MEDLINE, Cinahl, HEED, and NHS (Centre for Reviews and Dissemination). The term "obesity" was used to search HEED and NHS, (since these databases include only economic studies), while the searches in Cinahl and MEDLINE used the terms "obesity", "costs", and "cost analysis".

Most of the literature search was completed in January 2002, identifying over 300 references. After reviewing the titles and summaries, 230 articles that were found to be of little or no relevance were excluded. Over 70 articles were retrieved and reviewed for relevance. Some articles were added following a review of the reference lists in the recovered articles and through other sources. In total, 22 articles were found to be relevant for the purposes of the following discussion of the costs of obesity and obesity-related diseases.

1.4.3
Results

1.4.3.1 Studies Addressing Direct Costs of Obesity

One study calculated both the direct and the indirect costs of obesity and obesity-related diseases in the United States for 1986 [4]. The direct costs of obesity and its complications were calculated at 5.5 % of the total health care costs in the United States that year. The costs of obesity-related diseases will always be based on some assumptions concerning how large a proportion of the prevalence and incidence of various diseases can be related to obesity.

In a later study in the United States, in 1996, the costs of obesity-related diseases, i. e., diabetes, cardiovascular disease, hypertension, and gallstones, were calculated at the 1993 price level [25]. This study also calculated the cost distribution across various BMI ranges (23–24.9, 25–28.9, ≥ 29). Of the direct costs of obesity-related diseases, nearly 60 % could be attributed to the population with a BMI exceeding 29, i. e., the definition of obesity applied in this study. The authors claimed that the costs of obesity are actually underestimated because the study population was limited. The study shows that both risks and costs in the respective groups increase substantially at higher BMIs. However, the study is not presented in the summary in Table 1.3, since the costs of obesity as a proportion of the total direct costs of health care were not presented by this study.

A larger study, the Health Professional Followup Study, calculated the costs in the United States for 1995 [26]. The study included people with BMI 29 and above, and their relative risk of being affected by complications (diabetes, cardiovascular disease, high blood pressure, breast cancer, colon cancer, uterine cancer, and musculoskeletal diseases). Using information acquired from a large number of other studies, the direct costs of complications were calculated. (Over 60 % of the costs of care of type 2 diabetes were found to be related to obesity.) The total direct cost of obesity and obesity-related diseases was estimated at 5.7 % of the costs of health care in the United States in 1995. The indirect costs were estimated to be similar.

A study from California that included men with BMI ≥ 27.8 and women with BMI ≥ 27.3 estimated the costs of obesity in 1993 to be approximately 6 % of total health care cost [18].

Using a model, another study from the United States estimated the direct costs of obesity-related diseases in adults [1]. The direct costs in the model were calculated based on data from a study in 1998 [26]. The model is based on several assumptions, but the authors estimate that the direct costs comprise between 0.9 % and 4.3 % of total health care costs. The distribution of costs in this study clearly illustrates the uncertainty of the basic data used to calculate costs in this field.

A study from the Netherlands (1989) calculated the direct costs of obesity [21]. The authors first determined the increased risk of certain complications in an overweight population. The point of departure was a population study with self-reported data on weight and care consumption from the 1980s. It included the cost of ambulatory care, inpatient care, and drugs for several selected diseases. The study showed that the direct costs of obesity and obesity-related diseases were 4% of the total costs of health care.

A French study, which defined obesity as BMI > 27, calculated both the direct and indirect costs of obesity and obesity-related diseases [12]. Relatively reliable epidemiological data were used to estimate the percentage of overweight individuals, but the relative risk of developing various complications was based on uncertain associations reported in the literature. In France, the costs of obesity and obesity-related diseases were 2% of total health care costs in 1992. A relatively small group of severely obese people (BMI > 39) accounted for nearly 50% of the total costs of obesity and obesity-related diseases.

Another French study, which included 14 670 participants, collected data in 1991 and 1992 (Medical Care Household Survey) [5]. All care consumption during a three-month period was reported. The direct costs of obesity were calculated as all care consumption associated with obesity in individuals with a BMI > 30. These costs were estimated at between 0.7% and 1.5% of the total health care costs in France.

A study from New Zealand (1991) calculated the direct costs of obesity and obesity-related diseases at 2.5% of the total health care cost [23]. This study defined obesity as BMI > 30. Data on the prevalence of obesity was acquired from epidemiological studies. The estimates of direct costs included care for six diseases associated with obesity, where direct costs covered inpatient care, ambulatory care in and outside of the hospital, drugs, and laboratory services. The cost estimates were based on relatively broad general assumptions. The authors suggested that their method could underestimate the actual costs.

A study from Canada in the mid-1990s also found the direct costs to be similar, 2.4% of the total health care cost [2].

A study from Australia in 1989 showed the direct costs of obesity and obesity-related diseases to be approximately 2% of the costs of all health care [20]. In this study also, the authors suggested that the costs might have been underestimated, mainly because the costs of outpatient care were not included.

A review article noted that the estimates presented in published studies on the costs of obesity and obesity-related diseases are based on uncertain information. The article also pointed out deficiencies in studies based on the incidence approach [10]. An evaluation of these studies by SBU confirms this criticism. The studies are based on unconfirmed data and unconfirmed assumptions. They differ in regard to epidemiological conditions, definitions of risk groups, and methods for calculating risks and costs.

Table 1.4 summarizes the referenced studies. The table shows that the various studies reached different results concerning the direct costs of obesity. Some of these differences can be attributed to different definitions of obesity and different

Table 1.4.1 Direct costs for obesity as a percentage of total health care costs in different countries.

Author Year, reference	Country	Year	Definition	%
Colditz 1992 [4]	USA	1986	BMI >29	5.5
Wolf & Colditz 1998 [26]	USA	1995	BMI ≥ 29	5.7
Quesenberry et al. 1998 [18]	USA	1993	BMI ≥ 27.5	6.0
Allison et al. 1999 [1]	USA	1995	BMI ≥ 29	0.9–4.3
Seidell 1995 [21]	The Netherlands	1989	BMI >25	4.0
Lévy et al. 1995 [12]	France	1992	BMI >27	2.0
Detournay et al. 2000 [5]	France	1991/ 1992	BMI >30	0.7–1.5
Swinburn et al. 1997 [23]	New Zealand	1991	BMI >30	2.5
Birmingham et al. 1999 [2]	Canada	1997	BMI ≥ 27	2.4
Segal et al. 1994 [20]	Australia	1989	BMI >30	2.0

assumptions concerning the risk of obesity. Excluding the United States, the direct costs in these studies average 2.3 % of total health care costs. In the studies that used the same definition of obesity as applied by this SBU report, i.e., a BMI > 30, the direct costs vary from 0.7 % to 2.5 % of the costs of health care in the respective countries. Judging from these studies, the direct costs of obesity could fall between 1 % and 2 % of the total health care costs.

1.4.3.2 Studies Concerning Other Economic Aspects

Indirect costs A Swedish study of obese patients (BMI ≥ 28) examined the indirect costs of lost productivity due to absenteeism and early retirement [14]. The results suggested that the value of lost productivity due to absenteeism and early retirement caused by overweight and obesity among women in 1988 corresponded to approximately 10 % of the total indirect costs of absenteeism and early retirement in women that year.

Correlation between level of obesity and health care costs   The correlation between level of obesity and utilization of health services has been studied in the United States [18]. This study used data from a health study in 1993 among members of a large health maintenance organization (HMO) in Northern California. Slightly less than 60%, or approximately 19 000 of its members, participated in the study. Morbidity associated with obesity was determined using answers from a health questionnaire and analysis of drug prescriptions. Each participant's health care costs were determined from information on health services consumed during one year in conjunction with health check-ups. The study showed a strong correlation between BMI and total health care costs. If the reference value was set at 1 in the group with a BMI of 20–24.9, the costs of the remaining groups were as follows: BMI 25–29.9, 0.95; BMI 30–34.9, 1.25; BMI ≥ 35, 1.44. The cost difference between the reference group and the two groups with a higher BMI were statistically significant, which was not the case for the cost difference between the reference group and the group with BMI 25–29.9.

A model study calculated the lifetime cost of obesity-related diseases in different age groups and weight classes [24]. The risk of ill health (and consequent greater care costs) increased substantially with weight. The cost doubled for both men and women when BMI increased from 22.5 to 37.5.

Another study, based on reports from over 6000 employees in an American corporation, clearly showed an association between the degree of BMI, health care costs, and sick leave [3]. The results showed, e.g., a positive correlation between BMI and the percentage who were absent from work for more than 5 days due to illness at some time during the study period. The association between the costs of health care and the different BMI values yielded a J-shaped curve, with the lowest costs for those with a BMI around 25.

An American model study calculated how a weight reduction of 10% in body weight could potentially influence the risks and health care costs in type 2 diabetes, hypertension, blood lipid disorders, cardiovascular disease, and stroke [17]. A cohort of men and women aged 35 through 64 years with different BMI values (27.5, 32.5, and 37.5) was analyzed in the model. A weight loss of 10% was assumed to remain throughout life, and maximum life expectancy in the model was 99 years. The results of these calculations showed that a 10% weight reduction led to an average of 1.2 to 2.9 fewer years with hypertension, depending on gender, age, and initial BMI. Expected time with type 2 diabetes and blood lipid disorders was influenced somewhat less. The expected number of cases of heart disease and stroke declined by 1.2–3.8% and 0.1–1.3% respectively. The health care costs saved as a result of a 10% weight loss were estimated to range between 2300 USD and 5300 USD per person for the duration of life.

A large study in Sweden tracked drug consumption in a population of obese individuals for 6 years [16]. Consumption data for 1286 participants in the Swedish Obese Subjects (SOS) intervention study was compared with data for 958 individuals in a randomly selected reference group. The costs of drugs were 77% higher among individuals with obesity. The use of drugs for diabetes was 9 times higher.

A recently published study from the United States used data from an extensive telephone survey of approximately 10 000 individuals to determine the direct cost of care for obesity, alcohol abuse, and smoking [27]. The study shows that 23 % of the population met the criteria for obesity (BMI > 30). The direct care costs of obesity are higher than for the corresponding costs of diseases and health problems caused by alcohol abuse, smoking, and aging. In relative terms, the estimates showed that the costs of health care increased by 36 % due to obesity while costs increased by 21 % due to smoking. An epidemiological study of this type shows the relationship without establishing the causes. Furthermore, it is uncertain how widely the results can be applied. Hence, reliable conclusions cannot be drawn.

Correlation between level of obesity and income   The correlation between obesity and income has been investigated in several studies using relatively similar methodology, i. e., a regression model where income is the dependent variable. Obesity is included in the model as one of many explanatory variables. By using several explanatory variables, researchers attempt to isolate the possible effects that obesity might have on income.

An early American study from 1980 investigated the relationship between obesity and income [13]. A sample of 2356 men aged 51 to 65 years formed the basis for the study. The model found a correlation between obesity and income. Another study from Great Britain investigated the relationship between obesity and income in teenagers [19]. This cohort study included everyone born in England, Scotland, and Wales during the first week of March 1958. Followup occurred at ages 7, 11, 16, and 23 years. The relationship between obesity at age 11, 16, and 23 years and income at age 23 years could not be shown in men. In women who became obese at some point between 11 and 23 years of age, it was found that salaries were negatively affected at age 23 years.

An American study from 1981 investigated a sample of 10 039 individuals aged 16 to 24 years [6]. Followup occurred 7 years later. A significantly negative correlation between obesity and income was found in both men and women, i. e., the higher the obesity the lower the income. Furthermore, the authors found that obesity results in greater social consequences for the individual than other chronic, physical diseases. This was supported by the fact that the authors found no significant correlation between other chronic physical diseases and, e. g., self-esteem and the percentage of subjects who were married. However, they did find a negative correlation between obesity and self-esteem and the percentage of married subjects.

Since the authors defined obesity differently and did not used identical models, reliable conclusions cannot be drawn from the results. Both of the studies that included women suggest a negative correlation between obesity and income. In men, the results do not clearly point in either direction, and the correlation between obesity and income appears to be weaker.

Willingness to pay One way to determine how obese people value their poor health is to ask a sample how much they would be willing to pay for hypothetically effective treatment.

A study from Sweden surveyed 3549 individuals with an average BMI of 39.6 about their willingness to pay [15]. A positive correlation was found between willingness to pay and a high household income, high weight, high education, gender (women), and low age. On average, the respondents were willing to pay twice their monthly income for a treatment that would eliminate their overweight-related health problems.

1.4.3.3 Conclusions

- A general assessment of international studies suggests that the direct costs of obesity-related diseases are approximately 2 % of the expenditure on health care.
- Clearly, there is a positive correlation between increased BMI and increased cost of care and treatment.
- The scientific evidence for assessing indirect costs is limited. A Swedish (Göteborg) study suggests that the costs of lost productivity from short-term absenteeism and early retirement correspond to 10 % of total lost productivity in women during that year.
- The correlation between obesity and personal income has been studied, but the results are uncertain. Possibly, there is a negative correlation between obesity and income in women.

References Section 1.4

1. Allison DB, Zannolli R, Narayan KM. The direct health care costs of obesity in the United States. Am J Public Health 1999;89(8):1194-9.
2. Birmingham CL, Muller JL, Palepu A, Spinelli JJ, Anis AH. The cost of obesity in Canada. Cmaj 1999;160(4): 483-8.
3. Burton WN, Chen CY, Schultz AB, Edington DW. The economic costs associated with body mass index in a workplace. J Occup Environ Med 1998;40(9):786-92.
4. Colditz GA. Economic costs of obesity. Am J Clin Nutr 1992;55(2 Suppl): 503S-7S.
5. Detournay B, Fagnani F, Phillippo M, Pribil C, Charles MA, Sermet C, et al. Obesity morbidity and health care costs in France: an analysis of the 1991–1992 Medical Care Household Survey. Int J Obes Relat Metab Disord 2000;24(2):151-5.
6. Gortmaker SL, Must A, Perrin JM, Sobol AM, Dietz WH. Social and economic consequences of overweight in adolescence and young adulthood. N Engl J Med 1993;329(14):1008-12.
7. Henriksson F, Fredrikson S, Masterman T, Jonsson B. Costs, quality of life and disease severity in multiple sclerosis: a crosssectional study in Sweden. Eur J Neurol 2001;8(1): 27-35.
8. Holmberg H, Carlsson P, Kalman D, Varenhorst E. Impact on health service costs of medical technologies used in management of prostatic cancer. Scand J Urol Nephrol 1998;32(3):195-9.
9. Jonsson D, Husberg M. Samhällsekonomiska kostnader för reumatiska sjukdomar. CMT Rapport 5. Centrum för utvärdering av medicinsk teknologi, Hälsouniversitetet, Linköping; 1995.
10. Kortt MA, Langley PC, Cox ER. A review of cost-of-illness studies on obesity. Clin Ther 1998;20(4):772-9.
11. Leffler E, Gustavsson S, Karlson BM. Time trends in obesity surgery 1987 through 1996 in Sweden – a population-based study. Obes Surg 2000;10(6):543-8.
12. Levy E, Levy P, Le Pen C, Basdevant A. The economic cost of obesity: the French situation. Int J Obes Relat Metab Disord 1995;19(11):788-92.
13. McLean RA, Moon M. Health, obesity, and earnings. Am J Public Health 1980;70(9):1006-9.
14. Narbro K, Jonsson E, Larsson B, Waaler H, Wedel H, Sjöstrom L. Economic consequences of sick-leave and early retirement in obese Swedish women. Int J Obes Relat Metab Disord 1996;20(10):895-903.
15. Narbro K, Sjöstrom L. Willingness to pay for obesity treatment. Int J Technol Assess Health Care 2000;16(1):50-9.
16. Narbro K, Ågren G, Jonsson E, Näslund I, Sjöström L, Peltonen M. Pharmaceutical costs in obese: A comparison with randomly selected population sample, and long-term changes after conventional and surgical treatment. The SOS intervention study. I: Narbro K, Economic aspects

on obesity, Göteborgs universitet (avhandling); 2001.

17. Oster G, Thompson D, Edelsberg J, Bird AP, Colditz GA. Lifetime health and economic benefits of weight loss among obese persons. Am J Public Health 1999;89(10):1536-42.

18. Quesenberry CP, Jr, Caan B, Jacobson A. Obesity, health services use, and health care costs among members of a health maintenance organization. Arch Intern Med 1998;158(5):466-72.

19. Sargent JD, Blanchflower DG. Obesity and stature in adolescence and earnings in young adulthood. Analysis of a British birth cohort. Arch Pediatr Adolesc Med 1994;148(7):681-7.

20. Segal L, Carter R, Zimmet P. The cost of obesity: the Australian perspective. Pharmacoeconomics 1994;5(Suppl): 45-52.

21. Seidell JC. The impact of obesity on health status: some implications for health care costs. Int J Obes Relat Metab Disord 1995;19(Suppl 6):S13-6.

22. Socialstyrelsen. Hälso- och sjukvårds-statistisk årsbok 2000, (nätversion), Stockholm.

23. Swinburn B, Ashton T, Gillespie J, Cox B, Menon A, Simmons D, et al. Health care costs of obesity in New Zealand. Int J Obes Relat Metab Disord 1997;21(10):891-6.

24. Thompson D, Edelsberg J, Colditz GA, Bird AP, Oster G. Lifetime health and economic consequences of obesity. Arch Intern Med 1999;159(18): 2177-83.

25. Wolf AM, Colditz GA. Social and economic effects of body weight in the United States. Am J Clin Nutr 1996; 63(3 Suppl):466S-9S.

26. Wolf AM, Colditz GA. Current estimates of the economic cost of obesity in the United States. Obes Res 1998;6(2):97-106.

27. Sturm R. The effects of obesity, smoking, and drinking on medical problems and outranks both smoking and drinking in its deleterious effects on health and costs. Health Aff (Millwood) 2002;21(2):245-53.

2
Systematic Literature Review – Methods

2.1
Background

The systematic literature review upon which this book is based was initiated with the establishment of a project plan that outlined two main areas:

1. Prevention of obesity in adults, adolescents, and children
2. Treatment of obesity in adults, adolescents, and children.

Each Chapter was divided into Sections. Two members of the Project Group shared the primary responsibility for each Chapter in the report.

To ensure that all questions and treatment methods of relevance for patients and the public were included, the Project Group called a meeting of laypersons. This meeting included representatives from national patient organizations for overweight people and for people with diabetes, two members of the SBU group of laypersons, and a journalist. Some of the viewpoints and perspectives generated through this discussion were included in the project plan. This group was also included in the review and comment process for the summary of the report.

2.2
Literature Search

A literature search covered articles from 1966 to 2001 in the MEDLINE database and the Cochrane Library. The search was conducted separately for adults (over 18 years) and children (0-18 years). The main search terms are presented in Table 2.1. Other databases were used to search the following four areas:

1. Costs and health economic assessments: Cinahl, HEED, and NHS (Center for Reviews and Dissemination)
2. Alternative medicine: Embase, Cinahl
3. Ethics: PsycInfo
4. Quality of life: PsycInfo.

Treating and Preventing Obesity. Edited by J. Östman, M. Britton, E. Jonsson
Copyright © 2004 WILEY-VCH Verlag GmbH & Co. KGaA, Weinheim
ISBN 3-527-30818-0

Table 2.1 Main search terms and combined search terms used to search the literature

Studies of adults >18 years	Studies of children 0–18 years
Obesity:	Obesity:
prevention and control	diet therapy
exercise	drug therapy
exercise therapy	therapy
diet therapy	rehabilitation
dietary fiber	surgery
very low calorie diet	prevention and control
behavior therapy	
quality of life	
ephedrine and caffeine	
lipase inhibitors	
sibutramine	
drug therapy	
surgery	
gastric bypass	
sleep apnea	
infertility, female	
polycystic ovary syndrome	
costs and cost analysis, cost-effectiveness	
cost benefit, cost utility	
sick leave	
pension and disability	
ethics	
alternative medicine	

A search for additional studies was conducted via reference lists in relevant articles, conference reports, international contacts of Project Group members, and review articles. Studies on prevention may be classified in the databases under headings other than those presented in Table 2.1. Therefore, searches were also conducted via the SBU report on preventing cardiovascular disease (1997).

2.3
Literature Review and Quality Assessment

Review and classification of studies included three phases:

Phase 1

Abstracts were used to classify the studies. Two members of the Project Group, independently of each other, reviewed each abstract. The goal was to identify non-relevant studies: i.e., studies that did not address the subject of obesity, did not address the project questions, where the problem of obesity could not be distinguished from other issues in the study, case studies, editorials, comments, animal experiments, etc. The following languages were accepted: Danish, English, French, German, Norwegian, and Swedish. If a particularly relevant study was identified in another language it was also included. The section on alternative medicine/treatment methods (Section 4.7) includes studies in Chinese. The results from the two independent reviewers were compared, and studies that were judged as "potentially relevant" by one or both reviewers were included in Phase 2. Full text versions of published articles were acquired prior to Phase 2 of the review process.

Phase 2

Two members of the Project Group conducted a new review of the entire article. As in Phase 1, the goal continued to be the identification of non-relevant studies. During this phase, the reasons for eliminating studies were recorded. Previously specified minimum standards were applied to determine whether the study would proceed to Phase 3 of the literature review. The requirements were as follows:

- The studies should address obesity, i. e., BMI > 30 according to the WHO definition. In several studies that were conducted before the BMI concept was applied, overweight was reported in the number of kilograms or the percent above normal or "ideal" weight based on the "Metropolitan Height and Weight Tables". Therefore, this book also includes studies that to some extent may classify individuals as overweight but where many of the participants were actually obese according to the BMI definition. However, the conclusions presented in the Sections of this book are based mainly on findings from studies where obesity is confirmed.
- The followup period of the study should be at least 12 months. In most cases, shorter times (6 months) were accepted if no other material in the subject area could be found. This has been specifically noted and accounted for in the quality rating.
- A control group is required. In a few cases, however, studies without control groups, e. g., concerning surgery and alternative medicine, have been included since they were the only studies available.
- The study must contain relevant outcome variables, preferably weight loss/ weight stability and mortality, quality of life, and psychosocial consequences. Morbidity, e. g., myocardial infarction, stroke, sleep apnea, orthopedic load injuries, fertility improvement, sick leave, and hospitalization were also found to be relevant outcome variables. Other variables include recovery or improvement from diabetes, hypertension, and blood lipid disorders that are severe enough to require treatment.
- Reports on side effects and risks of various treatment methods were particularly sought after, and were included in the ongoing review.
- Health economic assessments, e. g., studies addressing the cost of obesity-related diseases, were reviewed based on the criteria presented in Section 1.4 and Chapter 8.

Phase 3

The final review included the studies judged by one or both of the reviewers to meet, or potentially meet, the minimum requirements. These studies were rated for quality based on the type of study and according to a three-grade scale that reflected high, medium, and low quality. In cases where the two reviewers did not agree on the quality grade, other members of the Project Group were asked to read the article, and it was either included or excluded following discussion.

Quality was assessed using the following criteria, which appear in order of priority from the highest to lowest quality:

Type
- Randomized studies
- Studies with matched controls/ecological controls
- Studies with uncertain or no control groups.

Followup
Treatment studies:
- More than 2 years
- 1–2 years
- In exceptional cases less than 1 year.

Prevention studies:
- More than 5 years
- 3–5 years
- 1–2 years.

Dropout
- Less than 20%
- 20–30%
- 30–40%.

Size, total number of patients followed
Treatment studies:
- More than 150
- 75–150
- 25–75.

Prevention studies:
- More than 1000
- 500–1000
- 200–500.

Studies that received high points for all variables were found to have *high quality* and studies with low points were found to have *low quality*. Studies that fell in between these parameters were judged to have *medium quality*. Furthermore, a *low score* was given to all studies having more than 40% dropout, with fewer than 25 patients treated, and with fewer than 200 individuals in studies of preventive interventions.

As mentioned above, different criteria were used to rate the health economic studies.

2.4
Reporting Facts and Conclusions

Facts were extracted from all studies with high or medium quality. In some areas where no other information could be found, even low quality studies were referenced. When study findings could be identified for males, females, and children, these figures were presented separately. A synthesis of the results from studies with high and medium quality was then conducted. Only statistically significant differences in results were included ($p < 0.05$). The absence of such a difference does not necessarily mean that the method has no effect, but that this effect could not be demonstrated.

The conclusions presented in this book have been rated based on the strength of the underlying scientific evidence in accordance with the following scale:

Grade 1 – Strong scientific evidence. At least two studies supported by high quality or a good systematic review. Nothing substantial contradicts the findings.

Grade 2 – Moderate scientific evidence. One study supported by high quality and at least two studies supported by medium quality. Nothing substantial contradicts the findings.

Grade 3 – Limited scientific evidence. At least two studies supported by medium quality. Nothing substantial contradicts the findings.

No conclusions were drawn on evidence judged to fall below Grade 3 in quality.

3
Preventing Obesity

3.1
Preventing Obesity in Adults

Summary

Eleven studies met the quality requirements established for this report. The goals of these studies have focused on preventing cardiovascular diseases by reducing smoking, treating hypertension, and treating high cholesterol. Only to a limited extent did the goals focus on preventing the onset of obesity. Information concerning diet and exercise was disseminated via the mass media and newsletters, or at the workplace. Two studies are based on high quality, five on medium quality, and four on low quality. The studies of low quality have short observation periods or substantial dropout.

A study in Sweden (Norsjö) achieved favorable effects on cholesterol levels and smoking, but not on the prevalence of obesity. Similar results were achieved in five large North American studies. Two of these studies showed the weight gain that normally occurs in a population to be somewhat lower in cities with intervention programs for prevention than in the control areas. An ambitious intervention program in a small region in Israel resulted in a lower prevalence of overweight.

Conclusions: Population-based intervention programs for prevention have focused mainly on cardiovascular diseases and not specifically on overweight or obesity. Findings from a few studies suggest there are opportunities to slow the rate of increase in obesity in the population. However, it is essential to design and assess new strategies that are adapted to a nation's population.

3.1.1
Introduction

Obesity generally develops over a relatively long period and in a context where many genetic, social, cultural, and behavioral factors interact to create an imbalance between the intake and the utilization of energy.

Modern society provides the conditions for obesity to develop. Yet, at the same time these conditions have increased life expectancy and improved the health status of the population in general. The structure of society leads to efficiency in food

Treating and Preventing Obesity. Edited by J. Östman, M. Britton, E. Jonsson
Copyright © 2004 WILEY-VCH Verlag GmbH & Co. KGaA, Weinheim
ISBN 3-527-30818-0

production, infrastructure, distribution, storage, and advertising (even for high-fat products), but also leads to many factors that play a role in obesity. Contemporary society also places a much lower demand for physical activity. Good communication, automated transport, escalators, elevators, etc. influence these trends as do the lower proportion of physically demanding work and higher access to sedentary entertainment and activities. From an evolutionary standpoint, humans have benefited from utilizing energy from food as efficiently as possible. One theory is that humans have genes programmed to store energy when food is abundant. This energy can be used when access to food becomes limited.

Theoretically, obesity can develop from relatively insignificant and barely measurable changes in the balance between intake and utilization of energy that continues for a sufficiently long period. After obesity has been established, human physiological processes attempt to maintain the weight achieved. The mechanism responsible for this phenomenon is largely unknown. In principle, obesity can be prevented by means of long-term strategies and basic dietary habits that correspond to an individual's energy requirements and/or through greater physical activity.

Studies addressing the effects of preventive measures in general, and the prevention of obesity in particular, involve many methodological and other problems which should be considered when assessing the results. To accurately interpret the results of preventive intervention, such studies must continue for many years. During this period, various conditions in society can influence either the control group or the reference region in the same way as the trial group or the intervention region.

Hence, it can be difficult to determine the differences among groups and areas and draw conclusions concerning the effects of preventive interventions. Another obstacle facing preventive interventions are the extremely powerful and contrary messages promoting fast food, chips, soft drinks, candy, and sedentary activities that are communicated via advertising in the mass media. In this environment, it becomes difficult to promote the findings from scientific studies. Another difficulty with preventive programs aimed at obesity is to identify, define, measure, and assess all relevant results from the interventions and isolate those interventions that actually have an effect on weight and other variables. Interest on the part of the research community in studies on the prevention of obesity has also been rather limited, which is reflected by the relatively small number of studies published in the field.

Most of the programs for prevention described in the scientific literature have been designed to prevent cardiovascular disease by means of interventions to reduce cholesterol, high blood pressure, smoking, and other risk factors. Even if these programs are not primarily targeted at preventing obesity, they are often based on informational activities that promote healthy diets and increased exercise. Hence, they provide indirect information about the results of preventing obesity.

Prevention may be *primary*, i.e., aimed at preventing the occurrence of a disease, or *secondary*, i.e., aimed at preventing recurrence. One of the goals in the area of obesity is to prevent weight gain in the entire adult population and hence the percentage of obese individuals. An analysis of weight change in several populations has estimated that the prevalence of obesity declines by approximately 25 % when BMI is reduced by 1 unit [11].

A health-oriented public policy may be population-based, i. e., include several different coordinated interventions aimed at improving dietary habits and increasing physical activity in the entire population. Controlled, population-based studies aimed at reducing risk factors for cardiovascular disease began in the mid 1970s. This type of study compared intervention and control groups from different geographic regions. Not only the intervention program itself, but also changes in the prevalence of risk factors of other causes over time can influence the results, making it more difficult to interpret them.

Hence, it is possible that even participants in the control cities improve their life-style because of the information disseminated.

The effects of intervention programs can be studied using a *cross-sectional design*, whereby studies are performed in different years on a large number of randomly selected individuals from both the intervention and the control regions. This method allows for causes other than the intervention program, e. g., changes over time.

Effects can also be monitored using a *cohort design*, i. e., following, for several years, only those individuals who were initially examined for the risk factors. This method has greater power to assess change, and the results can be related to certain initially defined groups of individuals. A disadvantage with this method is that the repeated contacts and examinations may influence the results in both the intervention and control groups. The strength of the evidence is high when the results of cross-sectional and cohort analysis are in agreement.

Strictly individual-based intervention studies can be considered to assess effects on individuals who fall within the risk zone for a disease, e. g., cardiovascular disease. This high-risk strategy is applicable to individuals with pronounced obesity and in those where obesity is associated with type 2 diabetes, hypertension, or blood lipid disorders.

3.1.2
Methods

A MEDLINE search was carried out using the search terms "obesity", "prevention", "randomized clinical trial", and "Minnesota Heart Health Program". In the first phase, the literature search identified 54 studies. An additional 15 studies were found in reference lists of studies that focused on prevention on cardiovascular disease. Based on the abstracts of these 69 articles, 53 studies were selected. The complete studies were evaluated, and 8 were found to meet the quality requirements established. Rejected studies were eliminated for the following reasons:

- 23 studies lacked primary data. These were mainly overviews or presented only hypotheses
- 17 studies did not focus on prevention
- 2 studies had excessive dropout

- 2 studies lacked relevant control groups
- 1 study had too few participants (< 200 individuals).

In later followup, 3 additional studies were found that met the quality criteria. Hence, the critical review includes 11 studies that were presented in 12 articles. All of these studies are population-based.

Furthermore, several individual-based studies were reviewed that focus on type 2 diabetes and hypertension. These studies are presented in Chapter 7 (Sections 7.1 and 7.2).

3.1.3
Results

An intervention study in Sweden (Norsjö, 1985–1990) included population-based interventions in combination with a high-risk strategy in regard to preventing cardiovascular risk factors, primarily hypertension, high cholesterol, and smoking (Table 3.1) [2]. The study invited everyone aged 30, 40, 50, and 60 years in each municipality (approximately 260 individuals per year), and 95 % participated in the study. The prevalence of obesity (BMI $\geq$ 30) was initially 13 % in men and 14 % in women, and did not change for the duration of the study.

The Stanford Three Project assessed the effects on traditional risk factors from a mass media campaign that focused on fat in the diet [5, 7]. Furthermore, high-risk patients in one of the two intervention cities received individualized instruction. Over 400 people (aged 35–59 years) participated in each city. After 2 years, smoking, hypertension, and cholesterol levels had declined in the intervention cities, but no effects were observed in weight trends, expressed as relative weight, (current/ ideal weight) [5]. At followup after 3 years, no difference was found between the intervention and the control cities [7, 12].

A 5-year intervention study using a cross-sectional design (Community Focused Program for the Control of Hypertension, Atherosclerosis, and Diabetes - CHAD), was introduced in the 1970s in Israel and included approximately 500 subjects and a control population (approximately 1500 people) in a nearby district [1]. The program was integrated into primary care. Compared to the control population, average body weight declined by 0.6 kg in the intervention group. The percentage of overweight men and women (BMI $\geq$ 28) declined by 23 % and 7 % respectively.

A broad program for primary prevention of cardiovascular disease was started in 1977 in two cities in Switzerland with 13 000 and 15 000 inhabitants respectively and two control cities [8]. The information was distributed via the mass media and local committees. Furthermore, attempts were made to influence dietary habits via food producers and restaurants. In the intervention cities, BMI increased insignificantly more than in the control cities. A major weakness is that only about one third of the total number invited actually participated in the program.

Several population-based interventions were performed within the framework of the Minnesota Heart Health Program (MHHP). The goal of this study, initiated in 1980 and carried out in a population of about 400 000 people, was to reduce the

Table 3.1 Effects on obesity/overweight in studies aimed at preventing cardiovascular diseases.

Author Year Reference	Study design	Inclusion criteria (Recruitment)	Intervention method	Followup period	No. Partici-pants/ (%= followed up)	Results BMI and weight	Results/Other	Study quality Comments
Brännström I et al. 1993 [2] Norsjö Sweden	CT	Interv: Norsjö. Annually approx. 260 individuals ex-amined aged 30, 40, 50, and 60 years. Contr: approx. 1600	Community-based information	5 years	Interv: (95 %) Contr: (80 %)	Cross-sectional analysis: % with BMI >30 unchanged in Interv and de-clined in Contr. Not significant	Interv: Cholesterol decreased. Smoking decreased in those with higher educa-tion. Antihyperten-sive therapy un-changed	Medium
Farquhar JW et al. 1977 [5] Stanford Three Community Study USA	CT	Three cities 35–59 years (California)	Interv 1: One city mass media infor-mation. Interv 2: One city ditto + individual therapy for high risk of cardiovascular disease Contr: One city	2 years	Interv 1: 427 (74 %) Interv 2: 449 (62 %) Contr: 418 (72 %)	No difference in relative weight	Systolic blood pressure and cholesterol decreased. Smoking decreased	Low
Fortmann SP et al. 1981 [7] Stanford Three Community Study USA Stern MP et al. 1976 [12] Stanford Three Community Study USA	CT	Three cities 35–59 years (California)	Interv 1: One city mass media infor-mation. Interv 2: One city, ditto + individual therapy for high risk of cardiovascular disease Contr: One city	3 years	Interv 1: 385 (58 %) Interv 2: 263 (68 %) Contr: 365 (66 %)	Relative weight unchanged in Interv and Contr	Cholesterol increased less in Interv than in Contr	Medium

See legend on page 70

Table continues on next page

Table 3.1 continued

Author Year Reference	Study design	Inclusion criteria (Recruitment)	Intervention method	Followup period	No. Partici-pants/ (%= followed up)	Results BMI and weight	Results/Other	Study quality Comments
Abramson JH et al. 1981 [1] CHAD Israel	CT	>35 years. Interv and Contr areas in West Jerusalem	Information via district physicians and nurses	5 years	1970 Interv: 574 (85 %) Contr: 1834 (91 %) 1975 Interv: 524 (91 %) Contr: 1512 (83 %)	Interv: Preva-lence of over-weight declined from 31.8 % to 27.6 %. (13 % net reduction com-pared to Contr*) M –23 % W –7 %	Interv: Prevalence of hypertension, smok-ing, and overweight decreased. No differ-ence in cholesterol between Interv and Contr	Medium
Gutzwiller F et al. 1985 [8] Switzerland	CT	Interv: Two cities Contr: Two cities 16–69 years	Massive informa-tion, activation of participants, envir-onmental interven-tions (restaurants and food producers)	3 years	Interv: 848 (27 %) Contr: 1358 (39 %)	Interv: BMI +0.4* Contr: BMI –0.1	Interv: Blood pressure increased, smoking decreased. Interv and Contr: Cholesterol declined	Low Poor participation
Forster JL et al. 1988 [6] USA	RCT	Approximately 3000 individuals contacted through MHHP	Interv: Dietary info through newsletter + economic reim-bursement Contr: No intervention	1 year	Interv: 103 Contr: 108 Total drop-out 8 %	Interv: –1.0 kg* Contr: –0.1 kg	Interv: Smoking decreased. Choles-terol and blood pressure unchanged	Low Poor participation
Jeffery RW et al. 1999 [9] USA	RCT	1226 contacted through MHHP (approx 1/3 low-income participants). Mainly women	Interv 1: Dietary info via newsletter Interv 2: Ditto + economic reimbur-sement Contr: No intervention	3 years	Interv 1: 414 Interv 2: 198 Contr: 197	Interv 1: +1.6 kg Interv 2: +1.5 kg Contr: +1.8 kg		Low

Jeffery RW et al. 1995 [10] USA	CT	MHHP with weight reduction for overweight. 25–74 years	Interv: Three cities received information via mass media, direct education, workplace information Contr: Three cities	7 years	Interv: 3527 Contr: 3525 Dropout 67%	BMI increased 1 unit in both Interv and Contr. Cross-sectional analysis and cohort analysis yielded same result	Interv: Cohort analysis showed that both cholesterol and obesity related diseases decreased	Medium
Taylor CB et al. 1991 [13] Stanford Five City project USA	CT partly RCT	12–74 years	Interv: Information via mass media in two cities Contr: Two cities	6 years	Cross-sectional analysis approx 800 and cohort 743 (64%)	Cross-sectional analysis: Interv: 0.57 kg* Contr: 1.25 kg Cohort analysis no difference		High
Carleton RA et al. 1995 [3] USA	RCT	Interv: Pawtucket Contr: Control city 18–64 years	Interv: Broad information Contr: No intervention	6 years	Interv: Approx 6000 (68%) Contr: Approx 1200 (68%)	Cross-sectional analysis: BMI increased less in Interv 0.25* than Contr 0.88. Cohort analysis no difference	Cross-sectional and cohort analysis: No difference between Interv and Contr regarding cholesterol, smoking, blood pressure	Medium
Tudor-Smith C et al. 1998 [14] Heartbeat Wales Program Great Britain	RCT	18–64 years Interv: Wales Contr: Two regions in East England	Interv: Broad mass media info on diet, exercise, smoking, and high accessibility to nutritious food. Contr: No intervention	5 years	Interv: 1985: 18 538 (88%) 1990: 13 045 (79%) Contr: 1985: 1483 (64%) 1990: 4534 (61%)	Interv: Prevalence of overweight increased from 43% to 46%. Contr: Prevalence of overweight unchanged 40% versus 41%.	In Interv and Contr groups, improved dietary choice and unchanged exercise. Interv: Reduced smoking	High

Table continues on next page

See legend on page 70

Table 3.1 continued

Author Year Reference	Study design	Inclusion criteria (Recruitment)	Intervention method	Followup period	No. Partici- pants/ (%= followed up)	Results BMI and weight	Results/Other	Study quality Comments
Dowse GK et al. 1995 [4] Mauritius	Pro- spec- tive	25–74 years in 11 regions	Information via mass media, schools, workplaces	5 years	1987: 5080 (86%) 1992: 5162 (96%)	BMI >30 M: +1.9% W: +4.8% BMI 25–30 M: +7.6% W: +5.3%	Hypertension, smok- ing, and high alcohol consumption de- creased. Cholesterol decreased. Exercise increased	Low

RCT = Randomized Controlled Trial
CT = Controlled Trial
Interv = Intervention group
Contr = Conrol group
M = Men
W = Women
CHAD = Community Focused Program for the Control of Hypertension, Atherosclerosis, and Diabetes
MHHP = Minnesota Heart Health Program
* = Statistical significance

incidence of cardiovascular disease by 15 % by reducing smoking, lowering blood pressure and cholesterol, and counteracting obesity. Participants from an earlier health study were recruited by letter and received monthly newsletters with instructions about diet and physical activity [6]. They also paid a fee that was returned in full following this study. The average weight loss based on self-reporting was greater in the intervention group (1.0 kg) than in the control group (0.1 kg). Against the background of the findings in this pilot study, in which only 7 % of all invited participated, Jeffery started a similar low-intensive, three-year educational program in several areas with high percentages of low-income residents [9]. The study included 1226 people (aged 20 to 45), mostly women. The participants were randomized to a control group and two intervention groups who received instruction about diet and physical activity, mainly via monthly newsletters. Free lottery tickets were used to encourage participation in one of the intervention groups. About 400 individuals dropped out, some because of pregnancy. The intervention group reported an average weight gain of 1.6 kg, which was insignificantly lower than in the control group.

Another part of the MHHP report studied the effects of improved dietary and exercise habits in preventing obesity [10]. The information was distributed via the mass media, in schools and home-based programs, at workplaces, supermarkets, and restaurants. In total, 3500 individuals started in the three intervention cities and an equal number in the three control cities. At the outset, the mean BMI was 26.6 in men and 25.0 in women. The report presents a cross-sectional analysis and an assessment of cohorts, with a dropout of approximately 30 %. The results, which were similar with the two methods, showed that in 7 years the BMI had increased by 1 unit, with no difference between the intervention and control cities.

Taylor et al. (Stanford Five-City Project) provided the public with health and dietary information via various mass media. The information was aimed at reducing the prevalence of cardiovascular risk factors, e. g., weight gain [13]. The inhabitants (n=1700) in two intervention cities and two control cities were randomized for a random sample study on four occasions. After 5 years, the average weight increase was 0.57 kg in the cities where information was provided and 1.25 kg in the control cities. The results varied both among the different age groups and between men and women. Some differences among the cities and among the time periods were difficult to explain. However, no difference was found among the cities in an analysis of the four cohorts, all of which had substantial dropout.

A comprehensive intervention study was conducted in Pawtucket Rhode Island (United States) from 1980 through 1993 [3]. BMI, blood cholesterol, blood pressure, and the prevalence of smoking were evaluated every second year in about 6000 individuals and an equal number in a reference city. A cross-sectional analysis showed that BMI increased substantially less in the intervention cities, while no difference was found in other risk factors. A cohort analysis did not find any differences among the cities.

In Wales, a randomized, stratified prevention study focused on cardiovascular diseases (Heartbeat Wales Program) [14]. The study targeted individuals aged 18 through 64 years. The primary goal was to improve diet and exercise habits and reduce smoking. Information was distributed via the mass media, e. g., repeated TV programs, while concurrently increasing the access to healthy food. The study used a cross-sectional design and included over 31 000 people in the intervention area (approximately 18 600 people in 1985 and 13 000 in 1990). Two reference areas in Eastern England had nearly 1500 participants in the first year and approximately 4500 at followup. Fifteen indicators in a written questionnaire were used for assessment. In the intervention area, 13 of these indicators had improved, e. g., chicken, fish, vegetables, and low-fat milk were more frequent in the diet in the intervention area. Smoking declined somewhat and physical activity remained unchanged. Nine indicators improved in the reference areas, e. g., those mentioned above. The prevalence of overweight increased in the intervention area from 43 % to 46 %, but remained unchanged in the reference areas. A reason why no effects from intervention were noted could be that the preventive interventions became known in the reference areas.

An interesting intervention program in Mauritius was assessed for 1987 through 1992 within the framework of a WHO initiative ("Interhealth") [4]. Intensive information about how to improve lifestyle was distributed via the mass media, at schools and at workplaces. Changes were made in legislation and taxes. Of over 5000 people invited, around 85 % participated in both examinations. BMI increased in both men and women and in all subgroups, independently of age and ethnicity. Obesity increased in men from 3.4 % to 5.3 % and in women from 10.4 % to 15.2 %. Contributing factors, according to the authors, could be lower employment and reduced tobacco smoking. The prevalence of both manifest diabetes and reduced glucose tolerance did not change. However, cholesterol levels declined, as did the prevalence of hypertension and smoking. Alcohol consumption also declined. Since there was no reference population, it is not possible to determine the extent to which the findings reflect a change over time or are related to actual changes in lifestyle through the intervention program. For this reason, the study was not used in formulating the conclusions of this Chapter.

3.1.4
Discussion

Large intervention studies addressing traditional risk factors for cardiovascular disease have been conducted in several countries, mainly in the United States. Since obesity has not been the primary focus, these studies have been difficult to identify.

Two of the studies meet the requirements for high quality [13, 14]. Five of the studies present low quality due to small study groups, short followup time, and dropout during recruitment of participants or followup. A common methodological weakness is that the outcome measures consist of average BMI and body weight or changes in these parameters. Three studies report on the change in prevalence of overweight/obesity, which is a more important outcome measure. The reason why no effect was shown from the intervention in one of these studies was that knowledge about the preventive interventions became known in the reference areas. In two studies, the results from cross-sectional analysis show that the intervention can, to some extent, counteract weight gain in the population, while the cohort analysis showed no effects. Hence, the effects of the intervention program are viewed as uncertain.

Apparently, preventing obesity is substantially more difficult than lowering blood cholesterol or reducing smoking. This can be explained by the fact that other risk factors receive higher priority than obesity and that interventions against obesity have not been effective.

The problems with this type of intervention involve deficient knowledge and the negative attitudes toward obesity treatment and prevention, even among well-educated staff. Better knowledge about the nature of the problem would probably improve the chances of success. Obesity can be particularly difficult to prevent since diet and exercise habits may be difficult to change. Also, various unknown physiological regulation mechanisms play a role.

Different types of interventions have been attempted. As regards the effects on blood pressure and blood cholesterol, it appears that broad information via the mass media and at the workplace can be relatively successful. However, it appears that informational brochures that encourage participation in educational programs are ineffective. Certain types of studies are lacking, e. g., studies that combine dietary information with encouragement and opportunities to increase physical activity in daily life.

References Section 3.1

1. Abramson JH, Gofin R, Hopp C, Gofin J, Donchin M, Habib J. Evaluation of a community program for the control of cardiovascular risk factors: the CHAD program in Jerusalem. Isr J Med Sci 1981;17(2-3):201-12.

2. Brännström I, Weinehall L, Persson LA, Wester PO, Wall S. Changing social patterns of risk factors for cardiovascular disease in a Swedish community intervention programme. Int J Epidemiol 1993;22(6):1026-37.

3. Carleton RA, Lasater TM, Assaf AR, Feldman HA, McKinlay S. The Pawtucket Heart Health Program: community changes in cardiovascular risk factors and projected disease risk. Am J Public Health 1995; 85(6):777-85.

4. Dowse GK, Gareeboo H, Alberti KG, Zimmet P, Tuomilehto J, Purran A, et al. Changes in population cholesterol concentrations and other cardiovascular risk factor levels after five years of the non-communicable disease intervention programme in Mauritius. Mauritius Non-communicable Disease Study Group. BMJ 1995; 311(7015):1255-9.

5. Farquhar JW, Maccoby N, Wood PD, Alexander JK, Breitrose H, Brown BW, Jr, et al. Community education for cardiovascular health. Lancet 1977;1(8023):1192-5.

6. Forster JL, Jeffery RW, Schmid TL, Kramer FM. Preventing weight gain in adults: a pound of prevention. Health Psychol 1988;7(6):515-25.

7. Fortmann SP, Williams PT, Hulley SB, Haskell WL, Farquhar JW. Effect of health education on dietary behavior: the Stanford Three Community Study. Am J Clin Nutr 1981;34(10):2030-8.

8. Gutzwiller F, Nater B, Martin J. Community-based primary prevention of cardiovascular disease in Switzerland: methods and results of the National Research Program (NRP 1A). Prev Med 1985;14(4):482-91.

9. Jeffery RW, French SA. Preventing weight gain in adults: the pound of prevention study. Am J Public Health 1999;89(5):747-51.

10. Jeffery RW, Gray CW, French SA, Hellerstedt WL, Murray D, Luepker RV, et al. Evaluation of weight reduction in a community intervention for cardiovascular disease risk: changes in body mass index in the Minnesota Heart Health Program. Int J Obes Relat Metab Disord 1995;19(1):30-9.

11. Rose G. Population distributions of risk and disease. Nutr Metab Cardiovasc Dis 1991;1:37-50.

12. Stern MP, Farquhar JW, McCoby N, Russell SH. Results of a two-year health education campaign on dietary behavior. The Stanford Three Community Study. Circulation 1976;54(5):826-33.

13. Taylor CB, Fortmann SP, Flora J, Kayman S, Barrett DC, Jatulis D, et al. Effect of long-term community health education on body mass index. The Stanford Five-City Project. Am J Epidemiol 1991;134(3):235-49.

14. Tudor-Smith C, Nutbeam D, Moore L, Catford J. Effects of the Heartbeat Wales programme over five years on behavioural risks for cardiovascular disease: quasiexperimental comparison of results from Wales and a matched reference area. BMJ 1998;316(7134):818 22.

3.2
Preventing Obesity in Children and Adolescents

Summary

Fourteen controlled studies were found on preventing obesity in children and adolescents. Eight of the studies presented high or medium quality, and all involved preschool and school-aged children aged 5 years and above. Most included programs to promote physical activity and good eating habits at the school. Several of the studies also included elements directly targeted at parents. The results were followed up after 2 to 5 years.

Results: The most relevant outcome measure, i. e., the percentage of overweight and obese children, was not used in more than 2 of the studies. One of the studies found no difference between the experimental and control groups. The second study showed a reduction in the percentage of overweight girls, but no change among boys in the experimental groups. The mean BMI was followed in the other studies. This declined in 2 of the studies, but was not influenced to a statistically significant degree in the other 4 studies presenting medium quality. Several studies reported improved blood lipids and reduced blood pressure in the treatment groups.

Conclusions: Of the 8 strongest studies, positive results were achieved in 3 studies, and no effects were shown in 5 studies. Consequently, reliable conclusions cannot be drawn.

3.2.1
Methods

A MEDLINE search for preventive interventions against obesity in children and adolescents yielded 158 abstracts. Of these, 132 were excluded because they did not focus on prevention or were based on overviews, opinions, editorials, or studies with no control groups. The 26 remaining publications were reviewed in their entirety in Phase 2. Within this group, 4 studies met the minimum criteria.

Several studies focused primarily on preventing cardiovascular diseases, and these studies were not identified by the search terms selected. A complementary search that focused on cardiovascular disease and a further review of earlier overview articles identified 6 studies. Also included were 4 recently published studies. In total, 14 studies were approved for review.

For the purpose of reporting on particularly interesting observations, 4 studies were included with followup times shorter than 2 years (2 studies), with incomplete data (1 study), or with inclusion of obviously selected groups that were not comparable (1 study). The observations were included to shed light on areas that might be of potential interest but where acceptable studies (i. e., studies that meet the inclusion criteria) were not available. These observations were not used as a basis for any of the conclusions presented in this Chapter.

The difficulty in identifying studies on the prevention of obesity can be illustrated by the fact that none of the 3 review articles published in 2001 presented all of the studies reported below. These review articles were from the Cochrane Collaboration in Australia and Germany [3, 4, 13]. Although this review identified more studies than earlier systematic literature reviews, it is not certain that all relevant studies were found.

Prevention can have a general purpose, i.e., reducing the number of overweight individuals in a total child and adolescent population. All of the studies reviewed have used this strategy. Another type of prevention is more individual-oriented, aimed at preventing the progression of obesity in certain risk group, e.g., individuals with certain genetic factors. One study appears to have this long-term goal, where overweight parents with normal weight children were identified, and an intervention aimed at changing dietary habits was started [22].

3.2.2
Results

All 14 studies that met the minimum criteria were targeted at school-aged children. The parents in all of these studies were always informed. In some cases the parents were targeted directly with educational activities. One of the studies aimed only at increasing physical activity [17].

The other studies included different programs to multidimensionally promote a healthier lifestyle, improve dietary habits, and increase exercise.

Eight of the studies used an educational package entitled "Know Your Body". This included special educational programs on diet, exercise, and drugs, and had a goal of lowering the risk factors for future cardiovascular disease (Table 3.2). The dietary advice was general and aimed at reducing fat intake and increasing fiber, fruit, and vegetables. Specially trained teachers conducted the program, and instruction was usually presented in the schools.

The study which was included in the so-called "North Karelia Youth Project" combined such a program with ads containing general information on healthy lifestyles that were targeted at adolescents. It used a more intensive intervention based on the "Know Your Body" model [14]. The study reported no effects on BMI or blood lipids after 2 years, when the participating schools were compared with schools in the control region. It also reported the number of overweight adolescents, and found no difference between the treatment and control schools. A limitation of the study is that the overweight rate was low (4%) in these areas when the study was implemented. In such a population, genetic factors probably dominate, and it is more difficult to achieve a reduced rate of overweight by influencing the environment.

A study by Walter et al. included about 1700 school children aged 8 to 10 years [21]. It involved 2 hours of teacher-led training per week for 5 school years in preschools. The teachers received training to deliver information and advice within a framework of a cognitive behavioral therapy approach. After 5 years, no weight difference was observed between the experimental and control schools. In the socio-

Table 3.2 Studies on preventing obesity in children and adolescents.

Author Year Reference Country	Study design	Inclusion criteria (Recruitment)	Intervention methods Study groups	Treatment period/ Extra followup period	Participants No. at start/ followed up	Results Weight change	Results/Other	Study quality Comments
Puska P et al. 1982 [14] Finland	CT	One city and one rural school in the intervention region and control region respectively. Students aged 13 years	Education based on "Know-Your-Body"[1]. Healthy lifestyle through information and newspaper ads. Group 1: Intensive school-oriented intervention Group 2: Control group from nearby region	2 years/0	966/851	No difference in mean BMI or BMI increase. No change in number of overweight (BMI>24) among the groups	Lower blood pressure in experiment group. No effect on blood lipids	Medium Primarily not aimed at weight loss. Study also measures number overweight. Very low overweight rate in both regions
Walter HJ et al. 1988 [21] USA	RCT Schools stratified by socioeconomic level	Recruitment from areas with different socioeconomic status Children 8–10 years	Education based on "Know-Your-Body"[1] 2 hours/week	5 years/0	2474/1765 whereof 911/733 and 1563/1032 respectively in the area with lower socioeconomic status	No significant difference in Ponderal index[2], but positive trends in both intervention areas	Statistically significant reduction in cholesterol in socioeconomic advantaged area compared to control. Similar trend, but not statistically significant, in less advantaged area	High Not primarily targeted at obesity

See legend on page 83

Table continues on next page

Table 3.2 continued

Author Year Reference Country	Study design	Inclusion criteria (Recruitment)	Intervention methods Study groups	Treatment period/ Extra followup period	Participants No. at start/ followed up	Results Weight change	Results/Other	Study quality Comments
Bush PJ et al. 1989 [2] USA	RCT	Schools reported according to socio-economic background and thereafter randomized. Average age at start was 10.5 years	Education based on "Know-Your-Body"[1]	5 years/0	1041 started. 66%, 59%, 33%, 20% remained after 1, 2, 3, 5 years respectively	No significant difference among groups regarding Ponderal index[2]	Statistically lower blood pressure in the intervention group after 5 years. Results uncertain since high dropout rate skewed the groups (more children with low socio-economic background in the control group)	Low Very high dropout
Tamir D et al. 1990 [20] Israel	CT	Arabic and Jewish schools with students from different socio-economic backgrounds were recruited, and similar schools were selected as control group. First-year students	Education based on "Know-Your-Body"[1] with 15–20 teaching hours/year, individual working material, info to parents, posters	2 years/0	829/406	Significantly reduced mean BMI in treatment schools	Lower cholesterol in the treatment schools	Low Very high dropout makes the study difficult to assess

Lionis C et al. 1991 [8] Greece	CT	One school is a control school, one a treatment school. Same socioeconomic conditions in both schools. Ages 13–14 years	Education based on "Know-Your-Body"[1]	9 months/ 3 months	171/147	Significantly lower increase in BMI in the intervention group. (BMI increase 0.21 and 0.72 respectively)	Lower LDL cholesterol increase in intervention group. Lower blood pressure increase in intervention group. Dropout group had a significantly higher BMI than others	Low Shows effects on BMI trend for whole group
Resnicow K et al. 1992 [15] USA	CT	Schools with lower socioeconomic status. Ages 5–9 years	Education based on "Know-Your-Body"[1]. Teacher-led instruction in healthy behavior at least 30–45 minutes/week+ general school activities (salad bar, more fiber in cafeteria student-led health committees, extra aerobic sessions, etc)	2.5 years/ 0	2383/1209	No difference in mean BMI	Lower cholesterol, lower systolic blood pressure and higher health awareness in the group that participated the entire intervention period (n=98). Some tendency toward dose-effect correlation between results and intervention time	Low High dropout. Small group was exposed the entire intervention period. Obesity and overweight prevalence not reported. Study not primarily targeted at obesity

See legend on page 83

Table continues on next page

Table 3.2 continued

Author Year Reference Country	Study design	Inclusion criteria (Recruitment)	Intervention methods Study groups	Treatment period/ Extra followup period	Participants No. at start/ followed up	Results Weight change	Results/Other	Study quality Comments
Manios Y et al. 1999 [11] Greece	CT	Two municipalities on Crete were selected as intervention areas and a third with the same socioeconomic background as the control area. 21 schools selected randomly for this analysis. Age at start, 6 years	Modified "Know-Your-Body"[1] program. Major effort at parent education including information about metabolism in childhood. Also increased school-based exercise	3 years/0	579/471	Significantly lower BMI in the intervention group after 3 years. Significantly lower increase in subcutaneous fat (skinfold) in the intervention group	Significantly increase in exercise during free time in intervention group. Significantly improved physical capacity (standing, jump, sit-ups) in intervention group after 3 years	Medium Percentage overweight not reported separately, but study shows a consistant information program can reduce mean BMI
Manios Y et al. 1998 [10] Greece	CT	Followup of another subgroup within study presented above	See above study	3 years/0	962 (whereof 424 in control schools) selected at followup	Significantly lower mean BMI and lower BMI increase in the intervention schools compared to the controls. Less subcutaneous fat in intervention group	Improved physical condition and strength in intervention groups	Medium Overweight not reported separately

| Sallis J et al. 1997 [17] USA | RCT Stratified by socioeconomic level | Six schools that accept randomization in Southern California were selected. Children 9–10 years | Physical exercise Group 1: Three 30-minute extra exercise sessions/week directed by gymnastic teacher Group 2: Corresponding exercise session led by other teacher + encouraged exercise outside of school hours Group 3: Usual school gymnastics | 1.5 year/0 | 740/547 | BMI significantly higher in both the treatment groups compared to the control groups after 6 and 12 months respectively. No difference after 1.5 y. Trend toward lower subcutaneous fat in the treatment groups, not significant | Medium The study does not report on overweight children but only the population average |
| Bal L et al. 1990 [1] Former Soviet Union | CT | 11–12 year old children in two districts in Moscow. "Overweight" children were identified for direct intervention in the intervention districts | Education concerning diet, obesity, cardiovascular diseases for children, teachers, and parents. Girls received training in preparing low calorie food. The "overweight" children also received focused behavior-oriented treatment | 3 years/0 | Interv. 1123/947 Contr. 1983/1403 | No difference in BMI between groups. No initial difference in subcutaneous fat. After 2 years, significantly lower subcutaneous fat in the intervention group. No difference by year 3 | Significantly lower blood pressure year 1. No difference by year 3 | Low The study is difficult to assess since the socioeconomic status in the district differed. Intervention group initially shorter |

See legend on page 83

Table continues on next page

Table 3.2 continued

Author Year Reference Country	Study design	Inclusion criteria (Recruitment)	Intervention methods Study groups	Treatment period/ Extra followup period	Participants No. at start/ followed up	Results Weight change	Results/Other	Study quality Comments
Donnelly JE et al. 1996 [5] USA	CT	Schools matched for ethnic and socioeconomic background. Children aged 8–11 years	Instruction in nutrition, increased number of exercise sessions, leaner and higher fiber school lunches within existing economic parameters. No changes in control schools	2 years/0	Interv: 102/100 Contr: 236/100	No difference in mean BMI before or after conclusion of study. No change in number of overweight	No difference in physical capacity, significantly higher HDL cholesterol in intervention group	Low
Luepker RV et al. 1996 [9] USA	CT	Third-year students (mean age 8.8 years) in 96 schools from 12 school districts	Group 1: 90-minute physical exercise per week + modified school meals + education in healthy living. Group 2: As above + interactive educational program with the parents. 28 schools in each intervention group and 56 schools in the control group	2.5 years	5106/4019	No difference between groups in mean BMI	No difference in cholesterol, blood pressure, or subcutaneous fat	High But the study did not primarily target obesity, and the percentage of overweight/ obese was not reported

Gortmaker SL et al. 1999 [6] USA	RCT	10 schools randomized to Intervention or Control schools. Ages 11–13 years	School-based program based on "Planet Health". Regular teacher instructed class in healthy living, including less TV watching, reduced intake of fat, and increased exercise	18 months/0	1295/1295 (only followup children included)	Percentage of overweight girls declined in the treatment schools from 23.6%* to 20.3%, and increased from 21.5% to 23.7% in the control schools (p=0.03). No difference found among boys	TV watching declined in Intervention schools compared to Control schools	Medium
Sahota P et al. 2001 [24] England	RCT	Periodic matching of 10 schools. Ages 7–11 years	Modification of school meals. School planning to increase exercise and dietary knowledge	12 months	613/595	No effect on BMI	No change in exercise. Significantly higher self-esteem in obese children in the intervention schools	Medium

RCT = Randomized Controlled Trial; CT = Controlled Trial, not randomized

* statistical significance

[1] "Know-Your-Body" = Classroom-based, teacher-led information and exercise, concerning diet, exercise, and smoking

[2] Ponderal Index = Weight in kilograms/height[3]

economically advantaged area, the experimental group showed significantly lower cholesterol levels compared to the control schools. The study aimed primarily at preventing cardiovascular diseases and smoking, and not at reducing overweight. It did not report if there were changes in the percentages of children with obesity.

A similar study by Bush investigated a little over 1000 adolescents, mainly black Americans in a socioeconomically disadvantaged environment [2]. No difference in weight was reported between the experimental and control groups. However, it is difficult to evaluate the study since only 20% of the participants could be followed up after 5 years. Furthermore, the numbers of adolescents with overweight or obesity were not reported.

A study from Jerusalem applied an adapted "Know Your Body" program. It investigated whether this program could influence weight and blood lipids among Arab and Jewish first grade students [20]. The study lasted 2 years. The program included teacher-led lectures, individual material for the students, workbooks and material sent home to the parents, and posters. The experimental and control schools were comparable at the start. After 2 years, the experimental schools had a significantly more favorable BMI trend and lower total cholesterol than the controls. However, the study was difficult to evaluate since dropout was high, i.e., above 50%.

A similar study performed in Crete showed a significantly lower increase in BMI in the experimental group [8]. The study included 171 children who received training for 9 months. The followup period was only 3 months; hence the results must be interpreted with caution.

A study by Ken Resnicow et al. assessed the "Know Your Body" model in children in an inner city environment in the United States [15]. The study included 1200 children aged 5 to 9 years and continued for 2.5 years. The intervention included teacher-led education for 30 to 45 minutes per week and school year, a change in the food offered at the school cafeterias, and various school activities through student-led health committees – meetings where students tried new foods and extra exercise sessions. The studies were not aimed primarily at obesity, and BMI did not differ among the groups at the end of the study. A significantly lower plasma cholesterol and systolic blood pressure could be identified in the group that had received the longest and most intensive intervention. This group, however, included only 98 students, and hence the results are difficult to assess.

In two more recent studies, the "Know Your Body" model has been modified according to local conditions on Crete [10, 11]. Both of the studies present 3-year data regarding a 6-year project. In two municipalities, an attempt was made to use information and increase physical activity to reduce obesity and thereby, in the long run, reduce cardiovascular mortality. The project actively engaged parents using advice and information about the physical health of the child based on test results and the degree of overweight. Both of the studies reported results from subgroup investigations. The program was directed at children aged 6 and 12 years, and the results were reported from approximately 1430 children aged 9 years. The children in the intervention schools had a significantly lower BMI, and had better physiological test results. One of the studies, where this topic was investigated, found better knowledge about diet and health in the intervention group [11].

The effects of increased physical activity were assessed in one study [17]. Sallis et al. investigated whether more exercise sessions at schools would influence physical development in children aged 9 to 10 years. Three 30-minute sessions per week, led by an athletics instructor or other teacher, showed a tendency toward reducing subcutaneous fat. This, however, was not statistically confirmed. Also, overweight *per se* was not reported.

A Russian study examined whether an informational program for all children in combination with a targeted treatment program for overweight children would reduce mean BMI and risk factors during a 3-year period [1]. The study included 3000 children (aged 11 to 15 years). However, this study is difficult to evaluate since the intervention region and the control region were not comparable in socioeconomic terms. After 3 years of intervention, the study was unable to confirm any difference in subcutaneous fat or BMI. Blood pressure declined in the intervention group after 1 year, but thereafter the differences were not observable.

An American study by Donnelly et al. attempted, for 2 years, to prevent overweight by changing the content in school lunches, increasing education about nutrition, and instituting exercise sessions 3 times per week [5]. The children were aged 8 to 11 years when the study started. No difference was found between the experimental and control schools as regards physical work capacity or weight trends. However, significantly higher HDL cholesterol was found in the intervention group. This study also followed children with high-grade obesity, but even in this subgroup no difference could be noted in weight trends between the experiment and control groups. This study was performed within the economic framework of the schools and includes no assessment concerning which parts of the program were actually implemented. Therefore, it is not possible to determine whether or not the planned interventions were effective.

An American study by Luepker et al. [9] randomized 96 schools with 5106 eight-year-olds into 3 groups. School lunches were modified at 28 schools. They also instituted an extra physical activity session per week and offered general education targeted primarily at reducing future heart disease. In addition, 28 schools offered education targeted at the children's parents. After 2.5 years, no differences were noted in average BMI, blood pressure, or cholesterol between the 56 experimental schools and the 40 control schools. The study was not primarily aimed at obesity/overweight, and the results for overweight could not be isolated.

A recent study from regions in the United States with a high prevalence of obesity (over 20 %) assessed a special weight reduction program called "Planet Health" [6]. The program included information concerning TV watching, exercise and physical activity, and dietary and nutritional advice. The educational aspects were carried out by school teachers, both in theoretical subjects and in school gymnastics. The study, which continued for 2 school years, resulted in a significantly reduced percentage of obese girls (from 23.6 % to 20.3 %). No change could be observed in the boys.

An English study investigated whether children aged 7 to 11 years would be less likely to become obese through a school-based intervention program. The program combined teacher-based education aimed at enhancing knowledge about diet and increasing interest in physical activity with modification of school meals and more physical activity sessions at schools [24]. The study lasted only 1 year. No significant differences were found between the control and treatment schools as regards weight trends, physical activity, and sedentary activity. At the conclusion of the study, however, children from the intervention schools reported a higher intake of vegetables.

3.2.3
Interesting Observations that do not Meet the Minimum Criteria

A study by Robinson (Table 3.3) analyzed whether it was possible to influence weight and physical performance by reducing the time spent on TV games and watching TV and video [16]. An attempt was made to teach children to be selective in watching TV and in implementing TV-free weeks. Furthermore, children and adolescents were helped to be observant in their TV watching by allowing the family, without cost, to use a monitoring unit that showed how much TV each of the family members watched. After 7 months, the children in the experimental group had reduced their TV watching and had a significantly lower increase in BMI and a lower volume of subcutaneous fat compared to the control group. The results suggest that it is possible to influence children's TV habits, at least in the short term. This also appears to impact on the degree of overweight. However, the evidence is weak since followup was only 7 months.

A study from Sweden compared 6-year old children (2 daycare centers) with similar socioeconomic backgrounds, but with different orientations concerning their external environment [7]. The study, which can be considered a case study, suggests that the design of the daycare environment can be important for the physical development of the child. Children in one daycare center had larger and more open play areas and were out-of-doors regardless of the weather. They had significantly better resilience and muscle strength than children at a conventional daycare center. However, it should be emphasized that no conclusions can be drawn from this study since the children were not randomly selected for the daycare with greater outdoor activities. It is probable that parents who placed their children in an "outdoor" daycare were themselves more physically active and influenced their children's physical capabilities through their own social and biological traits.

In a study from Thailand, Mo-suwan et al. investigated whether physical activity influenced the development of overweight in preschool children (average age 4.5 years) [12]. The experiment groups had a 15-minute walk in the morning and a 20-minute aerobic dancing session in the afternoon 3 times per week. The girls in the experimental group had a lower tendency to increase in BMI than did girls in the control group. BMI and the thickness of subcutaneous fat in the upper arm declined in both the experimental and the control groups. The evidence has low quality because of the short followup time. The study design carried a sub-

Table 3.3 Studies that presented interesting observations, but did not meet the inclusion criteria.

Author Year Reference Country	Study design	Inclusion criteria (Recruitment)	Intervention methods Study groups	Treatment period/ Extra followup period	Participants No. at start/ followed up	Results Weight change	Results/Other	Assessment Comments
Robinson TN 1999 [16] USA	RCT	Two schools socioeconomically matched. Ages 8–9 years	Less time spent on TV, video, TV games, included 10-day "TV Turn Off" and electronic TV-time measuring device attached to familyTV	7 months/0	198/192	Significantly lower increase in BMI (18.38–18.67, and 18.10–18.89) in the treatment than in the control groups	No difference in reported food intake and exercise. TV watching declined. Lower volume subcutaneous fat	Very short followup
Grahn P et al. 1997 [7] Sweden	CT	Daycare children aged 3–7 years. Mean 5.9 years	Comparison of usual daycare with "Out-of-doors" daycare based on certain concepts, i.e., much higher number of outdoor activities	Case studies during 1 year	26/26	No difference between groups in height and weight	The "Out-of-doors" daycare children had better balance, better gripping power in their hands, and better long jumping	Positive selection of trial group, consequently noncomparable groups
Mo-suwan L et al. 1998 [12] Thailand	RCT	Classes in two preschools randomized to treatment or control classes. Age 3.5–5.5 years	15-minute walk in the morning + 20-minute aerobic dancing in the afternoon 3 times/ week	29 weeks/0	292/292	Girls in treatment group had lower tendency toward increased BMI than the control girls	Percentage of children with subcutaneous fat above cutoff point for obesity declined in the treatment group from 12 % to 8.8 % and in the control group from 11.7 % to 9.7 % (differences not significant)	Some effect in the girls, but not in the boys. Very short study and risk for "contamination" between the treatment and the control classes

See legend on page 88

Table continues on next page

Table 3.3 continued

Author Year Reference Country	Study design	Inclusion criteria (Recruitment)	Intervention methods Study groups	Treatment period/ Extra followup period	Participants No. at start/ followed up	Results Weight change	Results/Other	Assessment Comments
Simonetti-D'Arca A et al. 1986 [18] Italy	CT	School children aged 3–9 years	Group 1: Education with written material, films, discussions with family and teachers Group 2: Only distribution of written material Group 3: Control group	12 months/0	1321 (only the number of followup reported, hence dropout cannot be assessed)	Percentage obesity declined from 13.3% to 11.7% in Group 1. Increased from 10.6% to 11.2% in Group 2. Increased from 11.4% to 12.1% in Group 3. No estimate of significance in the study	Of those initially overweight, 53.5% remained overweight in Group 1 and 37.4% became normal weight. In the control group the corresponding figures were 65.6% and 23.7% respectively. Significance was not calculated	Dropout not reported. No statistical calculations, but the study shows the importance of monitoring individuals development and not only mean BMI

= Randomized Controlled Trial; CT = Controlled Trial, not randomized
* statistical significance

stantial risk that the control and treatment groups could influence each other since different groups in the same daycare center participated in the study.

An Italian study by Simonetti D'Arca et al. [18] investigated whether weight trends in children aged 3 to 9 years were influenced by information programs directed at parents and children for 1 year. In total, 1300 children were followed, but dropout was not reported nor were differences which were potentially statistically significant. However, the study was of some value since it carefully reported changes over 1 year. Changes in the percentage of normal weight, overweight, and obese children were marginal in both the intervention and control groups. The rapid changes in body composition of children are well illustrated by the fact that only 50 % of the overweight children in the intervention group remained in this category after 1 year (37 % had become normal weight while 9 % had become obese). In the control group, 66 % of the overweight children remained overweight after 1 year, while 24 % had become normal weight, and 11 % had developed obesity. The aim with prevention studies is to prevent the development of obesity and overweight. In the treatment group, 87 % of the normal weight children maintained normal weight or underweight while slightly fewer than 13 % became overweight, and in the control group 85 % of the normal weight children maintained normal weight or underweight.

Finally, a German study by Müller is examining the effects of a combined school and family intervention to reduce the development of obesity and overweight [23]. After 1 year, the increase in subcutaneous fat was significantly less pronounced in children in the treatment schools compared with those in the control schools. The report, however, is not complete, and further results from this promising study are awaited with interest.

3.2.4
Discussion

The prevention studies show that it is difficult to achieve desired changes in mean BMI. Relatively powerful interventions for a longer period have been carried out, but apparently have been inadequate. Several of the studies did not focus on overweight problems, and therefore did not investigate whether the percentage of overweight changed with the interventions. Hence, it can be difficult to determine whether or not the prevalence of obesity changed among children. The intent of primary prevention studies is to change long-term behavior in normal weight children so they do not become overweight and obese. None of the studies that met the minimum criteria reported data that enabled this to be assessed. It can be questioned whether the effects achieved during one-year intervention were not more of a treatment effect, i. e., that the interventions helped overweight and obese children and their parents to change behavior to achieve weight reduction.

Several of the studies presented in Table 3.2 were conducted during the 1970s and 1980s when the prevalence of obesity was substantially lower than it is today. They included, e. g., studies by Puska and Walter et al. [14, 21]. They found no change in mean BMI, while a reduction could be noted in mean cholesterol in one of the intervention groups. When these studies were conducted, the genetic factors probably dominated, and therefore it was more difficult to achieve effects by influencing the environment. Now that the prevalence of obesity among children has now increased, interventions targeted at environmental factors should have a greater probability for success. Three of the most recently published studies, with medium quality, have reported more favorable results [6, 10, 11]. In the American study, the percentage of overweight girls declined during the intervention period, and in two of the Crete studies the mean BMI after 3 years of intervention was significantly lower in the intervention groups. The Greek studies were also targeted at children between 6 and 9 years of age. It is possible that the preventive efforts should be targeted at lower age groups to establish a healthy lifestyle early.

Eight of the 14 studies that the met the minimum criteria were conducted in the United States, and one older study was conducted in Scandinavia. It is not unlikely that cultural differences could have substantial importance for the interventions that can be effective in countries with different social structures, dietary habits, etc.

Preventing obesity during childhood and adolescent years is an important strategy for reducing the current rapid increase in obesity. Several studies are needed to determine which interventions are effective. They would, include, e. g., the impact of fat in the diet compared to food with low glycemic index or a high percentage of protein [19]. The importance of soft drinks also needs to be studied, since they appear to be less filling in relation to the calorie content compared to calories in other forms.

Another issue which has not been studied is whether eating disorders increase in schools where attempts are made to prevent overweight through diet and exercise counseling.

References Section 3.2

1. Bal L, Shugaeva EN, Deev AA, Maslova AR, Aleksandrov AA. Results of a three-year trial of arterial hypertension prevention in a population of children aged 11–15 years by overweight control. COR VASA 1990;32 (6):448-56.

2. Bush PJ, Zuckerman AE, Taggart VS, Theiss PK, Peleg EO, Smith SA. Cardiovascular risk factor prevention in black school children: The "know your body" evaluation project. Health Educ Q 1989;16(2):215-27.

3. Campbell K, Water E, O'Meara S, Summerbell C. Interventions for preventing obesity in children (Cochrane Review). In: The Cochrane Library. Oxford: Update Software; 2001. Report No 2.

4. Campbell K, Waters E, O'Meara S, Summerbell C. Interventions for preventing obesity in childhood. A systematic review. Obesity reviews 2001;2:149-57.

5. Donnelly JE, Jacobsen DJ, Whatley JE, Hill JO, Swift LL, Cherrington A, et al. Nutrition and physical activity program to attenuate obesity and promote physical and metabolic fitness in elementary school children. Obes Res 1996;4(3):229-43.

6. Gortmaker SL, Peterson K, Wiecha J, Sobol AM, Dixit S, Fox MK, et al. Reducing obesity via a school-based interdisciplinary intervention among youth: Planet Health. Arch Pediatr Adolesc Med 1999;153(4):409-18.

7. Grahn P, Mårtensson F, Lindblad B, Nilsson P, Ekman A. Ute på dagis – hur använder barn daghemsgården...? Movium/Inst för landskapsplanering, Stad & Land 1997;145.

8. Lionis C, Kafatos A, Vlachonikolis J, Vakaki M, Tzortzi M, Petraki A. The Effects of a Health Education Intervention Program among Cretan Adolescents. Preventive Medicine 1991;20:685-99.

9. Luepker RV, Perry CL, McKinlay SM, Nader PR, Parcel GS, Stone EJ, et al. Outcomes of a field trial to improve children's dietary patterns and physical activity. The Child and Adolescent Trial for Cardiovascular Health. CATCH collaborative group. JAMA 1996;275(10):768-76.

10. Manios Y, Kafatos A, Mamalakis G. The effects of a health education intervention initiated at first grade over a 3 year period: physical activity and fitness indices. Health Educ Res 1998;13(4):593-606.

11. Manios Y, Moschandreas J, Hatzis C, Kafatos A. Evaluation of a health and nutrition education program in primary school children of Crete over a three-year period. Prev Med 1999;28(2):149-59.

12. Mo-suwan L, Pongprapai S, Junjana C, Puetpaiboon A. Effects of a controlled trial of a school-based exercise program on the obesity indexes of preschool children. Am J Clin Nutr 1998;68(5):1006-11.

13. Müller M, Mast M, Asbeck I, Langnäse K, Grund A. Prevention of obesity – is it possible? Obesity reviews 2001;2:15-28.

14. Puska P, Vartiainen E, Pallonen U, Salonen JT, Pöyhiä P, Koskela K, et al. The North Karelia youth project: evaluation of two years of intervention on health behavior and CVD risk factors

among 13- to 15-year old children. Prev Med 1982;11:550-70.

15. Resnicow K, Cohn L, Reinhardt J, Cross D, Futterman R, Kirschner E, et al. A three-year evaluation of the know your body program in inner-city schoolchildren. Health Educ Q 1992;19(4):463-80.

16. Robinson TN. Reducing children's television viewing to prevent obesity: a randomized controlled trial. JAMA 1999;282(16):1561-7.

17. Sallis JF, McKenzie TL, Alcaraz JE, Kolody B, Faucette N, Hovell M. The effects of a 2-year physical education program (SPARK) on physical activity and fitness in elementary school students. Sports, Play and Active Recreation for Kids. Am J Public Health 1997;87(8):1328-34.

18. Simonetti D'Arca A, Tarsitani G, Cairella M, Siani V, De Filippis S, Mancinelli S, et al. Prevention of obesity in elementary and nursery school children. Public Health 1986;100(3):166-73.

19. Spieth LE, Harnish JD, Lenders CM, Raezer LB, Pereira MA, Hangen SJ, et al. A low-glycemic index diet in the treatment of pediatric obesity. Arch Pediatr Adolesc Med 2000;154(9):947-51.

20. Tamir D, Feurstein A, Brunner S, Halfon ST, Reshef A, Palti H. Primary prevention of cardiovascular diseases in childhood: changes in serum total cholesterol, high density lipoprotein, and body mass index after 2 years of intervention in Jerusalem schoolchildren age 7–9 years. Prev Med 1990;19(1):22-30.

21. Walter HJ, Hofman A, Vaughan RD, Wynder EL. Modification of risk factors for coronary heart disease. N Engl J Med 1988;318:1093-100.

22. Epstein LH, Gordy CC, Raynor HA, Beddome M, Kilanowski CK, Paluch R. Increasing fruit and vegetable intake and decreasing fat and sugar intake in families at risk for childhood obesity. Obes Res 2001;9(3):171-8.

23. Müller MJ, Asbeck I, Mast M, Langnase K, Grund A. Prevention of obesity – more than an intention. Concept and first results of the Kiel Obesity Prevention Study (KOPS). Int J Obes Relat Metab Disord 2001;(Suppl 1):S66-74.

24. Sahota P, Rudolf MC, Dixey R, Hill AJ, Barth JH, Cade J. Randomised controlled trial of primary school based intervention to reduce risk factors for obesity. BMJ 2001;323(7320):1029-32.

4
Treating Obesity in Adults

4.1
Dietary Treatment

Summary

Dietary treatment of obesity aims at limiting the intake of energy and thereby achieving a negative energy balance, which leads to weight reduction. A key question concerns which type and degree of dietary change is possible. Usually, dietary advice is given in combination with advice concerning increased physical activity. No clearly defined boundary separates dietary treatment from behavior therapy.

Dietary treatment involves counseling patients on the amount and proportions of food, energy (calorie) restrictions, limitations on fat content with or without energy restrictions, and vegetarian diets. Dietary treatment can also focus on meals and meal structure, or on replacing some meals with diet formulas.

Results: Twenty-five studies that met established criteria showed that weight loss averaging between 3 and 10 kilograms can be achieved during 1 year through dietary counseling by a dietician or other diet-knowledgeable individual or group (Evidence Grade 1). Substituting one or more main meals with products having a low energy content can promote weight reduction (Evidence Grade 2). In the few studies that monitored weight trends for a longer period (up to 5 years) patients usually returned to the original weight (Evidence Grade 2).

Carbohydrate-rich diets, in free amounts according to current recommendations, i.e., where at least 50–55 % of the energy comes from carbohydrates and a maximum of 30 % comes from fat (corresponding to 60 to 75 g fat per day), can yield one or more kilograms of weight loss during 6 months. Stricter energy restriction, where the amount of fat is usually limited to 20–30 g/day, results in more rapid weight loss, but is more difficult to tolerate for an extended period. An abundant amount of fruit and vegetables (general recommendation is 0.5 kilos/day) contributes to low fat content and low energy density. Other types of dietary treatment have been assessed to a much lesser extent. Protein-rich diets that include more fish, lean meat, and lean milk products appear to promote weight reduction, mainly because of greater satiety. Shopping lists, menus, and distribution of meals may contribute to success. Lactovegetarian diets are not shown to yield greater weight loss than mixed diets with a corresponding energy content.

Treating and Preventing Obesity. Edited by J. Östman, M. Britton, E. Jonsson
Copyright © 2004 WILEY-VCH Verlag GmbH & Co. KGaA, Weinheim
ISBN 3-527-30818-0

Conclusions: Weight reduction of 3 to 10 kilograms can be achieved during 1 year through dietary treatment. The studies that followed patients for more than 1 year show that most return to their original weight.

4.1.1
Introduction

All treatment that yields a negative energy balance, i. e., where the energy (calories) utilized exceeds that supplied by food, leads to weight reduction. If utilization is equal to intake, then body weight remains constant. This is a scientifically proven fact and does not require further proof. Instead, dietary treatment studies are aimed at investigating the methods to achieve this negative energy balance.

Strict dietary treatment, where the size and composition of the diet are controlled in detail, can be carried out only at a metabolic inpatient care unit where it is possible to closely monitor the intake of energy and nutrients in the trial subjects. In studies under realistic conditions, one often uses concurrent dietary restrictions to limit intake, and interventions to increase physical activity and hence utilization.

The literature search in this study by SBU primarily divided studies into diet, diet and behavior modification, and behavior modification. Studies with a special emphasis on behavior-changing methods are addressed in a separate Section, but, in this context, the boundaries defining behavior therapy are not clear. The influence of dietary habits is also a method of behavior therapy aimed at changing the trial subjects' attitude toward food.

Even a minor weight loss of 5 % to 10 % can, if permanent, have a substantial effect on obesity-related risk factors, e. g., elevated levels of blood pressure, blood glucose, serum insulin, and blood lipids. From a public health perspective, even small decreases in weight are of substantial interest. Since weight gain is normal with increasing age in a western "obesogenic" (obesity promoting) environment, maintaining a constant weight over time may be viewed as a positive result of an intervention. Long-term studies often report that mean body weight in the population increases by 3 to 4 kilograms per decade.

Long-term programs for weight reduction often involve an initial weight-reduction phase of 1 to 6 months followed by varying degrees of weight stability or possibly continued, often slower, weight loss. Few studies distinguish between strategies for weight reduction and weight stability, i. e., they work with the same type of intervention throughout. Most studies focus on the weight reduction phase, while patients/trial subjects often find it easier to lose weight than to avoid gaining weight. The long-term studies, i. e., studies longer than 6 to 12 months, analyzed in this project usually combined a weight reduction phase of a few months and a longer weight-stability and/or reversion phase.

Studies that use weight loss as an end point should be designed as randomized controlled trials (RCT). Studies that use weight loss as a method to influence risk factors or physiological variables, e. g., well-being, mood, etc., can seldom fulfill the RCT requirement, since treatment, i. e., weight loss, cannot be predicted, and therefore a defined "dose" cannot be prescribed. Since all obese patients can weigh themselves and check the results of therapy, all RCT programs must contain a component in the placebo/control group that is sufficiently active to prevent these patients from taking their own initiative outside the protocol or from dropping out of the study.

A particular problem in assessing long-term treatment for obesity concerns changes over time and the age-related increase in, e. g., insulin resistance, blood pressure, and weight that is usually found in Western societies.

A common source of error may be that individuals who wish to participate in studies have often participated in several programs previously, or have dieted on their own. This could mean that they have already reached a plateau. Repeated failed attempts also involve a substantial risk of continued failure.

There are two main categories of randomized controlled trials, i.e., crossover studies and parallel studies. In crossover studies, the trial subjects are initially randomized to one treatment or another, and then after a "washout" period they switch to the other treatment. This design has the greatest statistical power, but is difficult to implement in practice when it involves relatively complex dietary and lifestyle changes for at least 12 months, which a study should cover. Hence, a parallel control group is easier to implement, but yields greater variation and therefore requires larger experiment groups to achieve the same power.

4.1.2
Special Methodological Problems in Studies of Weight Loss

Clinical studies using an RCT design use controls to adjust for effects of factors other than treatment that can enhance or counteract the treatment effect. The results from the treatment group are compared with those from the control group, and the effects of treatment are represented by the differences between the groups. In obesity treatment, several factors exist that render a conventional RCT design more difficult:

1. Overweight study subjects who accept the invitation to participate in a study want to lose weight and often do lose weight during the study regardless of the treatment. Hence, the study itself has an effect, making the control group necessary but results difficult to evaluate.
2. It is impossible to design any regular placebo treatment for lifestyle changes, and the study cannot be blinded. Pure dietary studies, i.e., using diets with low or high fat content, can often be blinded, which strongly enhances their value.
3. In practice, the control group is often given some type of standard treatment, e. g., brief information about diet and conventional, written dietary advice, and participants are urged to increase physical activity. Essentially, one compares two types of treatment, the intervention one wants to study (intensive treatment) and "low-level" treatment instead of regular placebo. However, it is neither possible nor ethically defensible to deny these patients adequate treatment for a longer period.

Studies investigating the effects of weight loss on blood pressure and other risk factors must consider that various methods for achieving weight loss (diet, physical activity, drugs) may themselves have effects on the risk factors that one hopes to study. This is in addition to the difficulty of "dosing" weight reduction as mentioned above.

The discussion above is based largely on ME Lean's review, "Is long-term weight loss possible?", which also includes original references [21].

4.1.3
Methods

From the articles identified in the primary search, 279 were retrieved for evaluation in Phase 2. These are categorized as follows: diet (100 studies), diet and behavior (36 studies), behavior (120 studies), and quality of life (23 studies). Of the total, 61 articles fulfilled the criteria that allowed them to continue on to Phase 3. From an additional search, another 17 articles continued on to Phase 2 and 8 articles to Phase 3.

Of the articles that continued to Phase 3, there were 41 judged to be oriented mainly toward dietary treatment. Of these, 5 were review articles without original data, and 4 were sent on to other members in the group since they addressed treatment involving a starvation diet or very low calorie diet (VLCD).

Among the remaining 32 articles, closer review found that 13 did not meet the requirements for Phase 3 studies and were therefore not assessed further. The reasons were as follows: No control group (4 studies), large dropout without analysis (3 studies), insufficient data (3 studies), only 3 weeks of followup (1 study), studies of only fatty tissue distribution (1 study), other primary hypothesis (1 study). One additional study was added from the reference list of a study that was initially excluded.

A final search conducted on January 7, 2002 yielded 9 additional articles for Phase 2, of which 5 articles continued on to Phase 3.

The 25 studies that were finally reviewed may be classified into the following categories:

- General dietary advice/counseling, different types of programs (6 studies)
- Energy/calorie restrictions (5 studies)
- Meal replacement (6 studies)
- Fat restrictions with or without energy restrictions (4 studies)
- Carbohydrate type (1 study)
- Vegetarian diet (1 study)
- Weight Watchers (2 studies)

4.1.4
Results and Discussion (see Table 4.1)

4.1.4.1 General Dietary Counseling, Different Types of ProgramsDietary Counseling
A study including 325 participants used combined behavior therapy and diet modification through video programs and workbooks for overweight individuals (mean age 70 years, > 4.5 kg over ideal weight, mean BMI 30.8). This was complemented by group discussions, a "hotline", and individual counseling on both diet and exercise [44]. After 40 weeks, weight loss in the trial group was 3.2 kg. Blood glucose and HDL cholesterol had improved. No significant changes were observed in the control group, which had a lower average weight at the outset of the study (mean BMI 28.8).

Jeffrey et al. studied the possibility of enhancing the effects of dietary advice by providing trial subjects with suitable food products and meals [20, 43]. A well-designed study that included 202 individuals at two centers [20] showed that the groups who received 5 breakfasts and 5 lunches at home each week, along with recommendations for other meals, reduced their weight substantially more than those with dietary advice alone. Payment varying from 25 dollars per week for achieved target weight to 2.5 dollars for weight stability yielded no effects either alone or in combination with meal distribution. The authors concluded that meal distribution is superior to dietary advice alone.

The latter study goes further and tests whether it is meal recommendations, the food *per se*, or the fact that the food is free which is responsible for this effect [43]. The study included 163 overweight women and compares, as an adjunct to conventional behavior therapy, meal planning and shopping lists, meal planning and meals one pays for, and meal planning and free meals. Each of these groups lost significantly more weight than the control groups which received behavior therapy alone (at 6 months 11–12 kg vs 8 kg in the control group, and at follow-up 1 year later 7 kg vs 3 kg). However, there was no significant difference among the trial groups, which shows that the structured meal design and shopping lists mainly accounted for the effect, rather than the meals with or without charge.

Metz et al. compared conventional dietary treatment of individuals with obesity and high blood pressure/blood lipid disorders or diabetes with corresponding prepared meals that were ordered twice per week [28]. The amount of energy was based on reducing weight by a maximum of 0.9 kg per week. After 1 year, the weight loss in the blood pressure/blood lipid groups was 5.8 kg in those given prepared meals versus 1.7 kg in those given conventional dietary treatment. The corresponding figures in the diabetes group were 3.0 kg and 1.0 kg, respectively.

Three reviewed studies therefore provide evidence that prepared meals can be helpful in weight reduction programs.

In recent years, fruits and vegetables have received attention in dietary recommendations, mainly due to epidemiological data showing a protective effect against cardiovascular diseases and some types of cancer. In an overweight context, the low energy density, i. e., low calorie content per weight/unit-volume, is of special inter-

Table 4.1 Dietary treatment.

Author Year Reference	Study design	Inclusion criteria (Recruitment)	Intervention method and study groups	Treatment/ followup period
Wylie-Rosett J et al. 1994 [44]	CT	>4.5 kg overweight >55 years (mean 70.5) BMI 1: 30.8 BMI 2: 28.8	1. Combined behavior and diet modification, including increased physical activity 2. Controls	40 weeks/ 40 weeks
Jeffery RW et al. 1993 [20]	RCT	14–32 kg overweight 25–45 years non-smokers	1. Dietary advice 2. Dietary advice + delivery of 5 breakfasts and 5 dinners per week 3. Dietary advice + money at target weight and weight stability, respectively 4. Dietary advice + 2 + 3 5. Control group	20 weeks/ 6, 12 and 18 months
Wing RR et al. 1996 [43]	RCT	15–35 kg overweight 15–55 years Women only	1. Dietary advice (control group) 2. Dietary advice + structured meal plan and shopping list 3. As in 2 + groceries which the intervent. subjects pay for 4. As in 2 + groceries free of charge 1000–1500 kcal/day less than 20% fat Physical activity 1000 kcal/week	26 weeks/ 78 weeks (= 22 weeks intervention and last followup 78 weeks after start)
Metz JA et al. 2000 [28]	RCT	Men and women with BMI >41 (mean BMI 32–35) with A. Blood pressure 140–180/90–105 and cholesterol 4.7–7.8 and/or triglycerides 2.3–11.3 mmol/l B. Type 2 diabetes fasting blood glucose >7.8 mmol/l	1. Ready-cooked meals 1250–1450 kcal/day delivered twice/week free of charge 2. Instructions on the corresponding diet with financial reimbursement	1 year

See legend on page 108

No. of patients/ No. followed up	Results Weight change	Results/Other	Study quality Comments
1. 163 selected (137 started)/ 106 followed up 2. 162/121	1. –3.2 kg* 2. –0.1 kg	Significantly increased HDL cholesterol and decreased fasting glucose in 1	Low
1. 40/26 2. 40/36 3. 41/35 4. 41/34 5. 40/28 Half men Half women Two centers	12 months 1. –4.5 kg 2. –9.1 kg 3. –5.5 kg 4. –9 kg 5.0 18 months 1. –4.1 kg 2. –6.4 kg 3. –4.0 kg 4. –6.5 kg 5.0	Distribution of groceries facilitates weight loss	Medium
1. 40/35/32 2. 41/37/37 3. 41/36/37 4. 41/40/38	26 weeks 1. –8.0 kg 2. –12.0 kg 3. –11.7 kg 4. –11.4 kg 78 weeks 1. –3.3 kg 2. –6.9 kg 3. –7.5 kg 4. –6.6 kg	Structured meal plans and shopping lists facilitate weight loss	High
A1: 93/75 B1: 56/42 A2: 90/79 B2: 63/51	A1: –5.8 kg* B1: –3.0 kg* A2: –1.7 kg B2: –1.7 kg	Improvements in blood pressure, blood lipids, glycated hemoglobin, and quality of life for both treatments but more pronounced for more parameters in the groups receiving ready-cooked meals	Medium

Table continues on next page

Table 4.1 continued

Author Year Reference	Study design	Inclusion criteria (Recruitment)	Intervention method and study groups	Treatment/ followup period
Singh RB et al. 1994 [36]	RCT	Hospitalized men with symptomatic coronary artery disease the past 24 h. 204 were randomized to intervention group, 202 to control group	1. Dietary advice + 400 g of fruit and vegetables/day 2. Dietary advice	6 months
Sjöström M et al. 1999 [37]	Prospective	100 consecutive persons referred to Vindeln Patient Education Centre (of 2500 during a 10-year period). Overweight (mean BMI 30) and at least one risk factor. W=47, M=53, mean age 52 years. Previous failures with conventional counseling and pharmacotherapy	4-week intensive program Residential No control group	4 weeks/ 1 year and 5 years
Baum JG et al. 1991 [4]	RCT, matching by weight loss after weight loss programs	48 of 150 interested (adv). 43 fullfilled inclusion criteria. 32 finally randomized. 25–50 years 20 %–70 % above ideal weight Mean BMI 30.6	12-week program with diet–exercise counseling. Then during 3 months 4 followup sessions + letter/phone contact with the therapist for another 3 months (Group 1), or only written comments on the followup (Group 2)	12 weeks/ 3, 6 and 12 months
Jalkanen L 1991 [17]	RCT	35–59 years (mean 49) DBT >95 mmHg BMI 27–34 Sessions with lectures and discussions each week for 6 months, then every fourth week. Control group offered to participate later	Individual energy-reduced diet 1000–1500 kcal/day	12 months

See legend on page 108

No. of patients/ No. followed up	Results Weight change	Results/Other	Study quality Comments
1. 204/198	1. −5.3 kg*	TG, fasting glucose, Blood pressure decreased. HDL cholesterol increased.	Low quality due to short time and non obese
2. 202/197	2. −2.2 kg	Weight at start 66.6 ± 10.5 kg (mean value ± SD). Data on height lacking	
100/100	12 months Men −7.0 kg Women −4.2 kg 5 years Men −3.6 kg Women −1.8 kg	SBP −20 DBP −15 at 5-year followup 75 % with DBP >90 before had still <90 after 5 years	Medium
32/30 15 in each group. Of 43 initiallly interested 34 started, followup 15 per group	1. 3 months −5.3 kg* 6 months −5.6 kg* 12 months −3.6 kg* 2. 3 months −3.5 kg 6 months −2.7 kg 12 months −1.5 kg	Weight reduction during 3 months was significantly greater and was maintained significantly better when contact with therapist	Medium
50/49 Half women	1 year −4 kg* Mean weight declined from 86 to 82 kg. Control ± 0		Medium

Table continues on next page

Table 4.1 continued

Author Year Reference	Study design	Inclusion criteria (Recruitment)	Intervention method and study groups	Treatment/ followup period
Hakala P et al. 1993 [12]	RCT	22–54 years 50% overweight No serious disease <u>Women</u> G: (n=20) mean 41 y, 120.7 kg, BMI 43.6 I: (n=18) 37 y 119.2 kg, BMI 43.4 <u>Men</u> G: (n=10), mean 39 y, 143.6 kg, BMI 42.7 I: (n=10) 40 y, 137.6 kg, BMI 41.7	Group therapy (G) with 2-week intensive period, 1200 kcal/day at rehab center, then 15 hours of dietary education, 15 hours of physical activation, and 12 hours of workplace training Group I, or individual counseling with 20 min. doctor's appoint-ment per month the first year, and every fourth month the second year	2 years/5 years
Pritchard DA et al. 1999 [30]	RCT	Overweight and high blood pressure and/ or type 2 diabetes 25–65 years 28% men Mean weight D: 85.5 kg DD: 91.7 kg C: 89.1 kg	D: Six group counseling sessions by dietician for 12 months DD: As in D but doctor invited and participated in two sessions C: Control group without contact with a dietician. Doctor visits according to normal routines and preferences	12 months
Hensrud DD et al. 1995 [13]	CT Matched normal-weight controls	120%–150% of ideal weight, mean blood pressure >100 mmHg >5 years Mean age 59 years	1. 800 kcal/day until weight decreased 10 kg (mean –13 kg after 3–4 months). Followup 4 years later without further intervention 2. Normal-weight controls	4 years
Pascale RW et al. 1995 [29]	RCT	Women with type 2 diabetes (BMI 36.4) or heredity for type 2 diabetes (BMI 36.3)	16-week program with dietary-, exercise-, and behavior training. 1. Energy-reduced diet (1000–1500 kcal/day) 2. Energy-reduced diet + fat restriction (<20 energy percent fat)	16 weeks/1 year
Summerbell CD et al. 1998 [39]	RCT	45 persons >17 years, BMI >27 (mean 41–47) No diabetes, pregnancy or breast-feeding	16 weeks with energy-reduced diet (800 kcal) 1. Conventional diet 2. Milk 3. Milk + 1 groceries	16 weeks/ 16 weeks

See legend on page 108

No. of patients/ No. followed up	Results Weight change	Results/Other	Study quality Comments
G: 30 (whereof 20 women) 30 (2 y)/28 (5 y) I: 30 (whereof 20 women) 28 (2 y)/25 (5 y)	Women (kg) 　　　　G　　I 1 y　−15.7　−11.9 2 y　−5.4　−10.4* 5 y　−2.1　−3.4 Men (kg) 1 y　−13.1　−26.2* 2 y　−1.8　−15.6* 5 y　−3.0　−12.9	G: After 2 years signi-ficantly lower weight than baseline only in women I: Significantly lower weight after 2 years in both sexes. G/I: In women no diffe-rences in followup. In men significantly better results in I after 1 and 2 years	High Individual counseling better for men, used much more than group followup
D: 88/48 DD: 92/65 C: 90/64	All (at last occasion of attendance) "Intention to treat" D:　−5.6 kg/7.3 % DD: −6.7 kg/6.6 % All who fullfilled D:　−7.7 kg/9.1 % DD: −8.1 kg/8.8 % C:No change	Both treatment groups decreased considerably and equally in weight. Less dropout where doctor participated. Blood pressure decreased in both treatment groups, but not in control group. Economic analysis main purpose – see Chapt. 8	Medium
24/24	1. +11 kg 2. +2 kg	Shows the need of followup support to maintain rapid weight loss	Medium
Type 2 diabetes 1. 22/16 2. 22/15 Heredity for type 2 diabetes 1. 23/13 2. 23/16	Type 2 diabetes 1 y 1. −0.96 kg 2. −5.2 kg* Heredity for type 2 diabetes 1 y 1. −3.5 kg 2. −3.0 kg	Energy and fat restriction yields greater weight loss in diabetic subjects than energy restriction alone	Medium
1. 14/9 2. 14/11 3. 17/11	All randomized were followed up. Weight change 16 weeks All and those fullfilling the intervention, respectively. 1.−1.7 kg　−2.6 kg 2.−9.4 kg −11.2 kg 3.−7.0 kg　−8.2 kg		Low Short study (4 months) but important since it shows the effect from limiting to a few groceries

Table continues on next page

Table 4.1 continued

Author Year Reference	Study design	Inclusion criteria (Recruitment)	Intervention method and study groups	Treatment/ followup period
Ditschuneit HH et al. 1999 [10]	Phase 1: RCT Phase 2: All on same diet.	>18 years, 25<BMI<40 (Mean BMI 33–34) failed attempts at weight loss	Phase 1 3 months RCT with energy-reduced diet (1200–1500 kcal/day) A. Conventional	Phase 1 3 months
Flechtner-Mors M et al. 2000 [11]	Case-control analysis divided on cases which belonged to B in Phase 1 and controls from A in Phase 1	>3 months. A. 82% women B. 76% women	B. Two main courses and two snacks exchanged for formula (shake, soup, hot chocolate) Phase 2 Case-control study with followup after 2 years and 4 years resp. Cases from B above. One main course and one snack exchanged in the same manner. Matched controls from A	Phase 2 2 years and 4 years
Quinn Rothhacker D 2000 [31]	Matched controls	Overweight/obese but otherwise healthy men and women. Mean BMI 30–32	Weight-reduction program with milk-based meal replacement twice/day for 3 months. Then as needed to maintain the weight during 5 years (free of charge)	5 years
Ashley JM et al. 2001 [2]	RCT	Women 25–50 years BMI 25–35 Mean BMI 30 Healthy, not pregnant or breast-feeding	1. Dietician-led groups 1 hour per session each week for 3 months, then more rarely 2. As in Group 1 but 2 of 3 main meals replaced by products with 220 kcal 3. Meal replacement as in Group 2 with counseling managed by nurse or doctor 10–15 minutes equally often as above	1 year
Schlundt DG et al. 1993 [35]	RCT	>20% over ideal weight, advertisement. Mean BMI 30–37	1. Diet with a low fat content but unlimited energy content 2. Diet with low fat and limited calorie content	16–20 weeks/ 9–12 months

See legend on page 108

No. of patients/ No. followed up	Results Weight change	Results/Other	Study quality Comments
Phase 1 A. 50/50 B. 50/50 Phase 2 after 2 years 1. 31 from A above 32 from B above Phase 2 after 4 years After 3 years 42 patients had left – of these 32 were re-recruited. Distribution to group not apparent	Phase 1 A. Men –1.1 kg Women –1.2 kg B. Men –8.4 kg* Women –6.8 kg* Phase 2 A. –6.4 kg B. –3.3 kg A. –3.2 % (dropout 3.0 %) B. –8.4 % (dropout 8.5 %)	2-year followup: BP, TG, fasting Glucose decreased in relation to weight loss 4-year followup: 1. Lower fasting Glucose and serum insulin 2. Lower blood pressure TG, fasting Glucose, and serum insulin	Medium 2- and 4-year followups show that replacement of two meals per day with weight-reduction agents facilitates weight loss
108 women 50 men 144 followed up 3 x 141 matched controls 247 women 142 men	–4.2 kg* –5.8 kg* +6.5 kg +6.7 kg	Important to consider weight gain in controls in long studies. However not randomized study	High
1. 37/23 2. 38/26 3. 38/25	1. –3.4 kg 2. –7.7 kg* 3. –3.5 kg *significant compared to 1 and 3 (p<0.03)	Meal replacements yielded significantly greater weight loss than conventional diet with 1200 kcal/day	Low quality due to small database and high dropout
1. 30/25/17 2. 30/24/18 (started/ intervention/ followup)	16–20 weeks 1. –4.6 kg 2. –8.8 kg* 9–12 months 1. –2.6 kg 2. –5.5 kg	Low-fat diet with energy restriction yielded better results than low-fat diet alone after intervention, but no difference after 9–12 months	Low

Table continues on next page

Table 4.1 continued

Author Year Reference	Study design	Inclusion criteria (Recruitment)	Intervention method and study groups	Treatment/ followup period

Jeffery RW
et al.
1995
[19]
	RCT	Women 25–45 years,
		120 %–140 % of ideal
		weight, non-smokers,
		maximum 20 drinks/
		week
			Dietary counseling during
			18 months.
			1. Fat reduction to
			   20 g/day
			2. Energy reduction to
			   1000–1200 kcal/day
				18 months/
				18 months

Toubro S
et al.
1997
[41]
	RCT	From waiting list for
		obesity treatment,
		BMI 27–40,
		2 men, 39 women
			Phase 1
			Initial weight reduction phase
			1. 500 kcal/day for
			   8 weeks
			2. 1200 kcal/day for
			   17 weeks
			Phase 2
			Re-randomization to
			1. Low-fat diet in free amounts
			2. Fixed energy intake
			   1850 kcal/day
			   for 1 year
				Phase 1
				8 or 17 weeks
				
				Phase 2
				1 year
				
				Followup
				1 year

Skov AR
et al.
1999
[38]
	RCT	Advertisement
		18–56 years
		BMI 25–34
		Weight stability
		>2 months
			1. High content of carbo-
			   hydrates (59 energy percent)
			   and low content of fat
			   (<30 energy percent)
			2. High content of protein
			   (25 energy percent)
			   and low content of fat
			3. Control group
			   with common Danish diet
			   in free amount
				26 weeks/26 weeks

Saris WH
et al.
2000
[34]
CARMEN
	RCT
	
	Multicenter
	study in 5
	European
	countries, 80
	participants
	in each
	center
		20–55 years
		BMI 26<35
		(mean BMI 30–31)
		<5 kg weight loss
		past 6 months
			1. Diet with a low content of fat
			   (25 energy percent) and high
			   share of "simple" carbohy-
			   drates (saccharose)
			2. Low fat and high share of
			   "complex" carbohydrates
			   (starch)
			3. Control group with normal
			   Danish diet in free amount
			4. Another control group to
			   measure seasonal variation in
			   weight
				6 months/
				6 months

Marniemi J
et al.
1990
[25]
	RCT	Advertisement
		25–50 years
		30 %–50 %
		overweight
			1. Lactovegetarian diet
			   1200 kcal/day
			2. Mixed diet
			   1200 kcal/day
			3. Control group Nutritionist/
			   dietician sessions each week
			   in groups of 15, then 5
			   sessions during rest of year
				1 year/
				1 year

See legend on page 108

No. of patients/ No. followed up	Results Weight change	Results/Other	Study quality Comments
1. 61/39 2. 61/35	<u>6 months</u> 1. −4.6 kg 2. −3.7 kg <u>18 months</u> 1. +0.4 kg 2. +1.8 kg	Return to original weight after 18 months. However easier to tolerate fat-reduced diet. Reduced fat-intake better correlation to weight loss than energy-intake	Medium
Phase 1 1. 21/19 2. 22/19	Phase 1 1. −12.6 kg 2. −12.6 kg	Low-fat diet in free amounts more effective than energy-fixed diet in terms of maintaining weight after substantial-initial weight loss.	Medium
Phase 2 1. 17/17/13 2. 20/20/15 (started/ intervention/ followup	Phase 2 1. −13.2 kg (of initially 13.5 kg) 2. −9.7 kg (of initially 13.8 kg) Significant (p<0.03) weight return in G 1.	Rapid or slower initial weight loss had no impact on long-term result	
1. 25/23 2. 25/23 3. 15/14	1. −5.1 kg 2. −8.9 kg Controls 0 kg	Body fat 1. −4.3 kg 2. −7.6 kg Significantly (p<0.001) better weight loss on protein rich and carbo-hydrate rich diet than in carbohydrate rich diet alone in free amount	Medium Study important since it was conducted under realistic conditions
1. 97/76 2. 97/83 3. 96/77 4. 99/82/80	1. −0.9 kg 2. −1.8 kg 3. +0.8 kg 4. +0.1 kg	Body fat 1. −1.3 kg 2. −1.8 kg 3. +0.6 kg	Medium
Total dropout 18.6 %		Modest, but significant weight loss on diet with many carbohydrates accord-ing to recommendation. No difference on starch and sugar in solid foods	
36 started, i.e., total dropout is 19 %, not specifically reported, but probably largest in group 1	1. −10.4 kg 2. −9.2 kg 3. +1.6 kg Significant weight loss in both groups but no difference between the diets	Initial reduction of blood lipids. After 1 year significantly lower TG and higher HDL, particularly in the men	Medium

Table continues on next page

Table 4.1 continued

Author Year Reference	Study design	Inclusion criteria (Recruitment)	Intervention method and study groups	Treatment/ followup period
Heshka S et al. 2000 [15]	RCT	1Previous overweight- treatment. Advertisement 18–65 years BMI 27–40	1. Weight-watcher program 2. 2 x 20 minutes dietician advice + printed material	26 weeks (of 2 years)
Lowe MR et al. 2001 [23]	Followup. No control group	Target weight (BMI 20–25) 1–5 years previously with weight watchers		1–5 years

RCT = Randomized Controlled Trial; CT = Controlled Trial, not randomized; TG = Triglycerides
BP = Blood Pressure; SBP = Systolic Blood Pressure; DBP = Diastolic Blood Pressure; W = Women; M = Men
* = Statistical significance

est. This is due to high water content, low fat content, and relatively high fiber content.

An Indian study of 204 men who presented at hospital with acute myocardial infarction during the previous 24 hours were given, in addition to the usual dietary advice, instructions to eat at least 400 grams of fruit and vegetables per day based on the recommendations from WHO [36]. The trial subjects (Group 1) were recommended to eat fruit and vegetables, preferably salads, prior to meals. The control group (Group 2) of 202 men received similar dietary advice, but without the specific recommendations for fruit and vegetables. At 6-month followup, Group 1 ate, on average, 393 grams more fruit and vegetables per day than did Group 2, and had a 20 % lower intake of total and saturated fat. The energy intake was 13 % lower and the fiber intake nearly twice as high in Group 1. Weight loss in Group 1 was significantly more (5.3 kg versus 2.2 kg) and their waist/hip ratio had declined significantly more (0.05 versus 0.02), as had triglycerides and blood pressure. HDL cholesterol increased significantly by 0.1 mmol/L. The study shows that dietary advice focusing on an increased consumption of fruit and vegetables can be effective in terms of body weight and cardiovascular risk factors.

A Swedish study by Sjöström et al. investigated the short- and long-term effects of a 4-week residential program [37]. One hundred consecutive individuals, 53 men and 47 women, out of 2500 who had participated in the program, were overweight and had a least one risk factor for diabetes, cardiovascular disease, or high blood pressure. A model for behavioral and lifestyle changes was used, where diet and lifestyle changes are systematically planned and implemented based on the individual's situation. Nutritional food was purchased, prepared, and served in groups under the leadership of a dietician. At 1- and 5-year followup, a 3- to 4-day repetition program was conducted, including a review and revision of individual goals. Both weight and blood pressure dropped rapidly during the residential period. After 5 years, the average weight in men with an initial BMI above 30

No. of patients/ No. followed up	Results Weight change	Results/Other	Study quality Comments
Started/ followed up 1. 211/174 2. 212/172	1. −4.8 kg 2. −1.4 kg	Waist circumference and fat mass decreased more in Group 1 than in Group 2	Medium
Followup of 1002 persons	42.6 % maintained 5 % weight reduction or more. 18.8 % maintained 10 % weight reduction or more		Low

remained 5 kg lower, and diastolic and systolic blood pressure remained at 15 mmHg and 20 mmHg, respectively, lower than at the outset of the intervention. The study suggests a high potential for programs that begin with an intensive course using well-designed and established methods for lifestyle changes. However, this method requires substantial resources.

After an initial weight loss, nearly all studies reported at followup a rather rapid return toward or to the original weight. Baum et al. studied two degrees of therapeutic intervention in a 12-month followup of 32 individuals who had undergone a 12-week program of behavior therapy including physical activity [4]. Weight loss averaged 4 kg, corresponding to 1.5 BMI units. During the first 3 months of followup, half of the group (Group 1) underwent four sessions aimed at preventing relapse, and thereafter letters or telephone contact with a therapist for another 3 months. The control group (Group 2) had only letter contact and written comments on the results of the followups. Group 1 continued to lose weight at 3- and 6-month followup, and maintained a lower weight than Group 2, even after 12 months. The mean weight in Group 1 at that time was 3.6 kg below the original weight, i. e., about the same as that at the end of the initial 3-month treatment. However Group 2 had regained more than half of the original weight loss, reporting a mean weight only 1.5 kg below the original weight. Ongoing therapeutic contacts are therefore important for maintaining weight loss during the first year.

4.1.4.2 Energy (Calorie) Restriction

Five studies used dietary treatment with an emphasis on energy (calorie) restrictions, either at fixed levels or corresponding to a particular energy deficit compared with the individual need estimated. A deficit of 2 MJ (500 kcal) per day theoretically yields a weight reduction of approximately 0.5 kg per week and 4 MJ (1000 kcal) yields approximately 1 kg per week.

In a study of weight reduction and cardiovascular risk factors [17], individuals were given advice on exercise and diet (corresponding to 1000–1500 kcal per day) once per week for the first 6 months and thereafter every third week. Weight declined 4 kg in the intervention group, but did not change in the control group. The blood lipid profile improved, but blood pressure declined equally in both groups. The fact that the original weight was higher in the intervention group than in the control group (86 kg versus 80 kg) weakens this study. Despite successful weight reduction, the mean weight in the intervention group at 12-month followup therefore remained higher than that in the control group (82 kg vs 80 kg).

Hakala et al. compared overweight therapy in groups and individuals among substantially overweight women (40 individuals, BMI 42.2) and men (20 individuals, BMI 43.5) with 5-year followup [12]. After a 2-week intensive period at a hospital, with 1200 kcal per day, the patients were randomized to either group therapy with 15 hours of dietary instruction, 15 hours of physical activity, and 12 hours of workplace training, or to a 20-minute physician visit per month for the first year, and every fourth month the second year. A physician provided systematic dietary counseling with the goal of 1200 kcal per day. In the group receiving group therapy, weight reduction after 1 year, 2 years, and 5 years was 16 kg, 5 kg, and 2 kg respectively among the women, and 13 kg, 2 kg, and 3 kg among the men. In the group that received individual counseling, the corresponding figures for women were 12 kg, 10 kg, and 3 kg respectively and 26 kg, 16 kg, and 13 kg for men. The study is one of the few with a 5-year followup, and the authors maintain that the results are comparable to or better than other studies with conservative obesity treatment – only Björvell and Rössner have reported better long-term results [7]. Individual counseling by a physician in this study [12] yielded better results than group instruction/therapy. Participation in the group sessions was 69 % during the first year, but only 29 % the second year. In the individual group, 86 % of the appointments during the first year and 69 % during the second year were used, which should have contributed to the superior result in this group.

Another study by Pritchard et al., described in greater detail in Chapter 8, randomized overweight men and women to individual counseling on diet and exercise every second month for 1 year (initially 45 minutes and thereafter 15 minutes) with physician participation initially and at two of the counseling sessions [30]. Good weight loss was achieved in both groups, on average 7 % to 9 % of the original weight, with no differences between the groups. However, dropout was substantially lower in the group with physician participation. See Chapter 8 on economic assessment, which was the main objective of the study.

Hensrud et al. followed 24 overweight women (BMI 28) for 4 years. The subjects had a mean blood pressure exceeding 100 mmHg and normal glucose tolerance [13]. A diet of 800 kcal per day was used until a weight reduction of 10 kg was achieved. Blood pressure and blood lipids improved in different phases of weight reduction. After 4 years, the trial subjects had gained 11 kg, and had thereby returned to their original weight. The control group gained 2 kg during the same period. The participants who had voluntarily exercised had gained less weight than the inactive participants (6 kg versus 13 kg). Blood pressure and blood lipids had deteriorated once again, and the deterioration correlated with the degree of weight gain. An interesting conclusion of the study is that risk factors are influenced by body weight and not by the energy restrictions during the weight-loss period.

Should dietary counseling focus on energy (calorie) content, or should it also focus on fat? Pascale et al. studied this in 44 women with type 2 diabetes and 46 women with a family history of diabetes [29]. All underwent a 16-week program of behavioral change regarding diet and exercise. Dietary advice was focused on achieving 1000–1500 kcal per day. Furthermore, a goal in one of the groups was to limit fat intake to 20–30 grams per day, corresponding to 20 % of the energy intake. This group lost more weight (7.7 kg compared to 4.6 kg) and maintained their weight loss substantially better after 1 year (5.2 kg versus 1.0 kg). Another study showed that substantially more (54 % versus 20 %) of the original participants complied with a program involving an energy-reduced diet (1200–1500 kcal/day) for 18 months if the fat content was 35 % of the energy compared to 20 % [27]. This corresponds to approximately 55 g versus 30 g fat per day.

4.1.4.3 Meal Replacement

One study compared a conventional 800 kcal diet with an 800 kcal milk-only diet and an 800 kcal diet of milk and another food product, in 45 individuals with an average BMI > 40 [39]. After 16 weeks, weight loss was 9.4 kg and 7.0 kg in the groups that had received milk alone versus milk plus a food product, compared to only 1.7 kg in the conventionally treated control group. The authors concluded that dietary treatment with new, simple diets can yield results that are as good as the most successful pharmacological treatment.

Dieting formulas used as replacements for two main meals and two snacks have been assessed for 3 months in a study involving 100 subjects [10]. In another phase of the study, including 24 months of followup, one main meal and one snack were replaced. During the trial period, weight loss in the group receiving meal replacements was 11.3 kg compared to 5.9 kg in the control group. In the first phase, the trial group lost 7.1 kg versus 1.3 kg in the control group. In the trial group, triglycerides, glucose, and insulin levels declined significantly during the first 3-month period, while both of these risk factors and blood pressure declined in both of the groups after 27 months. This study provides support for the idea that defined meal replacements can facilitate both weight loss and weight stability.

In a followup study of 75 % of the originally recruited subjects, the average weight loss after 4 years was 8.4 % for the group receiving meal replacement versus 3.2 % in the control group. Both of the groups had significantly lower blood glucose and insulin, but only the trial group had improved in triglyceride values and blood pressure [11].

Another study followed 108 women and 50 men who received free meal replacement products for 5 years [31]. Two meals per day were replaced during the first 3 months, and one to two thereafter until the desired weight had been achieved. Then one or more meals were replaced as needed, depending on the weight trend. After 5 years, the average weight loss in women was 4.2 kg and in men it was 5.8 kg. Matched controls during the same time had gained 6.5 kg (women) and 6.7 kg (men) respectively.

Ashley et al. compared conventional dietician-led group interventions with women, 1 hour per session, with or without meal replacement products [2]. A third group was instructed by a physician or nurse to use meal replacement, 15 minutes per visit. After one year, the group treated by a dietician using meal replacements had lost an average of 7.6 kg, but the other groups lost only about 3 kg. These are statistically significant differences.

In summary, five studies provide support for the supposition that meal replacement can contribute to weight loss.

4.1.4.4 Fat Restriction, with or without Energy Limitations

As knowledge has increased regarding how fat and carbohydrates are metabolized during overconsumption of various nutrients, several studies have been based on the hypothesis that weight reduction and/or weight stability can be achieved without energy/calorie restrictions if the diet has a low fat content and high carbohydrate content. Schlundt, Hill et al. [35] randomized 60 individuals to diets with low fat content (LF) and free carbohydrate intake versus low fat and energy content (LFE) during a 16 to 20 week program. The LFE group lost more weight than the LF group (men 11.8 kg and women 8.2 kg versus 8.0 kg and 3.9 kg). Fat intake declined from 90 to 30 grams per day. After 9 to 12 months, 65 % of the subjects could be followed up. No significant differences were found in maintained weight reduction between the groups (LF 2.6 kg and LFE 5.5 kg).

Jeffery et al. compared dietary counseling focused on fat reduction to 20 grams per day with energy reduction to 1000–1200 kcal per day in 74 women with a mean BMI of 30 [19]. After 6 months, weight loss in the group that received fat restrictions alone was 4.6 kg versus 3.7 kg in the group that also received energy limitations. During the following 12 months, weight returned to the original level in both of the groups, despite continued dietary counseling.

Toubro and Astrup studied 43 people with BMI 27–40 who had lost weight, on average 13.5–13.8 kg, with dietary formulas or conventional, energy-reduced diet and medication (ephedrine/caffeine) [41]. During a 1-year followup, the participants were later re-randomized to a free diet with a low fat and high carbohydrate content, versus energy-reduced diet. Weight reduction in the former treatment group was more permanent, 13 kg versus 10 kg.

Several studies have shown that protein provides the greatest satiety per energy unit, followed by carbohydrates and fat (in last place). Based on this knowledge, Skov et al. compared two diets with reduced fat content according to current recommendations (less than 30 % energy fat), one with a low protein content (12 % energy) and high carbohydrate content (HC), and the other with a high protein content (25 %) (HP) [38]. The trial subjects who had a BMI of approximately 30 (25–34) at the outset of the trial reduced during 6 months 8.9 kg per HP diet and 5.1 kg per HC, while the control groups did not change in weight. In the HP group, 34 % of the trial subjects lost more than 10 kg. The corresponding figure for the HC group was 9 %. The HP group also showed significantly greater reduction in fat mass. No difference was found in the taste of the food in the different groups. The authors report better satiety and a higher thermogenic effect of protein as the probable mechanisms for greater weight reduction in the HP group. The higher protein content in this group was mainly achieved through greater amounts of lean meat and milk products with low fat content.

Astrup et al. performed a meta-analysis of 16 controlled studies using low-fat diet in free amounts covering a 2- to 12-month trial period and 1728 individuals, published between 1966 and 1998 [3]. On average, the weight following the trial was 3.2 kg lower in the low-fat groups, and weight reduction was greater in those with higher initial weights. None of the studies covered individuals with obesity, and in 12 of the 16 studies weight reduction was not the primary goal. The authors draw the conclusion that the greatest potential in low-fat – high carbohydrate diets can be in preventing weight gain.

4.1.4.5 Carbohydrates

Recommendations concerning greater carbohydrate intake call attention to the nutritional quality of carbohydrates. For example, do added low-molecular-weight carbohydrates in products with a high sugar content have different effects on obesity, diabetes, and cardiovascular risk factors than foods with a high starch content?

Cross-sectional studies show an inverse relationship between body weight and sugar consumption, i. e., overweight persons eat more fat and less sugar than normal weight persons. However, the weakness of such studies is that dietary habits may have changed as a result of obesity. Fructose, which is found naturally in fruits and berries, comprises half of the molecule in common sugar. Many studies show an initial triglyceride increase, which is usually found to be temporary in longer studies. Another potentially negative effect of changing to a low-fat, carbohydrate-rich diet is that HDL cholesterol drops. Concurrently, LDL cholesterol usually declines as well. Overall, based on current recommendations, a carbohydrate-rich diet is often found to have positive effects on blood lipids [1].

A multicenter study, CARMEN, is the first prospective, controlled, long-term study to compare low-fat/high-carbohydrate diets with high or low percentage of low-molecular-weight (simple) carbohydrates [34]. The group with a low percentage of sugars and high percentage of starches lost 1.8 kg in 6 months, while the group with a high percentage of sugars lost 0.9 kg. No significant weight change was found in two control groups. None of the high carbohydrate diets yielded significant effects on either cholesterol values or triglycerides. The study achieved differences in the carbohydrate composition by varying the sugar and starch content in solid foods that were otherwise similar. The fiber intake was the same. Intake of foods with a high starch content generally means that fiber intake also increases, which helps promote further weight loss. The role of a high consumption of sugar-sweetened drinks in overweight people needs to be studied further. A recently published prospective epidemiological study suggests an association between the consumption of sugar-sweetened drinks and obesity in children aged 11 years in the United States [24].

4.1.4.6 Lactovegetarian Diet

The possibility that a lactovegetarian diet could be superior to a mixed diet for weight reduction was investigated in two studies that met the criteria established for Phase 3 review. However, one was rejected because the diets were not fully defined, and the primary issue was not weight reduction. In the remaining Finnish study, including 106 subjects, the lactovegetarian diet and mixed diet yielded the same weight reduction after 1 year, i. e., 9.2 kg and 10.4 kg respectively [25]. Dietary advice, 1200 kcal per day, was given to groups of 15 individuals once per week for 10 weeks, and thereafter at 5 meetings during the remainder of the year. The study primarily focused on changes in blood lipids. After 1 year, significantly higher HDL/LDL-ratios remained in both of the groups, while there was a reversion from the initial decline in total cholesterol and triglycerides. Thus, lactovegetarian diets are not believed to yield greater weight loss than do mixed diets with a corresponding energy content.

4.1.4.7 Commercial Weight-Loss Programs

Commercial weight-loss programs which aim at treating obesity and overweight, e. g., Weight Watchers, are active in many countries. The primary principles of treatment involve the restriction of energy intake and recommendations to increase physical activity. Dietary treatment focuses mainly on reducing fat intake. The focus is placed on learning the elementary roles of nutrition with the help of illustrations and various recipes. Both knowledge and body weight are followed up. Treatment adheres to scientifically developed principles. Two scientific studies have recently been published on this method.

A multicenter study randomized 423 patients with BMI 27–40 from various centers to either a Weight Watchers program or printed material and counseling by a dietician in two 20-minute sessions at the outset and again after 12 weeks [15]. After 26 weeks, weight reduction was 4.8 kg and 1.7 kg respectively. Dropout was approximately 18 % and similar in the two groups. Continued followup showed weight loss after 1 and 2 years at 5.0 kg and 3.0 kg in the Weight Watchers group and 1.7 kg and 0.0 kg in the control groups respectively. At the 2-year checkup, dropout had increased to about 25 %. Weight loss among those who attended more than 78 % of the Weight Watcher sessions was 6.8 kg after 1 year and 5.3 kg after 2 years. The results were comparable with pharmacological treatment [14].

In another study, individuals were followed up who had reached their target weight (self-selected targets within the BMI interval 20–25) 1 to 5 years earlier [23]. After 5 years, 42.6 % had retained a weight loss of 5 % or more, and 18.8 % had retained a weight loss of 10 % or more. Although the study lacks a control group, it has value because of the long followup period.

4.1.4.8 Other Aspects

Glycemic index: The effect of various carbohydrates on blood glucose, which is reported to play an important role in diabetes, has received attention in recent years. It is expressed in terms of the glycemic index (GI), which is the area below the blood glucose curve based on a standardized amount of food expressed in percent by a corresponding area based on white bread or glucose solution with the same level of carbohydrates. The insulin levels are often affected concurrently, i.e., food with high glycemic index also yields high insulin levels. Food structure is an important factor which can yield low GI, mainly foods rich in starch (whole wheat bread, peas and beans with intact cells, protein network in pasta, compact surface in parboiled rice). The origin of the starch and the degree/type of heat applied, gelatin-forming types of dietary fiber, and organic acids, in, e.g., sourdough bread, are other factors that influence GI. The size of the molecule in the carbohydrates, i.e., "simple" and "complex" carbohydrates, have, however, in direct opposition to what was believed earlier, a subordinate importance (see, e.g., [5]).

Several studies, of 3 to 6 months, revealed the potential for improving the approach to type 2 diabetes through foods with a low glycemic index [8]. These studies and studies in healthy individuals also suggest positive effects of low GI on risk factors such as LDL cholesterol and PAI 1 (Plasminogen Activator Inhibitor 1) [18]. Epidemiological studies suggest a strong negative correlation between low glycemic load (amount of carbohydrate × GI) and the development of type 2 diabetes, particularly in combination with high intake of fiber from grains [32, 33]. These variables were also correlated to a reduced risk of cardiovascular disease [22].

Some studies suggest that foods with low GI yield increase satiety, but these studies are not conclusive. A variation in protein content can probably be a factor making interpretation difficult. As regards weight loss based on low GI, there is only one 3-month study and no long-term studies [6].

Additional studies are needed to test the importance of diet with a high level of natural carbohydrate and fiber-rich foods with low glycemic index for preventing and treating overweight and obesity in an industrialized country. Theoretically/mechanistically and epidemiologically, there is strong evidence of the importance of dietary changes in this direction, in agreement with current dietary recommendations, i.e., increased consumption of fruit/vegetables and optimally combined and processed grain products with low glycemic index instead of products high in fat. An expert group in FAO/WHO has recommended high intake of foods high in carbohydrates, preferably with low GI [1].

Fat and fat quality: Limiting fat intake to a maximum of 30 % of energy and saturated fatty acids (in recent years saturated and transfatty acids) to a maximum of 10 % has been a key recommendation, internationally, regarding nutrition since the 1970s. Reducing the cholesterol value (LDL cholesterol) to reduce the risk of cardiovascular disease was originally the primary motive. Protein should correspond to 10 % to 15 % of the energy and carbohydrates to 55 % to 60 % (Nordic Nutritional Recommendations, 1996). Because of the obesity epidemic in recent years, a maintained or reduced body weight has become an increasingly more important motive for fat reduction. Theoretically, there are several reasons why a diet with limited fat content, based on the recommendations, should facilitate weight reduction and reduce the risk of weight increase, particularly under normal conditions, i. e., without special restrictions on amounts:

1. Fat contains more than double the energy (calories) of protein and carbohydrates.
2. Carbohydrates are stored as glycogen while fat can be stored in unlimited amounts.
3. The surplus of carbohydrates and particularly protein are metabolized to a greater extent than fat.
4. Protein yields the best, and fat the worst, satiety per energy unit (calorie).
5. Natural carbohydrate-rich foods have greater volume per energy unit (lower energy density).

Saturated and unsaturated fats yield the same amount of energy, but the fat quality plays a role for LDL cholesterol that is increased by saturated fat. Animal trials show that polyunsaturated fat, particularly from the n-3-family (the type of polyunsaturated fat found in fish and certain oils), can influence metabolism so that fat is metabolized to a greater extent rather than being stored. Furthermore, the insulin sensitivity is improved (for an overview see [9]). These effects, however, have not been verified in humans. A multicenter study, however, showed that monounsaturated fat improves the insulin sensitivity in healthy subjects compared to saturated fat [42]. However, the effects were observed only at a fat intake < 37 % of the energy. Epidemiological studies provide support for the hypothesis that unsaturated fat should be able to contribute toward reducing the risk of diabetes [16].

Meal schedules: Dividing the same amount of food across several meals instead of two to three large meals is shown in some studies to have advantages, e. g., lower body weight and lower levels of risk factors such as blood pressure, blood glucose, and blood lipids. Jenkins et al. performed an extreme trial of this type, where the food of the day was distributed across 17 equally large portions that were consumed once per hour, but even 5 to 6 meals compared to 3 yielded similar effects in one study [26]. A recently published epidemiological study provides support for a correlation between mealtime frequency and cholesterol levels [40]. Experience shows that a regular schedule of meals is an important element in controlling how much one eats.

References Section 4.1

1. FAO/WHO Report 66, Carbohydrates in human nutrition. FAO, Rome; 1998.

2. Ashley JM, St Jeor ST, Schrage JP, Perumean-Chaney SE, Gilbertson MC, McCall NL, et al. Weight control in the physician's office. Arch Intern Med 2001;161(13):1599-604.

3. Astrup A, Grunwald GK, Melanson EL, Saris WH, Hill JO. The role of low-fat diets in body weight control: a meta-analysis of ad libitum dietary intervention studies. Int J Obes Relat Metab Disord 2000;24(12):1545-52.

4. Baum JG, Clark HB, Sandler J. Preventing relapse in obesity through post-treatment maintenance systems: comparing the relative efficacy of two levels of therapist support. J Behav Med 1991;14(3):287-302.

5. Björck I, Liljeberg H, Ostman E. Low glycaemic-index foods. Br J Nutr 2000;83(Suppl 1):S149-55.

6. Björck I, Elmeståhl H. Glykemiskt index. Metabolism och mättnadsgrad. Scand J Nutrition 2000;44:113-7.

7. Björvell H, Rössner S. A ten-year follow-up of weight change in severely obese subjects treated in a combined behavioural modification programme. Int J Obes Relat Metab Disord 1992;16(8):623-5.

8. Brand JC, Colagiuri S, Crossman S, Allen A, Roberts DC, Truswell AS. Low glycemic index foods improve long-term glycemic control in NIDDM. Diabetes Care 1991;14(2):95-101.

9. Clarke SD. Polyunsaturated fatty acid regulation of gene transcription: a mechanism to improve energy balance and insulin resistance. Br J Nutr 2000;83:S59-66.

10. Ditschuneit HH, Flechtner-Mors M, Johnson TD, Adler G. Metabolic and weight-loss effects of a long-term dietary intervention in obese patients. Am J Clin Nutr 1999;69(2):198-204.

11. Flechtner-Mors M, Ditschuneit HH, Johnson TD, Suchard MA, Adler G. Metabolic and weight loss effects of long-term dietary intervention in obese patients: four-year results. Obes Res 2000;8(5):399-402.

12. Hakala P, Karvetti RL, Ronnemaa T. Group vs individual weight reduction programmes in the treatment of severe obesity – a five-year follow-up study. Int J Obes Relat Metab Disord 1993;17(2):97-102.

13. Hensrud DD, Weinsier RL, Darnell BE, Hunter GR. Relationship of comorbidities of obesity to weight loss and four-year weight maintenance/rebound. Obes Res 1995;3(Suppl 2):217S-22S.

14. Heshka S, Anderson JW, Atkinson RL, Greenway F, Hill JO, Phinney S, et al. Self-help weight loss vs a structured commercial program: A two-year randomized controlled trial (Konferensabstrakt). Experimental Biology 2001.

15. Heshka S, Greenway F, Anderson JW, Atkinson RL, Hill JO, Phinney SD, et al. Self-help weight loss versus a structured commercial program after 26 weeks: a randomized controlled study. Am J Med 2000;109(4):282-7.

16. Hu FB, van Dam RM, Liu S. Diet and risk of Type II diabetes: the role of types of fat and carbohydrate. Diabetologia 2001;44(7):805-17.

17. Jalkanen L. The effect of a weight reduction program on cardiovascular risk

factors among overweight hypertensives in primary health care. Scand J Soc Med 1991;19(1):66-71.

18. Jarvi AE, Karlstrom BE, Granfeldt YE, Bjorck IE, Asp NG, Vessby BO. Improved glycemic control and lipid profile and normalized fibrinolytic activity on a low-glycemic index diet in type 2 diabetic patients. Diabetes Care 1999;22(1):10-8.

19. Jeffery RW, Hellerstedt WL, French SA, Baxter JE. A randomized trial of counseling for fat restriction versus calorie restriction in the treatment of obesity. Int J Obes Relat Metab Disord 1995;19(2):132-7.

20. Jeffery RW, Wing RR, Thorson C, Burton LR, Raether C, Harvey J, et al. Strengthening behavioral interventions for weight loss: a randomized trial of food provision and monetary incentives. J Consult Clin Psychol 1993;61(6):1038-45.

21. Lean ME. Is long-term weight loss possible? Br J Nutr 2000;83:S103-11.

22. Liu S, Willett WC, Stampfer MJ, Hu FB, Franz M, Sampson L, et al. A prospective study of dietary glycemic load, carbohydrate intake, and risk of coronary heart disease in US women. Am J Clin Nutr 2000;71(6):1455-61.

23. Lowe MR, Miller-Kovach K, Phelan S. Weight-loss maintenance in overweight individuals one to five years following successful completion of a commercial weight loss program. Int J Obes Relat Metab Disord 2001;25(3):325-31.

24. Ludwig DS, Peterson KE, Gortmaker SL. Relation between consumption of sugar-sweetened drinks and childhood obesity: a prospective, observational analysis. Lancet 2001;357(9255):505-8.

25. Marniemi J, Seppanen A, Hakala P. Long-term effects on lipid metabolism of weight reduction on lactovegetarian and mixed diet. Int J Obes 1990;14(2):113-25.

26. McGrath SA, Gibney MJ. The effects of altered frequency of eating on plasma lipids in free-living healthy males on normal self-selected diets. Eur J Clin Nutr 1994;48(6):402-7.

27. McManus K, Antinoro L, Sacks F. A randomized controlled trial of a moderate-fat, low-energy diet compared with a low-fat, low-energy diet for weight loss in overweight adults. Int J Obes Relat Metab Disord 2001;25(10):1503-11.

28. Metz JA, Stern JS, Kris-Etherton P, Reusser ME, Morris CD, Hatton DC, et al. A randomized trial of improved weight loss with a prepared meal plan in overweight and obese patients: impact on cardiovascular risk reduction. Arch Intern Med 2000;160(14):2150-8.

29. Pascale RW, Wing RR, Butler BA, Mullen M, Bononi P. Effects of a behavioural weight loss program stressing calorie restriction versus calorie plus fat restriction in obese individuals with NIDDM or a family history of diabetes. Diabetes Care 1995;18(9):1241-8.

30. Pritchard DA, Hyndman J, Taba F. Nutritional counselling in general practice: a cost effective analysis. J Epidemiol Community Health 1999;53(5):311-6.

31. Quinn Rothacker D. Five-year self-management of weight using meal replacements: comparison with matched controls in rural Wisconsin. Nutrition 2000;16(5):344-8.

32. Salmeron J, Ascherio A, Rimm EB, Colditz GA, Spiegelman D, Jenkins DJ, et al. Dietary fiber, glycemic load, and risk of NIDDM in men. Diabetes Care 1997;20(4):545-50.

33. Salmeron J, Manson JE, Stampfer MJ, Colditz GA, Wing AL, Willett WC. Dietary fiber, glycemic load, and risk of non-insulin-dependent diabetes mellitus in women. JAMA 1997;277(6):472-7.

34. Saris WH, Astrup A, Prentice AM, Zunft HJ, Formiguera X, Verboeket-van de Venne WP, et al. Randomized controlled trial of changes in dietary carbohydrate/fat ratio and simple vs complex carbohydrates on body weight and blood lipids: the CARMEN study. The Carbohydrate Ratio Management in European National diets. Int J Obes Relat Metab Disord 2000;24(10):1310-8.

35. Schlundt DG, Hill JO, Pope-Cordle J, Arnold D, Virts KL, Katahn M. Randomized evaluation of a low fat ad libitum carbohydrate diet for weight reduction. Int J Obes Relat Metab Disord 1993;17(11):623-9.

36. Singh RB, Niaz MA, Ghosh S. Effect on central obesity and associated disturbances of low-energy, fruit- and vegetable-enriched prudent diet in north Indians. Postgrad Med J 1994;70(830):895-900.

37. Sjöström M, Karlsson AB, Kaati G, Yngve A, Green LW, Bygren LO. A four week residential program for primary health care patients to control obesity and related heart risk factors: effective application of principles of learning and lifestyle change. Eur J Clin Nutr 1999;53(Suppl 2):S72-7.

38. Skov AR, Toubro S, Ronn B, Holm L, Astrup A. Randomized trial on protein vs carbohydrate in ad libitum fat-reduced diet for the treatment of obesity. Int J Obes Relat Metab Disord 1999;23(5):528-36.

39. Summerbell CD, Watts C, Higgins JP, Garrow JS. Randomised controlled trial of novel, simple, and well supervised weight reducing diets in outpatients. BMJ 1998; 317(7171):1487-9.

40. Titan SM, Bingham S, Welch A, Luben R, Oakes S, Day N, et al. Frequency of eating and concentrations of serum cholesterol in the Norfolk population of the European prospective investigation into cancer (EPIC-Norfolk): cross sectional study. BMJ 2001;323(7324): 1286-8.

41. Toubro S, Astrup A. Randomised comparison of diets for maintaining obese subjects' weight after major weight loss: ad lib, low fat, high carbohydrate diet vs fixed energy intake. BMJ 1997;314(7073):29-34.

42. Vessby B, Unsitupa M, Hermansen K, Riccardi G, Rivellese AA, Tapsell LC, et al. Substituting dietary saturated for monounsaturated fat impairs insulin sensitivity in healthy men and women: The KANWU Study. Diabetologia 2001;44(3):312-9.

43. Wing RR, Jeffery RW, Burton LR, Thorson C, Nissinoff KS, Baxter JE. Food provision vs structured meal plans in the behavioral treatment of obesity. Int J Obes Relat Metab Disord 1996;20(1):56-62.

44. Wylie-Rosett J, Swencionis C, Peters MH, Dornelas EA, Edlen-Nezin L, Kelly LD, et al. A weight reduction intervention that optimizes use of practitioner's time, lowers glucose level, and raises HDL cholesterol level in older adults. J Am Diet Assoc 1994;94(1):37-42.

4.2
Special Diets

4.2.1
Dietary Fiber

Summary

Dietary fiber is an integrated part of our nourishment. Distinguishing natural fiber in the diet from supplements where fiber is used in a pharmacological context leads to methodological problems. It is difficult to implement alternative strategies based on low and high fiber diets over a longer period. Different types of fiber also have varying characteristics in the gastrointestinal canal. Fiber in tablet form and fiber as part of a natural diet act differently. The favorable effects that dietary fiber has on the gastrointestinal tract and on fat and carbohydrate metabolism motivates increased use of high-fiber foods in overweight and obese individuals, regardless of their potential weight-reducing effects.

Results: Three studies presenting medium or low quality show that dietary fiber as a supplement to conventional low-energy diets has limited effects in achieving and maintaining lower weight. Weight loss, compared to a control group, ranges between 1 kg and 2 kg. Dropout in these studies is high, and followup is short. Hence, reliable conclusions cannot be drawn. Dietary fiber has no side effects.

Conclusions: Scientific documentation on the effects of dietary fiber as a supplement to energy-reduced diets in treating obesity is insufficient, mainly because the studies that have been published have short followup periods.

4.2.1.1 **Introduction**
Strict scientific studies of the importance of dietary fiber for facilitating and maintaining weight loss have substantial methodological weaknesses. There are several reasons for this.

If one increases the intake of dietary fiber in the normal diet, it is impossible to assess the effects of the fiber alone – changes in fiber content inevitably affect other components as well. In some contexts, researchers have attempted to design stricter scientific studies that used dietary fiber in the same way as medication, i.e., they attempted to create a type of placebo tablet. Such studies, however, face some problems – it is technically difficult to manufacture fiber tablets that contain more than approximately 0.50 gram of dietary fiber. If fiber intake is intended to influence body weight, and the daily intake ranges between 15 and 20 grams, it is reasonable to assume that a clinically meaningful fiber increase should be at least 5 to 10 grams per day. This means that a large number of tablets would be needed to supplement the diet, rendering it difficult to recruit patients.

Dietary fiber is a component of vegetables that is resistant to digestion. It consists mainly of components of the cell walls of plants. Fiber is a heterogeneous concept chemically, mechanically, and physiologically. Foods naturally rich in fiber contain a combination of soluble and insoluble fibers. In assessing the effects of dietary fiber, authors generally describe the mechanical effects on the stomach and intestinal function, peristalsis, etc, to be associated mainly with insoluble fibers (e. g., lignin, cellulose, hemicellulose), while the effects that have been registered on blood glucose and LDL cholesterol have bonded more to soluble fibers such as pectin. The few fiber products which have been assessed in strictly controlled and randomized scientific trials have generally combined, e. g., citrus pectin and insoluble fibers. It is uncertain whether it is the solubility or other specific characteristics in the fiber composition that has led to the effects reported with some fiber tablets.

4.2.1.2 Methods

A search of MEDLINE from 1966 through 1997 resulted in 73 references to dietary fiber. Of these, 16 articles were reviewed, of which three met the criteria for further review. The remaining 13 studies were excluded because followup times were shorter than 6 months, and they were not randomized controlled trials.

4.2.1.3 Results

The studies have been summarized in Table 4.2.

Ryttig's study initially showed increased weight loss in the treatment group compared to placebo, but at followup after up to 1 year the differences were insignificant [3]. The treatment group of middle-aged women also had an initial mean BMI of only 27.

A study by Rigaud included 6 months of treatment [2]. Dropout is high, and less than 50 % complied with 6 months of treatment. Under these conditions, a significantly greater weight reduction was noted in the fiber group (5.5 kg) compared to the placebo group (3.0 kg).

Pasman's study used a different method. Here, a 14-month supplement of fiber (20 g/day) was used following an initial weight loss via a VLCD (Very Low Calorie Diet) [1]. The study lacks controls to treatment with this high fiber dose. Hence, no effects were attributed to long-term fiber treatment in weight reduction beyond 14 months.

4.2.1.4 Discussion

One encounters substantial methodological problems in designing RCT studies of dietary fiber. It is difficult to create pharmacological products with a high fiber content without a marked difference from the reference tablets, and not less than 15 to 20 dietary fiber tablets per day must be taken in a clinically relevant study. It has not been determined whether dietary fiber should be given between meals, before meals, or as an evening meal to achieve the most favorable effects.

In summary, there are few dietary fiber studies to analyze if one applies strict criteria on scientific evidence, and these studies differ substantially. Of the 3 stud-

Table 4.2 Dietary Fiber.

Author Year Reference	Study design	Inclusion criteria (Recruitment)	Intervention method Study groups	Treatment period/ Extra followup time
Ryttig KR et al. 1989 [3]	RCT and DB	Women 18–55 years 110%–130% above ideal weight	Fiber suppl. (6–7 g/day) to low-energy diet (1200–1600 kcal/day) or free diet during three periods: 11, 16 and 25 weeks	52 weeks/0 For the placebo- group: 27 weeks
Rigaud D et al. 1990 [2]	CT	Completed VLCD treatment. 16–60 years BMI higher than 25 and weight stability 3 months	Individual dietary advice 25%–30% below need for weight stability. 1. +7 g fibers/day 2. Placebo	6 months/ 6 months
Pasman WJ et al. 1997 [1]	CT	Completed VLCD treatment	After 3 months of VLCD: 1. Suppl of guarana fiber 10 g x 2 (n=20) 2. No supplement (n=11)	14 months/0

DB = Dubbel Blind; RCT = Randomized Controlled Trial
CT = Controlled Trial, not randomized; VLCD = Very Low Calorie Diet
* Statistical significance

ies reviewed, 1 presents medium quality and 2 present low quality, since followup times did not exceed 1 year. Reliable conclusions cannot be drawn from these studies. Normally, dietary fiber is a natural part of the diet, and intake should be 25 to 35 grams per day through increased consumption of high-fiber foods, i. e., whole-wheat products, fruit, and vegetables. No side effects appear except for mild gastrointestinal difficulties that accompany a change in diet. Several reports show favorable effects on intestinal function and on the metabolism of fat and carbohydrates. Increased dietary fiber content is therefore desirable in overweight and obese people.

4.2.2
Low-Energy Diets

Summary

"Protein formulas" were previously viewed with skepticism because of their serious side effects in the treatment of obesity. Modern Very Low Calorie Diets (VLCDs) are safe and do not cause serious side effects if they are used in an integrated, long-term treatment program.

Results: No studies have been able to use VLCDs for a period up to 1 year. Current treatment periods are usually 12 weeks or, in some cases, up to 16 weeks.

No. at start/ No. followed up	Results Weight change	Results/Other	Study quality Comments
97/97 Fiber: 62 Placebo: 35	Period 1 1. Fiber: −4.9 kg* 2. Placebo: −3.3 kg Period 2 1. −3.8 kg* 2. −2.8 kg Period 3 1. −6.7 kg 2. Not studied	Significantly greater reduction in diastolic blood pressure in Group 1 during Period 2	Medium Dropout diffi- cult to assess. Mean BMI 27
52/23	1. −5.5 kg* 2. −3.0 kg	Sense of hunger more frequent in Group 1. No difference in diastolic blood pressure	Low High dropout in both groups
31/31	No effect of fiber supplement on weight trend	No difference in effect on blood pressure or cholesterol	Low No placebo for fiber – methodo- logical weakness

Assessment of the long-term results therefore measures the initial effects or the maintenance of weight loss. Eight randomized studies have been identified. Initially, a substantial weight reduction is achieved, often 15 to 20 kg, or more, greater than weight loss achieved by conventional energy-restrictive diets. The tendency to regain weight is great after treatment has stopped. Studies for 1 to 2 years, where a VLCD is used intermittently for shorter periods, have noted a sustained weight loss of several kilograms more than with dietary treatment alone (Evidence Grade 3).

Conclusions: Weight reduction is greater during the initial period of 6 to 12 weeks with a VLCD than with a conventional energy-reduced diet. Intermittent maintenance treatment with VLCD yields a small lasting weight reduction up to 1–2 years.

4.2.2.1 Introduction

Low-energy diets (Very Low Calorie Diet, VLCD) are defined as products which provide a balanced, adequate diet of between 400 and 800 kilocalories (kcal) per day. Today, these products are manufactured using adequate protein sources, such as milk or soy products. Essential fatty acids, vitamins, minerals, and trace elements are added to fulfill current nutritional recommendations. Examples of VLCD products include Cambridge, Herbalife, Modifast, Nupo, Nutrilette, and Optifast. In the past, VLCD had a poor reputation because unbalanced formulas were used, resulting in unwanted consequences. A liquid protein diet based on hydrolyzed connective tissue protein with incomplete amino acid structures led to several deaths in the United States, leading to considerable concern and a strong public reaction. Modern balanced VLCD formulas can be used for many weeks without medical risk. Case studies have described the use of VLCD for 1 year without serious side effects.

Currently, VLCD is used mainly in combination with a long-term diet, exercise, and behavior-oriented treatment program. Many commercial products with low energy content have been developed, mainly in the United States, where corporations concurrently offer complete educational programs and participate in establishing weight reduction clinics.

VLCD can be used either for several weeks of total nutrition replacement or replacement of individual meals. Treatment with balanced products can be used without medical supervision for up to 2 weeks. Treatment is surprisingly simple to follow. The side effects that can appear are chills, hair loss, and at times euphoria. With rapid weight reduction, as with other treatment methods, gallstone problems and gout attacks may appear. After several days, when energy intake is comprised only of protein formulas and liquids, the hunger sensation disappears. The probable explanation is that the ketones that are formed during the breakdown of body fat have anorectic and, in some cases, even mildly euphoric effects. Attempts to combine VLCD with food generally make it more difficult to maintain the diet in the long term since the advantages of having a high level of ketones in the blood disappears.

Although the safety level of VLCD treatment is high when used correctly, the EU is increasingly recommending that a higher energy intake (800–1200 calories per day) be defined as a low calorie diet (LCD). The carbohydrate content of the products is generally higher, which means that elevated levels of ketones in the blood do not develop. The temptation which accompanies cooking can be avoided by using LCD products, but otherwise they are comparable to a general low-energy diet.

4.2.2.2 Method

The literature review of studies concerning the long-term effects of VLCD is limited by the fact that VLCD is routinely an initial form of therapy which is later followed by conventional treatment methods involving diet, exercise, and behavior change. In studies defined as 1-year, long-term therapy, VLCD is never used as the only treatment. The studies which have been presented are based on followup times of at least 1 year, with VLCD used on one or more occasions.

The MEDLINE search for the period 1966 through 2000 resulted in 206 references. The search was limited to studies of adults or a mix of age groups. Furthermore, case reports and articles in Russian, Polish, or Spanish were excluded. Of the 206 references, 23 met the criteria for further review. Many of the older studies are not systematic. Control groups are lacking and dropout has not been clearly reported. Not infrequently the analyses are retrospective after 5 years of followup. Eight of the studies met the established selection criteria.

4.2.2.3 **Results**

Wadden presents a randomized control trial (RCT) of 49 patients, of whom 40 were followed for 1 year (Table 4.3) [9]. After 6 weeks the VLCD group (420 kcal per day for 16 weeks) had reduced significantly, 21.5 kg compared to 11.9 kg in the group which received only behavioral therapy and low-energy diet. After 1 year, the difference was not significant, 12.2 versus 10.9 kg.

Wing studied the effects of VLCD in 93 individuals with type 2 diabetes, who were randomized to low-energy diets alone (1000–1200 kcal per day) or intermittent VLCD treatment for two 12-week periods [10]. Dropout (total of 26) was similar in both groups. Greater weight loss was achieved in the VLCD program (14.2 kg) than in the control group (10.5 kg). Furthermore, improved glucose metabolism control (HbA$_1$) and some blood pressure reduction was noted in the VLCD group.

A randomized controlled trial by Ryttig and Rössner included 60 patients, of whom 45 complied with 64 weeks of treatment (VLCD was given for the first 12 weeks) [6]. Initially, greater weight loss was achieved in the VLCD group than in the group that received a low-energy diet with the same energy content, but after 1 year there was no significant difference. Current risk factors for cardiovascular disease (blood pressure, blood glucose, and blood lipids) improved in relation to weight loss.

Ryttig, Flaten, and Rössner randomized 81 patients to 8 weeks of treatment with VLCD (420 kcal per day) or balanced low-energy diet (1600 kcal per day) [5]. Weight loss in the VLCD group was initially greater, but after 26 months of treatment no difference was observed. Dropout in the study was 47%. Temporary hair loss was noted as a seldom-reported side effect during VLCD treatment.

Rössner and Flaten monitored 93 patients for 1 year using three different types of VLCD and LCD (420, 530, or 880 kcal per day) for 6 weeks. Similar weight loss in all three groups suggests that energy intake can be raised to 880 kcal per day without changing the long-term results [4]. In patients who could be followed up after 1 year (60%), lasting weight reduction was 10% to 14% of the original body weight.

Torgerson randomized 113 patients to either VLCD or to Dietsconventional diet and behavior programs, with similar energy content in the low-energy diet, for 12 weeks [8]. In both treatment groups, lasting weight loss was observed after 2 years, but the more pronounced weight reduction in the VLCD group early in treatment did not remain. The study showed that the VLCD program in the initial phase resulted in greater weight loss in men.

Torgerson (1999) also studied the importance of consistency in the use of VLCD treatment [7]. In total, 121 men and women were randomized to three groups, i. e., strict VLCD treatment for 16 weeks, the same treatment but with intensive supervision at the metabolic unit during the first week of treatment, and finally a group who received more liberal instructions including two free meal selections per week. A lasting weight reduction of 10% was found in the 60% who complied with the study.

VLCD treatment resulted in significantly better weight loss in patients who complied with the strict 16 week treatment program and 1-year followup. An initial

Table 4.3 VLCD (Very Low Calorie Diet).

Author Year Reference	Study design	Inclusion criteria (Recruitment)	Intervention method and study groups	Treatment period/ Extra followup time
Wadden TA et al. 1994 [9]	RCT	Women >25 kg overweight	Behavior therapy for both groups. 1. VLCD (420 kcal/ day for 16 weeks) then a balanced diet (1200 kcal/day) 2. Balanced diet (1200 kcal/day)	1 year
Wing RR et al. 1994 [10]	RCT	30–70 years Type 2 diabetes 18 kg above ideal weight	Basic program of the Pittsburgh group with group therapy 1. VLCD (800 kcal/day), 12 + 12 weeks, a balanced diet in-between (1000–1200 kcal/day) 2. Balanced diet (1000–1200 kcal/day)	1 year
Ryttig KR et al. 1995 [6]	RCT	BMI >30, Weight-stability ± 3 kg for 2 months	After VLCD (330 kcal/day) for 12 weeks. Then randomization to 1 year 1. VLCD (120 kcal/day) + balanced diet 1480 kcal/day 2. Balanced diet (1600 kcal/day)	1 year
Ryttig KR et al. 1997 [5]	RCT	21–64 years BMI >30, Weight-stability ± 3 kg for 2 months	1. VLCD (420 kcal/day) for 8 weeks. Then a) Balanced diet 1600 kcal/day b) Balanced diet + VLCD (240 kcal/day) Total of 1600 kcal/day 2. Balanced diet (1600 kcal/day) + behavior therapy	26 months
Rössner S et al. 1997 [4]	RCT	20–65 years BMI >30	VLCD 6 + 2 weeks: 1. 420 kcal/day 2. 530 kcal/day 3. 880 kcal/day Balanced diet 1600 kcal/day w 7–25 + w 28–52	1 year
Torgerson JS et al. 1997 [8]	RCT	37–60 years BMI >32	1. VLCD 12 weeks + balanced diet 92 weeks 2. Balanced diet 104 weeks M: 1400–1800 kcal/day W: 1200–1400 kcal/day	2 years

See legend on page 128

No. of patients/ No. followed up	Results Weight change	Results/Other	Study quality Comments
49/40	<u>16 weeks</u> 1. −21.5 kg* 2. −11.9 kg <u>1 year</u> 1. −12.2 kg 2. −10.9 kg		Medium
93/67	<u>1 year</u> 1. −14.2 kg 2. −10.5 kg	Group 1 lower fasting glucose, cholesterol, and diastolic blood pressure, and higher HDL cholesterol	Medium Randomization procedure not well described
60/45	<u>12 weeks</u> −20.8 kg <u>1 year</u> 1. −12.8 kg (39 %)* 2. −8.5 kg (54 %)	Blood pressure dropped first 12 weeks, then rose some-what more in Group 2	Medium
1a) 27/15 1 1b) 27/11 2. 27/16	<u>26 months</u> 1a. −10 % 1b. −9.5 % 2. −7 % of initial weight	Cholesterol, TG, fasting glucose, HDL Cholesterol no group difference	Low
1. 30/29 2. 32/19 3. 31/17	<u>1 year</u> 1. −12.9 kg 2. −11.2 kg 3. −10.0 kg	Blood pressure, TG, Cholesterol, fasting glucose no group difference	Medium
1. 58/45 2. 55/45	<u>Men</u> 1. −15.5 kg* 2. −5.3 kg <u>Women</u> 1. −6.8 kg 2. −5.6 kg		Medium

Table continues on next page

Table 4.3 continued

Author Year Reference	Study design	Inclusion criteria (Recruitment)	Intervention method and study groups	Treatment period/ Extra followup time

Torgerson JS
et al.
1999
[7]
	RCT	21–50 years
		BMI >30
			VLCD (456 kcal/
			day) for 16 weeks.
			1. Strict VLCD
			2. Care at metabolic
			  unit 1 week
			3. Two meals/week with a
			  balanced diet. Up to
			  1 year with a balanced diet
			  (−500 kcal/day)
				1 year

RCT = Randomized Controlled Trial; CT = Controlled Trial, not randomized
TG = Triglycerides; M = Men; W = Women
* Statistical significance

period at the metabolic unit did not yield better treatment results. The treatment regime alone made the treatment program difficult to follow, and after 1 year it yielded less weight loss (8.6 kg) than VLCD treatment (12.3 kg).

4.2.3
Fasting

Summary

Fasting has been used as a weight reduction method, but it has never been systematically assessed by adequate scientific methods. For treatment to be risk free, patients must be administered adequate amounts of vitamins, minerals, trace elements, and water.

Results: Three noncontrolled studies have been identified. Two of these studies reported that the weight loss remained up to 3 years, but a return to the original weight was common.

Conclusion: There is no scientific documentation on the lasting effects which total fasting, fasting, or "zero-diets" may have on weight.

4.2.3.1   Introduction
Earlier strategies for treating obesity included total fasting. In principle, this involves supervision to ensure that patients have adequate fluids, minerals, vitamins, trace elements, and electrolytes, but no food components containing energy. Total fasting is a treatment alternative that was practiced in the 1960s and 1970s and led to substantial weight reduction. Currently, the method is only of historical interest since it has become apparent that total fasting leads to a substantial degradation of not only of fat tissue but also of muscle mass.

No. of patients/ No. followed up	Results Weight change	Results/Other	Study quality Comments
1. 41/32 2. 39/24 3. 41/27	16 weeks 1. −16.4 kg 2. −16.0 kg 3. −13.8 kg 1 year 1. −12.3 kg 2. −10.2 kg 3. −8.6 kg		Low High dropout

4.2.3.2 **Results**

A study by Berger et al. followed up 42 of 45 patients for an average of 21 months after fasting [11]. Fourteen patients had lost weight and nine weighed more than they did at the outset. This study showed that psychosocial background variables did not influence the outcome. However, the study contained no statistical analyses.

A study by H Goschke et al. followed 162 patients for an average 2.8 years on a so-called Diets"zero-diet". Nearly 50% of these subjects were described as "successfully treated", but no systematic statistical assessment was performed [13].

A study from California treated 207 patients by fasting for 2 months. Mean weight at the outset of the study was 143 kg. After fasting, an average weight loss of 28.6 kg was reported [12]. One fourth of the group fasted for less than 1 month, while another one fourth fasted for more than 2 months. Followup of 121 patients for an average of 7.3 years showed that weight loss had been maintained for up to one and one half years. Within 2 years, 50% of the patients had returned to their original weight, and only 7 patients had retained their weight loss at the later followups. The authors concluded that fasting had temporary effects, but did not have lasting results. Total fasting requires medical supervision. Therefore, it is resource-demanding and probably indicated only in special cases. Recent surgical treatment methods have generally replaced this type of treatment.

Fasting, (so-called liquid fasting) has been widely used at health spas, etc. However, the results from these programs have not been systematically reviewed. The studies presented above do not meet the requirements or standards for scientific evidence, and therefore no conclusions can be drawn.

References Section 4.2

1. Pasman WJ, Westerterp-Plantenga MS, Muls E, Vansant G, van Ree J, Saris WH. The effectiveness of long-term fibre supplementation on weight maintenance in weight-reduced women. Int J Obes Relat Metab Disord 1997;21(7):548-55.

2. Rigaud D, Ryttig KR, Angel LA, Apfelbaum M. Overweight treated with energy restriction and a dietary fibre supplement: a 6-month randomized, doubleblind, placebo-controlled trial. Int J Obes 1990;14(9):763-9.

3. Ryttig KR, Tellnes G, Haegh L, Boe E, Fagerthun H. A dietary fibre supplement and weight maintenance after weight reduction: a randomized, double-blind, placebo-controlled long-term trial. Int J Obes 1989;13(2):165-71.

4. Rössner S, Flaten H. VLCD versus LCD in long-term treatment of obesity. Int J Obes Relat Metab Disord 1997;21(1):22-6.

5. Ryttig KR, Flaten H, Rössner S. Long-term effects of a very low calorie diet (Nutrilett) in obesity treatment. A prospective, randomized, comparison between VLCD and a hypocaloric diet + behaviour modification and their combination. Int J Obes Relat Metab Disord 1997;21(7):574-9.

6. Ryttig KR, Rössner S. Weight maintenance after a very low calorie diet (VLCD) weight reduction period and the effects of VLCD supplementation. A prospective, randomized, comparative, controlled long-term trial. J Intern Med 1995;238(4):299-306.

7. Torgerson JS, Ågren L, Sjöstrom L. Effects on body weight of strict or liberal adherence to an initial period of VLCD treatment. A randomised, one-year clinical trial of obese subjects. Int J Obes Relat Metab Disord 1999;23(2):190-7.

8. Torgerson JS, Lissner L, Lindroos AK, Kruijer H, Sjöström L. VLCD plus dietary and behavioural support versus support alone in the treatment of severe obesity. A randomised two-year clinical trial. Int J Obes Relat Metab Disord 1997;21(11):987-94.

9. Wadden TA, Foster GD, Letizia KA. One-year behavioral treatment of obesity: comparison of moderate and severe caloric restriction and the effects of weight maintenance therapy. J Consult Clin Psychol 1994;62(1):165-71.

10. Wing RR, Blair E, Marcus M, Epstein LH, Harvey J. Year-long weight loss treatment for obese patients with type II diabetes: does including an intermittent very-low-calorie diet improve outcome? Am J Med 1994;97(4):354-62.

11. Berger M, Granz M, Berchtold P, Kruskemper GM, Zimmermann H. Serial studies of the long-term effects of a total fasting regimen (author's translation). Dtsch Med Wochenschr 1976;101(16):601-5.

12. Drenick EJ, Johnson D. Weight reduction by fasting and semistarvation in morbid obesity: long-term follow-up. Int J Obes 1978;2(2):123-32.

13. Goschke H, Hausser R, Lauffenburger TH, Maier I, Ott S, Vogel M. Long-term results of fasting. Results from 132 consecutive patients after 1–6 1/2 years. Schweiz Med Wochenschr 1976;106(21):713-7.

4.3
Behavior Therapy

Summary

Behavior analysis and behavior therapy are scientifically grounded and tested methods used in problem-solving situations or for training certain skills. Using behavior therapy to treat obesity aims at changing diet and exercise habits to achieve weight loss.

Results: Behavior therapy may be included as a component for different types of treatment, and it is difficult to isolate the effects of this treatment. Four randomized controlled trials have attempted to analyze the effects of various types of behavior therapy. A study presenting high quality showed that behavior therapies of different types in combination with different types of dietary counseling/treatment achieved a moderate but significantly greater weight loss than in the control group. Two other studies, presenting medium quality, found no significant differences in weight loss after 1 to 2 years compared with the control groups.

Conclusions: Reliable conclusions cannot be drawn.

4.3.1
Introduction

Behavior can be defined as a reaction to an external signal. Behavioral modification refers to methods aimed at changing the environment in a structured way so as to give individuals an opportunity to control their environments themselves to design, influence, and organize their lives and their way of living.

Behavioral modification has been used in several fields, mainly in treating dependency problems. In treating obesity, behavioral modification may consist of all or some of the following components:

1. Develop social skills, e. g., the ability to say no without guilt and anxiety
2. Prevent relapse in weight gain
3. Exchange unwanted thought patterns for more effective interventions against obesity
4. Control signals and behavior that lead to or maintain obesity
5. Change unilateral thinking (either success or failure) for more complex and flexible solutions
6. Regain normal behavior in meal-time situations by registering feelings while eating
7. Positive reinforcement and recognition of success in weight reduction
8. Basic nutritional skills and physiology
9. Adapted physical activity

The basis for a well-structured treatment program for obesity involves diet, exercise, and behavioral change. Most programs of behavioral modification therefore include combinations of several of the components mentioned above. Several other Sections in this book also present studies that address changes in behavior.

4.3.2
Methods

A literature search in MEDLINE (using the search terms "obesity", "behavior therapy", "adults", "randomized controlled trials") identified 293 articles. Review articles and reference lists were acquired from 12 additional studies in other searches.

Using the summaries from these articles, 120 articles were selected for relevance by two reviewers during Phase 1. The articles were studied in their entirety during Phase 2. Most of the articles that were eliminated were based on small patient databases, lacked control groups, reported high dropout, or had short followup times (less than 6 months). Only four studies met the established quality standards. Two studies included patients with type 2 diabetes. In addition, four articles presented a study that was neither randomized nor controlled, but had an observation time of several years and was relatively comprehensive [1].

4.3.3
Results

A large study compared the effects of four behavioral modification treatment strategies with those in control groups of conventionally treated patients (Table 4.4) [3].

Through advertising, approximately 200 men and women who were 14 kg to 32 kg overweight (mean BMI > 30) were recruited. These subjects were randomized to four intervention groups and a control group that did not receive intervention. The first intervention group, Group 1, initially received behavioral therapy in a group. The participants received recommendations about diet and exercise once per week for 20 weeks. In addition, Group 2 received prepared meals for 18 months, Group 3 received an economic reward for successful weight loss and maintained weight, and Group 4 received both meals and economic rewards. In total, nearly 90% of the participants complied with treatment for up to 30 months. In the four intervention groups, weight loss after 30 months was moderate (on average 1.4-2.2 kg) but significantly better than in the control group, which increased in weight by an average of 0.6 kg. However, there was no difference among the treatment groups. In these groups, between 8% and 17% of the participants achieved weight loss exceeding 9 kg. Early, successful weight loss suggested long-term success. The variables that best related to both initial weight loss and maintenance were reduced fat intake, knowledge about diet, regular exercise, and insight concerning the difficulties in maintaining new habits.

Sbrocco et al. presented results from a study of 24 women with an original mean BMI of 32. These were randomized to two different behavior therapies, the traditional model (TBT) and behavior therapy with a choice of food (VBT) [4]. In the TBT group, treatment consisted of group meetings each week to receive dietary information. The participants were recommended an energy intake of 1200 kcal per day with reduced fat content. Different changes in eating behavior were included in the treatment. Participants in the VBT group received advice to stop special dietary treatment and dieting food, and instead were given free choice. The participants set their own priorities with regard to means and objectives. The intent was to achieve a slower but more permanent weight loss and a positive experience from exercising. Treatment times were 13 weeks with followup after 6 and 12 months. Energy intake was higher than the target (1200 kcal) in the TBT group and lower than the target (1800 kcal) in the VBT group. The level of physical activity was the same in both groups. Both of the groups improved to the same degree from a psychological perspective. After 6 and 12 months, the participants in the VBT group had better results than those of the participants in the TBT group. After 12 months, the VBT group achieved greater weight loss (10.1 kg) than the TBT group (4.3 kg).

One study included 53 patients with type 2 diabetes, of whom 75 % received tablets, and 63 % of these received treatment for high blood pressure [5]. The mean value for BMI was 34.8. A high percentage (73 %) had already attempted dietary treatment at least 10 times. All participants paid a fee (85 USD). The amount of the deposit refunded depended on active participation and goal achievement. Patients were randomized to three groups: dietary information, behavior therapy, and standard treatment for people with diabetes. Treatment time was 16 weeks. The two intervention groups receiving behavior therapy and dietary information held meetings every week while only four meetings were held in the control group. All of the groups had the same dietary recommendations of at least 1000 kcal per day. Group treatment involving behavior therapy included:

1. Information about reduced energy and high-fiber diets
2. Physical exercise by walking, intended to use 1000 kcal per week
3. Changes in meal habits and eating behavior
4. Motivation to change personal perspectives on food and diabetes.

Standard treatment included the routine clinical information given to people with diabetes along with four group meetings during 16 weeks. After 4 months, the group that received behavior therapy had lost significantly more weight (6.3 kg), but in followup at 16 months no difference was observed among the three groups. The changes in the fasting values of glucose, cholesterol, and triglycerides and the diastolic blood pressure co-varied with the degree of weight loss. Registration of behavior changes showed that a change in one variable was often followed by changes in others. Self-reported depression decreased during the first 4 months, mostly in the group who received behavior therapy. There was a correlation between the degree of weight loss and the onset of self-reported depression.

Another study randomized patients with type 2 diabetes and BMI > 27 to a conventional weight loss program (n = 26) and to an expanded program (n = 27) including behavior therapy and physical exercise [2]. At every visit, the meals from the three preceding days were recorded. Behavior therapy was led by a psychologist and was conducted in groups once per week for the first 2 months, and thereafter

Table 4.4 Studies addressing the effect of behavior therapy on body weight and certain metabolic and psychological variables

Author Year Reference	Study design	Recruitment	Inclusion criteria	Exclusion criteria	Study groups
Jeffery RW et al. 1995 [3]	RCT	Advertisement	Men and W: 25–45 years Overweight: 14–32 kg Mean value: BMI 31	Smokers Ongoing prescription medicine Current disease	Group treatment during 20 weeks, then: 1. Behavior therapy + diet (1000–1500 kcal/day) + physical activity (250–1000 kcal/w) 2. Behavior therapy + ready-cooked food 3. Behavior therapy + reward when fullfilling goal 4. Behavior therapy + ready-cooked food + reward 5. Control group
Sbrocco T et al. 1999 [4]	RCT	Newspaper advertisement	Women Non-smokers 30%–60% overweight Doctor's consent to participate	Weight reduction >4.5 kg past month or >9 kg past 6 months	Group treatment: 1. Behavior therapy with optional diet (1800 kcal) 2. Traditional behavior therapy (1200 kcal)
Wing RR et al. 1985 [5]	RCT	Advertisement in local press and letter to treating physician	30–70 years >20% over-weight Mean BMI 34.8 Type 2 diabetes treated with tablets or diet only. Deposit $85		Group treatment: 1. Dietary information 2. Behavior therapy 3. Control group
Blonk MC et al. 1994 [2]	RCT	Patients at outpatient clinic	BMI >27 Type 2 diabetes	Heart disease treatment with insulin, diuretics, beta-blockers, lipid-lowering agents	Run-in period 3 months, then randomization to 24 months of group Treatment concerning: 1. Conventional (dietary) treatment 2. With addition of education in behavior treatment and training with 2-month intervals

RCT = Randomized Controlled Trial; CT = Controlled Trial, not randomized
SBP = Systolic blood pressure; DBP = Diastolic blood pressure; TG = Triglycerides; W = Women
* = Statistical significance

Treatment/ Followup period	No. of patients/ No. followed up	Results Body weight	Metabolic and psychological variables	Study quality Comments
6, 12, 18, 30 months	101 women and 101 men (177; 88%)	Result 30 months 1. −1.4 kg* 2. −2.2 kg* 3. −1.6 kg* 4. −1.6 kg* 5. +0.6 kg		High
13 weeks/ 6, 12 months	24/22	6 months 1. −7.0 kg* 2. −4.5 kg 12 months 1. −10 kg* 2. −4.3 kg	Improved sense of well-being with weight loss	Medium
16 weeks/ 16 months	53 (50)	16 weeks 1. −3.9 kg 2. −6.3 kg* 3. −2.9 kg 16 months 1. −3.0 kg 2. −3.4 kg 3. −1.8 kg	16 months Reduction of: HbA$_{1C}$ 0.3 fasting glucose −7.2 TG −0.1 mmol/l Cholesterol −0.24 mmol/l SBP −4.8 Depressive symptoms decreased in intervention group	Medium
years	40 women and 20 men 1. 30/27 2. 30/26	1. −2.1 kg 2. −3.5 kg	After 2 years no difference concerning HbA1C, fasting insulin, SBP, DBP, TG, cholesterol	Medium

quarterly up to 20 months. Exercise was led by a physiotherapist 1 or 2 times per week. After 6 months, weight loss was 2.9 kg in the expanded program and 1.2 kg in the conventional program. After 24 months, weight loss was 3.5 kg and 2.1 kg respectively, which did not represent a significant difference between the groups. The metabolic variables HbA_1, blood glucose, and blood lipids, as well as blood pressure levels dropped markedly in both treatment groups. Correlation analyses show strong associations between weight loss and HbA_{1c} levels at 6 months but not at 24 months. The most important predictors of weight loss were high values of HbA_{1c} and mild overweight in the family. It was concluded that the expanded program had only a temporary effect on glycemic control and had no effect on weight beyond the results reported in the control group.

A nonrandomized study from Sweden reported results after 4 years of treatment for severely overweight men and women [1]. The mean BMI was 41 in women and 43 in men. The treatment program included 68 patients, 56 of whom could be traced after 4 years. All had made several attempts at weight loss and reported physical and/or psychological complications. The participants were divided into a group treated with behavior therapy and a control group selected from volunteer patients. Treatment consisted of group meetings at a day unit with a maximum of five participants for 6 weeks. Behavior therapy aimed at changing habits, including strategies to prevent relapse, was combined with dietary information. The daily energy intake was 600 kcal. Group or individual exercise was included three times per week. Individual weekly schedules were developed for other physical activity. During the remaining time, up to 4 years, patients were temporarily given an opportunity to participate once or twice per week in followup involving weighing and dietary advice. The patients who did not participate were contacted regularly. To avoid relapse, 2-week treatment sessions were offered regularly at the department. After one year, weight loss was 15.0 kg in women and 30.9 kg in men who were primarily participants in the intervention group. Weight loss in the control group averaged 6.8 kg. At 4-year followup (intervention group only), the lasting weight loss in women was 11.5 kg and in men 18.4 kg. Hence, this study found that weight loss in individuals who were severely obese could be achieved and maintained with consistent monitoring, followup, and contact over a longer period. This method, however, requires substantial resources.

4.3.4
Discussion

The studies referred to here often used a combination of behavior therapy methods and education on diet and physical exercise. Even in other respects, the studies were designed in a way that makes interpretation difficult. Furthermore, recruitment of participants to the studies varied substantially. One study is based on volunteers at different levels of BMI who were recruited by advertising. These participants paid a deposit, which was later refunded completely, or in part, depending on goal achievement. Other studies are based on overweight patients with type 2 diabetes, which may have importance as regards motivation and dropout and which can diminish the possibilities to reproduce the results in other patient groups.

Hence, one encounters major methodological difficulties in assessing behavior therapy. The methods vary widely, and are always integrated with dietary information and information about physical exercise. Also, the therapist probably plays a major role. Behavior therapy requires more than an isolated intervention. It requires substantial intervention, time, and personal resources. Continuity and long-term contact with the therapist are particularly important. Several studies suggest that the patient's well-being increases with treatment and care. However, these studies involve only a small number of patients, and the difficulties with controlled studies are substantial. Of the studies reviewed, no particular type of behavior therapy demonstrated better effects than any of the others. The long-term effects are modest when the supportive function in behavior therapy is absent. There is a need for studies based on evidence-based methods to assess different types of behavior-modifying interventions.

References Section 4.3

1. Björvell H, Rössner S. Long term treatment of severe obesity: four-year follow up of results of combined behavioural modification programme. BMJ (Clin Res Ed) 1985;291(6492): 379-82.
2. Blonk MC, Jacobs MA, Biesheuvel EH, Weeda-Mannak WL, Heine RJ. Influences on weight loss in type 2 diabetic patients: little long-term benefit from group behaviour therapy and exercise training. Diabet Med 1994;11(5): 449-57.
3. Jeffery RW, Wing RR. Long-term effects of interventions for weight loss using food provision and monetary incentives. J Consult Clin Psychol 1995;63(5):793-6.
4. Sbrocco T, Nedegaard RC, Stone JM, Lewis EL. Behavioral choice treatment promotes continuing weight loss: preliminary results of a cognitive-behavioral decision-based treatment for obesity. J Consult Clin Psychol 1999;67(2):260-6.
5. Wing RR, Epstein LH, Nowalk MP, Koeske R, Hagg S. Behavior change, weight loss, and physiological improvements in type II diabetic patients. J Consult Clin Psychol 1985;53(1): 111-22.

4.4
Physical Exercise

Summary

Increased physical activity is one of the cornerstones in treating obesity. Regardless of weight loss, physical exercise has favorable effects on risk factors such as diabetes and cardiovascular disease.

Results: Four studies, two of which present high quality, highlight the effects of physical exercise combined with traditional dietary treatment to reduce fat intake. Major weight loss, averaging about 4 kg within 1 year, can be achieved with regular exercise, usually walking but even jogging among younger individuals (Evidence Grade 1). Increased physical exercise as the only intervention is less effective than current dietary treatment according to one study of medium quality.

It has not been demonstrated whether regular physical exercise can counteract the weight gain which usually occurs within 1 to 2 years after initially successful obesity treatment.

Conclusions: Increased physical activity has few side effects and leads to greater well-being. Physical exercise along with dietary treatment can yield moderate weight loss in obese patients. Physical exercise alone is less effective than dietary treatment.

4.4.1
Introduction

The utilization of energy in the body increases, with all types of physical activity, in relation to intensity and duration. Furthermore, a positive relationship exists between energy utilization and the body weight of the individual. Programs aimed at increasing physical activity are therefore a logical component in obesity treatment. The main purpose of the review has been to determine the extent to which physical activity alone, or in addition to dietary advice, can lead to weight loss in obese individuals. The type, intensity, and frequency of exercise programs for obese individuals greatly affect the outcome, since exercise should continue over a longer period.

4.4.2
Special Methodological Problems in Studies of Physical Exercise

Studies of increased physical activity in the treatment of obesity face several methodological problems. One problem is that factors controlling food intake cannot be confirmed. There is reason to suspect that increased exercise influences dietary habits. Changes could possibly be attributed to various regulatory mechanisms that cause a spontaneous loss in appetite. Also, individuals could consciously reduce their energy intake. The opposite is also conceivable, to compensate for an increased need for energy. Although it is possible for a study to achieve complete control of these factors, in practice it is very demanding. This greatly limits the opportunities for long-term studies of sufficiently large study groups. Another problem is that the methods for quantifying physical activity started to be developed and assessed only in recent years. Nevertheless, studies for a limited time period and in small groups show that physical exercise reduces fat mass in the body with unchanged energy intake, which is a result that can be expected thermodynamically. For example, the studies by Wood et al. [15, 16] continually followed up energy intake, but the results depend on what the trial subjects report. The conclusion that can be drawn is that physical activity enhances the weight loss achieved by energy restriction alone.

The high dropout rate among trial subjects is another methodological problem in studying the effects of physical exercise on obesity. Therefore, it is important to design physical activity so that the intensity is reasonable and that the program intrudes as little as possible on normal lifestyle [6]. This problem has been discussed recently [5]. Mainly, overweight women hesitate to participate in exercise programs because of the anxiety about negative attitudes. Motivation for physical activity is often low, but it can be enhanced if women become more aware of the medical advantages and receive active support, mainly from the group leader and relatives. Clearly, simple exercise programs are more likely to be carried out over longer periods than programs which require special preparation, equipment, or clothing.

4.4.3
Methods

The MEDLINE search resulted in 186 articles on physical exercise and obesity. A search of studies about the effects of physical activity on other conditions, e.g., myocardial infarction, yielded 10 articles. Reference lists and review articles yielded another 31 articles, i.e., a total of 227 articles (Phase 1). The group selected 78 articles from the abstracts (Phase 2). Two copies of the articles were acquired and read by two members of the project group. A limit for observation time was established at 12 months, except in isolated studies with particularly valuable information. Six scientific studies remained for final assessment. One or more causes for exclusion in Phase 2 and Phase 3 were

- Obesity not the focus: 10
- Followup too short: 11
- Dropout too high ($> 40\%$): 10
- Control group missing: 12
- Insufficient number of subjects in the study groups: 24
- Physical activity not the focus: 42
- Lack of primary data (review articles): 29
- Same material published more than once: 2
- Uncertain design: 1

4.4.4
Results

Five studies were included in the review. In addition, a meta-analysis and several other studies were presented because of special circumstances (Table 4.5).

One study compared the effects of self-selected physical exercise (45 minutes, 3 to 7 times per week for 12 months) with dietary treatment (reduction of 500 kcal/day) [9]. Weight loss was greater in the dietary group (6.3 kg) than in the exercise group (2.6 kg). The loss of fat mass was largely the same in both groups (approximately 2–2.5 kg), while muscle mass was maintained only in the exercise group. The exercise programs were individually adapted, but were too strenuous for individuals with high-grade obesity.

Two reports from a randomized controlled trial compared the effects of physical exercise in addition to an energy-restrictive diet [10, 11]. The study included 121 overweight women. Aerobic-type exercises were combined with body building three times per week (total of 1.5 hours) for 12 weeks. Weight loss was greater in the group that received both exercise and energy-restrictive diet (10.9 kg) than that in the group that received only the energy-restrictive diet (6.6 kg). At followup 6 months later, the original weight had been reduced by approximately 8 kilos in both groups.

Compared with the control group, the level of triglycerides was lower, while total cholesterol and LDL cholesterol remained unchanged. Both experimental groups reported a reduction in total bone density in the body of about 3% and in the bone density of the lumbar vertebrae of just below 3%.

Part of a study reported in one article addressed individuals with type 2 diabetes (mean BMI 38) who were randomized to restrictive energy intake (less than 1000 kcal per day) alone or along with an exercise program involving a 5-kilometer walk three to four times per week [14]. After 10 weeks, weight loss was greater in the exercise groups (9.3 kg) than in the control groups (5.6 kg). After 12 months, the weight in both groups had increased somewhat, but the difference in weight loss remained (7.9 kg and 3.8 kg respectively).

Dietary treatment and physical exercise were compared in two randomized and controlled studies, both designed to reduce weight by 1 kg per week [15, 16]. Compliance regarding both diet and individually adapted exercise programs (walks or jogging three to four times per week) was checked continually. In the first study (including men weighing 120% to 160% of ideal weight), body weight had decreased more after 1 year in the diet group (7.2 kg) than in the exercise group that jogged an average 20 km per week (4.0 kg) [15]. Body fat and triglycerides decreased and HDL cholesterol increased equally in both groups. The second study included both men and women weighing 120% to 160% of ideal weight [16]. The participants were randomized to an energy-restrictive diet alone or diet in combination with regular exercise (walks or jogging 25–45 minutes three times per week). After 1 year, the average weight loss in men was substantially greater in the diet and the exercise group (8.7 kg) than in the diet group (5.1 kg). No difference was noted among women. Exercise was accompanied by a reduction

Table 4.5 Studies addressing the effect of physical activity on body weight and certain metabolic variables.

Author Year Reference	Study design	Inclusion criteria (Recruitment)	Intervention method Study groups	Treatment/ followup period
Pritchard JE et al. 1997 [9]	RCT	Men: overweight Mean BMI 29	1. Diet: Reduction with approx. 500 kcal/day by low content of fat 2. 65 %–75 % of max physical capacity 45 minutes 3–7 times/week 3. Controls	12 months/0
Svendsen OL et al. 1994 [11]	RCT	Women: 49–58 years BMI 25–42	1. Diet (4.2 MJ/day) 2. Diet (as above) + physical activity (submax aerobics and body-building 1–1.5 week) 3. Controls	12 weeks/6 months
Wing RR et al. 1988 [14]	RCT	Women: 30–65 years with type 2 diabetes >20 % above ideal weight	1. Diet (–1000 kcal/day) + training (+ 3 miles, 3 times/week) 2. Free diet + training (+ 3 miles, 4 times/week) 3. Diet + stretching	12 months/0
Wood PD et al. 1988 [15]	RCT	Men: overweight 120 %–160 %	1. Diet with expected weight loss 1 kg/week, fat intake reduced by 30 % 2. Individual instruction corresponding to 1 kg weight loss/week Training: 60 %–80 % of max physical capacity 40–50 minutes, 3–4 times/week 3. Controls	1 year/0
Wood PD et al. 1991 [16]	RCT	Men and women: 25–49 years Overweight 120 %–160 %	1. Diet (moderate reduction of energy, fat and cholesterol) 2. Diet (as above) + physical activity (60 %–80 % of max) 25–45 minutes, 3 times/week	1 year/0

RCT = Randomized Controlled Trial; CT = Controlled Trial, not randomized
LBM = "Lean Body Mass" expresses muscle mass; TG = Triglycerides
* = Statistical significance

No. of patients/ No. followed up	Results Weight, Fat weight	Other results	Study quality Comments
66/60	1. −6.3 kg* 2. −2.6 kg 3. +0.9 kg	Energy intake as fat decreased 1. −32,0 %* 2. +1.0 % 3. +0.4 % Activity 1. +5.9 %* 2. +14.6 % 3. +6.5 %	Medium Diet self-controlled
1. 51/47 2. 49/47 3. 21/16	12 weeks 1. −6.6 kg* 2. −10.9 kg* 3. 0 kg 6 months 1 and 2: −approx. 8 kg* 3. 0 kg	TG decreased, HDL cholesterol increased. No effect from physical activity	Medium
1. 12 2. 15 3. 13	1 and 2: −7.9 kg* 3. −3.8 kg	1 and 2: HbA1 reduced and need for tablets reduced	Medium
1. 51/42 2. 52/47 3. 52/42	1. −7.2 kg* 2. −4.0 kg* 3. +0.6 kg Body fat 1. −5.9 kg* 2. −4.1 kg* 3. −0.3 kg	TG (mmol/l) 1. −0.27* 2. −0.16* 3. +0.1 HDL cholesterol (mmol/l) 1. +0.12* 2. +0.11* 3. −0.02	High Diet and physical activity yield the same reduction in weight and fat weight at same negative calorie balance
1. 87/71 2. 90/81 3. 87/79	Men 1. −5.1 kg* 2. −8.7 kg* 3. +1.7 kg Women 1. −4.1 kg* 2. −5.5 kg* 3. +1.3 kg	Blood pressure decreased (both Group 1 and 2) TG decreased in Group 2 (men). Cholesterol decreased (women) (both Group 1 and 2). HDL cholesterol increased in Group 2 (both men and women)	High

in triglycerides in men and an increase in HDL cholesterol in both men and women. Blood pressure decreased in both of the study groups.

As an addition to an energy-restrictive diet, two types of exercise programs of low to moderate intensity were compared in obese women (mean BMI 34) [6]. Several short (10–15 minutes) exercise sessions per day were compared with a longer exercise session per day. Probably because of better compliance, the short program resulted in greater physical activity over the entire 20-week period. A tendency toward better weight loss (8.9 kg) was noted in this group than in the group with the longer program (6.4 kg). It is uncertain whether or not the diet was the same in the two exercise programs, since energy intake was self-reported.

The value of increased physical activity as a way to prevent weight gain was studied in obese women (mean BMI 34) [3]. After a 12-week weight loss program, the participants were randomized to 40 weeks of dietary treatment, exercise programs involving walking 2–3 hours per week, or walking 4–6 hours per week. At followup 1 year later, the average reduction from the original weight was basically the same (0.6–0.7 kg) in the exercise groups, while weight had increased by 2 kg in the diet group.

A randomized pilot study investigated the effects of an exercise program of walking in obese elderly patients with osteoarthrosis-type knee problems (age and load changes) [7]. Participants in one of the exercise groups were treated with energy-restrictive diet aimed at reducing weight by 6.8 kg within 6 months. Only 3 of the 24 participants dropped out of the study. Weight loss was greater in the combination group (8.5 kg) than in the diet group (1.8 kg). In both of the study groups, knee problems decreased and knee function improved.

A meta-analysis compared the effects of physical exercise with the effects of low-energy diet and a combination of both methods [8]. For the period 1966 through 1994, 21 studies, which included at least 100 participants, were identified. In 493 subjects (as many men as women) the mean BMI was 33. Participants in the exercise program were younger and less overweight, and the intervention period was longer (on average 21 weeks) than in the other groups (about 15 weeks). Weight loss was greater (about 11 kg) if low-energy diets were included in the treatment program than if the program consisted of physical exercise alone (3 kg). The results after 1 year were reported for a smaller number of studies in the meta-analysis, and these studies reported no significant differences between physical exercise alone (8.7 kg), diet (9.0 kg), and diet in combination with physical exercise (11.8 kg).

4.4.5
Discussion

The results of these studies show that weight loss is achieved by physical exercise as the only type of therapy or as an adjunct to dietary treatment. Weight loss is primarily attributed to fat loss, while other body mass is preserved, in contrast to dietary treatment alone [11, 15, 16]. Weight loss per month, which has been estimated at approximately 0.1 kg to 0.3 kg, varies, e. g., with the design and intensity of the exercise program. Weight loss is also achieved in individuals with type 2 diabetes by dietary treatment and tablets [14]. However, the effects often diminish with time.

The type and level of increase in physical activity that obese people select is important, since obese people usually find it difficult to sustain intensive programs for a long period. An important finding is that brisk walking and self-selected activities result in weight loss [9, 15]. Both of the interventions are probably well suited for long-term intervention.

Randomized controlled trials are not available to show the effects of physical exercise on mortality and morbidity. This deficiency is attributed to the methodological and other problems involved in performing such studies. However, some information is available from studies in related medical fields. Physical exercise is shown to have positive effects in preventing myocardial infarction or type 2 diabetes (primary intervention) or in preventing new infarction (secondary prevention) [2, 4]. In other studies, reliable conclusions could not be drawn because of high dropout rates [13]. Many of these patients have been overweight and have lost weight during the intervention.

The review not only shows favorable effects on body weight and fat, but also positive effects on diabetes and blood lipids [14–16]. The positive effects on insulin resistance, lipids, and blood pressure are often more pronounced than the effects on body fat. Some studies show effects on several concurrent diseases, independently of the effects of physical exercise on circulation, referred to as "metabolic fitness" [12]. These effects are valuable regardless of weight loss.

Reports that did not focus primarily on obesity have shown that physical exercise generally increases well-being [4]. This important fact is particularly well demonstrated in studies by Blair et al., and has been summarized in a consensus statement [1]. These studies did not carry out an intervention, but nearly 22 000 people were followed up for 8 years. The participants were classified according to underweight, normal weight, and overweight/obesity, and were examined using cycle-ergometers to determine maximum physical work capacity. The studies concluded that physical exercise reduced many of the health risks associated with obesity. In fact, thin people who were physically inactive had greater risks than physically active obese people, which suggests that the risks associated with physical inactivity are greater than the risks associated with obesity. The analysis covered all types of mortality where it was possible to assess the risks for cardiovascular disease and diabetes. Some might object that physical exercise *per se* did not determine the outcome since this is not an intervention study. Furthermore, the willingness to exercise may involve protective selection factors beyond the exercise itself. Because of the problems mentioned above, it would be nearly impossible to implement a study without some objections. The results, however, suggest that physical exercise may have a preventive effect without influencing the degree of obesity. However, if obesity were also reduced, one would expect further risk reduction similar to that reported by the studies presented here.

Quality of life has not been discussed in the studies reviewed. Weight loss is generally limited, which can mean that any direct, weight-related improvement in the quality of life has been relatively minor.

Likewise, complications have not been reported in the studies reviewed here. Other studies have reported on mild (trauma) or severe (myocardial infarction) complications, but these are rather infrequent since different contraindications, common mainly in individuals with high-grade obesity, are usually observed.

References Section 4.4

1. Blair S, Kohl HW, Brill PA. Behavioural adaption to physical activity in Exercise, Fitness and Health (Bouchard C, Shephard RJ, Stephens T, Sutton JR, McPherson BD, eds). Champaign, Illinois, USA: Human Kinetic Books; 1990.

2. Eriksson KF, Lindgärde F. Prevention of type 2 (non-insulin-dependent) diabetes mellitus by diet and physical exercise. The 6-year Malmo feasibility study. Diabetologia 1991;34(12):891-8.

3. Fogelholm M, Kukkonen-Harjula K, Nenonen A, Pasanen M. Effects of walking training on weight maintenance after a very-low-energy diet in premenopausal obese women: a randomized controlled trial. Arch Intern Med 2000;160(14):2177-84.

4. Froelicher VF. Exercise, fitness and coronary heart disease. In Exercise, Fitness and Health. Champaign, Illinois, USA: Human Kinetic Books; 1990.

5. Hemmingsson E, Page A, Fox K, Rössner S. Influencing adherence to physical activity behaviour change in obese adults. Scandinavian Journal of Nutrition/Näringsforskning 2001;45(3):114-9.

6. Jakicic JM, Wing RR, Butler BA, Robertson RJ. Prescribing exercise in multiple short bouts versus one continuous bout: effects on adherence, cardiorespiratory fitness, and weight loss in overweight women. Int J Obes Relat Metab Disord 1995;19(12): 893-901.

7. Messier SP, Loeser RF, Mitchell MN, Valle G, Morgan TP, Rejeski WJ, et al. Exercise and weight loss in obese older adults with knee osteoarthritis: a preliminary study. J Am Geriatr Soc 2000;48(9):1062-72.

8. Miller WC, Koceja DM, Hamilton EJ. A meta-analysis of the past 25 years of weight loss research using diet, exercise or diet plus exercise intervention. Int J Obes Relat Metab Disord 1997;21(10):941-7.

9. Pritchard JE, Nowson CA, Wark JD. A worksite program for overweight middle-aged men achieves less weight loss with exercise than with dietary change. J Am Diet Assoc 1997;97(1):37-42.

10. Svendsen OL, Hassager C, Christiansen C. Effect of an energy-restrictive diet, with or without exercise, on lean tissue mass, resting metabolic rate, cardiovascular risk factors, and bone in overweight postmenopausal women. Am J Med 1993;95(2):131-40.

11. Svendsen OL, Hassager C, Christiansen C. Six months' follow-up on exercise added to a short-term diet in overweight postmenopausal women – effects on body composition, resting metabolic rate, cardiovascular risk factors and bone. Int J Obes Relat Metab Disord 1994;18(10):692-8.

12. Tremblay A, Doucet E, Imbeault P, Mauriege P, Despres JP, Richard D. Metabolic fitness in active reduced-obese individuals. Obes Res 1999;7(6):556-63.

13. Wilhelmsen L, Sanne H, Elmfeldt D, Grimby G, Tibblin G, Wedel H. A controlled trial of physical training after myocardial infarction. Effects on risk factors, nonfatal reinfarction, and death. Prev Med 1975;4(4):491-508.

14. Wing RR, Epstein LH, Paternostro-Bayles M, Kriska A, Nowalk MP, Gooding W. Exercise in a behavioural weight control programme for obese patients with type 2 (non-insulin-dependent) diabetes. Diabetologia 1988;31(12):902-9.

15. Wood PD, Stefanick ML, Dreon DM, Frey-Hewitt B, Garay SC, Williams PT, et al. Changes in plasma lipids and lipoproteins in overweight men during weight loss through dieting as compared with exercise. N Engl J Med 1988;319(18):1173-9.

16. Wood PD, Stefanick ML, Williams PT, Haskell WL. The effects on plasma lipoproteins of a prudent weight-reducing diet, with or without exercise, in overweight men and women. N Engl J Med 1991;325(7):461-6.

4.5
Pharmacotherapy

Summary

Drugs for treating obesity have been available for many years in a large number of countries. Pharmacotherapy in obesity is approached in at least three main ways, i.e., by influencing appetite-regulating mechanisms in the brain, by inhibiting the uptake of the fat, and by stimulating energy utilization. New pharmacological strategies for treating obesity are based on recent knowledge of the factors that direct appetite regulation and metabolism. The main focus of this chapter is on orlistat and sibutramine, two agents used to promote weight loss.

Results: This review includes 9 randomized, placebo-controlled studies of orlistat and sibutramine, drugs based on different modes of action. The 6 studies of orlistat included approximately 2500 patients on active therapy and present results based on medium quality after 1 year of treatment. Two of the four studies showing results after 2 years of treatment present low quality because of high dropout. On average, weight loss after 1 year was approximately 3 kg greater with orlistat treatment than that with placebo treatment. About 20 % of the patients in the studies achieved a weight loss of at least 10 % of their original weight, which was twice as many as in the placebo groups (Evidence Grade 2).

The 3 studies of sibutramine included approximately 1400 on active therapy and use a somewhat different design, which renders interpretation difficult. However, all present medium quality. In 2 studies, sibutramine yields weight loss which is about 4 kg greater after approximately 1 year than that in the placebo groups. In the largest study, "Sibutramine Trial of Obesity Reduction and Maintenance" (the STORM study), weight reduction after 2 years is more than 5 kg greater in those completing the study than in the control group. The share of patients who lost at least 10 % of their original weight was approximately twice as high in the sibutramine groups as that in the control groups, 25 % and 10 %, respectively (Evidence Grade 2). There are currently no studies of orlistat or sibutramine with a treatment time longer than 2 years.

The side effects associated with orlistat are related to the intended effect of the drug and to the diarrhea that occurs with continued intake of a high-fat diet during treatment. Because of the effects of the agent, sibutramine produces a lesser reduction in blood pressure than would correspond to the weight loss. Otherwise, sibutramine initially has the expected side effects, e. g., sleep problems, mouth dryness, and constipation.

Conclusion: The documented effects of orlistat and sibutramine show a weight loss of 2 kg to 5 kg greater than that in the control groups in treatment up to 2 years.

4.5.1
Introduction

Pharmacological treatment of obesity can be based on at least three main principles. Some drugs act via appetite-regulating mechanisms in the brain. Other agents can reduce the uptake of the fat, and thereby energy, from food. Yet other agents stimulate energy expenditure in the body. The basis for new pharmacological strategies in the treatment of obesity has been the result of new knowledge of factors which direct appetite regulation and metabolism in the body. This is evident from an extensive literature review [5].

Drugs for treating obesity have been available for many years in a large number of countries, but primarily in the United States.

4.5.2
Methodological Aspects of Drug Studies

Assessing the medical appropriateness of drugs used in treating obesity is difficult since authorities in several countries have limited the treatment time to 3 months. Therefore, agents must be evaluated as part of a more long-term program, making it difficult to isolate individual components.

Assessing pharmacological therapy for obesity also presents other methodological problems. In contrast to clinical trials in, e. g., hypertension and diabetes, patients who participate in obesity studies can easily see if treatment has the desired effect. Hence, clinical trials must be designed so that patients in placebo groups also experience sufficient weight loss so that they do not drop out of the study.

Therefore, particularly during long-term studies, the placebo group also receives, e. g., active contact with a dietician, supportive counseling, and group sessions. Weight loss in the control group can vary widely from one study to another depending on differences in treatment programs.

In attempting to identify patients who can be expected to respond favorably to treatment, many of the clinical trials with drugs begin with an open or single-blind introductory period, usually 4 weeks. The protocol usually sets out the treatment goals for participants in the main part of the study, primarily regarding compliance with prescribed medication, the percentage of drugs taken, and weight loss. This strategy aims to include patients who have managed to change their diet.

Experience from long-term studies of anti-obesity drugs shows that many patients discontinue the treatment. In estimating the scope of a study researchers often calculate that up to 50 % of the patients may drop out of treatment within 1 year. For this reason, recruitment of patients should take into consideration the expected high dropout rate, and adjust statistical calculations accordingly. Three main principles are used to calculate treatment outcome:

1. "Intention to treat" (ITT), where every patient who has received at least one dose of the drug is included in the final evaluation.

2. "Last observation carried forward" (LOCF), where the last value measured from the patient is used, regardless of when in the study the patient dropped out, and this value is used in the evaluation.
3. Completers, where treatment results are included only for patients who completed the entire study according to the criteria established beforehand.

Most studies present and compare the different methods, but generally there is not much difference in the results.

4.5.3
Orlistat and Sibutramine

Orlistat is a substance that blocks the effect of lipases, i.e., enzymes that break down the neutral fats (triglycerides) in the diet into fatty acids. This reduces the uptake of fatty acids, cholesterol, and fat-soluble vitamins (A, D, E, and K) in the gastrointestinal tract. Orlistat was developed primarily as a drug to reduce blood cholesterol levels. However, in animal studies the drug also demonstrated characteristics indicating that it could be used to treat obesity. In 1997 it was approved by the US Food and Drug Administration (FDA). Orlistat acts by transporting a greater amount of fat to the colon, thus increasing the volume of bowel content. Furthermore, the fats are partly broken down by the bacteria of the colon to gut motility-stimulating agents and gases. The most common side effects of orlistat mainly involve the gastrointestinal tract. During the first year of treatment, the most commonly observed side effects were oily discharge from the rectum (27% of the patients), gas accompanying bowel evacuation (24% of the patients), urgency in bowel evacuation (22% of the patients), increased bowel evacuation (11% of the patients), and fecal incontinence (8% of the patients) [2]. Since these side effects are the result of greater amounts of fat in the bowel, restricting the intake of fat in the diet reduces these problems. The prevalence of side effects decreased with continued use of orlistat, probably because the patients who continued the treatment ate less fatty food. Rare cases of hypersensitivity have been reported. The main clinical symptoms are pruritus, skin rash, urticaria, and other hypersensitivity reactions. Very rare cases of elevated aminotransferases and alkaline phosphatase and occasional cases of hepatitis, which may be severe, have been reported. Clinical trials have reported some reduction of fat-soluble vitamin levels in the blood, although usually within normal limits. No clinical cases of vitamin deficiency have been reported. Orlistat was approved for use within the European Union (EU) in 1999. The trade name of the drug is Xenical®.

Sibutramine was originally developed in England as a potential agent for treating depression. Researchers believed that an agent with this structure was a new serotonin-noradrenalin-reuptake inhibitor and, as such, could be used to treat moderate depression. The agent was tested for this indication, but was ineffective. However, weight loss was identified as one of the side effects. Experimental animal studies showed that sibutramine reduced food intake by earlier satiety, and that this effect was associated mainly with noradrenergic mechanisms. During the

1990s, sibutramine was evaluated in increasingly larger clinical trials, and was shown to be effective in treating obesity.

Since sibutramine has both noradrenergic and serotonergic effects, the cardio-vascular, gastrointestinal, and central nervous side effects of the drug can be explained completely or in part.

An average increase in resting systolic and diastolic blood pressure of 2 to 3 mm Hg and an average increase in heart rate of 3 to 7 beats per minute have been observed [1]. Sibutramine partly counteracts the antihypertensive effect of weight loss. Further increase in blood pressure and heart rate cannot be excluded in individual cases. Clinically significant increases in blood pressure and heart rate occur, and tend to happen during the first 4 to 12 weeks. In patients with at least a 10% weight reduction, blood pressure decreases as much after treatment with sibutramine (10 mg × 1) as after placebo. With a higher sibutramine dose (15 mg × 1), blood pressure drops less than in the placebo group. Most other side effects occur during the first 4 weeks of the treatment and decrease in intensity and frequency with time. Generally, they are transient and not serious. Very common (> 10%) side effects include loss of appetite, constipation, mouth dryness, and sleep problems. Common (1% – 10%) side effects include rapid heart rate, palpitations, elevated blood pressure, heat sensation with flushing, nausea, dizziness, numbness, headache, anxiety, sweating, and altered taste sensation. Occasional cases of side effects which have occurred during treatment with sibutramine, and considered to be of clinical importance, include different forms of acute inflammatory processes of the kidneys, seizures, lack of platelets and transient elevation in liver enzymes. In rare cases, symptoms such as headache and increased appetite have been observed when the drug is discontinued. Sibutramine was approved in 1998 in the United States under the name Reductil®.

4.5.4
Other Drugs

Cimetidine (used to treat depression) and caffeine/ephedrine are agents which have also been used in the treatment of obesity.

4.5.5
Method

In the initial literature search, 31 articles were found, whereof 14 remained after Phase 2, and 7 remained after Phase 3 (see Chapter 2 "Method"). All of these studies were RCTs, and most reported results after a followup of at least 1 year. Some studies were excluded because treatment of obesity was not the main focus. By extending the literature search, 9 articles could ultimately be included in the report (Table 4.6).

4.5.6
Results

4.5.6.1 **Orlistat**

Six long-term studies of Orlistat have been published [6–8, 10–12]. Sjöström monitored 435 patients in an RCT of orlistat (120 mg × 3) or placebo, plus a low-energy diet for all patients for 1 year. Thereafter they were re-randomized to orlistat/placebo for another year. Concurrently, dietary advice became more liberal [12]. After 1 year, significantly greater weight loss was observed in the orlistat group than in the placebo group (10.2 % vs 6.1 %). After re-randomization, the placebo patients showed a greater weight gain than those continuing with the drug. However, the patients who were initially treated with orlistat lost somewhat more when re-randomized to placebo. In patients who remained on orlistat, their weight only increased by half the weight increase of the control group during the second year. Those who were transferred from placebo to orlistat lost an additional 0.9 kg during this period. The side effects involving the gastrointestinal tract were as expected – troublesome diarrhea at a high intake of fat. Dropout at 2 years was 37 %.

Davidson conducted a 2-year randomized controlled study of orlistat and placebo [6]. The study was a multicenter study involving 892 patients. To determine "intention to treat", 224 placebo and 668 orlistat patients were evaluated. After 1 year, weight loss was significantly greater in the orlistat group (120 mg × 3), 8.8 kg, than in the placebo group, 5.8 kg. The patients were then re-randomized to orlistat (120 mg × 3 or 60 mg × 3) or placebo. One year later, the weight increase was lowest in the group treated with 120 mg × 3 compared to 60 mg × 3 or placebo. The cardiovascular risk profiles (elevated blood pressure, blood lipid disorders, and blood glucose) improved in relation to weight reduction.

In a 2-year study, Rössner compared 729 patients who received placebo, orlistat 60 mg × 3, or 120 mg × 3. He reported greater weight loss and greater maintained weight loss in the group treated with the higher dose of orlistat compared to the groups on a low dose of orlistat and placebo [11]. Using a standardized questionnaire, quality of life was found to improve mainly in the group experiencing the greatest weight reduction. Traditional risk factors such as blood lipids, blood pressure, and blood glucose were improved in relation to weight reduction.

Lindgärde studied the effect of 1 year of orlistat treatment on body weight and cardiovascular risk factors in 376 patients [10]. Mean weight had decreased somewhat more (5.9 %) in the orlistat group compared to the control group (4.6 %). Furthermore, total cholesterol, LDL cholesterol, fasting blood glucose level, and HbA_{1C} had improved. This concerned both non-diabetics and those with type 2 diabetes.

Hollander studied the effect of orlistat treatment in type 2 diabetics [8]. The study lasted for 57 weeks, was randomized, double-blind, and placebo-controlled. Orlistat (120 mg × 3) or placebo was given together with a low-energy diet to 391 patients with a BMI of 28–40. The patients had stable glucose control during ongoing treatment with oral antidiabetics. After 1 year of treatment, patients in the orlistat group had lost 6.2 % of their initial weight, compared to 4.3 % in the placebo

Table 4.6 Randomized placebo-controlled trials of pharmacotherapy in obsesity.

Author Year Reference	Study design	Inclusion criteria (Recruitment)	Intervention method Study groups	Treatment period
Sjöström L et al. 1998 [12]	RCT + DB. Re-randomiza-tion after 1 year	From waiting lists or advertisements. > 18 years BMI 28–47	"Single-blind" 4-week introduction. 1. Orlistat 120 mg × 3 2. Placebo × 3 Energy-reduced diet (−600 kcal/day). After 1 year re-randomization of patients with complying with medication	1 year/2 years
Davidson MH et al. 1999 [6]	RCT DB	BMI 30–43	4-week intro period with placebo and low-energy diet Year 1 1. Orlistat 120 mg × 3 2. Placebo 1 × 3 with continued low-energy diet Year 2 After re-randomization 1a. Orlistat 120 mg × 3 1b. Orlistat 60 mg × 3 1c. Placebo 1 × 3 2. Placebo	1 year/2 years
Rössner S et al. 2000 [11]	RCT DB Multicenter	Over 18 years BMI 28–43 Adults, no metabolic complications W=approx. 80%	1. Orlistat 120 mg × 3 + diet 2. Orlistat 60 mg × 3 3. Placebo × 3 (Energy-reduced diet −600 kcal/day in all groups)	1 year/2 years
Lindgärde F 2000 [10]	RCT DB	18–75 years BMI 28–38 Comobidity: hypertension, diabetes, and lipid disorders W=approx. 65%	1. Orlistat (120 mg × 3) 2. Placebo (1 × 3) Energy-reduced diet (−600 kcal/day) for 2 weeks and after 6 months	1 year

See legend on page 158

No. of patients/ No. followed up	Results Weight change	Results/Other Responders	Study quality Comments
Year 1 1. 345/284 2. 343/260 Year 2 Total 526/435	After 1 year 1. −10.2%* (10.3 kg) 2. −6.1% (6.1 kg) After 2 years Olistat reduces body weight compared to placebo, difference 3.6 kg. Orlistat reduces weight gain compared to placebo, difference 2.4 kg	Blood lipids, fasting glucose decreased significantly more in group 1. Responders (%): 1 year 　　　　　5%　10% 1. Orlistat　32　30* 2. Placebo　30　16 2 years 　　　　　5%　10% 1. Orlistat　57*　nr 2. Placebo　37　nr	Medium
Year 1 1. 668/458 2. 224/133 Year 2 1a. 153/109 1b. 152/102 1c. 138/95 2. 133/97	Year 1 1. −8.8 kg (−10%)* 2. −5.8 kg (−6%) Year 2 1a. 3.2 kg* 1b. 4.3 kig* (1c + 2) 5.6 kg	Orlistat treatment 120 mg × 3 showed lower LDL cholesterol Responders (%): 1 year 　　　　　5%　10% 1. Orlistat　66*　39* 2. Placebo　44　25 2 years 　　　　　5%　10% 1. Orlistat　nr　34* 2. Placebo　nr　18	Medium, Year 1. Low, Year 2 due to high drop-out
1. 244/181/159 2. 242/185/140 3. 243/158/136	1 year 1. −9.7%* 2. −8.6%* 3. −6.6%* 2 years 1. −7.6%* 2. −6.8% 3. −4.5%	In the orlistat groups improved quality of life and after 2 years reduction in cholesterol and LDL cholesterol. Responders (%): 1 year 　　　　　5%　10% 1. Orlistat　64*　38* 2. Orlistat 3. Placebo　44　19 2 years 　　　　　5%　10% 1. Orlistat　67*　28* 2. Orlistat 2. Placebo　39　19	Medium
1. 190/159 2. 186/164	1. −5.9% 2. −4.6%	Lowering of cholesterol, LDL cholesterol, and fasting glucose. Responders (%): 1 year 　　　　　5%　10% 1. Orlistat　54　19 2. Placebo　41　15 2 years 　　　　　5%　10% 1. Orlistat　nr　nr 2. Placebo　nr　nr	Medium

Table continues on next page

Table 4.6 continued

Author Year Reference	Study design	Inclusion criteria (Recruitment)	Intervention method Study groups	Treatment period
Hollander PA et al. 1998 [8]	RCT DB Placebo	BMI 28–40 Diabetic subjects ≥ 18 years. Similar distribution in women and men	1. Orlistat (120 mg × 3) 2. Placebo (1 × 3) Low-energy diet in both groups	57 weeks
Hauptman J et al. 2000 [7]	RCT DB Primary care	> 18 years BMI 30–44	4 weeks of placebo intro period and low-energy diet. <u>Year 1</u> 1. Orlistat 120 mg × 3 2. Orlistat 60 mg × 3 3. Placebo, low-energy diet <u>Year 2</u> 1. Orlistat 120 mg × 3 2. Orlistat 60 mg × 3 3. Placebo, no energy reduction for those with stable weight. Some increase in calories for patients who lost weight.	1 year/2 years
Apfelbaum M et al. 1999 [3]	Open VLCD 1 month. Then RCT DB	BMI > 30 18–55 years No hypertension or diabetes	1. Sibutramine 10 mg 2. Placebo	1 year
James WP et al. STORM 2000 [9]	Weight loss 6 months RCT DB Multicenter	BMI 30–45 17–65 years No hypertension or diabetes	1. Sibutramine 10–20 mg 2. Placebo	18 month

See legend on page 158

No. of patients/ No. followed up	Results Weight change	Results/Other Responders	Study quality Comments

1. 162/139
2. 159/115
	1 year
	1. −6.2%*
	2. −4.3%
		Improved glycemic control in Group 1. Decreased antidiabetic medication in Group 1.
		Responders (%):
		1 year
		
		               5% 10%
		1. Orlistat 49* 18*
		2. Placebo 23 9
		
		2 years
		               5% 10%
		1. Orlistat Not studied
		2. Placebo Not studied
			Medium

1. 210/151/113
2. 213/154/119
3. 212/122/91
	Year 1
	1. −7.9 kg*
	2. −7.1 kg*
	3. −4.1 kg
	Year 2
	1. −5.0 kg*
	2. −4.5 kg*
	3. −1.7 kg
	Concerns ITT, equivalent results for those completing the study
		Cholesterol level decreased.
		Responders (%):
		1 year
		               5% 10%
		1. Orlistat 51* 29*
		2. Orlistat 49* 24*
		3. Placebo 31 11
		
		2 years
		               5% 10%
		1. Orlistat 34* 19*
		2. Orlistat 34* 15*
		Placebo 24 7
			Medium, Year 1.
			Low, Year 2
			due to high dropout

1. 81/54 2. 78/45	1. −5.2 kg* 2. +0.5 kg	Proportion maintained weight loss: 1. 75% 2. 42% TG decreased and HDL cholesterol increased. Responders (%): 1 year 5% 10% Sibutramine 86* 54* Placebo 55* 23*	Medium
1. 352/204 2. 115/57	1. −10.2 kg* 2. −4.7 kg (0–24 mo)	> 80% maintained weight loss 6–24 months. 1. 43% 2. 16% TG decreased HDL cholesterol increased BP increased: Group 1: 28 Group 2: 24 DBP Group 1: +2 mmHg Responders (%): 18 months 5% 10% 1. Sibutramine 51* 29* 2. Placebo 49 19	Medium

Table continues on next page

Table 4.6 continued

Author Year Reference	Study design	Inclusion criteria (Recruitment)	Intervention method Study groups	Treatment period
Wirth A et al. 2001 [13]	RCT DB Multicenter	BMI 30–40 18–65 years who during 4 weeks with Sibutramine 15 mg × 1 lost ≥ 2% in weight or at least 2 kg	1. Sibutramine 15 mg ×1 2. Sibutramine 15 mg × 3 intermittently during three 12-week periods 3. Placebo	44 weeks

RCT = Randomized Controlled Trial; CT = Controlled Trial, not randomized
DB = Double Blind; W = Women; VLCD = Very Low Calorie Diet
ITT = Intention to Treat; TG = Triglycerides; BP = Blood Pressure; DBP = Diastolisc Blood Pressure
* = Statistical significance
nr = not reported

group. Combined orlistat and dietary treatment yielded significant improvement in glucose control when compared to placebo and diet. This could be measured by a significant reduction in the HbA_{1C} level, fasting blood glucose level, and the reduced dosage of diabetes medication. Improvement in blood lipids was also noted.

Hauptman reported on a 2-year orlistat study that included 796 patients from 17 primary care units [7]. After a single-blind placebo period of 4 weeks on a low-energy diet, the patients were randomized to treatment with orlistat (120 mg × 3 and 60 mg × 3, respectively) or placebo in combination with a low-energy diet during the first year. After this period, weight loss (ITT) was greater (7.9 kg and 7.1 kg, respectively) in the orlistat groups than in the placebo group. The differences between the study groups was somewhat smaller after 2 years when the dropout was very high (on average 50%), but greatest in the placebo group. In approximately one fourth of the patients treated with the higher orlistat dosage, dropout was attributed to problems in the gastrointestinal tract. A significant reduction in blood cholesterol and some reduction in blood pressure was noted in the orlistat group. After 1 year, the share of patients who had lost at least 10% of their original weight averaged 22% (16%–27%) in the six orlistat studies and 11% in the placebo groups.

4.5.6.2 Sibutramine

Three long-term studies have been published on sibutramine [3, 9, 13]. Apfelbaum treated a group of patients with VLCD (Very Low Calorie Diet), 220–800 kcal per day) for approximately 4 weeks [3]. Patients who had lost at least 6 kg were then randomized to either sibutramine (10 mg per day) or placebo for another 12 months. Approximately two thirds of the 159 patients who started the second phase completed the study. An intention-to-treat analysis noted an average weight

No. of patients/ No. followed up	Results Weight change	Results/Other Responders	Study quality Comments
1. 405/312 2. 395/303 3. 209/137	1. −3.8 kg* 2. −3.3 kg* 3. 0.2 kg	TG decrease in Group 1 and 2. No differences in blood pressure between Group 1, 2 and 3 Responders (%): 48 weeks |		5%	10%
---	---	---
1. Sibutramine	65*	32*
2. Sibutramine	63*	33*
3. Placebo	35	13		Medium

loss, beyond the VLCD effect, of 5.2 kg in the sibutramine group and a weight gain of 0.5 kg in the placebo group. In the two study groups, 75 % and 42 % of patients, respectively, maintained their weight loss after the VLCD period. HDL cholesterol increased in the sibutramine group.

James et al. studied the effect of sibutramine in a double-blind placebo-controlled study (the so-called STORM study), which was preceded by 6 months of introductory open treatment with sibutramine (10 mg per day) [9]. In this multicenter study (initially 605 patients), an individually energy-adjusted diet was prescribed, considering basic metabolism. Patients who had lost at least 5 kg during the first 6 months and had not gained more than 2 kg during the past 3 months (467 patients) were randomized (3:1 ratio) to continued treatment with sibutramine or placebo during the following 18 months. Individualized advice on diet and exercise was also given.

The study protocol offered the possibility for a double-blind increase in the dose of sibutramine to 15 mg or 20 mg if the expected therapeutic effect failed to appear. Of 204 patients treated with sibutramine who completed the study, 58 % maintained more than 80 % of the weight loss achieved during the initial period, i.e., an average weight loss of approximately 10 kg since the start of the study. Of those in the placebo group who completed the study (57 patients), 16 % maintained the weight loss, and their weight loss since the start of the study was around 5 kg. A similar percentage of men and women responded to the treatment. Dropout in the study groups (42 % and 50 %, respectively) was mainly attributed to side effects. Average blood pressure was unchanged, but sibutramine treatment in 5 % of the patients was interrupted when blood pressure exceeded predetermined limits. In the sibutramine group, reductions in the risk factors of triglycerides, LDL cholesterol, insulin, C-peptide, and uric acid were noted. HDL cholesterol increased by 21 %, which was more than in the placebo group (12 %).

Wirth conducted a multicenter study involving 1102 patients having a BMI of 30–40. The study was randomized, double-blind, and placebo-controlled [13]. After an open 4-week introductory period with 15 mg per day, all but one patient had lost at least 2 kg. The patients were then randomized to 44 weeks of treatment. The study compared sibutramine treatment in two ways, either continuously (15 mg × 1) or intermittently (15 mg × 3) during weeks 1–12, 19–30, and 37–48, with placebo during the weeks when sibutramine was not used. In addition, one group was treated continuously with placebo. The mean weight loss in the intention-to-treat group was 3.8 kg among those receiving sibutramine continuously and 3.3 kg in the group that received intermittent therapy, while the placebo group gained 0.2 kg. The two groups that received sibutramine were similar as regards weight. Usual risk parameters, such as waist circumference and blood lipid levels, improved during sibutramine treatment, and the effects on blood pressure were equal in the three groups.

In these three sibutramine studies, on average 40% of the participants had lost at least 10% of their original weight after 1 to 1.5 years. This figure was more than double that in the placebo group.

4.5.6.3 Caffeine/Ephedrine

Astrup studied 180 patients who were treated for 24 weeks with caffeine and ephedrine in combination, or separately, or with placebo [4]. Comparability among the groups in the study was good. From a total of 180 patients, 141 were followed up. The study showed that the caffeine and ephedrine group achieved the greatest weight loss. The differences between the other three study groups were not significant. Side effects were more frequent in the combination group.

References Section 4.5

1. Produktresumé för Reductil®. www.emea.org.
2. Produktresumé för Xenical®. www.emea.org.
3. Apfelbaum M, Vague P, Ziegler O, Hanotin C, Thomas F, Leutenegger E. Long-term maintenance of weight loss after a very-low-calorie diet: a randomized blinded trial of the efficacy and tolerability of sibutramine. Am J Med 1999;106(2):179-84.
4. Astrup A, Breum L, Toubro S, Hein P, Quaade F. The effect and safety of an ephedrine/caffeine compound compared to ephedrine, caffeine and placebo in obese subjects on an energy-restricted diet. A double blind trial. Int J Obes Relat Metab Disord 1992;16(4):269-77.
5. Bray GA, Greenway FL. Current and potential drugs for treatment of obesity. Endocr Rev 1999;20(6):805-75.
6. Davidson MH, Hauptman J, DiGirolamo M, Foreyt JP, Halsted CH, Heber D, et al. Weight control and risk factor reduction in obese subjects treated for 2 years with orlistat: a randomized controlled trial. JAMA 1999;281(3):235-42.
7. Hauptman J, Lucas C, Boldrin MN, Collins H, Segal KR. Orlistat in the long-term treatment of obesity in primary care settings. Arch Fam Med 2000;9(2):160-7.
8. Hollander PA, Elbein SC, Hirsch IB, Kelley D, McGill J, Taylor T, et al. Role of orlistat in the treatment of obese patients with type 2 diabetes. A 1-year randomized double-blind study. Diabetes Care 1998; 21(8):1288-94.
9. James WP, Astrup A, Finer N, Hilsted J, Kopelman P, Rössner S, et al. Effect of sibutramine on weight maintenance after weight loss: a randomised trial. STORM Study Group. Sibutramine Trial of Obesity Reduction and Maintenance. Lancet 2000; 356(9248): 2119-25.
10. Lindgärde F. The effect of orlistat on body weight and coronary heart disease risk profile in obese patients: the Swedish Multimorbidity Study. J Intern Med 2000;248(3):245-54.
11. Rössner S, Sjöstrom L, Noack R, Meinders AE, Noseda G. Weight loss, weight maintenance, and improved cardiovascular risk factors after 2 years treatment with orlistat for obesity. European Orlistat Obesity Study Group. Obes Res 2000;8(1):49-61.
12. Sjöstrom L, Rissanen A, Andersen T, Boldrin M, Golay A, Koppeschaar HP, et al. Randomised placebo-controlled trial of orlistat for weight loss and prevention of weight regain in obese patients. European Multicentre Orlistat Study Group. Lancet 1998;352(9123):167-72.
13. Wirth A, Krause J. Long-term weight loss with sibutramine: a randomized controlled trial. JAMA 2001;286 (11):1331-9.

4.6

Surgery

Summary

Surgical treatment of obesity may be appropriate for severely overweight patients, generally when other treatment measures have not yielded results. Commonly accepted cutoff points for surgical treatment of obesity are BMI > 40, or BMI > 35 in cases of severe comorbid conditions [9].

Results: Seventeen randomized studies, numerous long-term followups (at least 5 years) and 15 nonrandomized comparative studies form the basis for the conclusions presented in this section. Furthermore, the Swedish Obese Subjects (SOS) study has reported extensively on the effects of weight loss on morbidity, risk factors, and quality of life. The SOS study compares 2000 surgically treated patients to an equally large matched control group that was monitored in primary care. However, the SOS investigation is not a randomized study.

In severely obese patients, surgical treatment yields greater weight reduction than the nonsurgical methods currently available (Evidence Grade 1). After 1 to 2 years, weight loss amounts to approximately 50 % to 75 % of the overweight prior to surgery, which is equal to 30 kg to 40 kg of weight reduction for a person weighing 125 kg and with a height of 170 cm. The long-term effects (5–10 years) of surgical treatment are well documented.

Weight loss after surgery leads to a significant reduction in new cases of diabetes and almost entirely normalizes the glucose level in persons with type-2 diabetes (Evidence Grade 1). Weight loss also has a major positive effect on health-related quality of life (Evidence Grade 2). It is currently unknown whether intentional weight reduction in obesity, regardless of the treatment method, leads to lower total mortality or to fewer cases of myocardial infarction and stroke. Surgical treatment of obesity, however, does not increase total mortality compared to nonsurgical treatment.

Several different types of surgical procedures are available to treat obesity. Gastric bypass (GBP) achieves the best results in relation to side effects, and it is also the best-documented method (Evidence Grade 1). The effects of vertical banded gastroplasty (VBG) are also well documented. VBG is easier to perform than gastric bypass and it lacks some of the disadvantages of the latter procedure. However, VBG results in less weight reduction than gastric bypass (10–15 kg less) (Evidence Grade 1), and long-term studies have shown that patients with weight gain may be candidates for reoperation. Many studies have shown that gastric banding (adjustable and nonadjustable) has yielded relatively poor long-term weight loss and have also reported high reoperation rates (approximately 20 % during the first 5 years). Nonrandomized studies and two controlled, randomized trials of gastric bypass, VBG, and gastric banding by laparoscopic surgery suggest there are possibilities to reduce postsurgical discomfort and complications. However, more well-controlled studies need to be performed to adequately evaluate the advantages and disadvantages of laparoscopic surgery.

Conclusions: Surgical treatment of obesity has a substantial and well-documented long-term effect on weight and risk factors in individuals with an initial BMI ≥ 40. Gastric bypass yields the best results and is the best documented of the surgical methods available.

4.6.1
Introduction

Surgical treatment of obesity may be appropriate for patients with very severe overweight, generally when other treatment measures have not been effective. Commonly accepted cutoff points for surgical treatment of obesity are BMI > 40, or BMI > 35 in cases of obesity-related comorbidities [9]. These cutoff points are not based on systematic studies, but have been adopted with experience, e. g., in association with a consensus conference at NIH (National Institutes of Health, USA) in 1991. When surgery for obesity was introduced 50 years ago, the average weight loss was approximately 45 kg for persons weighing 125 to 145 kg. The indication for surgery was therefore arbitrarily set at approximately 45 kg above "normal weight". In someone of average height, this corresponds to a BMI of approximately 40.

Experiences from the SOS study indicate that other inclusion weights can be accepted. The SOS study used a BMI of 34 as a lower limit in men and a BMI of 38 in women. In analyzing outcomes (weight loss, change in secondary disease, quality of life, psychosocial function, complications), no significant differences are reported between the groups of patients above or below a BMI of 40 [86].

Age 60 years is usually accepted as the upper age limit for surgical treatment of obesity. The lower age limit is usually reported as 18 to 20 years of age. However, there are reports of surgery in patients outside of these upper and lower limits. The importance of the age limits has yet to be addressed in systematic studies [1, 19, 38, 65, 76, 105, 120]. Usually, other requirements are also placed on candidates for surgery, e. g., serious attempts at weight loss using conservative treatment methods. Nearly all patients who are considered for surgical treatment of obesity have already made many unsuccessful attempts to lose weight [117]. Mental disorders, alcohol or drug abuse, eating disorders, and ulcers are other factors which may suggest that surgical treatment should not be used. However, scientific studies have yet to present evidence for these inclusion and exclusion criteria.

The first surgical procedures for obesity date back to the 1950s. It was observed that patients lost weight following surgery, e. g., for ulcers or other disorders, when the small intestine was shortened. As the technique has been modified and refined, surgery has become a prominent method for treating severe obesity. Several different surgical methods are available. Many of these methods have undergone incremental modification since they were introduced, but all can be performed by open surgery or laparoscopic methods.

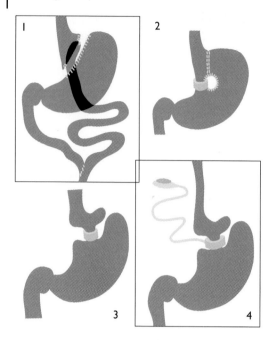

Figure 4.1 Diagram of:
1. Gastric bypass
2. Vertical banded gastroplasty
3. Gastric banding with nonadjustable band
4. Gastric banding with adjustable band.

The describes following surgical methods are described in greater detail in Section 4.6.6.2. Figure 4.1 illustrates the first three listed below, showing the most common surgical methods.

Gastric banding (GB)
Gastric bypass (GBP)
Vertical banded gastroplasty (VBG)
Horizontal gastroplasties (HGPL)
Intestinal bypass
Bileopancreatic bypass (BPB)
Duodenal switch (DS).

Two other invasive methods should also be mentioned, namely liposuction and intragastric balloon treatment. However, neither of these methods has a place in the treatment of obesity. The indication for liposuction is mainly cosmetic, and intragastric balloon treatment has no effect.

4.6.2
Literature Search

A systematic literature search identified 113 articles judged as relevant for this evidence evaluation. Thirty studies were known by the reviewers or identified during review of other reference lists, and eight studies addressed so-called intragastric balloon treatment. The reference list to this Section also includes 24 descriptive and technical studies that describe surgery as an approach for treating obesity.

Only randomized controlled trials (RCT) having a followup time of at least 1 year were considered. An average followup time of at least 5 years was required for studies that simply described effects over time, i.e., comparing to the preoperative situation without a control group. The rationale is that weight reduction after surgery often takes place during a longer period (1–2 years), and that it is important to allow time for both negative and positive effects on therapy or obesity-related morbidity to appear.

This Section also reports on several published reports from the SOS study (Swedish Obese Subjects). The study is an extensive intervention study with a surgical treatment group and a matched control group that received conventional treatment. The value of the scientific evidence presented in the SOS study is considered to be high because of the controlled conditions and the lengthy followup time (over 10 years) of the study.

4.6.3
Findings on Weight Reduction and Complications

4.6.3.1 Gastric Bypass (GBP)
Randomized controlled trials: Seven studies on GBP have been identified (Table 4.7, Figure 4.2). All studies show a statistically significantly better weight loss for GBP compared to other techniques studied. Greater weight loss was not associated with greater complications. In all studies, the number of reoperations was also lower for GBP than for other methods.

Four studies compared different forms of GBP (Table 4.8). Brolin compared the results of GBP with shorter and longer retained segments of small intestine (length of Roux-loop 75 and 150 cm, respectively) in surgery of 45 persons with very severe obesity (> 91 kg overweight) [20]. Weight loss was significantly greater in the group of patients that retained a longer segment of small intestine where the food passes without mixture of bile and pancreatic juice. In an RCT, Fobi et al. also compared two different variants of GBP [35].

Westling and Gustavsson reported results from a study of laparoscopic and open GBP, respectively [134]. Many (23 %) of those who were candidates for laparoscopic surgery were transferred to open surgery. A high frequency of obstruction of the small intestine (ileus) unexpectedly occurred in the group that received laparoscopic surgery during the observation period. The patients in the study were the surgeons' and the institution's initial experience of laparoscopic obesity surgery, and the study was interrupted prematurely. Hence, the evidence is of limited value.

Parts of another, ongoing, study of laparoscopic versus open GBP have been published and address, e. g., coagulation conditions, peroperative abdominal pressure, fluid requirements, and body temperature [88, 91, 92, 94]. Weight reduction after 1 year is similar in the groups. The group receiving laparoscopic surgery had somewhat shorter episodes of care and recovery time and a lower rate of wound-related complications [89].

Long-term followup of gastric bypass: Several nonrandomized studies report at least 5 years of followup (Table 4.10). Weight loss after 5 years corresponded to 50 % to

Table 4.7 Randomized controlled trials (RCT) of gastric bypass (treatment group) versus other stomach operations.

Author Year Reference	Control group	Number Treatm. Grp./ Contr. Grp.	Women %	Followup, months
Lechner GW et al. 1981 [58] 1983 [59]	HGPL	50/50	93/93	24 (−36)
Pories WJ et al. 1982 [101]	HGPL	42/45	81/78	18
Näslund I et al. 1986 [87] 1987 [85]	HGPL	29/28	90/89	36
Sugerman HJ et al. 1987 [122]	VBG	20/20	90/90	36
Hall JC et al. 1990 [40]	VBG, HGPL	99/106/105	95/92/91	36
MacLean LD et al. 1993 [69] 2000 [68]	VBG	52/54	nr	Approx. 36 (60)
Howard L et al. 1995 [47]	VBG	20/22	75/82	60

Contr. Grp. = Control group
Treatm. Grp. = Treatment group
HGPL = Horizontal gastroplasty
VBG = Vertical banded gastroplasty
nr = Not reported
%EWL = % of preoperative excessive weight lost
%BW = % of preoperative body weight lost
kg = Weight loss in kg
RCT = Randomized controlled trial
 * = $p < 0.05$
 ** = $p < 0.01$
*** = $p < 0.001$

75 % of the preoperative overweight. Long-term complications have been few, apart from anemia and incisional hernia.

Overall assessment of gastric bypass evidence: Several randomized controlled trials and other long-term followups show that GBP yields greater weight loss than other forms of gastroplasty. GBP did not result in higher rates of reoperation or early or late complications. Hence, GBP should be considered the standard against which other methods can be compared.

Weight loss Treatm. Grp vs Contr. Grp	Early complications	Late reop (revision) % Treatm. Grp. vs Contr. Grp.	Study quality Comments
%EWL: 77 vs 55*** %BW: 38 vs 26*** kg: 46 vs 29***	Equivalent	5% vs 14%	Medium
%BW: 40 vs 19*** kg: 51,5 vs 30***	Equivalent	0 vs 40%	Medium to high
%EWL: 64 vs 42*** %BW: 32 vs 21*** kg: 38 vs 25***	Somewhat more in treatm grp.	0 vs 36%	Medium to high
%EWL: 62 vs 36** %BW: 32 vs 20** kg: 41 vs 27**	Equivalent	0 vs 20%	Medium to high
% av pat with %EWL >50%: 66 vs 44 vs 16***	Equivalent	6% vs 14% vs 20%	High
% av pat with %EWL 50%: 58 vs 39	Equivalent	23% vs 43%	High
%EWL: 71 vs 36* % av pat with %EWL >50%: 100% vs 0%	Equivalent	12% vs 0%	Low

4.6.3.2 Horizontal Gastroplasty (HGPL)

Randomized controlled trials: The four randomized controlled trials where GBP formed the comparison group to HGPL are presented in Table 4.7 and Figure 4.2 [40, 59, 85, 101]. All studies show significantly better results for GBP than for HGPL.

A comparative study of HGPL, VBG, and GBP found that the success rates (defined as more than 50% reduction of initial overweight) after 3 years were 17% in HGPL (gastroanastomosis), 48% in VBG, and 67% in GBP [40]. In a comparison with VBG, it was shown that HGPL was less effective (Table 4.9) [5].

Table 4.8 Randomized controlled trials (RCT) of different types of gastric bypass.

Author Year Reference	Treatment group	Control group	Number Treatm. grp/ Contr. grp	Women %	Followup, months
Brolin RE et al. 1992 [20]	Roux-loop 75 cm	Roux-loop 150 cm	22/23	82/65	36 (12–78)
Fobi MA et al. 2001 [35]	Stapled in situ stomach	Divided stomach	25/25	96/88	72
Westling A et al. 2001 [134]	Laparoscopic surgery	Open surgery	30/21	94	≥ 12
Nguyen NT et al. 2001 [89]	Laparoscopic surgery	Open surgery	79/76	nr	1–23

Contr. Grp. = Control group Treatm. Grp. = Treatment group nr = Not reported %EWL = % of preoperative excessive weight lost %BW = % of preoperative body weight lost kg = Weight loss in kg dBMI = Reduction (number of BMI units) of BMI from preoperative value ns = Not significant RCT = Randomized controlled trial * = p<0.05

Although, in comparison with other surgical methods, HGPL appeared to be a poorer method, one RCT found it to be superior to conventional medical treatment (diet) [6]. Maximum weight reduction did not differ between the groups (26 and 22 kg, respectively) but the diet group could not maintain the weight loss. After 2 years, the retained weight loss was 8.2 kg in the diet group, but 30.6 kg in the HGPL group. In a 5-year followup that was difficult to interpret, HGPL was still considered superior (Table 4.9) [7].

Long-term followups of HGPL: Of no current interest.

Overall assessment of HGPL evidence: The method is no longer used, but has been of importance for the technical advancement of surgery for obesity.

4.6.3.3 Vertical Banded Gastroplasty (VBG)

Randomized controlled trials: Four studies have shown VBG to yield less weight loss than GBP (Table 4.7, Figure 4.2) [40, 47, 68, 122]. Three of the studies also reported that more reoperations were required after VBG than after GBP. One exception was the study by Howard where the GBP patients also received a Marlex Mesh® reinforcement around the stoma [47]. In the latter study, 25 % of the patients

Weight loss	Complications	Late reop (revision) % Treatm. Grp vs Contr. Grp	Comments	Study quality
kg: 52 vs 75* dBMI: 18 vs 25	No difference	4% vs 0	Only super-obese with >91 kg overweight included	Medium
%BW: 34 vs 33 ns kg: 48 vs 48 ns %EWL: 69 vs 68 ns	Gastrogastric fistula: 8 (32%) vs 1 (4%)*	9 (36%) vs 4 (16%)	Hypothesis about the advantage of transection confirmed	Medium
dBMI: 14 vs 13 ns	Bowel obstr: 6 vs 0 7 laparoscopic surgeries converted to open surgery	nr	Early in learning curve. Study interrupted prematurely	Low
12 months: %EWL: 68 vs 62 ns	2 laparoscopic surgeries converted Serious complications 8% vs 9%, minor complications 19% vs 16%	none	Quality of life measurements better at 1 and 3 months in Treatm. Grp. at 6 months no differences. Several other part studies published [88, 91–94]	Medium

who received GBP experienced bleeding in the stomach, and reoperation was required in half of these cases. The authors concluded, in accordance with the usual practice in GBP, that reinforcement of the GBP anastomosis with foreign material should be avoided. Compared to HGPL, vertical banded gastroplasty yields greater weight loss and fewer reoperations (Table 4.7) [40].

A randomized clinical trial by Lundell et al. compared VBG to open nonadjustable gastric banding (GB) (Table 4.9) [63, 64]. The study was actually designed to study weight-loss mechanisms and the effects of both techniques on gastroesophageal reflux. The study randomized 24 patients to VBG and 26 patients to GB. After 12 months, no difference was found between the groups in terms of weight loss (from BMI 42.5 to BMI 34.5), nor was any difference found between the methods concerning reflux symptoms or measured acid reflux.

Long-term followup of VBG: Several studies report a followup time of more than 5 years. These studies are in agreement, as presented in Table 4.11. VBG yielded a weight loss of between 50% and 75% of the preoperative overweight. After this maximum weight loss during the first and second year after the operation, there was a tendency for later slow weight gain, resulting in a long-term weight loss equivalent to 40% to 65% of the preoperative overweight. Approximately one in

Table 4.9 All other randomized controlled trials apart from those already presented in tables 4.7 and 4.8

Author Year Reference	Treatment group	Control group	Number Treatm. Grp./ Contr. Grp.	Women %	Folllowup, months
Danish obes proj 1979 [8]	Intestinal bypass	Conventional (nonsurgical)	130/66	Equivalent between the groups	>24
Andersen T et al. 1984 [6] 1988 [7]	HGPL	VLCD (not surgical)	27/30	89/87	2 years 5 years
Griffen WO et al. 1977 [39]	GBP	Intestinal bypass	32/27	72/48	12
Andersen T et al. 1987 [5]	HGPL	VBG	22/23	81	12
Lundell L et al. 1987 [63] 1997 [64]	VBG	GB	24/26	54	12
de Wit LT et al. 1999 [135]	Lap GB	Open GB	25/25	Equivalent between the groups	12

Contr. Grp. = Control group; Treatm. Grp. = Treatment group
HGPL = Horizontal gastroplasty; VBG = Vertical banded gastroplasty
GB = Gastric banding; GBP = Gastric bypass; VLCD = Very Low Calorie Diet, low-energy diet
RCT = Randomized controlled trial
nr = Not reported
%EWL = % of preoperative exessive weight lost
%BW = % of preoperative body weight lost
kg = Weight loss in kg
dBMI = Reduction (number of BMI units) of BMI from preoperative value
ns = Not significant
* = $p<0.05$; ** = $p<0.01$; *** = $p<0.001$

Weight loss	Complications	Late reop (revision) % Treatm. Grp. vs Contr. Grp.	Study quality Comments
24 months kg: 42.9 vs 5.9***	More and more serious in Treatm. Grp. Better quality of life measure in Treatm. Grp.	nr	High
2 years kg: 31 vs 7* 5 years 16% vs 3%* defined as successful cases	Treatm. Grp.: 2 intra-abdominal abscesses, otherwise no difference between the groups	none	Medium Surgical method obsolete
kg: 51 vs 58	Early compl. somewhat higher in Treatm. Grp. Late compl. more and more severe, particularly liver compl. in Contr. Grp.	3 vs 3	High quality despite small groups and short observation time due to significant findings
kg: 33 vs 49* %EWL: 56 vs 80**	Equivalent between the groups	none	Preoperative weight loss with VLCD
dBMI: 8 in both groups	nr	nr	Main puprose of the study to study gastro-esophageal reflux
kg: 35 vs 34 dBMI: 11.6 vs 10.6	More incisional hernias in open surgery group	none	Low

Table 4.6.4 Long-term followup of gastric bypass (GBP) (mean followup >5 years).

Author Year Reference	Number, (% women)	Followup, years	Followed up %	Weight loss
Pories WJ et al. 1987 [100]	5 years: 57 (nr) 6 years: 26 (nr)	5 and 6 years respectively	98	5 years: %BW=69% 6 years: %BW=71%
Yale CE 1989 [137]	251 (83%)	>5 years	90	%EWL=60% kg=41
Fobi MA 1993 [33]	100 (94%)	10 years	46	%EWL=55% in not re-operated
Reinhold RB 1994 [106]	153 (nr)	>5 years (r=5–16 years)	56	%EWL=51%
van de Weijgert EJ et al. 1999 [130]	100 (84%)	m=9.9 years	75	7 years: %EWL=67%
Cook CM 1999 [24]	100 (95%)	m=7 years	100	kg=42.2
MacLean LD et al. 2000 [68]	274 (nr)	m=5.5 years	89	dBMI=16.7
Mitchell JE et al. 2001 [80]	100 (83%)	r=13–15 years	78	kg=30.1 dBMI=11

Followup time has been reported as the mean value for the entire group (m), or range (r) or if all followed up the same length of time; unit = years.

Contr. Grp. = Control group   r = Range (interval)
Treatm. Grp. = Treatment group   %EWL = % of preoperative excessive weight lost
GBP = Gastric bypass   %BW = % of preoperative body weight lost
nr = Not reported   kg = Weight loss in kg
m = Mean value   dBMI = Reduction (number of BMI units) of BMI from preop. value

Late complications	Late reop. (revision) %	Effect on comorbidity	Study quality Comments
Described in detail	0 (not clearly stated)	99 % euglycemic postop	Hig Study mainly of diabetics
21 % hernia 8 % staple line rupture 2 % ileus 4 % stomal ulcer	3 %	nr	High Also reports results after gastroplasties
6 % anemia	26 %	nr	Low Low % of patients followed up
4 % hernia kg=37	19 %	Hypertension decreased from 17 % to 13 %, diabetes from 12 % to 6 %, heart disease 7 % to 5 %	Long followup
33 % iron deficiency (10 years) 48 % B12 deficiency (10 years) 8 % folate deficiency (10 years)	43 %	Very significant improvements, reported in detail	Medium GBP method now obsolete Preoperative weight reduction program
nr	nr	nr	Low Study population randomly selected from 8000 operated in Utah to study living habits after GBP
24 % needed gall bladder surgery during observation time 6 hernia	0	nr	High
Described in detail	0	Described in detail including psychopathology and eating behavior	Low to Medium Retrospective. Detailed description

Table 4.11   Long-term followup of Vertical Banded Gastroplasty (VBG) (mean followup >5 years).

Author Year Reference	Number, (% women)	Followup, years	Followed up %	Weight loss
MacLean LD et al. 1990 [66]	57 (nr)	5 years	98%	%EWL/60%
Field RJ et al. 1992 [32]	36 (94%)	m/6.4 years	69%	dBMI/6.5
Mason EE et al. 1992 [75]	313 (78%)	≥5 years	nr (>40%)	%EWL=49%
Fobi MA 1993 [33]	100 (nr)	>10 years	43%	%EWL=42%[1]
Sweet W et al. 1994 [127]	118 (85%)	r: 10–12 years and 5–10 years, respectively	47% and 60% respectively	%EWL=46% and 54%, respectively
Ramsey-Stewart G 1995 [104]	60 (nr)	m/5.7 y (r/2–7 y) m/9.6 y (r/4–11 y)	97% and 75%, respectively	%EWL/63% and 53%, respectively
van Gemert WG et al. 1997 [131]	49 (69%)	m/6.8 years	94%	8 years: dBMI/15
Näslund E et al. 1997 [82]	198 (nr)	5 and 7 years, respectively	89%	5 years and 7 years: dBMI/10
Baltasar A et al. 1998 [13]	100 (73%)	5–11 years	5 years/93%	%EWL/54%
Verselewel de Wit 1999 [132]	40 (93%)	m=7.4 years	85%	7 years: %EWL=46% dB
van de Weijgert EJ 1999 [130]	100 (84%)	m=7.2 years	78%	%EWL=63%
Alper D et al. 2000 [3]	450 (73%)	m=5.2 years m=3.2 years	29% and 67%, respectively	5.2 years: %EWL=59%

See legend on page 176

Late complications	Late reop. (revision) %	Effect on comorbidity	Study quality Comments
48 % staple line-rupture	19 %	nr	High Results described in detail
2 sudden cardiac deaths 6 hernias	None	Hypertension decreased from 47 % to 32 % Diabetes from 28 % to 14 % Back-joint problems from 69 % to 32 %	Small group
Reported by Mason in other studies	6 %	nr	Medium Poorer results in women >225 % overweight comp <225 %
10 % hernia	12 %	nr	Low Phone interview
nr	1% per year	nr	Medium Phone interview
None	2 %	nr	Somewhat brief report
Reported in detail – eg, 24 % band-related compli-cations	24 %	nr	Retrospecive study focusing on possible difference between Dacron and Marlex bands
21 % hernia 29 % esophagitis 27 % staple line rupture 3 % band erosion	6 % per year for 1–7 years	nr	Thorough review of complications
	25 %	nr	High
r	18 %	nr	Small group, but detailed report of weight changes
	18 %	nr	High
ncisional hernia 26 %, bstruction of stoma % , surgical method omplications 6 %	5 %	nr	Low. Silicon ring Vertical gastroplasty

Table continues on next page

Table 4.11 Long-term followup of Vertical Banded Gastroplasty (VBG) (mean followup >5 years).

Author Year Reference	Number, (% women)	Followup, years	Followed up %	Weight loss
Balsiger BM et al. 2000 [12]	73 (75%)	≥10 years	99%	%EWL/37%
Hernandez-Estefania R et al. 2000 [43]	34 (85%)	5 years	100% (not clearly stated)	dBMI/7

Followup time has been stated as mean value for the entire group (m),
or range (r) or whether all followed up same length of time; unit = years.
1 = Reoperated patients excluded in this information
m = Mean
r = Range (interval)
nr = Not reported
%EWL = % of preoperative excessive weight lost
%BW = % of preoperative body weight lost
kg = Weight reduction in kg
dBMI = Reduction (number of BMI units) of BMI from preoperative value

five patients were reported to have needed a reoperation within 5 to 10 years after the initial surgery. Apart from this weight gain and the need for reoperation, few serious side effects from VBG were reported.

Overall assessment of VBG evidence: This method has been widely used, and its long-term results are well documented. Weight loss with VBG is not as great as weight loss with GBP, but it is easier to perform and maintains the normal route of food through the gastrointestinal tract. Laparoscopic VBG should be evaluated in adequately controlled studies before it is accepted as routine clinical practice.

4.6.3.4 Gastric Banding (GB)

Randomized trials: Although laparoscopic, adjustable GB has been in use since the early 1990s, and although it has been widely used (around two thirds of all lectures at the annual international obesity surgery conferences during 1999 through 2001 concerned GB), not a single RCT has compared the value of GB to GBP, and only one study has compared GB to VBG (Table 4.9) [63, 64].

However, one published RCT has compared open GB to laparoscopic GB [135]. Twenty-five patients were randomized to each group. The duration of the operation was significantly longer for laparoscopic surgery. It was necessary to convert two patients to open surgery. No differences were found between the groups with respect to early complications. The length of the hospital stay was shorter for those receiving laparoscopic surgery. During the first year, weight reduction was similar in both groups (from approximately 150 kg to approximately 115 kg),

Late complications	Late reop. (revision) %	Effect on comorbidity	Study quality Comments
Incisional hernia 23 % Reflux >7 %	19 %	nr	High Prospective
nr	>18 %	nr	Study focuses on eating behavior in a group monitored 3 years (n=67) and subgroup with 5 years (n=34)

but those receiving open surgery had more readmissions to hospital for complications, mainly incisional hernia. Also, nonrandomized studies of adjustable GB by open and laparoscopic methods have yielded similar weight loss, but less pain, shorter duration of medical care, and fewer wound complications for those receiving laparoscopic surgery [15, 49].

Long-term followup of gastric banding: Few studies reporting on long-term results after GB have been published. A small study investigated 26 patients from Norway 14 years, on average, after having received open nonadjustable GB. The bands had been removed in approximately 35 % of the patients because of complications. Those with bands still intact had retained only a moderate weight loss [129]. Using the same surgical technique, Fried and Peskova reported a weight loss of 37 kg, equivalent to 13 BMI units, in 58 % of 155 patients who could be monitored for 5 years [36]. Twelve percent of the patients had esophagitis. The reoperation rate was not reported.

The best report on long-term effects after laparoscopic adjustable GB is the prospective outcome followup by O'Brien et al., with up to 4 years of followup [96]. In contrast to the relatively low complication rate in this prospective study, is a report from Uppsala, where 35 % of the patients were reoperated mainly due to band migration or esophagitis (median followup time of 35 months) [133]. Numerous studies with short followup periods have reported substantial problems with pouch dilatation, functional stoma stenosis, band slippage, and erosion, all of which resulted in a substantial need for reoperation [27, 30].

The SOS study reported that weight loss after GB and VBG was similar for 2 to 10 years (Figure 4.3), but GB was associated with a higher reoperation rate.

Overall assessment of gastric banding evidence: There is no RCT-based evidence of the value of GB in relation to other methods. There is a substantial need for studies comparing laparoscopic adjustable GB to other methods.

4.6.3.5 Complications Following Stomach Procedures

All stomach procedures involve a risk for obstruction of the anastomosis between the upper small stomach pouch and the small intestine (as in GBP), or the lower, and larger, part of the stomach (as in gastroplasties). This may cause vomiting and inflammation of the esophagus and, if left untreated, may cause nutritional complications and malnourishment. Several case reports of serious complications have been published, e. g., by Mason [73]. However, the complication rate is so low that it is not noted in the RCT and long-term reports listed in Tables 4.7–4.11.

Vitamin B12-deficiency is a side effect specific to GBP. (A low intake of B12 in combination with blockage of intrinsic factors is probably the cause). All GBP patients should supplement their intake of vitamin B12 throughout life [4]. Iron deficiency is also relatively common. One fifth to one third of patients receiving stomach surgery [85], particularly women with menses [121] require medication with iron agents. This deficiency is mainly attributed to a low intake of iron, but an additional cause in GBP is that the main part of the stomach and upper part of the small intestine (which play a major role in the uptake of iron from the gastrointestinal tract) are bypassed.

Theoretically, particularly in GBP, there should also be a risk of osteoporosis resulting from a change in the metabolism of calcium. This has not been studied in depth, however, probably due to the lack of case reports and observations in long-term followup (> 10 years).

Other complications are similar to those that occur with any type of open surgery or laparoscopic surgery in the upper part of the abdomen. [41, 86]

4.6.3.6 Intestinal Bypass

Long-term results of intestinal bypass: The results concerning weight loss are good. Most studies have reported an average weight loss of approximately 75 % of overweight, or 30 % to 40 % of the original weight. At long-term followup, weight loss had been maintained in the group of patients not requiring reoperation.

Intestinal bypass has been associated with a range of problems [16]. During the first 2 years, many patients required hospital care on repeated occasions due to disabling diarrhea involving electrolyte and fluid imbalance. Calcium is saponified in the intestine because of insufficient uptake of fat, which in the long run causes hyperoxaluria and formation of kidney stones. Late joint symptoms similar to rheumatoid arthritis are common. They are usually relieved temporarily with antibiotics. Clinical findings and animal experiment studies indicate that bacterial growth in the bypassed intestine is an important cause of arthritis. Liver damage also appears and is permanent in some cases.

An RCT randomized 32 patients to GBP and 27 to intestinal bypass (jejunoileal bypass) (Table 4.9) [39]. Preoperatively, the average weight was 152 kg, and after 1 year the difference in weight loss was not statistically significant, 51 kg for GBP and 58 kg for intestinal bypass. Early side effects were more common after GBP, while late complications were much more common and severe after intestinal bypass. In the patients accepting pre- and postoperative liver biopsies after the GBP, a significant improvement in the degree of steatosis (fatty degeneration) was observed in 10 of 12 subjects. After intestinal bypass, 12 of 15 patients showed deterioration in the liver changes. In this small group of patients, one patient died from liver complications and the shunt in one patient had to be closed because of impending liver failure. In many patients, intestinal shunts have been closed or reoperated using other surgical methods.

Comprehensive evidence evaluation of intestinal bypass: A major NIH consensus conference on obesity surgery in 1991, which took a position against the use of intestinal bypass, has been an important reason why the use of this technique has now practically ceased [9]. At this conference, the literature available was summarized as follows:

1. Intestinal bypass can yield substantial weight loss.
2. The patients are usually satisfied with the results, and psychosocial improvement is satisfactory.
3. Mortality during surgery can be limited to 0.5 % and wound infections to 3 %.
4. All patients get diarrhea.
5. Electrolyte disorders can be controlled.
6. Half of the patients develop some type of metabolic complication.
7. Liver failure, kidney stones, autoimmune joint inflammation, or skin disease occurred in 20 % of those receiving intestinal bypass surgery, and these complications often occur late, more than 10 years after the operation [97].

4.6.3.7 Bileopancreatic Bypass (BPB) and Duodenal Switch (DS)

RCTs have not been conducted for either of these methods. For BPB, several other types of studies are available, even studies with long followup times. Most of these studies come from Italy. In 1998, Scopinario et al. reported on 2241 BPB patients followed between 1 and 21 years [110]. There are no controlled comparisons between BPB and other methods, but nonrandomized comparisons suggest that BPB yields a greater weight loss than GB [11], VBG [21], and GBP [81]. BPB is, however, associated with serious malabsorptive problems such as albumin deficiency in the blood and vitamin deficiencies [11, 21, 81].

Two nonrandomized comparative studies of DS are available. For more than 4–8 years, Marceau et al. followed the results in 252 BPB patients and 465 DS patients [70]. DS was associated with greater weight loss and fewer side effects. In the second study, Rabkin found that DS did not yield a greater weight loss than GBP [102].

Overall assessment of the evidence: DS and BPB need to be further evaluated in randomized, comparative studies before they can be assessed in relation to other types of surgery and recommended for general use.

4.6.3.8 Laparoscopic or Open Surgery

The surgical methods described above can be performed either by laparoscopic or open surgery. In principal, the gastrointestinal procedure is the same, and hence the same long-term results should be expected in terms of efficacy, including side effects and complications. This, however, has not been studied. There is a difference in the surgical trauma itself and in the access time of the procedure. An open procedure probably involves greater stress during surgery and could result in more wound complications after surgery, e. g., wound infection and incisional hernia. The laparoscopic instruments and the surgical system, e. g., stapling devices, differ from those used in open surgery, although they are designed according to the same principles. Somewhat surprisingly, more small bowel obstructions have been reported after laparoscopic surgery than would be expected based on experience with the corresponding open procedures [93, 134].

Several nonrandomized studies have compared open and laparoscopic VBG [25, 62, 83], open and laparoscopic adjustable GB [26, 49], open and laparoscopic GBP [90], and open VBG and laparoscopic adjustable GB [10, 125, 126]. In these noncontrolled studies, the laparoscopic method was associated with a more rapid recovery, less postoperative pain, better postoperative respiratory status, and shorter time in hospital. Three large (n = 1040, 500, and 275) noncomparative studies of laparoscopic GBP reported speedy rehabilitation, excellent weight loss, and relatively few complications [45, 109, 136]. In a smaller study (n = 40) of laparoscopic DS, the median length of stay was 4 days [107].

Although most reports are positive toward laparoscopic methods, some authors report poor results [22, 28, 30, 133].

A specific problem associated with laparoscopic procedures is their long learning curve. In several studies, e. g., two RCTs, the first cases treated by the surgeon and institution have been included in the laparoscopic group [134, 135]. This may influence the outcome of that group negatively. The large differences in the need for reoperation, from 35 % to a few percent, can perhaps be explained by such learning differences [29, 79, 96, 133]. Several authors report even higher complication rates in early cases compared to later cases in the same series [95, 126].

It is too early to determine the role of laparoscopic surgery in the treatment of obesity. Will the obvious advantages of less access trauma, and thereby fewer wound complications, justify taking the risk of a technically more demanding surgical technique? Are the long-term results of laparoscopic procedures at least as good as the results of open procedures? There is a need for well-designed, comparative studies of open and laparoscopic surgery for obesity, where technical learning problems are adequately managed.

Appendix 4.6.2 presents important technical requirements related to obesity surgery.

4.6.4
Surgery Compared to Conservative Treatment and Effects on Risk Factors

Two RCTs have compared surgery with conventional treatment. In both cases, surgery yielded a better weight loss than conventional dietary treatment even though the latter was given at specialized obesity clinics. These studies are of limited value, since the surgical method applied was intestinal bypass, which is no longer in general use [6-8, 119].

In addition to the 2 randomized trials, there is an extensive intervention study with matched controls, i.e., for each surgery patient, a conventionally treated patient of the same sex, age, weight, risk factors (18 different variables) was studied. This study, the so-called SOS study (Swedish Obese Subjects), is judged as having high quality and is described in greater detail below.

4.6.5
The SOS Study

4.6.5.1 Aim and Design
The main purpose of the SOS study is to study whether intentional, major, and long-term weight loss can reduce the increased levels of mortality and morbidity in overweight individuals. The SOS study also includes other aims related to genetics, quality of life, and health economics [116, 117].

SOS consists of a registry study and an intervention study. In addition, there is a reference group of 1135 individuals who were randomly selected from the general population. The registry study includes 6328 individuals who received health examinations at 480 of the approximately 700 community health centers in Sweden. The treatment group included 2010 persons who received GB, VBG, or GBP. The control group included an equally large number of matched obese subjects treated and monitored at the community health centers, where they were offered the conventional treatment available. Drugs for treating obesity have not been available during most of the study. Apart from being a resident of one of the 18 participating county councils, the criteria for inclusion were age between 37 and 60 years and a BMI of > 34 for men and > 38 for women.

SOS is not a randomized trial. However, an extensive matching process was used to select the control group. This model was chosen since, at the time when the study was planned (1985–1987), ethical acceptance of a randomized trial could not be obtained. This was because mortality from obesity surgery at the time was considered to be 1–5 %, and it was not ethically acceptable to place the patient in a situation where random chance determined whether high-risk or low-risk treatment would be used. Individuals in the registry study, who were approved based on the inclusion and exclusion criteria of the intervention study, could decide for themselves if they wanted to have surgical treatment for obesity. For each surgical case approved, an automated matching program based on 18 variables (sex, weight, height, smoking, biochemistry, and psychological variables) selected the optimal control at the time from among those requesting conventional treatment and who had been approved based on the same inclusion and exclusion criteria used in the surgical cases. To the greatest extent possible, the matching procedure was designed to eliminate confounders, e. g., different personality traits among those who select or reject surgery.

Inclusion in the study was completed on January 31, 2001. The patients in the treatment and control groups are followed up at 0.5, 1, 2, 3, 4, 6, 8, 10, 15, and 20 years. Prior to inclusion, and 2, 10, 15, and 20 years after inclusion, blood samples are taken for extensive analysis.

Several interim reports have been published. Since the study is still ongoing, the numbers of patients in these reports vary. The main findings concerning total mortality, and the incidence of, or mortality from, heart attack and stroke are not available to the study leaders, but are supervised by a separate safety committee. The results concerning these outcome measures will probably not be published before 2005.

4.6.5.2 Weight Loss in the SOS Study

Changes in weight are illustrated in Figure 4.3, which shows 8 years of followup in 346 surgically treated patients and the same number of controls, of whom 251 (73 % of available cases) surgical patients and 232 (67 %) controls had completed the 8-year study [115]. Similar weight changes to those presented in Figure 4.3 are found in reports of greater shares of the patient population with shorter followup [114] and for the first 63 surgical patients and the corresponding control group, which was monitored for 10 years [117].

In the three surgical methods used in SOS, patients achieved maximum weight loss after 1 year (Figure 4.3). Between 1 and 6–8 years, a tendency toward weight gain was observed. Between 8 and 10 years of followup, weight appears to be stabilized [117]. At all time points, GBP resulted in 6–13 % greater weight loss than with other methods. After 2 years, weight loss was observed (percent of the preoperative weight) of 33 % + 10 % for GBP, 23 % + 10 % for VBG, and 21 % + 12 % for GB [50]. After 10 years, weight loss in the surgical group as a whole was 16.7 %.

Figure 4.3 also illustrates that conventional, nonpharmacological treatment of obesity does not result in weight loss. Body weight in the control group of the SOS study increased by 1.1 % in 10 years [117].

4.6.5.3 Surgical Complications in the SOS Study

Five patients (0.25 %) died as a consequence of the intervention itself, three because of leakage, and two because of myocardial infarction [41, 86]. Mortality is much lower than that reported during the 1980s and 1990s (1–5 %).

Complications and reoperations during the primary episode of care have been reported in the first 1164 patients [86]. In 151 (13 %) patients, 193 complications were determined to require surgical intervention and at least one additional day in hospital. The complications reported were bleeding (0.8 %), blood clot in the lung and/or in the legs (0.8 %), wound infection or rupture of the surgical wound (1.8 %), deep infection with an abscess in the abdomen and/or leakage due to anastomosis rupture (2.1 %), lung complications (6.2 %), and others (4.8 %). Approximately 2 % (26 subjects) were reoperated because of these complications, mainly for leakage. Similar figures have been reported for the total SOS treatment group [41].

In 4 years of followup, 12 % of the first 1164 surgical cases in the SOS study were reoperated using some method of revision. Reasons included poor weight loss or technical complications, e. g., rupture of the stapled wound. The reoperation rate, around 3 % annually, was highest for the GB patients. Those who initially received VBG and GB were often reoperated using GBP [86].

4.6.5.4 Effects on Risk Factors in the SOS Study

An analysis of 282 men and 560 women from the surgical and control groups identified a change in risk factors related to weight change [112, 113]. A weight loss of 10 kg was sufficient to achieve a clinically significant improvement in all traditional risk factors except total cholesterol (Figure 4.4). Although other studies have reported that total cholesterol is reduced in the short term (1–6 months) by moderate weight loss, Figure 4.4 shows that maintained weight loss of 30–40 kg is required to achieve a reduction in total cholesterol after 2 years.

Another 2-year report of 767 surgical patients and 712 controls showed that weight loss resulted in a dramatic reduction in the incidence of hypertension, diabetes, hyperinsulinemia, hypertriglyceridemia, and hypo-HDL-cholesterolemia [114]. For diabetes, the reduction in incidence was dramatic (32 times). However, the incidence of hypercholesterolemia was not affected. In another analysis, it was found that minor weight loss (<4 kg) and weight gain were associated with a diabetes incidence of 7–9 % over 2 years. An average weight loss of 7 % was associated with a 2-year incidence of 3 %, while no new cases of diabetes occurred in groups with a weight loss of 12 % or more. In an 8-year followup, the incidence of diabetes remained five times lower in the surgical group than in the control group [115]. However, no difference was found between the groups concerning the incidence of high blood pressure after 8 years (Figure 4.5).

4.6.5.5 Effects on the Cardiovascular System in the SOS Study

Left ventricle structure and function has been studied before inclusion and 1 to 4 years after. Prior to inclusion, a surgical treatment group (n = 41) and an overweight control group (n = 31) were compared to a reference group from the normal population (n = 43) [52, 53]. Compared to normal-weight persons, obese individuals had elevated values of systolic and diastolic blood pressure, left ventricular mass, and relative heart muscle thickness, while the ejection fraction (measure of systolic function) and E:A ratio[1] (measure of diastolic function) were decreased.

1) The peak E-wave and A-wave velocities were measured. EW = early filling wave, AW = late filling wave.

After 1 year, all of these values had improved in the surgical group, but did not improve in the control group, which remained at an unchanged high weight. Reduction in left ventricular mass and improvement in diastolic function were related to the degree of weight loss. Both weight gain and poor weight loss after 1 year were associated with a measurable deterioration in diastolic function.

The variation in heart rate and the catecholamine secretion were studied in other SOS subgroups, [51]. The findings indicate that overweight persons, compared to normal-weight persons, have increased sympathetic activity (one of the involuntary nervous and hormone systems which is activated mainly by stress, combat, and fear) and decreased vagal activity (the other involuntary nervous system, which is activated mainly by rest, peace, and security), with an associated morbid reduction in heartrate variability. These impairments were normalized after 1 year in the surgical group, but not in the control group.

Information from questionnaires prior to and 2 years after inclusion in SOS were analyzed from the first 1210 surgical cases, and the first 1099 control cases were analyzed as regards different heart and lung symptoms [50]. At inclusion, the groups were comparable in most respects. After 2 years, shortness of breath and chest pain had decreased in a much higher percentage of the surgical treatment group compared to the control group. At inclusion, 87% of the surgical cases reported shortness of breath from walking up two flights of stairs, while only 19% experienced these symptoms 2 years later. In the overweight control group, the corresponding figures were 69% and 57%, respectively. A high probability for sleep apnea was observed in 23% of the surgical cases before treatment, but in only 8% of these cases 2 years after treatment. The corresponding figures for the control group were 22% and 20%, respectively.

The same study reported that 46% of the surgical patients were physically inactive before weight loss, while only 17% were inactive 2 years after the operation. The corresponding figures in the control group were 33% and 29%, respectively. Traditionally, physical inactivity is considered to contribute toward the development of obesity. The SOS findings indicate that obesity can also prevent physical activity, and that this vicious cycle can be broken by significant weight loss.

SOS is the first published study to show that intentional weight loss can inhibit the atherosclerotic process [54]. The annual increase in this process was nearly three times as high in the obese control group as in the normal weight reference group. In the surgical treatment group, the rate of increase was normalized.

4.6.5.6   Quality of Life in SOS Before and After Weight Loss

Cross-sectional data from 800 obese men and 943 obese women in the SOS registry study show that these individuals have a much poorer health-related quality of life than the age-matched reference groups [123]. The measurements are based on several different general rating scales and an obesity-specific psychosocial scale. (The scales were evaluated under Swedish conditions.)

A 2-year study (55) and a 4-year study (124) demonstrated how all of the instruments mentioned above registered considerable improvements in quality of life and psychosocial function. These improvements were proportional to weight loss, i. e., the greater the weight loss the greater the improvement in health-related quality of life. (See Chapter 6 on quality of life.)

4.6.5.7 Health Economics and SOS

The SOS also includes an economic component, discussed separately in Chapter 8 of this report.

4.6.6
Appendix: Glossary and Surgical Details

4.6.6.1 Glossary

Access trauma   The stress and the injury to the body (e. g., on the abdominal wall) caused by the part of the operation required to gain access to perform the procedure. Particularly important as regards the difference between open and laparoscopic surgery.

Anastomosis   Surgical connection of two tubular structures, e. g., gastrointestinal organs in gastric bypass between stomach and small intestine.

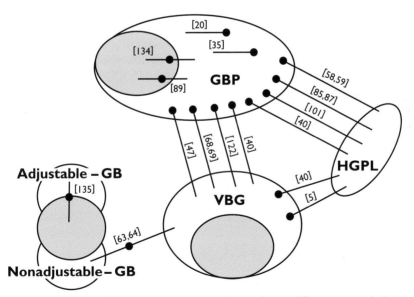

Figure 4.2   Diagram of RCT with stomach operations.
Shaded field indicates laparoscopic surgery and white field indicates open surgery. The beginning and end of the line show the two methods compared. A mark in the middle of the line indicates that no difference in weight loss was found between the methods. A mark at the end of the line indicates the method with the statistically significant greatest weight loss. The numbers of the lines correspond to the citation numbers in the reference list.

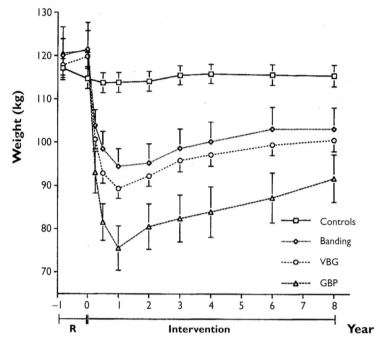

Figure 4.3 Weight changes in the SOS study with +95% confidence interval. In total, 252 surgically treated patients and 232 obese subjects in control group from the maching study until the 8-year control. Figure includes only cases followed up during the entire period. R = Registry study when matching variables were collected.

Banding = gastric banding, n=63. VBG, n=164. GBP, n=24.
Each of the surgical groups had a statistically significant (p<0.01) weight loss greater than that in the control group. (Reproduced from [115])

BPB   Biliopancreatic bypass. A more extensive surgical procedure which is basically a combination of gastric bypass and intestinal bypass (see Section 4.8.2).

DS   Duodenal switch. Variant of BPB (see Section 4.8.2).

Erosive esophagitis   Corrosion of the esophagus.

Gastroesophageal reflux   Stomach content returns to the esophagus where it can cause corrosion and esophagitis.

Gastroplasty   Collective term for all surgical methods for obesity where the normal course of the gastrointestinal tract is preserved but the passage is affected by a narrow stoma.

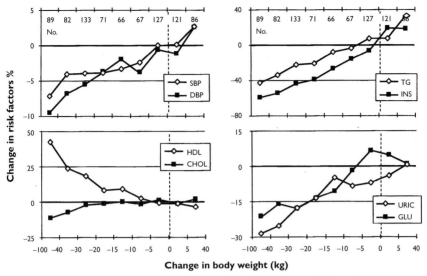

Figure 4.4 Change of risk factors in weight loss. Adjusted percentage change in risk factors in relation to weight change (kg) for 2 years in 842 overweight men and women combined from the surgical group and the control group in the SOS study. The percentage of change for each risk factor has been adjusted with regard to the baseline value of the risk factor studied, initial body weight, gender, age, and body height. Number in each weight group stated at the top of each figure. SBP = systolic blood pressure. DBP = diastolic blood pressure. HDL = serum HDL cholesterol. CHOL = total serum cholesterol. TG = triglycerides. INS = serum insulin. URIC = serum uric acid. GLU = blood glucose. All serum samples are fasting samples. (Reproduced with permission from [112]).

GB   Gastric banding (see Section 4.8.2).

GBP   Gastric bypass (see Section 4.8.2).

Hernia   Rupture – in this context, abdominal wall hernia in the surgical incision.

HGPL   Horizontal gastroplasty (see Section 4.8.2).

Hyperinsulinemia   Excessive level of insulin in the blood.

Hyperoxaluria   Excessive level of oxalic acid in the blood.

Hypertriglyceridemia   Excessive level of lipids in the blood.

Hypo-HLD-cholesterolemia   Decreased level of HDL cholesterol in the blood.

Ileum   Lowest part of the small intestine.

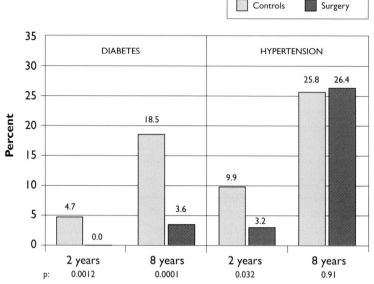

Figure 4.5 Two- and eight-year incidence (new cases) of diabetes and hypertension in 251 surgically treated patients (black columns) and 232 obese subjects in the control group (gray columns) in the SOS study. Calculations are based on patients completing the entire study. (Reproduced with permission from [115])

Ileus Bowel obstruction.

Incidence Frequency of cases of a particular disease occurring in a particular population during a particular period.

Intestinal bypass See Section 4.8.2.

Intrinsic factor A protein formed in the mucous membrane of the stomach which has major importance for the uptake of vitamin B12 in the body.

Invasive method Diagnostic or treatment method involving a procedure in the body, e. g., an operation, insertion of a catheter or foreign material, sampling of tissue.

Jejunum Upper part of the small intestine.

Laparoscopic operation "Keyhole" surgery in the abdominal cavity.

Lap band One of two commercial systems for laparoscopic adjustable gastric banding.

Neuro-humoral feedback   Feedback system mediated by hormones and/or nerve signals triggered by the small intestine.

Obstruction   Clogging, blockage in the gastrointestinal tract (or blood vessel).

Pouch dilatation   Enlargement of the stomach pouch, usually leading to weight gain relapse.

RCT   Randomized Controlled Trial.

Reflux   The content of the stomach returns to the esophagus.

Roux-en-Y   "(Bowel) loop like a Y", a manner of connecting the stomach with the bowel in stomach surgery. One of the loops of the Y goes to the stomach, the other to the duodenum, gall- and pancreatic duct. Another way of connecting stomach and bowel is called the "Omega loop".

SAGB   One of two commercial systems for adjustable gastric banding. Is also sometimes called "the Swedish band" after its originator, Dag Hallberg.

Shunt   Connection (anastomosis) between two channels in the body whereby a part is bypassed. Synonym is bypass.

SOS   Swedish Obese Subjects. A study on the effect of weight loss where 2000 surgically treated patients are compared to an equally large matched control group and followed for more than 10 years.

Staple line   Mechanical suture line is used instead of a manual suture line. Can also be used with certain anastomoses. Its advantage lies in greater safety compared to a manual suture line.

Steatosis   Degeneration of fat (mainly of the liver).

Stoma   Synonym is anastomosis.

Stomach pouch   The small proximal part (usually approximately 1–2 % of the maximum volume of the stomach), which in GBP and gastroplasties is separated with a stoma before this part of the stomach empties into the small intestine or remaining part of the stomach.

Stomal ulcer   Ulcer in an anastomosis.

Suture line   See Staple line.

VBG   Vertical banded gastroplasty (see Section 4.8.2).

%EWL %Excess Weight Loss. Percentage of reduction from preoperative over-weight. A common reference point used in North American literature for 0 % over-weight is the Metropolitan Life Insurance table of ideal weight. The corresponding reference point used in more recent literature is BMI = 25 kg/m². The former method of calculating yields somewhat higher values for overweight, but the difference between theses two references is small and has no practical clinical importance.

4.6.6.2 Description of Surgical Methods

Gastric bypass (GBP) GBP was the first surgical stomach operation intended to treat obesity [74]. In its original form, the operation involved a horizontal pouch and a so-called omega loop. The method has since undergone several changes, but since the beginning of the 1990s the anatomical design is fairly standardized in both laparoscopic and open surgery, with an upper small vertical stomach pouch (see section on surgical methods, Appendix 4.6.2) connected with the small bowel via the Roux procedure. This has been described in detail by, e.g., Fobi [34]. In the United States, this method was used in approximately three fourths of the 46 000 operations performed during year 2000 by surgeons associated with the American Society for Bariatric Surgery. GBP is performed both as open and laparoscopic surgery. (Figure 4.1)

Horizontal gastroplasty (HGPL) HGPL was developed in an attempt to simplify GBP. It was assumed that GBP involved a purely mechanical, restrictive mechanism where only the size of pouch and the volume of outflow mattered. Therefore, pouch and outflow were constructed based on the same design as in GBP, but the pouch emptied into the remaining main stomach instead of into the bowel. Many different variations of HGPL were tested in the late 1970s and early 1980s. The variations mainly differ in the manner of constructing the outflow of the upper small pouch (location of the anastomosis, suture machine or manual sutures, reinforcement or not). There are no adequate comparisons between these different variants of HGPL. However, there is no reason to assume that there would be any essential differences. Because of rapid regain in weight after an initial weight loss, none of these HGPL methods are used today. Nevertheless, they played a major part in the development of gastroplasties in use today, particularly vertical banded gastroplasty (VBG) and gastric banding (GB).

Vertical banded gastroplasty (VBG) Edward Mason drew on experience with different gastroplasties to develop techniques using the VBG method [71, 72]. In this method, stomach pouches, similar to a short extension of the esophagus, were introduced along the more sturdy upper right area of the stomach. A band of foreign material kept the outflow from this pouch from expanding (polypropylene, see Section 4.6.6.3 Technical Considerations). This method dominated during the late 1980s and the 1990s. Either laparoscopic or open surgery can be used (Figure 4.1). A variant of VBG is silastic ring vertical gastroplasty [31].

Gastric banding (GB)   GB involves drawing a band tightly around the upper part of the stomach. Hence, the gastrointestinal tract does not need to be opened. The method was developed concurrently at several different places in the world, independently of each other, e. g., by Bö in Norway [18]. The method was applied widely without performing randomized comparisons [30]. Complications and weight gain after the initial postoperative weight loss occurred in many patients, and the need for reoperation was high. Consequently, enthusiasm decreased, not only for GB but in many places even for obesity surgery in general (Figure 4.1).

Adjustable GB is an improvement over GB. The band can be filled with fluid via a subcutaneous injection port. By varying the amount of fluid in the system it is possible to narrow or widen the outflow (stoma) from the stomach pouch. Two commercial systems are available, based on somewhat different designs and principles. They have never been compared in a randomized clinical trial. Nonrandomized comparisons between the two bands indicate similar results [79]. The one system, the so-called Swedish Adjustable Band® (Obteck), was originally developed by Professor Dag Hallberg. The other band, LapBand® (BioEnterics) allows for less adjustment in the diameter of the stoma. Both bands are developed for easy application in laparoscopic surgery (Figure 4.1).

During the late 1990s, laparoscopic adjustable/variable GB had become a popular procedure, not least in countries with little experience of obesity surgery.

Intestinal bypass   The first operation for obesity was performed by Viktor Henrikson (Göteborg, Sweden) in the early 1950s [42]. In two female patients, he removed 105 cm of small bowel and achieved good weight loss without complications. However, no one followed in his footsteps. The actual breakthrough in obesity surgery came with intestinal bypass. Kremen and Linnér performed animal experiment studies as early as 1954 [57], and, following reports by Paynes [98, 99], intestinal bypass received broad acceptance.

Intestinal bypass does not involve the removal of bowel. Rather, most of the small intestine is reconnected as a blind loop. After the operation, the gastrointestinal tract consists functionally, after Treitz's ligament, of approximately 40 cm of jejunum (upper small bowel), approximately 15 cm ileum (lower small bowel), and the entire colon. The surgical procedure results in malabsorption contributing to the weight change. However, studies have shown that the most important explanation for weight loss is a reduction in the intake of food, probably conditioned by some type of neurohumoral feedback system from the small bowel [14, 23, 56]. Many patients, worldwide, received intestinal bypass during the 1960s and 1970s.

Bileopancreatic bypass (BPB) and duodenal switch (DS)   BPB was developed by Scopinario (Italy) in an attempt to deal with the side effects of intestinal bypass [111]. The procedure involves removing three fourths of the stomach and closing the duodenum. (Alternative methods have been reported from other groups, where the upper part of the stomach only bypasses the lower part, basically as in GBP.) The bowel is divided 250 cm from the ileocecal valve (i.e., where the small bowel enters the colon), and the lower end is anastomosed to the remaining part of the stomach. The upper end of the divided ileum is then anastomosed end-to-side to the ileum 50 cm from the ileocecal valve. Expressed in lay terms, BPB is a combination of a stomach shunt (GBP) and an intestinal bypass.

A modification of BPB, known as a "duodenal switch" (DS) [44] has been developed in an attempt to reduce the side effects of classic BPB. In this procedure, reduction of the stomach volume is performed differently. (Function of the pylorus and antrum is maintained by a longitudinal resection from the pylorus to the cardia region of the major side. The duodenum is divided below the pylorus, and the distal small intestinal loop is anastomosed to the proximal duodenal division. The distal duodenal division is closed. Otherwise, the method resembles BPB.) BPB and DS are seldom used in northern Europe.

Other Invasive Methods *Intragastric balloon*: The method involves the use of a gastroscope to insert an air–filled plastic balloon (200–600 mL) into the stomach. Several studies have investigated the effects of the intragastric balloon. Eight RCTs were identified, whereof seven did not find any statistically significant difference in weight loss [17, 37, 46, 60, 77, 78, 108]. One of the studies [103] reported a weak effect (7 kg versus 3 kg, $p < 0.05$). Several of the studies described complications from balloon treatment. Clearly, this method does not have a place in the treatment of obesity. Apart from this summary, the method is not addressed further in this report.

Liposuction: Liposuction is not a treatment method for obesity. Rather, it is a surgical method for removing a limited amount of subcutaneous fat in a limited area of the body. The indication is mainly cosmetic. Hence, the method is not addressed further in this report.

4.6.6.3
Technical Considerations in Obesity Surgery

Stoma Size A statistically significant correlation between stoma size and weight loss has been shown by using endoscopic [84] or X-ray methods [63] to measure postoperative stoma diameter after gastroplasties. This also serves as the theoretical foundation for development of adjustable bands in gastric banding.

While stoma size is of importance for weight loss in purely restrictive surgical methods such as VBG and GB, it is not related to weight loss after GBP [63, 84]. Nevertheless, some types of GBP use an external, nonexpandable band around the stoma or upper stomach pouch. Fobi [34] uses a silicone ring and Linner [61] uses a band of fascia (tendon sheath) from the patient's abdominal wall. In a randomized clinical trial, Howard [47] showed that reinforcement of the GBP stoma results in higher complication rates, e. g., stomal ulceration and band migration (migration and perforation of the stomach wall).

Foreign Material In gastroplasties, i. e., GB and VBG, foreign material is used to reinforce the stoma. The main materials used are propylene net (MarlexMesh®), polytetra-urethane ethylene (Gore-Tex®), silicone, or vascular grafts of dacron. VBG mainly involves the use of MarlexMesh® and, to some degree, Gore-Tex®. Non-adjustable GB mainly involves Gore-Tex® but also MarlexMesh® and dacron. The balloon bands in adjustable GB have been treated with silicone. There are many opinions about the choice of material, but few solid facts. No studies were found that used adequate methodology to compare the choice of material.

Pouch Size surgeryThe volume of the upper pouch has been changed gradually from approximately 200 mL in the 1960s and 1970s to approximately 15 mL during the past decade. The reason for superior long-term results with an initially smaller pouch is that it probably resists dilatation better. Tension in the wall can be presumed to increase more rapidly according to Hook's biomechanical law. Experimental data have shown that pouch volume measured during the operation correlates with weight loss after gastroplasty, but not after gastric bypass [87]. Lundell could not show any correlation between weight loss and pouch volume in gastroplasty when it was studied postoperatively by X-ray methods [63]. Despite the importance of optimum pouch size on surgical technique, no RCTs have been found (apart from the two mentioned above). This deficiency can probably be explained by the fact that a simple and valid measurement method is not available for evaluating the anatomic situation postoperatively.

Suture Line The introduction of suturing devices greatly facilitated the surgical treatment of obesity [2]. When Griffen introduced stapling *in situ* without division of the stomach wall, these procedures became both more simplified and more popularized [39]. High rupture rates (gastrogastric fistula) in the stapled suture lines were occasionally reported. Although minor breaks in the suture line do not cause immediate weight gain [87, 128], when the suture lines rupture, patients cease to lose weight and experience weight relapse [48]. Attempts were made to prevent ruptures in suture lines by making alterations in the suturing devices and by applying more lines of staples. Controlled studies of the different changes have not been published, and the problem of staple line rupture has become increasingly evident. Two studies, where all patients (even those who were symptom free) were examined by gastroscopy and/or X-ray, identified ruptures in over 40% of staple lines after VBG [66, 128]. An RCT by Fobi [35] (Table 4.8) showed that gastrogastric fistulas could be prevented in GBP by dividing the stomach. Likewise, MacLean [67] also found in VBG that ruptures in the vertical staple line decreased if the stomach wall was divided in a similar fashion.

References Section 4.6

1. Abu-Abeid S, Keidar A, Szold A. Resolution of chronic medical conditions after laparoscopic adjustable silicone gastric banding for the treatment of morbid obesity in the elderly. Surg Endosc 2001;15(2):132-4.

2. Alden JF. Gastric and jejunoileal bypass. A comparison in the treatment of morbid obesity. Arch Surg 1977;112(7):799-806.

3. Alper D, Ramadan E, Vishne T, Belavsky R, Avraham Z, Seror D, et al. Silastic ring vertical gastroplasty – longterm results and complications. Obes Surg 2000;10(3):250-4.

4. Amaral JF, Thompson WR, Caldwell MD, Martin HF, Randall HT. Prospective hematologic evaluation of gastric exclusion surgery for morbid obesity. Ann Surg 1985;201(2):186-93.

5. Andersen T, Backer OG, Astrup A, Quaade F. Horizontal or vertical banded gastroplasty after pretreatment with very-low-calorie formula diet: a randomized trial. Int J Obes 1987;11(3):295-304.

6. Andersen T, Backer OG, Stokholm KH, Quaade F. Randomized trial of diet and gastroplasty compared with diet alone in morbid obesity. N Engl J Med 1984;310(6):352-6.

7. Andersen T, Stokholm KH, Backer OG, Quaade F. Long-term (5-year) results after either horizontal gastroplasty or very-low-calorie diet for morbid obesity. Int J Obes 1988;12(4):277-84.

8. Anonymous. Randomised trial of jejunoileal bypass versus medical treatment in morbid obesity. The Danish Obesity Project. Lancet 1979;2(8155):1255-8.

9. Anonymous. Gastrointestinal surgery for severe obesity. Proceedings of a National Institutes of Health Consensus Development Conference. March 25–27, 1991, Bethesda, MD. Am J Clin Nutr 1992;55(2 Suppl): 487S-619S.

10. Ashy AR, Merdad AA. A prospective study comparing vertical banded gastroplasty versus laparoscopic adjustable gastric banding in the treatment of morbid and super-obesity. Int Surg 1998;83(2):108-10.

11. Bajardi G, Ricevuto G, Mastrandrea G, Branca M, Rinaudo G, Cali F, et al. Surgical treatment of morbid obesity with biliopancreatic diversion and gastric banding: report on an 8-year experience involving 235 cases. Ann Chir 2000;125(2):155-62.

12. Balsiger BM, Poggio JL, Mai J, Kelly KA, Sarr MG. Ten and more years after vertical banded gastroplasty as primary operation for morbid obesity. J Gastrointest Surg 2000;4(6):598-605.

13. Baltasar A, Bou R, Arlandis F, Martinez R, Serra C, Bengochea M, et al. Vertical banded gastroplasty at more than 5 years. Obes Surg 1998;8(1): 29-34.

14. Barry RE, Barisch J, Bray GA, Sperling MA, Morin RJ, Benfield J. Intestinal adaptation after jejunoileal bypass in man. Am J Clin Nutr 1977;30(1):32-42.

15. Belachew M, Legrand M, Vincent V, Lismonde M, Le Docte N, Deschamps V. Laparoscopic adjustable gastric banding. World J Surg 1998;22(9): 955-63.

16. Benfield J, Castelnuovo-Tedesco P, Drenick P, Passaro E. Intestinal bypass

operations as a treatment for obesity. Ann Inter Med 1976;85:97-109.

17. Benjamin SB, Maher KA, Cattau EL, Collen MJ, Fleischer DE, Lewis JH, et al. Double-blind controlled trial of the Garren-Edwards gastric bubble: an adjunctive treatment for exogenous obesity. Gastroenterology 1988;95(3): 581-8.

18. Bö O, Modalsli O. Gastric banding, a surgical method of treating morbid obesity: preliminary report. Int J Obes 1983;7(5):493-9.

19. Breaux CW. Obesity surgery in children. Obes Surg 1995;5(3):279-84.

20. Brolin RE, Kenler HA, Gorman JH, Cody RP. Long-limb gastric bypass in the superobese. A prospective randomized study. Ann Surg 1992;215(4):387-95.

21. Chapin BL, LeMar HJ, Knodel DH, Carter PL. Secondary hyperparathyroidism following biliopancreatic diversion. Arch Surg 1996;131(10):1048-52; discussion 53.

22. Chelala E, Cadiere GB, Favretti F, Himpens J, Vertruyen M, Bruyns J, et al. Conversions and complications in 185 laparoscopic adjustable silicone gastric banding cases. Surg Endosc 1997;11(3):268-71.

23. Condon SC, Janes NJ, Wise L, Alpers DH. Role of caloric intake in the weight loss after jejunoileal bypass for obesity. Gastroenterology 1978;74(1):34-7.

24. Cook CM, Edwards C. Success habits of long-term gastric bypass patients. Obes Surg 1999;9(1):80-2.

25. Davila-Cervantes A, Ganci-Cerrud G, Gamino R, Gallegos-Martinez J, Gonzalez-Barranco J, Herrera MF. Open vs laparoscopic vertical banded gastroplasty: A case control study with a 1-year follow-up. Obes Surg 2000;10(5):409-12.

26. De Luca M, de Werra C, Formato A, Formisano C, Loffredo A, Naddeo M, et al. Laparotomic vs laparoscopic lapband: 4-year results with early and intermediate complications. Obes Surg 2000;10(3):266-8.

27. DeMaria EJ, Sugerman HJ. A critical look at laparoscopic adjustable silicone gastric banding for surgical treatment of morbid obesity: does it measure up? Surg Endosc 2000;14(8):697-9.

28. DeMaria EJ, Sugerman HJ, Meador JG, Doty JM, Kellum JM, Wolfe L, et al. High failure rate after laparoscopic adjustable silicone gastric banding for treatment of morbid obesity. Ann Surg 2001;233(6):809-18.

29. Dixon JB, O'Brien PE. Gastroesophageal reflux in obesity: the effect of lap-band placement. Obes Surg 1999;9(6):527-31.

30. Doherty C, Maher JW, Heitshusen DS. An interval report on prospective investigation of adjustable silicone gastric banding devices for the treatment of severe obesity. Eur J Gastroenterol Hepatol 1999;11(2):115-9.

31. Eckhout GV, Willbanks OL, Moore JT. Vertical ring gastroplasty for morbid obesity. Five year experience with 1463 patients. Am J Surg 1986;152(6):713-6.

32. Field RJ, Jr, Field RJ 3rd, Park SY. Vertical banded gastroplasty: is obesity worth it? J Miss State Med Assoc 1992;33(12):423-32.

33. Fobi MA. Vertical banded gastroplasty vs gastric bypass: 10 years follow-up. Obes Surg 1993;3:161-4.

34. Fobi MA, Lee H, Holness R, Cabinda D. Gastric bypass operation for obesity. World J Surg 1998;22(9):925-35.

35. Fobi MA, Lee H, Igwe D, Jr, Stanczyk M, Tambi JN. Prospective comparative evaluation of stapled versus transected silastic ring gastric bypass: 6-year follow-up. Obes Surg 2001;11(1):18-24.

36. Fried M, Peskova M. Gastric banding in the treatment of morbid obesity. Hepato-Gastroenterology 1997;44(14):582-7.

37. Geliebter A, Melton PM, Gage D, McCray RS, Hashim SA. Gastric balloon to treat obesity: a double-blind study in nondieting subjects. Am J Clin Nutr 1990;51(4):584-8.

38. Greenstein RJ, Rabner JG. Is adolescent gastric-restrictive antiobesity surgery warranted? Obes Surg 1995;5(2):138-44.

39. Griffen WO, Jr, Young VL, Stevenson CC. A prospective comparison of gastric and jejunoileal bypass procedures

for morbid obesity. Ann Surg 1977;186(4):500-9.

40. Hall JC, Watts JM, O'Brien PE, Dunstan RE, Walsh JF, Slavotinek AH, et al. Gastric surgery for morbid obesity. The Adelaide Study. Ann Surg 1990;211(4):419-27.

41. Hedenbro J, Näslund I, Ågren G, Lindroos A-K, Sjöström L. 2010 operations for obesity in the Swedish SOS study: methods, hospital time and complications. Obes Surg 2001;11:392.

42. Henrikson V. Kan tunntarmsresektion försvaras som terapi mot fettsot? Nordisk Medicin 1952;47:744.

43. Hernandez-Estefania R, Gonzalez-Lamuno D, Garcia-Ribes M, Garcia-Fuentes M, Cagigas JC, Ingelmo A, et al. Variables affecting BMI evolution at 2 and 5 years after vertical banded gastroplasty. Obes Surg 2000;10(2): 160-6.

44. Hess DS, Hess DW. Biliopancreatic diversion with a duodenal switch. Obes Surg 1998;8(3):267-82.

45. Higa KD, Boone KB, Ho T. Complications of the laparoscopic Roux-en-Y gastric bypass: 1040 patients – what have we learned? Obes Surg 2000;10(6):509-13.

46. Hogan RB, Johnston JH, Long BW, Sones JQ, Hinton LA, Bunge J, et al. A double-blind, randomized, sham-controlled trial of the gastric bubble for obesity. Gastrointest Endosc 1989;35(5):381-5.

47. Howard L, Malone M, Michalek A, Carter J, Alger S, van Woert J. Gastric bypass and vertical banded gastroplasty – a prospective randomized comparison and 5-year follow-up. Obes Surg 1995;5:55-60.

48. Husemann BJ. Obesity: an innately incurable disease? Obes Surg 1999;9(3):244-9.

49. Juvin P, Marmuse JP, Delerme S, Lecomte P, Mantz J, Demetriou M, et al. Post-operative course after conventional or laparoscopic gastroplasty in morbidly obese patients. Eur J Anaesth 1999; 16(6):400-3.

50. Karason K, Lindroos AK, Stenlof K, Sjöstrom L. Relief of cardiorespiratory symptoms and increased physical activity after surgically induced weight loss: results from the Swedish Obese Subjects study. Arch Intern Med 2000;160(12):1797-802.

51. Karason K, Molgaard H, Wikstrand J, Sjöstrom L. Heart rate variability in obesity and the effect of weight loss. Am J Cardiology 1999;83(8):1242-7.

52. Karason K, Wallentin I, Larsson B, Sjöström L. Effects of obesity and weight loss on left ventricular mass and relative wall thickness: survey and intervention study. BMJ 1997;315(7113):912-6.

53. Karason K, Wallentin I, Larsson B, Sjöström L. Effects of obesity and weight loss on cardiac function and valvular performance. Obes Res 1998;6(6):422-9.

54. Karason K, Wikstrand J, Sjöström L, Wendelhag I. Weight loss and progression of early atherosclerosis in the carotid artery: a four-year controlled study of obese subjects. Int J Obes Relat Metab Disord 1999;23(9): 948-56.

55. Karlsson J, Sjöström L, Sullivan M. Swedish obese subjects (SOS) – an intervention study of obesity. Two-year followup of health-related quality of life (HRQL) and eating behavior after gastric surgery for severe obesity. Int J Obes Relat Metab Disord 1998;22(2):113-26.

56. Koopmans HS, Sclafani A. Control of body weight by lower gut signals. Int J Obes 1981;5(5):491-5.

57. Kremen A, Linner J, Nelson C. An experimental evaluation of the nutritional importance of proximal and distal small bowel. Ann Surg 1954;140:439-48.

58. Lechner GW, Callender AK. Subtotal gastric exclusion and gastric partitioning: a randomized prospective comparison of one hundred patients. Surgery 1981;90(4):637-44.

59. Lechner GW, Elliott DW. Comparison of weight loss after gastric exclusion and partitioning. Arch Surg 1983;118(6):685-92.

60. Lindor KD, Hughes RW, Ilstrup DM, Jensen MD. Intragastric balloons in comparison with standard therapy for

obesity – a randomized, double-blind trial. Mayo Clin Proc 1987;62(11):992-6.

61. Linner J. Anterior Roux-en-Y gastric bypass with fascial support. In: Mason EE, editor. Problems in general surgery. Philadelphia: Lippincott; 1992:251-9.

62. Lonroth H, Dalenback J, Haglind E, Josefsson K, Olbe L, Fagevik Olsen M, et al. Vertical banded gastroplasty by laparoscopic technique in the treatment of morbid obesity. Surg Laparosc Endosc 1996;6(2):102-7.

63. Lundell L, Forssell H, Jensen J, Leth R, Lind T, Lycke G, et al. Measurement of pouch volume and stoma diameter after gastroplasty. Int J Obes 1987;11(2):169-74.

64. Lundell L, Ruth M, Olbe L. Vertical banded gastroplasty or gastric banding for morbid obesity: effects on gastro-oesophageal reflux. Eur J Surg 1997;163(7):525-31.

65. Macgregor AM, Rand CS. Gastric surgery in morbid obesity. Outcome in patients aged 55 years and older. Arch Surg 1993;128(10):1153-7.

66. MacLean LD, Rhode BM, Forse RA. Late results of vertical banded gastroplasty for morbid and super obesity. Surgery 1990;107(1):20-7.

67. MacLean LD, Rhode BM, Forse RA. A gastroplasty that avoids stapling in continuity. Surgery 1993;113(4):380-8.

68. MacLean LD, Rhode BM, Nohr CW. Late outcome of isolated gastric bypass. Ann Surg 2000;231(4):524-8.

69. MacLean LD, Rhode BM, Sampalis J, Forse RA. Results of the surgical treatment of obesity. Am J Surg 1993;165(1):155-60; discussion 60-2.

70. Marceau P, Hould FS, Simard S, Lebel S, Bourque RA, Potvin M, et al. Bilio-pancreatic diversion with duodenal switch. World J Surg 1998;22(9):947-54.

71. Mason EE. Vertical banded gastroplasty for obesity. Arch Surg 1982;117(5):701-6.

72. Mason EE. Morbid obesity: use of vertical banded gastroplasty. Surg Clin North Am 1987;67(3):521-37.

73. Mason EE. Starvation injury after gastric reduction for obesity. World J Surg 1998;22(9):1002-7.

74. Mason EE, Ito C. Gastric bypass in obesity. Surg Clin North Am 1967;47(6):1345-51.

75. Mason EE, Maher JW, Scott D, Rodriguez EM, Doherty C. Ten years of vertical banded gastroplasty for severe obesity. In: Mason EE (ed) Problems in general surgery. Philadelphia: Lippincott Company; 1992:280-9.

76. Mason EE, Scott D, Doherty C, Cullen JJ, Rodriguez EM, Maher JW, et al. Vertical banded gastroplasty in the severely obese under the age of twenty-one. Obes Surg 1995;5(1):23-33.

77. Mathus-Vliegen EM, Tytgat GN, Veldhuyzen-Offermans EA. Intragastric balloon in the treatment of super-morbid obesity. Double-blind, sham-controlled, crossover evaluation of 500-milliliter balloon. Gastroenterology 1990;99(2):362-9.

78. Meshkinpour H, Hsu D, Farivar S. Effect of gastric bubble as a weight reduction device: a controlled, crossover study. Gastroenterology 1988;95(3):589-92.

79. Miller K, Hell E. Laparoscopic adjustable gastric banding: a prospective 4-year followup study. Obes Surg 1999;9(2):183-7.

80. Mitchell JE, Lancaster KL, Burgard AM, Howell LM, Krahn DD, Crosby RD, et al. Long-term follow-up of patients' status after gastric bypass. Obes Surg 2001;11:464-8.

81. Murr MM, Balsiger BM, Kennedy FP, Mai JL, Sarr MG. Malabsorptive procedures for severe obesity: comparison of pancreaticobiliary bypass and very long limb Roux-en-Y gastric bypass. J Gastrointest Surg 1999;3(6):607-12.

82. Näslund E, Backman L, Granström L, Stockeld D. Seven year results of vertical banded gastroplasty for morbid obesity. Eur J Surg 1997;163(4):281-6.

83. Näslund E, Freedman J, Lagergren J, Stockeld D, Granström L. Three-year results of laparoscopic vertical banded gastroplasty. Obes Surg 1999;9(4):369-73.

84. Näslund I. The size of the gastric outlet and the outcome of surgery for obesity. Acta Chir Scand 1986; 152:205-10.

85. Näslund I. Gastric bypass versus gastroplasty. A prospective study of differences in two surgical procedures for morbid obesity. Acta Chir Scand – Suppl 1987;536:1-60.

86. Näslund I. Effects and side-effects of obesity surgery in patients with BMI below or above 40 kg/m² in the SOS – (Swedish Obese Subjects) – study. In: Guy-Grand B, Ailhaud G (eds.) Progress in Obesity Research:8. London: John Libbey Company; 1999:815-21.

87. Näslund I, Wickbom G, Christoffersson E, Agren G. A prospective randomized comparison of gastric bypass and gastroplasty. Complications and early results. Acta Chir Scand 1986;152:681-9.

88. Nguyen NT, Fleming AW, Singh A, Lee SJ, Goldman C, Wolfe BM. Evaluation of core temperature during laparoscopic and open gastric bypass. Obes Surg 2001;11:570-5.

89. Nguyen NT, Goldman C, Rosenquist CJ, Arango A, Cole CJ, Lee SJ, et al. Laparoscopic versus open gastric bypass: a randomized study of outcomes, quality of life, and costs. Ann Surg 2001;234(3): 279-89; discussion 89-91.

90. Nguyen NT, Ho HS, Palmer LS, Wolfe BM. A comparison study of laparoscopic versus open gastric bypass for morbid obesity. J Am Coll Surg 2000;191(2):149-55; discussion 55-7.

91. Nguyen NT, Lee SL, Anderson JT, Palmer LS, Canet F, Wolfe BM. Evaluation of intra-abdominal pressure after laparoscopic and open gastric bypass. Obes Surg 2001;11(1):40-5.

92. Nguyen NT, Lee SL, Goldman C, Fleming N, Arango A, McFall R, et al. Comparison of pulmonary function and postoperative pain after laparoscopic versus open gastric bypass: a randomized trial. J Am Coll Surg 2001;192(4):469-76; discussion 76-7.

93. Nguyen NT, Neuhaus AM, Ho HS, Palmer LS, Furdui GG, Wolfe BM. A prospective evaluation of intracorporeal laparoscopic small bowel anastomosis during gastric bypass. Obes Surg 2001;11(2):196-9.

94. Nguyen NT, Owings JT, Gosselin R, Pevec WC, Lee SJ, Goldman C, et al. Systemic coagulation and fibrinolysis after laparoscopic and open gastric bypass. Arch Surg 2001;136(8):909-16.

95. O'Brien P, Brown W, Dixon J. Revisional surgery for morbid obesity – conversion to the Lap-Band system. Obes Surg 2000;10(6):557-63.

96. O'Brien PE, Brown WA, Smith A, McMurrick PJ, Stephens M. Prospective study of a laparoscopically placed, adjustable gastric band in the treatment of morbid obesity. Br J Surg 1999;86(1):113-8.

97. O'Leary JP. Gastrointestinal malabsorptive procedures. Am J Clin Nutr 1992;55(2 Suppl):567S-70S.

98. Payne JH, De Wind L, Commons R. Metabolic observations in patients with jejunocolic shunts. Am J Surg 1963;106:273-89.

99. Payne JH, DeWind LT. Surgical treatment of obesity. Am J Surg 1969;118(2):141-7.

100. Pories WJ, Caro JF, Flickinger EG, Meelheim HD, Swanson MS. The control of diabetes mellitus (NIDDM) in the morbidly obese with the Greenville Gastric Bypass. Ann Surg 1987;206(3):316-23.

101. Pories WJ, Flickinger EG, Meelheim D, Van Rij AM, Thomas FT. The effectiveness of gastric bypass over gastric partition in morbid obesity: consequence of distal gastric and duodenal exclusion. Ann Surg 1982;196(4):389-99.

102. Rabkin RA. Distal gastric bypass/duodenal switch procedure, Roux-en-Y gastric bypass and biliopancreatic diversion in a community practice. Obes Surg 1998;8(1):53-9.

103. Ramhamadany EM, Fowler J, Baird IM. Effect of the gastric balloon versus sham procedure on weight loss in obese subjects. Gut 1989;30(8):1054-7.

104. Ramsey-Stewart G. Vertical banded gastroplasty for morbid obesity: weight loss at short- and long-term follow up. Aust N Z J Surg 1995;65(1):4-7.

105. Rand CS, Macgregor AM. Adolescents having obesity surgery: a 6-year follow-up. South Med J 1994;87(12):1208-13.

106. Reinhold RB. Late results of gastric bypass surgery for morbid obesity. J Am Coll Nutr 1994;13(4):326-31.

107. Ren CJ, Patterson E, Gagner M. Early results of laparoscopic biliopancreatic diversion with duodenal switch: a case series of 40 consecutive patients. Obes Surg 2000; 10(6):514-23; discussion 24.

108. Rigaud D, Trostler N, Rozen R, Vallot T, Apfelbaum M. Gastric distension, hunger and energy intake after balloon implantation in severe obesity. Int J Obes Relat Metab Disord 1995;19(7):489-95.

109. Schauer PR, Ikramuddin S, Gourash W, Ramanathan R, Luketich J. Outcomes after laparoscopic Roux-en-Y gastric bypass for morbid obesity. Ann Surg 2000;232(4):515-29.

110. Scopinaro N, Adami GF, Marinari GM, Gianetta E, Traverso E, Friedman D, et al. Biliopancreatic diversion. World J Surg 1998;22(9):936-46.

111. Scopinaro N, Gianetta E, Friedman D, Traverso E, Adami GF, Vitale B, et al. Bileopancreatic diversion for obesity. In: Mason EE, editor. Problems in general surgery. Philadelphia: Lippincott Company; 1992:362-79.

112. Sjöström CD, Hakangard AC, Lissner L, Sjöström L. Body compartment and subcutaneous adipose tissue distribution – risk factor patterns in obese subjects. Obes Res 1995;3(1):9-22.

113. Sjöström CD, Lissner L, Sjöström L. Relationships between changes in body composition and changes in cardiovascular risk factors: the SOS Intervention Study. Swedish Obese Subjects. Obes Res 1997;5(6):519-30.

114. Sjöström CD, Lissner L, Wedel H, Sjöström L. Reduction in incidence of diabetes, hypertension and lipid disturbances after intentional weight loss induced by bariatric surgery: the SOS Intervention Study. Obes Res 1999;7(5):477-84.

115. Sjöström CD, Peltonen M, Wedel H, Sjöström L. Differentiated long-term effects of intentional weight loss on diabetes and hypertension. Hypertension 2000;36(1):20-5.

116. Sjöström L. Surgical intervention as a strategy for treatment of obesity. Endocrine 2000;13(2):213-30.

117. Sjöström L. Surgical treatment of obesity. An overview and results from SOS study. In: Bouchard C, Bray GA, editors. Handbook of obesity. New York: Marcel-Dekker; 2002.

118. Sjöström L, Rissanen A, Andersen T, Boldrin M, Golay A, Koppeschaar HP, et al. Randomised placebo-controlled trial of orlistat for weight loss and prevention of weight regain in obese patients. EuropeanMulticentre Orlistat Study Group. Lancet 1998;352(9123):167-72.

119. Stokholm KH, Nielsen PE, Quaade F. Correlation between initial blood pressure and blood pressure decrease after weight loss: A study in patients with jejunoileal bypass versus medical treatment for morbid obesity. Int J Obes 1982;6(3):307-12.

120. Strauss RS, Bradley LJ, Brolin RE. Gastric bypass surgery in adolescents with morbid obesity. J Pediatr 2001;138(4):499-504.

121. Sugerman HJ, Londrey GL, Kellum JM, Wolf L, Liszka T, Engle KM, et al. Weight loss with vertical banded gastroplasty and Roux-Y gastric bypass for morbid obesity with selective versus random assignment. Am J Surg 1989;157(1):93-102.

122. Sugerman HJ, Starkey JV, Birkenhauer R. A randomized prospective trial of gastric bypass versus vertical banded gastroplasty for morbid obesity and their effects on sweets versus non-sweets eaters. Ann Surg 1987;205(6):613-24.

123. Sullivan M, Karlsson J, Sjöström L, Backman L, Bengtsson C, Bouchard C, et al. Swedish obese subjects (SOS) – an intervention study of obesity. Baseline evaluation of health and psychosocial functioning in the first 1743 subjects examined. Int J Obes Relat Metab Disord 1993;17(9): 503-12.

124. Sullivan M, Karlsson J, Sjöström L, Taft C. Why quality of life measures should be used in the treatment of patients with obesity. In: Bjorntorp B (ed.) International textbook of obesity. Chichester: John Wiley and Sons; 2001:485-510.

125. Suter M, Bettschart V, Giusti V, Heraief E, Jayet A. A 3-year experience with

laparoscopic gastric banding for obesity. Surg Endosc 2000;14(6):532-6.

126. Suter M, Giusti V, Heraief E, Jayet C, Jayet A. Early results of laparoscopic gastric banding compared with open vertical banded gastroplasty. Obes Surg 1999;9(4):374-80.

127. Sweet W. Vertical banded gastroplasty: Stable trends in weight control at 10 or more years. Obes Surg 1994;4:149-52.

128. Svenheden KE, Åkesson LA, Holmdahl C, Näslund I. Staple disruption in vertical banded gastroplasty. Obes Surg 1997;7(2):136-8; discussion 9-41.

129. Valen B, Munk AC. Long term effects of gastric banding for weight reduction. Norwegian. Tidsskr Nor Laegeforing 2000;120(17):1995-6.

130. van de Weijgert EJ, Ruseler CH, Elte JW. Long-term follow-up after gastric surgery for morbid obesity: preoperative weight loss improves the long-term control of morbid obesity after vertical banded gastroplasty. Obes Surg 1999;9(5):426-32.

131. van Gemert WG, Greve JW, Soeters PB. Long-term results of vertical banded gastroplasty: Marlex versus Dacron banding. Obes Surg 1997;7(2):128-35.

132. Verselewel de Witt, Hamer PC, Hunfeld MA, Tuinebreijer WE. Obesity surgery: discouraging long term results with Mason's vertical banded gastroplasty. Eur J Surg 1999;165(9):855-60.

133. Westling A, Bjurling K, Ohrvall M, Gustavsson S. Silicone-adjustable gastric banding: disappointing results. Obes Surg 1998;8(4):467-74.

134. Westling A, Gustavsson S. Laparoscopic vs open Roux-en-Y gastric bypass: a prospective, randomized trial. Obes Surg 2001;11:284-92.

135. de Wit LT, Mathus-Vliegen L, Hey C, Rademaker B, Gouma DJ, Obertop H. Open versus laparoscopic adjustable silicone gastric banding: a prospective randomized trial for treatment of morbid obesity. Ann Surg 1999;230(6):800-5; discussion 5-7.

136. Wittgrove AC, Clark GW. Laparoscopic gastric bypass, Roux-en-Y 500 patients: technique and results, with 3–60 month follow-up. Obes Surg 2000;10(3):233-9.

137. Yale CE. Gastric surgery for morbid obesity. Complications and long-term weight control. Arch Surg 1989;124(8):941-6.

4.7
Alternative Medicine

Summary

Since conventional treatment of obesity is often unsuccessful in the long term, obese people often turn to the treatment methods found in alternative medicine, e. g., vinegar, acupuncture, herbs, and aromatherapy. The following section reviews the scientific evidence available on these treatment methods.

Method: In addition to the previously described literature search, a new and expanded search was performed in numerous databases. Chinese databases were comprehensively reviewed, as were many Internet pages. The inclusion criteria were broader than those applied in the rest of the report. However, uniform measures were used to review the studies, and conclusions were drawn based on the principles applied to the report as a whole.

Results: The search yielded 517 published studies, of which 81 were found to be original studies. Of these, only 11 met the established minimum criteria. Most of the excluded studies reported on followup times that were too short, usually only a few weeks. Of the studies accepted, 3 presented medium quality and 8 presented low quality. Two of the studies presenting medium quality were on hypnosis. The subjects were followed for 1.5 to 2 years. One study showed significant positive results while the second, smaller study did not. Two studies of low quality were positive. Although none of the conclusions could be confirmed, there is a tendency for hypnosis to enhance the effects of behavior therapy. Four studies on acupuncture presented low or very low quality, which renders it impossible to draw conclusions. This was also the case for a study on chromium treatment and one on aromatherapy. One study presenting medium quality on chromium-enhanced dietary supplements after weight loss showed no significant effects in terms of permanent weight loss. The review of Chinese databases yielded 50 references, but none of these studies presented significant results upon which to base conclusions.

Conclusions: No conclusions can be drawn concerning the effects of any alternative medical treatment for obesity, despite an extensive literature search and review of studies selected on broad inclusion criteria.

4.7.1
Introduction

Conventional treatment for obesity often fails in the longer term, and many persons who have been dieting return to their original weight with time. People with weight problems often want to test alternative treatment methods after having made repeated, and failed, attempts to lose weight. These alternatives are often advertised in unrealistically positive terms. It is difficult to identify what is actually of proven value, what is hopeful, and what is pure marketing.

The use of alternative medical health care has increased since the 1980s. A study in one major city (Stockholm) found that 22 % of the population had visited a provider of alternative medicine. An interview survey from year 2000 showed, however, that 49 % stated that they had, at some time, visited what they would call a provider of alternative or complementary medical care [3]. Hence, it was judged to be of value to systematically study the scientific basis for alternative medical treatment of obesity.

The field of alternative medicine offers a very wide variety of approaches and treatment methods. When it comes to treating obesity, however, only a limited number of therapies are presented in scientific magazines and the general press. The most common methods are described briefly here.

4.7.2
Definition of Alternative Medicine

Alternative medicine is difficult to define and is clearly dependent on culture and time; e. g., it is not defined in the same way in China as it is in some Western nations. There has been a shift toward using the term "complementary medicine" instead of "alternative medicine".

One review article presented a definition of alternative medicine based on exclusion [5].

Thus, alternative medical treatment of obesity is everything that is not

1. A drug currently approved by the FDA (Food and Drug Administration in the United States) or a drug under development by a pharmaceutical company
2. Surgery
3. Cognitive or behavior therapy methods to enhance weight loss by diet and exercise habits.

The definition used in the following discussion is in accordance with that used by the Cochrane Collaboration:

"Complementary or alternative medicine includes all forms of health care which – in a particular society or in a particular culture during a particular historical period – exists outside the politically predominant health care system" [3].

4.7.3
Alternative Medicine Methods Used to Treat Obesity

Acupuncture is a method used in traditional Chinese medicine (which also involves herbs and exercise). The theoretical basis is an ancient philosophical view of health as a balance of life energy flowing in the body. This flow takes place along "meridians" and can be influenced at the points where these meridians meet. At times, modern researchers use explanatory models where acupuncture influences hormone and nervous systems by the use of the needles on peripheral nerve endings. More recently, acupuncture has won respect in western medicine, mainly applied to pain relief. Reported side effects from acupuncture have been systematically reviewed up to 1996 [13]. Infections dominated, but occasional cases of lung puncture, impaired pacemaker function, etc. have been described.

Acupressure is a form of therapy that influences the same points as in acupuncture, but pressure is used instead of needles.

Aroma therapy. Scents are the unifying factor, e. g., massage using scented oils.

Ayurvedic medicine is based on traditional Indian teachings having roots many thousands of years ago. Herbs are the basis for treatment. Ayurvedic medicine exists in parallel with western medicine in India. A herb used in ayurvedic medicine for weight loss is commiphora mukul (also called guggul). The mode of action usually claimed is that the high iodine content increases the release of thyroid hormone, which causes an increase in metabolism. There are no reports on side effects [22].

Caffeine is said to stimulate weight loss by increasing heat production and possibly by increasing the degradation of fat in the adipose tissue via an increase in the activity in the nervous system. Caffeine in high doses has side effects, e. g., nervousness, anxiety, problems in the gastrointestinal tract, and cardiac dysrhythmia. It is also addictive [10].

Calcium exists in high levels in bone and in the diet. Studies indicate that a high intake of calcium correlates with a lower risk of overweight [9, 24].

Capsaicin is the agent that gives chili its strong taste. Any weight loss associated with capsaicin and ginger is explained by the increase in heat production after "hot" meals. Also, starting a meal with a spicy first course is thought to reduce the intake of food [10].

Carnitine is an amino acid needed to transport fat into the cells, where it is combusted to generate energy. The body can itself produce carnitine from other amino acids [24].

Chitosan consists of ground shells from crab, shrimp, and lobster. It is claimed that the active substance can bind the fat of the food and thereby inhibit the uptake of fat in the bowel. Hence, the effect is said to be similar to that of orlistat [10].

Chromium is a metal and a trace element in the body needed for normal energy metabolism processes. **Chromium picolinate** is said to increase satiety and increase the expenditure of energy by increased heat production [10].

Conjugated linoleic acid (CLA) is a fatty acid with a somewhat different structure from that of common linoleic acid, which is a building block in fat molecules. Conjugated linoleic acid inhibits an enzyme needed to deposit fat, increases the oxidative process, and contains transfatty acids, which in higher doses may negatively influence some health parameters [24, 26].

Guarana is a plant from which Brazilian Indians brew a stimulating drink. This contains 2 to 3 times as much caffeine as coffee.

Hydroxycitric acid exists naturally in garcinia cambogia, a fruit, and has been shown to reduce appetite and food intake in animal studies. The mode of action might be inhibition of an enzyme needed for new formation of fatty acids in the body. However, it is uncertain how great an impact this process has on storage of fat in the body. Reported side effects of higher doses include a strong laxative effect, abdominal pain, and vomiting [22].

Hypnosis is a method of treating different types of problems by putting the patient in a state of consciousness where he or she is susceptible to suggestion. For example, to treat obesity, the hypnotherapist might say to the patient in trance how he/she should alter his/her dietary habits or attitudes towards him/herself and to food. There are reports of relatively serious side effects in hypnosis, e. g., anxiety and split personality, but the extent to which they occur is uncertain [5].

Local treatment involving lotions have been tested as a means to reduce the local collection of unwanted fat deposits. These lotions contain pharmacological agents that are intended to penetrate the skin and increase fat mobilization in the underlying adipose tissue. **Liposuction** is also a method used for local removal of fat deposits. Neither treatment with lotions nor liposuction can be considered as treatments for obesity. Likewise, since they do not really qualify as alternative medicine, these methods are not addressed further here.

Pyruvate is an agent formed during the process of sugar degradation in the cells. There is no explanatory model for the claimed effect of weight loss, nor are there any reports of side effects [5].

Vinegar has been promoted in different contexts as a miracle cure for obesity. Vinegar is thought to flatten the blood sugar curve after a meal and prolong satiety. There are no data on side effects [24].

4.7.4
Costs

Costs related to the various treatment methods in alternative medicine vary widely by method and by country. Drinking vinegar mixed with water prior to a meal is not costly. However, vinegar is sold in capsule form by health food stores at a substantially higher cost per month. Four weeks of chitosan treatment cost approximately 25 USD, while 4 weeks of Xenical® treatment (which has a proven effect) may cost 65 USD [2]. Examples of more expensive methods include hypnosis and acupuncture, both of which require active treatment by a therapist. The cost of psychotherapy can range from 50 to 80 USD or more for 45 minutes of individual therapy. Studies of hypnosis report that at least five sessions have been given at a cost of approximately 250 USD for the series.

4.7.5
Methods

The literature search was based on the strategy described in the "Methods" section of Chapter 2. The search terms used were "obesity" and "alternative medicine". The MEDLINE, Cochrane Library, and Embase databases were originally searched for material published up to 1998. The search was later complemented in December of 2001. To ensure comprehensiveness, the search included both general search terms and specific terms concerning the different treatment methods described

Table 4.12 Search terms used in the database search.

Obesity (MeSH term)	Electroacupuncture (MeSH term)
Overweight	Aroma therapy
Therapy	Ayurvedic medicine
Alternative medicine (MeSH term)	Chitosan
Anti obesity agent	Chitin (MeSH term)
Chiropractic	Guarana
Anthroposophy	Caffeine (MeSH term)
Anthroposophic	Hydroxycitric acid
Homeopathy	Hypnosis (MeSH term)
Homeopathic	Calcium/therapeutic use (MeSH term)
Reflexotherapy	Capsaicin
Plants (MeSH term)	Carnitine (MeSH term)
Plants, medicinal (MeSH term)	Linoleic acids (MeSH term)
Medicine, herbal (MeSH term)	Conjugated linoleic acids, CLA
Commiphora	Chromium (MeSH term)
Ginger	Pyruvate
Garcinia	Vinegar
Acupuncture (MeSH term)	Acetic acid/therapeutic use (MeSH term)
Acupressure (MeSH term)	

above in this Section. The complementary search included MEDLINE (1966–2001), SweMed+ (1977–2001), Amed (former CATS, 1985–2001), and the Cochrane Controlled Trials Register (2001). The search terms used are presented in Table 4.12.

Five Internet addresses recommended in a review article, and 20 additional addresses were searched [22]. Also included were articles of potential interest from the reference lists from five review articles [5, 9-11, 22] and other relevant studies.

4.7.6
Critical Review of Studies

Having eliminated the irrelevant publications, an instrument was needed to distinguish which of the remaining studies were of sufficient quality to warrant further critical review. To ensure that interesting findings were not overlooked, the requirements here were somewhat less stringent than in other parts of the report. Furthermore, a survey was conducted to determine the number and quality of the alternative medicine studies. The following minimum criteria were established to identify the studies which could proceed toward a more thorough review:

1. Intervention using alternative medicine to treat obesity or overweight according to established definitions
2. Commercially available
3. Followup time of at least 6 months
4. Outcome measures: mortality, morbidity, quality of life, or body weight
5. The effects of alternative medicine must be distinguishable from other effects of concurrent interventions, e. g., diet and exercise. (Note that a control group was not required for inclusion).

To move forward in the review process, a study was first required to meet the first two criteria. If it did, and if it followed patients for 6 months or more, it moved on for further evaluation. Reasons for excluding a study were recorded. Studies that met the criteria received a full evaluation.

Hence, the inclusion criteria for these studies were broader than the criteria that applied to the rest of this report, but the evidence presented was judged according to the same standards. Any conclusions were also assessed in the manner described under the methods section in Chapter 2.

4.7.7
Results

The literature search yielded 517 references. These were reviewed in part to identify the original studies of interest. Duplicate articles were then eliminated as were editorials, comments, letters to the editor, review articles, and case studies (however, not case series), and animal studies. A few studies in Chinese were excluded since these were reviewed separately. References without a summary in the database were considered based on their title and classification, and the article was retrieved for evaluation in cases of uncertainty.

As a result of the elimination process, 95 of the 517 articles remained. Another 14 studies on caffeine were excluded since the effects of caffeine could not be distinguished from the effects of ephedrine or phenylpropanolamine, which are registered as pharmaceutical agents. With the 81 studies that remained, the next phase involved checking whether or not the minimum criteria were fulfilled.

Table 4.13 summarizes the number of studies reviewed by type of treatment and the reason(s) for exclusion. Of the 81 studies, 70 were excluded and 11 accepted. Of the excluded studies, 62 had followup times that were too short, often only a few weeks. Of the remaining studies, 3 were excluded because the effects of the alternative method could not be distinguished from the effects of other concurrent interventions. One study involved fewer than 10 test subjects, and 4 studies used unacceptable outcome measures. The table shows that most of the studies addressed acupuncture, hypnosis, and chromium. Most of the studies that fulfilled the minimum criteria were also within these categories. Only isolated studies in other treatment areas were identified.

4.7.8
Studies Fulfilling the Minimum Criteria

Of the 11 studies that met the minimum criteria, 4 were on acupuncture, 4 on hypnosis, 1 on chromium, 1 on aroma therapy, and 1 on a dietary supplement containing chromium picolinate, caffeine, carbohydrates, and soluble fibers. Three studies presented medium quality, and the remainder presented low quality. A review of the studies is given below and in Tables 4.14–4.17.

Table 4.13 Primarily selected studies addressing different treatment methods in alternative medicine and the number of studies that did not meet the minimum criteria. (Complete reference list of the studies in the table is available from SBU.)

Treatment method	Primarily selected studies No.	Criteria were not met Short followup period	Reason Endpoint not relevant	Other	Criteria were met Number
Acupuncture/ Acupressure	34	30	25	2	3	4
Hypnosis	12	8	7	0	1	4
Chromium	6	5	5	0	0	1
Pyruvate	5	5	5	0	0	0
Ayurvedic medicine (including Guggul/ Commiphora Mukul)	4	4	3	1	0	0
Chitin (Chitosan)	4	4	4	0	0	0
Conjugated linoleic acid (CLA)	4	4	3	1	0	0
Traditional Chinese medicine	3	3	3	0	0	0
Caffeine (Guarana)	2	2	2	0	0	0
Aroma therapy	1	0	0	0	0	1
Homeopathy	1	1	1	0	0	0
Hydroxycitric acid (Garcinia)	1	1	1	0	0	0
Hydroxycitric acid/ caffeine	1	1	1	0	0	0
Chromium/capsaicin (chili pepper)	1	1	1	0	0	0
Chromium/caffeine	1	0	0	0	0	1
L-carnitine	1	1	1	0	0	0
Ginger	0	0	0	0	0	0
Calcium	0	0	0	0	0	0
Vinegar	0	0	0	0	0	0
Total	81	70	62	4	4	11

4.7.8.1 Acupuncture

Acupuncture was used to treat 42 obese patients from Nigeria in a case study by Lei (1988, see Table 4.14). Obesity was defined as a body weight of 10 % above the standard weight for body height [18]. After three treatment sessions of 1 month each, the results were categorized as weight loss less than 1 kg, 1–5 kg, or more than 5 kg. The author also reported on a followup study of 7 patients from the group with the best result and 11 patients from the mid-range group. After 6 months, these 18 subjects had regained 0.75 kg on average. The study presents little detail, a high dropout rate, and no statistical analysis.

Liu et al. reported on a case study of traditional Chinese medicine from Nanjing College (1992) [19]. In total, 380 participants were treated by individualized ear and body acupuncture, using 1–3 treatment sessions of approximately 1 month each. Only the 167 participants who had not received any other treatment during

Table 4.14 Review of acupuncture studies that met the minimum criteria.

Author Year Reference Country	Treatment method	Study design Duration (Followup)	Study population Number (No. followed up) Gender distribution (% w) Recruitment Weight classification
Lei Z 1988 [18] China	Acupuncture	Case series 1–3 months (6 months after completed treatment)	n = 42 (18) 81 % women Outpatients At least 10 % overweight
Liu Z et al. 1992 [19] China	Acupuncture	Case series 1–3 months (1 year)	n = 380 (167) 92 % women Outpatients At least 20 % overweight
Zhan J 1993 [31] China	Acupuncture	Case series + RCT 10 days (6 months, 1 year)	n = 393 (case series) n = 76 (RCT) 100 % women (RCT) At least 20 % overweight
Tong et al. 1994 [30] China	Acupuncture, cupping, magnet therapy	CT 1–6 months (1 year)	n = 356 (50) 66 % women Random selection of outpatients Mean overweight 31.2 %

RCT = Randomized Controlled Trial
CT = Controlled Trial, not randomized
W = Women

the year were followed up. After 1 year, these participants had lost, on average, 4.27 kg.

In 1993, Zhan treated a group of 393 patients by ear acupressure [31]. The same study included a smaller test where 76 persons were randomized to ear acupressure or to a control group. The treatment lasted for 10 days. The treatment group lost 2.4 kg and the control group 0.8 kg, a statistically significant difference. After 1 year, 27 patients were followed up, reflecting a high dropout rate. At followup, the patients' weight was within 1.5 kg of the weight after treatment. Hence, the treatment appears to have had some lasting effect.

Tong et al. studied 356 patients who were treated either by ear and body acupuncture or by magnetic therapy (ear acupressure with magnetic spheres) [30]. No information was given on how the patients were assigned to groups. The patients were given 1–6 treatment sessions of about 1 month each. The results reflect

Intervention in respective group	Results	Study quality Comments
Individualized acupuncture	Weight loss after 3 treatment sessions 1. 14 patients >5 kg 2. 17 patients 1–5 kg 3. 1 patients <1 kg Followup of 7 patients from Group 1 and 11 patients from Group 2, 6 months after treatment Weight gain average 0.75 kg	Low Dropout 57 % at followup Outcome report only reports 32 patients. Misprint in article? Statistical analysis lacking
Individualized acupuncture + moxibustion	Original weight: 72.3 (10.36) kg After 1 year: 68.03 (10.14) kg Difference: −4.27 kg	Low Of 380 treated the 167 who did not receive any other treatment for overweight during the year were followed up
Case series: Individualized ear acupressure RCT: 1. Individualized ear acupressure 2. No treatment	After treatment 1. −2.4 (0.4) kg 2. −0.8 (0.1) kg After 6 months (n = 58) and 1 year (n = 27) all stayed within 1.5 kg weight gain	Low Dropout cannot be calculated since it is not apparent to which group the patients follwed up belonged
1. Acupuncture + cupping 2. Magnet therapy	After 1–6 treatment sessions (% of the patients who lost at least 5 kg): 1. 97.2 % 2. 93.8 % After 1 year (50 patients): 47 patients no weight gain	Low 50 followed up of 356 treated. No statistical analysis. Very briefly reported study

the groups directly after completed treatment, but 50 patients were also followed up 1 year after treatment start and 47 patients had maintained their weight loss. Statistical analysis is lacking, and the dropout rate at followup was high and undefined.

4.7.8.2 Hypnosis

In 1981, Goldstein compared two groups treated with hypnosis to a control group treated with behavior therapy (Table 4.15) [14]. One of the groups treated with hypnosis was given "evidence" (i. e., arm levitation) of being in a trance. Followup after 6 months showed statistically significant differences between the "evidence group" and the others, but no differences were shown between the second hypnosis group and the behavior group. The weight loss in all groups was clinically relevant, but the followup time was short.

Table 4.15   Review of studies on hypnosis that met the minimum criteria.

Author Year Reference Country	Treatment method	Study design Duration (Followup)	Study population Number (No. followed up) Gender distribution (% w) Recruitment Weight classification
Goldstein Y 1981 [14] USA	Hypnosis	RCT 4 weeks (6 months)	n=73 (60) 100 % women Patients were referred to psychologist for weight loss
Bolocofsky DN et al. 1985 [7] USA	Hypnosis	RCT 9 weeks (6 months, 2 years)	n=156 (109) 99 % women Advertisement 0.4 %–104.7 % overweight
Cochrane G et al. 1986 [8] Canada	Hypnosis	RCT 4 weeks (6 months)	n=60 (54) 100 % women Advertisement At least 20 % overweight according to MHWT
Stradling J et al. 1998 [29] Great Britain	Hypnosis	RCT 1 month (3, 6, 9, 12, 15 and 18 months)	n=60 (46) 18 % women Advertisement, sleep apnea syndrome treated by positive pressure BMI >30

RCT = Randomized Controlled Trial
W = Women
MHWT = Metropolitan Height and Weight Tables
SEM = Standard Error of the Mean
SD = Standard Deviation
1 pound = approx. 0.45 kg

A study by Bolocofsky et al. compared 9 weeks of hypnosis treatment to behavioral therapy [7]. Followup took place after 6 months and again after 2 years. The study was randomized, but not blinded, and the number of patients (156 persons) was relatively high. After completed treatment, the outcome was the same in both groups, but at 2-year followup the weight reduction was 9.9 kg in the group receiving hypnosis versus 3.1 kg in the group receiving behavior therapy. The difference is statistically significant. However, the study has deficiencies, mainly a dropout of 30 %, which was equally high in both groups.

In 1986, a three-armed randomized study was performed in Canada where 24 hours of hypnosis treatment and followup self-hypnosis by means of a cassette tape was compared to 24 hours of hypnosis without a cassette tape and no treatment [8]. Each group contained 20 patients. Followup was after 6 months. At that time, the two treatment groups had lost 17–18 pounds (7.7–8.2 kg) compared to the 0.5 pounds (0.23 kg) in the control group. Three

Intervention in respective group	Results	Study quality Comments
1. Hypnosis with determination of trance + behavior therapy 2. Hypnosis without determination of trance + behavior therapy 3. Behavior therapy only	Weight loss (mean; median) after 6 months 1. 36.2*; 39.3* pounds 2. 24.2; 24.7 pounds 3. 25.3; 25,6 pounds	Low Dropout 18 %
1. Hypnosis + behavior therapy once/week 2. Behavior therapy only once/week	9 weeks, 6 months, 2 years 1. −4.0, −8.2*, −9.9* kg 2. −3.0, −3.2, −3.1 kg	Medium Dropout 30 %
1. Hypnosis (24 h) + cassette 2. Hypnosis only (24 h) 3. No treatment	After 1 month and 6 months, mean 1. −6.53*, −17.82* 2. −8.00*, −17.12* 3. +1.50, −0.50 No weight unit stated in the study	Low Droput 10 % No treatment compared to 24 h of active treatment
1. Stress-reducing hypnosis + diet and exercise advice 2. Eating attitude change hypnosis + dietary and exercise advice 3. Dietary and exercise advice only	After 1 year and 18 months, % 1. −2.73, −3.33 2. −1.90, −1.23 3. −0.67, −2.00 After 18 months (kg) 1. −3.8 2. −1.6 3. −3.1	Medium Dropout 25 % No significant difference between the groups at any individual measure point, only Group 1 showed a significant weight loss at 18 months

persons in the treatment group and none in the control group dropped out. The possibility that this influenced the outcome cannot be excluded. One group received no treatment, and hence there was no control for nonspecific placebo effects.

A study by Stradling et al. in 1998 randomized 60 participants to two different groups with hypnosis and to a control group [29]. Concurrently, general advice was given on diet and exercise. The 20 participants in the control group received only advice on diet and exercise. Those treated with hypnosis also received a cassette for self-hypnosis after the active treatment. All had a BMI above 30 and were treated for obstructive sleep apnea syndrome. Followup was done on several occasions up until 18 months after the start of the study. No statistically significant differences between the groups could be shown at any of the followups. Only one of the groups treated with hypnosis (i.e., stress-reducing hypnosis) had a statistically significant remaining weight loss at 18-month followup.

Table 4.16 Review of other studies that met the minimum criteria.

Author Year Reference Country	Treatment method	Study design Duration (Followup)	Study population Number (No. followed up) Gender distribution (% w) Recruitment Weight classification
Bahadori B et al. 1997 [6] Austria	Chromium	RCT 6 months	n=36 (24) 80% women BMI >27
Pasman WJ et al. 1997 [25] The Netherlands	Chromium caffeine, dietary fiber	RCT 16 months	n=49 (33) 100% women BMI 31.2
Hirsch AR et al. 1995 [15] USA	Aroma therapy	Uncontrolled 6 months	n=3 193 86% women At least 10 pounds overweight

RCT = Randomized Controlled Trial
VLCD = Very Low Calorie Diet
LBM = Lean Body Mass
W = Women
1 pound = approx. 0.45 kg

4.7.8.3 Other Studies

The only refined study on chromium treatment was published in German in 1997 (Table 4.16) [6]. The study randomized 36 overweight persons to three groups. Initially, all were given VLCD (800 kcal/day for 8 weeks), later followed by chromium picolinate or chromium yeast equivalent to 200 µg chromium/day or placebo until followup after 18 weeks (6 months after study start). No differences in BMI could be shown between the groups at followup.

In 1997, Pasman et al. studied the weight-preserving effect of a dietary supplement for 14 months after an 8-week program on VLCD [25]. The supplement contained 50 g carbohydrates, 200 µg chromium picolinate, 20 g soluble dietary fiber, and 100 mg caffeine. This was compared to a group who received only 50 g carbohydrates after the 8 weeks and to a control group who received no treatment supplement afterward. The patients were randomly distributed, and the supplement was assigned via a double-blind procedure. There were 49 patients at the start of the study, but the analysis included only the 33 who completed the study. Hence, the chance of identifying differences among the three groups was low. Mean weight loss after 8 weeks of caloric reduction was 9 kg. The results are presented as a percentage of the weight loss at the different followup times. No statis-

Intervention in respective group	Results	Study quality Comments
8 weeks VLCD, then: 1. 200 µg chromium (chromium picolinate) + fiber supplement 2. 200 µg chromium (chromium yeast) + fiber supplement 3. Fiber supplement only	Weight loss after 6 months, not statistically significant (BMI) LBM increased in 1. by 0.8 (2.7) kg	Low Dropout 33 %
8 weeks VLCD, then: 1. Supplement of carbohydrates, caffeine, chromium picolinate and soluble fibers 2. Suppl. of carbohydrates only 3. No treatment	All reduced to 89.5 % of the original body weight after 8 weeks. At 16 months % of regained weight loss 1. 51.1 2. 68.1 3. 85.6	Medium Dropout 33 %
Inhalation of aromatic mixture at feeling of hunger, instructed not to change dietary and exercise habits	Weight loss in selected group −4.7 pounds/month (2.1 % of the body weight)	Low The results apply to a subgroup, size not reported

tically significant difference could be shown between the groups at the final followup 16 months after the study started.

In a study from 1995, Hirsch and Gomez tried giving an inhaler containing a scent (peppermint, banana, or green apple) to a large number of test subjects who wanted to lose weight [15]. This agent was changed once per month, and the subjects were instructed to inhale three times in each nostril when they felt hungry. Otherwise, the test subjects were instructed not change their diet or exercise habits. There was no control group. The characteristics of the test subjects were surveyed by psychological tests and self-rating forms, and their sense of smell was tested. The result after 6 months is reported as a mean value of weight loss in a selected group. That group fulfilled most of the conditions which, in the study, had shown a statistical association with successful weight loss, e. g., eating 2–4 meals per day, feeling guilty for eating too much but not for one's self as a person. Frequent use of the inhaler showed a statistical association with weight loss, but this could also be interpreted as a measure of the motivation to lose weight.

4.7.8.4 **Discussion and Conclusionsalternative treatments**

In summary, 11 studies were reviewed in greater detail: 4 on acupuncture, 4 on hypnosis, 1 on chromium, 1 on aroma therapy, and 1 on dietary supplements containing chromium picolinate, caffeine, carbohydrates, and soluble fibers. Three studies were found to present medium quality and the remainder presented low quality. Two studies on hypnosis presented medium quality, one of which showed a positive result for hypnosis. The other one did not present any statistically significant results. The two studies with low quality were positive toward hypnosis. No confirmed conclusions can be drawn as to whether or not hypnosis is an active treatment for obesity. However, hypnosis shows a tendency toward enhancing the effects achieved by behavior therapy.

All of the acupuncture studies had major weaknesses and presented low quality. Hence, no conclusions could be drawn. The dietary supplement study presented medium quality, but could not demonstrate any positive treatment effects. The scientific foundation is either too small or of insufficient quality to draw any conclusions on the benefits of alternative medicine in the treatment of obesity.

Apart from the original studies, a few meta-analyses and critical reviews were also found. One of these reviewed the general effects of hypnosis and seemed to observe a strong effect on obesity [17]. A new analysis that addressed only this field confirmed the findings [16]. Six studies were included, and a total weight loss of 5.37 kg in the intervention group was found versus 2.72 kg in the group receiving behavior therapy alone.

Allison criticized this meta-analysis and recalculated the data, whereupon the effects were considerably less certain [4]. He suggested that hypnosis yielded only a marginal additional effect beyond that from behavior therapy. Of the 6 studies analyzed by these authors, 4 were not accepted in the present report because of short followup periods. Two of the studies are included in this report, as are two other studies with longer followup periods. The conclusions differ somewhat since studies of very short duration were accepted. Valid evidence is not available that would allow a more positive interpretation of the effects than that presented in this report.

A critical review of acupuncture analyzed the four studies that had been excluded from this review because followup was no longer than 3–12 weeks [11]. Although two of these studies demonstrated better effects in the test groups, the author did not draw any conclusions on the value of acupuncture. An assessment of the effect of acupuncture on obesity, by the NHS (The National Health Service Center for Reviews and Dissemination) in York, referred to the review mentioned above and to two more recent publications [1]. These studies were also excluded because the followup periods were too short, i. e., 4 and 12 weeks, respectively [21, 27]. One of the studies reported no effect and the other reported a better effect in the test group than in the placebo group. None of the 4 studies identified were included in the reviews mentioned, and the 6 studies analyzed in the reviews were not accepted for this report. Even when combining the 10 studies and applying very low standards, there is no reliable evidence that acupuncture has any effect in the treatment of obesity.

All studies in a meta-analysis of chitosan showed some effect from chitosan, compared to placebo, as a supplement to a low-energy diet for 4 weeks [12]. The studies were performed by Italian research groups and published in the same Italian journal during a 2-year period. For this reason, independent studies are needed to confirm these results on the effect of chitosan. Since the followup period was not longer than 4 weeks in any of these studies, they were not accepted for this report.

The last meta-analysis addressed studies of calcium intake, which were originally made to study bone variables from a weight perspective [9]. The studies included a randomized controlled trial that tested a calcium supplement against placebo to determine whether the number of vertebral fractures decreased. A secondary finding was that both groups had decreased in weight during just less than 4 years of observation. Weight loss was 0.67 kg per year in the calcium group and 0.33 kg per year in the placebo group, a statistically significant difference. Hence, an association was found between a low calcium intake and overweight, but the authors expressed some reservations since it was previously shown that a low calcium intake is also an indicator for a generally poor diet.

Despite extraordinary search procedures, wide inclusion criteria, and a review of many references, there was not sufficient material of acceptable quality to permit any conclusions to be drawn. Followup time was the most common deficiency. Many studies in the field of alternative medicine report only a few weeks of observation time. Also, many of the studies were too small to have any statistical power. Furthermore, publication bias, i.e., the tendency to publish positive but not negative results, may have played a role.

Financing research in the field of alternative medicine may be a problem. Not many pharmaceutical companies have a special interest in the field. Likewise, health food companies do not have great incentive to conduct research. If an agent is found to have a sufficient medical effect, there may be interest in registering it as a pharmaceutical, and it then shifts to another market, e.g., glucosamine [23]. This dilemma should receive greater attention.

A general deficiency in the literature on alternative medicine concerns reliable facts on side effects. Such data have not been systematically collected. Hence, it becomes easy to believe that no reports on side effects means no side effects. Since many substances clearly have some effect on the body, it would be unreasonable to assume that there were not also some side effects. This is an area that needs to be more thoroughly investigated, and systematic reports are needed.

The scientific base for assessing the effects and side effects of treating obesity by alternative medicine is inadequate. Consequently, there is no scientific basis for recommending such treatment. The patients must weigh their decisions based on their perceptions of hopes, risks, and costs.

4.7.9
Overview of Recent Chinese Studies

A Chinese physician affiliated with the Project Group at SBU compiled an overview of recent Chinese studies. Since the studies were published in Chinese, only one person reviewed the text, but the SBU Project Group evaluated and interpreted the results.

4.7.9.1 Literature Search

The literature search was conducted in the China Biological Medicine database (CBM-disc) from 1995 to 2000 using the terms "obesity", "overweight", "intervention", and "treatment". Only studies published in Chinese and in Chinese medical journals were included.

The same inclusion criteria were applied in the review of Chinese studies as for other studies in alternative medicine, i.e., must address treatment methods in alternative medicine based on a given definition, must address overweight or obese subjects, and must use the same outcome measures, at least as regards weight reduction. The followup time should also be at least 6 months. However, when information on the followup time was lacking, which was often the case, these studies were also included. Weight loss that was not reported in kilograms, but as the percentage of the patients achieving an effective result, e.g., weight loss of at least 5 kg, was usually accepted.

4.7.9.2 Results

In total, 50 studies on the treatment of obesity were identified. Of these, 41 were found to address unconventional treatment methods. None of the Chinese studies on acupuncture presented in Table 4.14 were included here since these were published in English.

All studies were found to present low quality, and some did not fulfill the minimum criteria. Of the 41 studies on unconventional methods, 15 were excluded because the substances were not readily available elsewhere. Furthermore, 6 studies addressed liposuction, which is not considered to be a method for treating obesity.

Ultimately, 20 studies remained for further review (Table 4.17). Most addressed acupuncture, including ear acupressure, and other variants using plasters and various combinations. Herbal treatment and physical therapy involving vibration and electric stimulation were also studied. Upon further review, half of the selected studies were found to lack a description of both study design and outcome. Hence, these studies did not receive further review. The remaining 10 studies also presented low quality. Three of the larger studies (all without a control group) are mentioned below as examples:

Table 4.17 Primarily selected studies addressing the different Chinese therapy methods, and number that proceeded to second of review.[1]

	Description of studies and results lacking	Proceeded to 2nd phase of review	Total number
Acupuncture	3	6	9
Herbs/Tea/Mineral water	3	1	4
Umbilical plaster	–	1	1
L-carnitine	–	1	1
Qi-gong and similar	1	1	2
Physical treatments, including variants	3	–	3
Total	**10**	**10**	**10**

[1] Complete reference list of Chinese studies found is on file at SBU

1. A study of 526 persons, who were followed up for 3 to 6 months, treated obesity by using a hypodermic needle to bury catgut under acupoints. The results showed that 60 % of those treated achieved a weight loss greater than 6 kg [28].
2. A combination of electroexercise of the abdominal muscles and acupressure on the ears was administered to 152 obese individuals, who were followed up for 6 months. In 96 % of the cases, waist circumference decreased substantially to moderately [20].
3. A type of auricular plaster treatment in combination with stimulation was applied in a study of 200 persons, 90 % of whom lost more than 5 kg. No followup period was reported [32].

4.7.9.3 Discussion and Conclusions

Despite the access to a Chinese physician and the literature in Chinese databases, only a few studies on alternative medicine in obesity could be identified. The treatment methods, study design, and presentation differ considerably from Western studies, and hence they are difficult to assess. None of the studies fulfilled the established criteria used in other parts of the report, and it is impossible to draw conclusions on the effectiveness of the different treatment methods.

References Section 4.7

1. Acupuncture: NHS Centre for reviews and dissemination, University of York; 2001.
2. FASS – Läkemedel i Sverige. Stockholm: LINFO läkemedelsinformation AB; 2001.
3. Stockholmare och den komplementära medicinen: befolkningsstudie angående inställning till och användning av komplementär medicin genomförd under år 2000 i Stockholms läns landsting. Stockholm: Hälso- och sjukvårdsnämnden, Stockholms läns landsting; 2001.
4. Allison DB, Faith MS. Hypnosis as an adjunct to cognitive-behavioral psychotherapy for obesity: a meta-analytic reappraisal. J Consult Clin Psychol 1996;64(3):513-6.
5. Allison DB, Fontaine KR, et al. Alternative treatments for weight loss: a critical review. Critical Reviews in Food Science and Nutrition 2001;41(1):1-28.
6. Bahadori B, Wallner S, Schneider H, Wascher TC, Toplak H. Effect of chromium yeast and chromium picolinate on body composition of obese, non-diabetic patients during and after a formula diet. Acta Med Austriaca 1997;24(5):185-7.
7. Bolocofsky DN, Spinler D, Coulthard-Morris L. Effectiveness of hypnosis as an adjunct to behavioural weight management. J Clin Psychol 1985;41(1):35-41.
8. Cochrane G, Friesen J. Hypnotherapy in weight loss treatment. J Consult Clin Psychol 1986;54(4):489-92.
9. Davies KM, Heaney RP, et al. Calcium intake and body weight. J Clin Endocrinol Metab 2000;85(12):4635-8.
10. Egger G, Cameron-Smith D, Stanton R. The effectiveness of popular, non-prescription weight loss supplements. MJA 1999;171(6):604-8.
11. Ernst E. Acupuncture/Acupressure for weight reduction? A systematic review. Wien Klin Wochenschr 1997;109(2):60-2.
12. Ernst E. Chitosan as a treatment for body weight reduction? A meta-analysis. Perfusion 1998;11:461-5.
13. Ernst E, White A. Life-threatening adverse reactions after acupuncture? A systematic review. Pain 1997;71(2):123-6.
14. Goldstein Y. The effect of demonstrating to a subject that she is in a hypnotic trance as a variable in hypnotic interventions with obese women. Int J Clin Exp Hypn 1981;29(1):15-23.
15. Hirsch AR, Gomez R. Weight reduction through inhalation of odorants. J Neurol Orthop Med Surg 1995;16:28-31.
16. Kirsch I. Hypnotic enhancement of cognitive-behavioral weight loss treatments – another meta-reanalysis. J Consult Clin Psychol 1996;64(3):517-9.
17. Kirsch I, Montgomery G, Sapirstein G. Hypnosis as an adjunct to cognitive-behavioral psychotherapy: a meta-analysis. J Consult Clin Psychol 1995;63(2):214-20.
18. Lei Z. Treatment of 42 cases of obesity with acupuncture. J Trad Chin Med 1988;8(2):125-6.
19. Liu Z, et al. The long-term therapeutic effect of acupuncture and moxibustion in 167 cases of simple obesity. Int J Clin Acupunct 1992;3(2):99-107.

20. Mao W. Treatment of 152 cases with abdominal obesity by electroexercise and earpoints press therapy. Chinese Physical Therapy Journal 1997;20(1):30-2.

21. Mazzoni R, Mannucci E, Rizzello SM, Ricca V, Rotella CM. Failure of acupuncture in the treatment of obesity: a pilot study. Eat Weight Disord 1999;4(4):198-202.

22. Morelli V, Zoorob RJ. Alternative therapies: Part I. Depression, diabetes, obesity. American Family Physician 2000;62(5):1051-60.

23. Näsmark M. Är glukosaminets saga all? ProSana 2001(3):4-5.

24. Olsson E. Banta med piller – fungerar det? Hälsa 2001(10):18-24.

25. Pasman WJ, Westerterp-Plantenga MS, Saris WH. The effectiveness of long-term supplementation of carbohydrate, chromium, fibre and caffeine on weight maintenance. Int J Obes Relat Metab Disord 1997;21(12):1143-51.

26. Paulún F. Hur banta bäst? ProSana 2001(3):18-9.

27. Richards D, Marley J. Stimulation of auricular acupuncture points in weight loss. Aust Fam Physician 1998; 27:S73-7.

28. Sheng J, Hu B, Li J, Li H, Zhang Y, Chu L, et al. Experiences in treatment of obesity by burying catgut under acupoints. Practical Journal of Chinese Medicine Combined with Western Medicine 1998;11(4):362.

29. Stradling J, Roberts D, Wilson A, Lovelock F. Controlled trial of hypnotherapy for weight loss in patients with obstructive sleep apnoea. Int J Obes Relat Metab Disord 1998;22(3):278-81.

30. Tong S, et al. Treatment of obesity by integrating needling, cupping and magnetic therapy: a report of 356 cases. Int J Clin Acupunct 1994;5(3):337-9.

31. Zhan J. Observations on the treatment of 393 cases of obesity by semen pressure on auricular points. J Trad Chin Med 1993;13(1):27-30.

32. Zhou Y, Cheng S. 200 cases report of auricular-plaster combined with Jingluo Joanfei apparatus in the treatment of obesity. Hujian Medicine and Drug Journal 1997;19(2):122-3.

4.8
Negative Effects of Weight Loss

Complications that can arise in treating obesity with drugs or surgery were reported in Sections 4.5 and 4.6. Weight loss *per se* may also have certain negative
effects. For example, the scientific literature has documented a decrease in bone
density and an increase in the formation of gallstones.

A search of the literature in MEDLINE through December 2001 identified 19
studies on the topic, whereof 6 addressed questions about the possible negative
effects of weight loss. Five of these were randomized controlled trials. Various
combinations of the following search terms were used: "diet therapy", "alternative
medicine", "psychotherapy", "physical therapy", and "adverse effects", excluding
"obesity drug therapy" and "obesity surgery".

Results: Five studies, three of which were randomized, investigated the effects of
weight loss on bone density. One study randomized 66 men with a mean BMI of
29 to three groups, whereof one group was treated with a low-fat diet, another
group with physical activity, and a third group received no treatment [8]. Only in
the dietary group, where the average weight loss was 6.4 kg, was a reduction
(1.4 %) in bone density observed.

The effects of regular body-building exercises were assessed in a randomized
study of 21 overweight women [1]. One group received a balanced, energy-restricted diet for 24 weeks, while the other group received the diet and body-building
exercises for 90 minutes per week. In both groups, weight loss was around 19 kg,
and bone density declined in various parts of the femur by approximately 1 % and
3 % respectively.

A study of 27 postmenopausal women who had lost 10 kg after 6 months on a
balanced, low-energy diet noted that total bone density had declined by approximately 1 % [9].

The total bone density declined by approximately 2.5 % in a noncontrolled prospective study of 13 women who lost approximately 16 kg using VLCD treatment
for 10 weeks [3]. In followup 10 months later, both body weight and bone density
had returned to the original levels. Changes in bone density and body fat co-varied.
Simultaneous measurements of total bone density yielded values that were within
the reference range for women of the same age.

In summary, small but well-executed studies have shown that weight loss that
can be achieved after 6 months by nonsurgical methods involves a reduction in
bone density of a few percent (Evidence Grade 2).

Several nonrandomized studies have shown that formation of cholesterol-rich
gallstones increases in approximately 25 % of those who are overweight/obese
who had lost weight quickly [2, 6, 13]. The factors responsible are suggested to
be increased mobilization of cholesterol from the fat depots and reduced synthesis
of bile acid in the liver.

The only randomized study compared 13 patients (mean BMI 37) with two diet
regimens differing in both energy and fat content (520 kcal with 2 g fat and 900
kcal with 30 g fat, respectively) [4]. After 24 weeks, weight loss was equal in

both groups, on average 22 %. Gallstone formation was found in 4 of 6 patients with low fat intake, but not among any in the group with higher fat intake. This is attributed to better preservation of the emptying of the functions of the gall bladder resulting from higher intake of dietary fat.

Prospective epidemiological studies have shown that individuals whose weight is highly stable run a lower risk of cardiovascular disease and mortality than people whose body weight changes in either direction [5, 7]. These findings are based on followup of people with nearly normal weight, and the study does not report whether or not the weight loss was intentional. Against the background of these epidemiological findings, an ongoing debate concerns the potentially negative consequences for obese individuals who repeatedly gain and lose weight, so-called weight cyclers. Clinical studies have not shown whether, or to what extent, wide variations in body weight might elevate the risk of cardiovascular disease in overweight or obese people. Randomized studies of sufficient duration would be difficult to conduct.

A noncontrolled, prospective study for 30 months studied the effects of weight change, in 153 women, on abdominal obesity, blood lipids, and blood pressure [12]. No association was found between weight change and risk factors in an analysis of 7 patient groups who were categorized according to weight variation and its degree and direction.

A literature review addressed the extent to which weight variation in conjunction with obesity treatment has negative effects, e. g., on the distribution of body fat [11]. Three of four studies reported that the amount of abdominal fat had not changed. Furthermore, no findings suggested that basal metabolism would be lowered or that unfavorable redistribution would occur between body fat and non-fat tissues. Three of four published studies could not show that weight gain following a period of treatment had negative effects on renewed treatment.

The correlation between negative psychological parameters and weight variation in conjunction with obesity treatment was studied retrospectively in 120 women (mean BMI about 36) [10]. Weight variation did not have any negative psychological effects, but occurred more often among individuals with binge-eating disorders (BED).

References Section 4.8

1. Andersen RE, Wadden TA, Herzog RJ. Changes in bone mineral content in obese dieting women. Metabolism 1997;46(8):857-61.

2. Broomfield PH, Chopra R, Sheinbaum RC, Bonorris GG, Silverman A, Schoenfield LJ, et al. Effects of urso-deoxycholic acid and aspirin on the formation of lithogenic bile and gallstones during loss of weight. N Engl J Med 1988;319(24):1567-72.

3. Compston JE, Laskey MA, Croucher PI, Coxon A, Kreitzman S. Effect of diet-induced weight loss on total body bone mass. Clin Sci (Lond) 1992;82(4):429-32.

4. Gebhard RL, Prigge WF, Ansel HJ, Schlasner L, Ketover SR, Sande D, et al. The role of gall bladder emptying in gallstone formation during diet-induced rapid weight loss. Hepatology 1996;24(3):544-8.

5. Iribarren C, Sharp DS, Burchfiel CM, Petrovitch H. Association of weight loss and weight fluctuation with mortality among Japanese American men. N Engl J Med 1995;333(11):686-92.

6. Liddle RA, Goldstein RB, Saxton J. Gallstone formation during weight-reduction dieting. Arch Intern Med 1989;149(8):1750-3.

7. Lissner L, Odell PM, D'Agostino RB, Stokes J 3rd, Kreger BE, Belanger AJ, et al. Variability of body weight and health outcomes in the Framingham population. N Engl J Med 1991;324(26):1839-44.

8. Pritchard JE, Nowson CA, Wark JD. Bone loss accompanying diet-induced or exercise-induced weight loss: a randomised controlled study. Int J Obes Relat Metab Disord 1996;20(6):513-20.

9. Ricci TA, Heymsfield SB, Pierson RN Jr, Stahl T, Chowdhury HA, Shapses SA. Moderate energy restriction increases bone resorption in obese postmenopausal women. Am J Clin Nutr 2001;73(2):347-52.

10. Venditti EM, Wing RR, Jakicic JM, Butler BA, Marcus MD. Weight cycling, psychological health, and binge eating in obese women. J Consult Clin Psychol 1996;64(2):400-5.

11. Wing R. Weight cycling in humans: a review of the literature. Ann Behav Med 1992;14(2):113-9.

12. Wing RR, Jeffery RW, Hellerstedt WL. A prospective study of effects of weight cycling on cardiovascular risk factors. Arch Intern Med 1995;155(13):1416-22.

13. Yang H, Petersen GM, Roth MP, Schoenfield LJ, Marks JW. Risk factors for gallstone formation during rapid loss of weight. Dig Dis Sci 1992;37(6):912-8.

4.9
Maintaining Weight Loss

Anyone who is obese and who follows a treatment program for 6 months usually achieves clinically significant weight loss. However, for the majority, body weight eventually returns to the original weight, or higher, and only a small fraction of people can sustain their weight loss for many years. Hence, it is important to review the studies which address factors that may be responsible for a favorable prognosis in maintaining weight loss.

Many studies have addressed the relationship between weight loss on one hand and social support, psychological characteristics, demographic facts, and body weight prior to treatment on the other. All of these studies are weak, mainly because the study populations have been small and/or the study variables have been few. Hence, this question has been explored using meta-analyses or other types of studies that offer large patient databases.

A comprehensive meta-analysis is based on studies from the United States from 1970 to 1999 and included patients who participated in structured treatment programs [1]. In about half of the 29 studies included, the treatment was VLCD (median time 22 weeks) and in about an equal number of studies the treatment was balanced, energy-reduced diet (median time of 12 weeks). The study groups varied between 10 and 621 participants. Nearly 70 % maintained their weight loss after 1 year. In 11 studies, with more than 1000 participants in total, the followup time was 4 to 5 years. The average weight loss among these participants was 3 kg, which represents 23 % of the initial weight loss. The best results were achieved if the initial weight loss was at least 20 kg, which was often the case following VLCD. When weight loss was below 10 kg, the long-term effects were substantially lower. The effects of physical activity could be assessed in 6 studies, 5 of which used VLCD. They showed that after a median time of 2.7 years, weight loss was substantially greater in patients who reported regular physical activity (15 kg), than in those who did not report this (7.5 %). Since there was no control group, comparisons could be made only with the weight at outset. Because of this fact, the authors refer to studies which show that spontaneous weight gain in women who were not treated for overweight was approximately 6 kg during a 5-year period. In assessing the findings, consideration should be given to the fact that these findings applied only to patients who had completed the studies. Furthermore, they are based exclusively on self-reported weight data.

Another type of study concerns patients' data that were collected in the "National Weight Control Registry" (NWCR). Through advertising and other methods, information was acquired from patients who met the criteria that they had lost at least 13.6 kg (30 pounds) during at least 1 year. One of many studies from this database analyzes a comprehensive written questionnaire that was answered by nearly 800 respondents, the great majority being women [2]. Followup averaged 5.5 years. Weight trends during the period were self-reported, but were largely validated by, e. g., journal information and photographs. The results showed that body weight in women had decreased on average from 95 kg to 66 kg and BMI had decreased from 35 to 24. In men, weight had decreased from 121 kg to 86 kg and BMI from 37 to 26.

The questionnaire responses yielded several findings. Nearly 45 % reported that overweight/obesity appeared prior to 11 years of age. Approximately 45 % reported that they had succeeded in losing weight with improved dietary habits, mainly substantial reduction in fat intake, as a rule in combination with increased physical exercise. No less than 40 % reported that it was easier to maintain weight loss than to initially lose weight. Nearly 95 % reported improved quality of life. Less than 0.5 % experienced psychological problems.

Several different reasons for maintaining weight loss, which admittedly lasted only 2 years, were studied with the help of an extensive questionnaire that was answered by 509 participants (35 %) in an 8-week treatment program [3]. In women, weight loss following the treatment period was 7.8 kg, and after 2 years it was 4.2 kg. In men, the corresponding figures were 13.6 kg and 10.8 kg respectively. The maintained weight loss co-varied mainly with male gender, physical exercise, original weight loss, original weight, and frequency of participation during the treatment period. Less than one third of the favorable long-term effects could be explained by the 16 variables in the study.

In summary, three studies show that more than a small percentage of obese people can sustain a weight loss up to about 5 years. These studies are not completely free of methodological reservations and mainly include highly selected patients. From a prognostic perspective, the most favorable factors for maintaining weight loss appear to be substantial initial weight loss and physical exercise.

References Section 4.9

1. Anderson JW, Konz EC, Frederich RC, Wood CL. Long-term weight-loss maintenance: a meta-analysis of US studies. Am J Clin Nutr 2001;74(5):579-84.
2. Klem ML, Wing RR, McGuire MT, Seagle HM, Hill JO. A descriptive study of individuals successful at long-term maintenance of substantial weight loss. Am J Clin Nutr 1997;66(2):239-46.
3. Lavery MA, Loewy JW. Identifying predictive variables for long-term weight change after participation in a weight loss program. J Am Diet Assoc 1993;93(9):1017-24.

5
Treating Obesity in Children and Adolescents

Summary

Twenty studies were found to meet the minimum criteria for treatment by diet, exercise, and behavior modification. None of the studies addressing other treatment methods met the minimum criteria. Nevertheless, five studies on surgery for obesity and three studies on VLCD (very low energy diet) are presented here. Also presented are four studies concerning the side effects of obesity treatment, three of which address height growth and one addresses self-esteem.

Results: Three studies compared no treatment to treatment by diet, exercise, and behavior modification for 6 to 12 months. The treatment groups reduced relative weight by approximately 10%, while the control groups stayed around ±3% during the year studied (Evidence Grade 3). Two studies using longer treatment periods suggest that longer treatment can yield better long-term results, but the evidence was found to be insufficient for drawing conclusions. The differences among the various treatment strategies, e. g., with or without parent participation, family therapy, or bodybuilding, cannot be confirmed. Long-term followup (3–10 years) after 6–12 months of treatment was reported in 5 studies. Some of the studies reported modest, sustained weight loss while others did not. The evidence was judged to be insufficient for drawing conclusions.

Surgery has yielded positive treatment results in extremely overweight adolescents, but the lack of adequate studies does not allow one to draw reliable conclusions. Pharmacotherapy has not been studied in children. VLCD can be used in children and adolescents, but no data are available to evaluate the results for more than a few months. Rapid weight loss can influence height growth, especially in a 1-year perspective. Elevated self-esteem following successful treatment and lower self-esteem following unsuccessful treatment have been reported.

Conclusions: Diet, exercise, and behavior modification have resulted in an average weight loss of 10% during 1 year. The long-term results are uncertain.

Methods: A MEDLINE search identified 168 articles on treating obesity in children and adolescents. After the irrelevant material was removed, 76 articles remained for further assessment. Reasons for later exclusion were that the articles were actually editorials or overviews, the studies did not include control groups, or the followup period was less than 1 year. In some cases the studies were rejected because of insufficient patient data (4 studies). Although some studies did not

Treating and Preventing Obesity. Edited by J. Östman, M. Britton, E. Jonsson
Copyright © 2004 WILEY-VCH Verlag GmbH & Co. KGaA, Weinheim
ISBN 3-527-30818-0

meet the quality criteria, they were included because they provided information about particular types of treatment. A renewed MEDLINE search in December 2001 added another 3 references. The literature review ultimately included 28 studies.

This literature review does not address rare syndromes and special conditions such as Prader-Willi syndrome or obesity following surgery in the central nervous system, etc. Few patients are found in these categories, and the scientific evidence for treatment is lacking. This chapter reviews only those studies that address interventions for common overweight and obesity.

5.1
Dietary Intervention, Exercise, and Behavior Modification/Family Therapy

The models of combined interventions including dietary counseling, exercise, behavior therapy, etc. that have been tested in children and adolescents do not differ in principle from those used in adults. Most of the studies use specific dietary and exercise intervention in combination with different methods of supporting change in behavior regarding eating patterns and physical activity. Frequently, studies compare groups who have received similar interventions, with the exception of a single variable, the effect of which can then be studied in terms of body weight. To varying degrees, treatment has been targeted at parents and overweight children. For ethical reasons, control groups have received some type of treatment. Studies that included untreated control groups were either nonrandomized studies or the control groups of children and adolescents who were waiting to receive treatment at a later date. It may be questioned whether such a group can actually be considered a control group in a true sense. The extent to which expectations on future treatment influenced weight progression during the waiting period is not known.

Family therapy is a general concept that includes several orientations with at least three different theoretical backgrounds. *Systemic family therapy* attempts to influence the interaction between individuals without initially attempting to define the causes of the behavior that one hopes to change. *Cognitive family therapy* also focuses on change, but aims more directly at identifying and changing behaviors in those situations that lead to undesirable behavior. *Family therapy based on psychoanalytical theory* aims at understanding the underlying disturbance in the child's and the parent's individual development. The intent is to improve interaction in the family and promote positive behavior.

5.1.1
Results

In several studies by Epstein et al., children aged 6–12 years with mild to moderate obesity were investigated. Families where a child or parent was above 100% overweight were excluded, as were children with psychological or psychosocial problems. Basically, these studies attempted to modify long-term eating behavior by using "traffic light diets" ("Green" = low calorie food, vegetables, and most fruits; "Yellow" = basic foods that should be eaten every day; and "Red" = high-fat, high-sugar, energy-dense foods that should be avoided).

One study [18] randomized overweight children in 61 families to three groups:

1. To minimize TV watching and other similar sedentary activities
2. To engage in a given number of exercise sessions per week for 12 months
3. To receive both types of exercise advice.

The group that only received advice to minimize sedentary activities lost, on average, 20% of their percentage of overweight[1] after 1 year, while the other groups in the study lost approximately 10% (Table 5.1). The suggested mechanisms were that a reduction in sedentary style had a direct effect on the amount of low-intensity exercise, and that children developed their own choices for physical activity which could be more easily integrated into daily routines and thereby yielded more permanent effects.

The results could not be reproduced in a major, recently-published, study by the same research group, where 92 adolescents were divided into 4 groups, which, in addition to dietary advice and support for behavior modification, received a directive to reduce their amount of sedentary time or to increase their physical activity [13]. In all groups, the percentage of overweight decreased by about 20–25% after 6 months. Thereafter, they increased in weight, but not up to their initial weight, during the 2 years of followup. No differences were observed among the groups.

One study randomized 44 families to individualized and stepped training programs for 12 months [12]. Demands were placed on families in the treatment group to achieve the skills and behavioral changes required by each step of the treatment program before they were allowed to continue on to the next step. No demands were placed on the control group to achieve behavioral change before continuing with training. Rather, this group continued according to a schedule that had been planned from the outset. Weight loss in the treatment group was significantly greater than in the control group, particularly after 6 months. The difference was less pronounced after 24 months.

Another study by Epstein et al. investigated whether behavior modification aimed at problem solving improved the potential to lose weight [14]. Based on a specific program, children and parents practiced how to solve specific problems and conflicts that arise while attempting to modify their diets. In one group, the children did this alone; in another they worked together with the parents. The study continued for 6 months, with a followup period of 18 months. At the end of the study, no significant differences were noted between the groups. Based on a questionnaire, there appeared to be a significant decline in behavior problems as compared to the outset of the study. No differences were observed between the groups.

---

1) Percentage of overweight = the percentage above ideal weight for age, gender, and height.
   Related term: relative body weight.

Table 5.1 Dietary advice, exercise, and behavior modification/family therapy.

Author Year Reference Country	Study design	Inclusion criteria (Recruitment)	Intervention method Study groups	Treatment/ Followup time
Epstein LH 1995 [18] USA	RCT	Families recruited via ads in the media and referrals from MDs and school nurses. 61 of 92 screened families accepted. Children aged 8–12 years. Overweight 20%–100%	All receive traffic-light diet[1] + written information on physical activity. 1. Encouraged to reduce sedentary behavior 2. Encouraged to increase physical activity 3. Reduced sedentary behavior + increased physical activity	1 year/0
Epstein LH et al. 2000 [13] USA	RCT	20%–100% overweight No parent more than 100% overweight No current psychiatric treatment	Traffic-light diet advice[1] + financial incentives to all	6 months + 18 months
Epstein LH et al. 1994 [12] USA	RCT	Children 8–12 years Overweight 20%–100% Mean overweight 56% At least 1 parent overweight	Both groups receive traffic-light diet[1] + exercise advice. Interv group receives reinforcement and gradually modified advice depending on how previous advice was assimilated. Contr group receives the entire package without consideration to modified behavior	1 year/1 year
Epstein LH et al. 2000 [14] USA	RCT	Children over 120% in weight and over 8 years of age. Parents less than 100% overweight	Cognitive behavior therapy, traffic-light diet[1], advice on physical activity to all groups. One group focused on learning problem solving for parents/children. One group of children only and one group with instructor	6 months/ 18 months
Israel AC et al. 1994 [27] USA	RCT	Families recruited via pediatrician, school nurses, and newspaper ads. Children 8–13 years Overweight >20%	Family therapy. 1. Parental responsibility emphasized 2. Childs efforts emphasized	6 months/ 2 years

See legend on page 234

No. of patients/ No. followed up	Results Weight change	Results/Other	Study quality Comments
61/55	1. −20 % 2. −10 % 3. −10 % Group 1 significantly better than Group 2 and 3	All three patient groups significantly increased their physical fitness	Medium
92/92	No difference between the groups. After 6 mo the degree of over-weight decreased by approx. 25 %. After 2 years 15 % of weight loss maintained (significant)	No difference between the groups in physical working capacity	Medium
44 families/ 39 families	Group 1: −26.5 %* Contr group: −16.7 % after 1 year After 2 years no significant difference between groups	Relative weight decreased approx. 12 % in both groups after 2 years	Medium
67/62	No difference between groups in BMI, SD 2.8/2.6/2.7 before treatment. After 2 years 2.3/1.7/1.6	Significantly reduced psychological problems after 2 years compared to study start. Here the groups are not reported separately	Medium
34/20	6 mo: 1. −46 % 2. −33 % 2.5 y: No difference between groups, but significantly more in Group 2 are below achieved weight during treatment time		Low quality High dropout

Table continues on next page

Table 5.1 continued

Author Year Reference Country	Study design	Inclusion criteria (Recruitment)	Intervention method Study groups	Treatment/ Followup time
Golan M et al. 1998 [24] Israel	RCT	60 children recruited via school, aged 6–11 y. >20% overweight who live with both parents and lack of mental disorder	1. Only parents participate in group sessions, once/week at start and then less often 2. Dietary advice to the children via group treatments sessions	1 year/ 6 months
Brownell KD et al. 1983 [5] USA	RCT	12–16 years, more than 20% overweight (average 55.7%) 33 girls and 9 boys	Weekly group meetings to change behavior, diet and exercise. 1. Children only without parental participation 2. Separate meetings for mother and child 3. Mother and child together Otherwise same treatment (1 hour group sessions on diet, exercise, behavior once/week for 16 weeks. Then every second month)	1 year/0
Mellin LM et al. 1987 [30] USA	CT	Adolescents 12–18 y who responded to ad on treatment of overweight. 13%–113% overweight	Group treatment once/week, behavior modification + exercise training. Two parental meeting. Contr group waiting for treatment	2 months/ 1 year
Braet C et al. 1997 [3] Belgium	CT (RCT between Group 1 and 2)	Children 7–16 years Group 1–4 sought treatment for overweight	1. Individual behavior therapy (7 × 90 min and 7 followups with parents) 2. Group therapy. Otherwise as above 3. Advice on one occasion + brochure 4. 10 days of summer camp for children, monthly followup for parents 5. Control group. Weighing once/years	6 months/ 6 months
Flodmark CE et al. 1993 [22] Sweden	RCT between Group 1 and 2 (CT between Group 1 and 3)	Screening of 1906 school children 10–11 years, of whom 49 BMI >23. 44 accepted participation	1. Family therapy 2. Conventional counseling (3. Control group screening of 1 568 school children where 50 had a BMI >23)	1 year/1 year

See legend on page 234

No. of patients/ No. followed up	Results Weight change	Results/Other	Study quality Comments
1. 30/29 2. 30/21	Both groups significant weight loss after 1 year. After 18 months: 1. −14.6 %* 2. − 8.1 %	Significantly reduced overweight among the parents in Group 1, but not in Group 2	Medium Experimental design where two extremes in therapy focus are put up against each other
42/36	Mother and child separately reduced percentage of overweight by 20 %*. Other two groups reduced by 5 % after 1 year.	Systolic and diastolic blood pressure decreases significantly during treatment year	Medium
37/33 29 in control-group	Intervention group down 10 %*. Control group 0.1 %.	Statistically significant improved self-image in the interv group	Medium Wide range in age and relative weight renders findings difficult to interpret
1 + 2: 93/78 3. 57/74 4. 55/45 5. 54/42	1. −10 %* 2. −3 %* 3. −7 %* 4. −15 %* 5. +3 % No difference between the intervention groups. Intervention groups differed significantly from control group		Medium Selection in comparision group makes results uncertain
.. 24/20 2. 19/19 3. 50/48)	No significant differences between Group 1 and Group 2. (Less BMI increase in Group 1 than in Group 3 +5 % and +12 %, respectively)	Significant better physical fitness in Group 1 (40 %−45 % dropout in this study)	Medium High dropout in family therapy sessions. Uncertain comparability with non-randomized control group

Table continues on next page

Table 5.1 continued

Author Year Reference Country	Study design	Inclusion criteria (Recruitment)	Intervention method Study groups	Treatment/ Followup time
Ylitalo VM 1982 [43] Finland	CT	Children 7–15 years referred to pediatric clinic where every 3rd child consecutively was placed in the low-activity group	Diet instructions and training program for physical exercie identical in both groups. Active group checked 1–4 times/month and low-activity group once every 3 to 6 months	2 years/1 year
Nuutinen O et al. 1992 [33] Finland	CT	Children 6–16 years >20 % overweight. 32 consecutively admitted children to hospital. 16 children probably recruited differently	1. MD appointment and contact with dietician 2. MD appointment and group sessions with psychologist 3. Control group meets school nurse once/month	1 year/1 year
Schwingshandl J et al. 1999 [38] Austria	RCT	Children and adoles- cents aged 6–19 years recruited. Method of recruiting not reported. SDs from mean BMI were 2.78–10.95	Both groups receive diet instructions every 4th week for 12 weeks. Group A also had two fitness training sessions per week for 12 weeks	12 weeks/ 9 months
Christakis G et al. 1966 [8] USA	RCT	10 school classes with boys aged 13–14 years stratified by school performance	Physical fitness training sessions twice per week. Diet education, diet information, and information about risks of overweight. Control classes received usual school gymnastics	18 months/0
Sothern MS et al. 2000 [39] USA	CT	Children aged 7–12 y included in treatment study and control group selected from children who had previous intervention	Sessions once/week aimed at behavior modification + VLCD. Intervention group also received fitness training and control group recom- mended to take walks 3 times/week	10 weeks/ 9 months

1 Traffic-light diet = advice on diet based on assigning a color to foods. "Red" foods can only be eaten in a small amount, "yellow" foods are staples which should be eaten every day in a limited amount, and "green" foods (mainly vegetables and certain fruits) can be eaten in any amount.
RCT = Randomized Controlled Trial
CT = Controlled Trial, not randomized
* = Statistical significance
Interv = Intervention group
Contr = Control group
SD = Standard Deviation
VLCD = Very Low Calorie Diet

No. of patients/ No. followed up	Results Weight change	Results/Other	Study quality Comments
Active: 41/41 Low-active: 20/20	Mean obesity Activity group: −1.0 SD units* Low-activity group: no change (BMI and body weight not given)	No retardation of growth. Marginal effects on blood lipids and glucose tolerance	Medium No randomization. The study clearly shows that the prospects of succeeding with the treatment in- creases with a high frequency of treat- ment contact
48/48	1+2: −12.8 % 3: −3.7 % No significant differences		Medium No randomization. Control group significantly lower degree of overweight
30/20	Not clearly stated but 4 lost some weight and 16 increased in weight, however change in relative weight not specified	Weak statistically significant association between increase in muscle mass during the first 12 weeks of training and favorable weight trend after 1 year	Medium Very wide range in age and puberty stages and high dropout makes results uncertain
Intervention group: 55/49 Control group: 35/33	Overweight percent: −10.9* interv group −2.3 contr group		Medium Unusual study design; intensified training and educa- tion to entire class for over- weight to lose weight
9 interv + 48 contr/ 5 + 17	No difference in percentage overweight between the groups (no numbers stated in the article)	Both groups had significantly lower percentage of over- weight after 1 year compared with study start	Low Small number of patients. High dropout. Control group selected from previous studies

A few studies have assessed parental participation in treating childhood obesity. A randomized trial by Israel et al. studied therapy aimed at supporting the child's own abilities for self control compared to therapy aimed at increasing the parents' ability to control their children [27]. There were no significant differences between the groups in terms of overweight, either after 6 months of treatment or after 2 years of followup. However, the treatment group that focused on children's own capacity for self control showed that more children maintained the weight loss achieved during the treatment period.

Another study randomized children aged 6–11 years to a treatment group where the children self-controlled their weight and participated alone in the group meetings, and this was compared to a group where the parents alone attended regular counseling sessions [24]. The hypothesis assessed was that children would be less negatively influenced by their obesity if they did not need to participate. After 18 months, weight loss was significantly better among the children in the group where the parents alone received counseling. Furthermore, dropout was less in this group. However, the strategies used can be discussed. It is a lot to ask of a child in this age group, without parent participation, to take full responsibility for diet and exercise. On the other hand, it can be questioned whether a child's participation in taking responsibility for himself or herself should be completely avoided.

A study by Brownell et al. investigated the participation by parents in helping adolescents aged 12–18 years to lose weight [5]. Treatment was targeted at diet, exercise, and behavior modification. The adolescents were assigned by lottery to a group where they received support in group sessions, to a group where the mothers and their children separately received counseling and support, and to a group where parents and their children participated together. After 1 year, the results were significantly better in the group where the mothers and their children received support separately (mean change –20 % of overweight) compared to the other groups (–5 %).

Mellin et al. studied how a 3-month standardized program for both parents and adolescents aged 12–18 years, aimed at behavior modification and exercise, influenced weight after 1 year of followup [30]. The control group was made up of adolescents who were waiting for treatment. The treatment group lost, on average, about 10 % of body weight, while weight in the control group remained unchanged. Weight loss was statistically significant in the treatment group. This group also reported an improvement in self-esteem. Dropout was only 16 %. Despite some concerns about the study design, selection of control group, recruitment, etc., the study suggests that a defined program of this type can at least have some effect during the period of 1 year.

Braet et al. reported similar results in comparing different types of treatment [3]. The children received group therapy, individualized therapy, or treatment at summer camp. In addition, a fourth group consisted of children who could not participate in any of the other types of treatment. They received counseling on a single occasion and an informational brochure. All of the groups were compared with a control group that did not actively seek treatment and weighed significantly less. Each of the 4 treatment groups reported a significantly reduced degree of overweight after 1 year. Weight loss varied from 3% to 15% among the groups, but there were no significant differences among them. The control group reported a weight increase of 3% during the same period.

Flodmark et al. studied systemic family therapy [22]. Family therapy (6 treatment sessions) during 1 year was compared with a group receiving conventional treatment where the children had contact with a dietician and visited a physician on 5 occasions. Dropout from treatment was high in both groups. More than 50% of the family treatment sessions were attended by 15 of 24 children, while 7 children participated once or not at all. The followup reported on 5 children who were weighed by a school nurse plus the 15 who complied with the treatment. After 1 year of treatment plus 1 year of followup, no differences were found between the family therapy group and the conventional treatment group as regards mean BMI, mean BMI increase, or the number of severely overweight children. Compared to a nonrandomized and untreated control group, there was a significantly lower increase in BMI among the family therapy group and also a significantly smaller number of severely obese children. These results are, however, difficult to assess because of possible selection. Furthermore, the number of severely overweight children in the groups prior to the start of the study was not reported.

Ylitalo et al. studied the influence of visit rates on treatment outcome [43]. This Finnish investigation included 41 children aged 7–15 years who received frequent dietary and exercise counseling (once per week to once per month), while 20 children received identical counseling but only once every 3–6 months. After 2 years, a statistically significant lower mean weight was found in the group that had a higher frequency of counseling than did the lower frequency group. The differences remained after another year of followup.

Nuutinen and Knip also studied whether an intensive treatment program had positive effects on weight trends [33]. Children aged 6–16 years were placed into three groups, depending on when they had contact with the hospital. One group visited a physician once per month and a dietician five times during the treatment year. The second group visited a physician once per month, and there were 7 group sessions where 2–4 children met a psychologist and 2–8 parents met psychiatrists. They also met with a dietician in joint parent-child groups. The third group met with a school nurse once per month (without parental participation) during the treatment year. After 1 treatment year and 1 followup year, no significant difference in mean weight loss was observed among any of the groups. Both of the intensive treatment groups reported an average weight loss of 12.8%, and the group that visited the nurse once per month reported a weight loss of 3.7% (not significant).

A study by Schwingshandl et al. investigated whether a standardized bodybuilding exercise session twice per week for 12 weeks influenced weight trends after 1 year [38]. The children were aged 6–19 years. The groups were not presented separately. However, there is a weak but statistically significant correlation between the increase in muscle mass during the first 12 weeks of exercise and more favorable weight trends after 1 year. The results are questionable because of the wide age range and a dropout rate of 30%.

A study that was performed nearly 40 years ago investigated whether two fitness training and bodybuilding exercise sessions per week, dietary counseling, dietary information, etc. aimed at school classes had any effect on obese boys in these classes [8]. Fitness training, games, and bodybuilding exercise sessions were especially adapted to overweight students. The study continued for 18 months, the boys being 13–14 years old at the outset. The overweight boys lost 10.9 % in the treatment group and 2.3 % in the control group (significant difference). The design of this study was unusual since the direct intent was not to prevent overweight, but to have the overweight participants lose weight.

Sothern et al. investigated whether bodybuilding sessions for a 10-week VLCD period would improve the results for the year [39]. Treatment was carried out at home and consisted of fitness training and bodybuilding exercises. The control children (who were recruited 1–2 years earlier) were instructed to take walks 3 times per week for 60 minutes. Following a 1-year followup, it was not possible to observe any differences between the groups or any side effects, e. g., from injuries related to bodybuilding. Both of the groups lost considerable weight during the initial 10 weeks. During the remainder of the year there were no significant differences between them, but some of the weight loss remained.

5.2
Long-Term Effects of Different Treatments

Five long-term followups (4 years or longer) of children treated for obesity have been published. Epstein et al. conducted two 10-year followups of their treatment groups, and dropout was low despite the long followup period (Table 5.2) [16, 17].

One of the studies addressed long-term followup of 8 months of treatment where various types of diet, exercise, and behavior modification were tested in families with children between 6 and 12 years [16]. All three groups received advice concerning diet and exercise, while two groups received more direct support and encouragement for behavior modification. In one of these groups, treatment was aimed at the children, while in the other group both the parents and the children were encouraged to lose weight. Of the 76 patients who participated in the study, 61 (80 %) were followed up. The authors found a lower average degree of overweight (statistically significant) in the groups that received support and encouragement than that in the control group. The percent of overweight declined in all three groups during the treatment period. In group 1, after 20 months, body weight was relatively constant at 30 % overweight. In group 2, body weight increased between 20 and 60 months and thereafter remained constant at 40 % overweight. The difference between these groups was not significant. In group 3, body weight increased between 20 and 60 months and thereafter remained constant at 55 % overweight. There was, however, a wide distribution in all groups.

In the second 10-year followup by Epstein et al., data from four 1-year treatment studies, where both the children and at least one of the parents were overweight, were summarized [17]. Of the 185 children, 85 % were followed up. Ten years later, there was a lower degree of overweight (statistically significant) where therapists had been targeting both the overweight of the parents and the children than where they had focused on the children alone. Furthermore, there were significantly better long-term results in the groups that received advice and encouragement toward a more active lifestyle or advice concerning exercise sessions than in the groups that did not receive this advice. In total, approximately 30% of the controlled children had normal weight after 10 years of followup. These figures should be viewed in relation to the data concerning spontaneous correction of childhood obesity. As discussed earlier in Chapter 1.2, several concurrent epidemiological studies show that between 40 and 60% of overweight children aged 6–12 years become normal weight as young adults.

A 4-year followup of the study by Nuutinen et al. found that among 45 re-investigated children, there were no differences between those in family therapy and those who had their weight checked by the school nurse once per month [32]. The outcome was defined as the number of children with a sustained reduction in relative overweight of more than 10%.

A long-term followup of the study presented above by Braet et al. followed 109 of 136 children [2]. The treatment groups received cognitive behavior therapy individually, in groups, or at a 10-day summer camp. The control group, which was not randomized, received advice on one occasion. The therapy groups together showed an average weight loss of 15%. The children who received advice on a single occasion showed a weight loss of 6%. No differences were found between the groups who received individual therapy and those who received group therapy. Only 18% of the children achieved normal weight. During followup, this study also monitored the development of eating disorders. None of the children developed anorexia nervosa, and the authors did not find any more children with eating disorders than would normally be expected in this age group.

Finally, Johnson et al. conducted a telephone followup after 5 years of 18 patients who were treated by diet, exercise, and support for behavior modification for 16 weeks [28]. They found that the treatment group had a lower percentage of overweight than the control group (statistically significant). The findings are uncertain because of the methodology and a dropout rate exceeding 40%.

5.2.1
Observations that do not Meet the Minimum Criteria

It is uncertain which type of dietary advice yields the best compliance and weight loss. In a study by Spieth et al., one group was given dietary advice concerning low-fat, balanced, low-energy diets and the other group was given food with a low glycemic index, i.e., food which yields a slower increase in blood glucose (Table 5.3) [40]. Both of the groups received family counseling involving problem-focused behavior therapy. After 4 months, BMI and body weight had dropped significantly more in the group that had been recommended food with a low glycemic index. The study is short, and several sources of error could explain the findings. Hence, the value of the evidence is poor.

Table 5.2 Long-term followup (more than 4 years) after dietary treatment and behavior therapy in overweight children and adolescents.

Author Year Reference Country	Study design	Inclusion criteria (Recruitment)	Intervention method Study groups	Treatment/ Followup time
Epstein LH et al. 1990 [16] USA	RCT	Ad recruitment. >20% above ideal weight for age, height, sex. At least one parent obese and the parents live together	Diet, exercise, behavior modification. Group 1: Both parents and children encouraged to lose weight Group 2: Treatment directed at children Group 3: Participation generally encouraged	8 months/ 10 years
Epstein LH et al. 1994 [17] USA	CT	Followup of 4 studies (study above included), patients randomized to different groups. Age at treatment start 7–12 years, 20% overweight, and stable family situation. Some studies also included in the study above	All groups received general diet and exercise advice. Study 1 reported above. Study 2 compared two slim parents vs at least one overweight. Study 3 compared light exercise vs increased physical activity. Study 4 general exercise advice vs diet alone	1 year/10 years
Nuutinen O et al. 1992 [32] Finland	CT (long-term followup by Nuutinen 1992) reported in Table 5.1	Children 6–16 years, >20% overweight	MD appointment + dietician contact or MD appointment and group sessions with psychologist. Control group met school nurse once/month	1 year/4 years
Braet C 2000 [2]	CT (followup of [3] Braet 1997) reported in Table 5.1	Children 7–16 years	Cognitive behavior therapy individually/ group therapy/10 days summer camp. Control group received advice on 1 occasion and consists of those who can not/do not want to participate in other activites	6 months/ 4 years
Johnson WG et al. 1997 [28] USA	RCT	Newspaper ads Age 8–16 years 20% overweight	Support and advice and economic rewards. Group 1: 7 weeks diet, then 7 weeks diet + exercise Group 2: 7 weeks exercise and then 7 weeks exercise + diet Group 3: Information only (control group)	16 weeks/3.5 years

RCT = Randomized Controlled Trial
CT = Controlled Trial, not randomized

No. of patients/ No. followed up	Results Weight change	Results/Other	Study quality Comments
76/61	Group 1: 30 % overweight Group 2: 40 % overweight Group 3: 55 % overweight No significant difference between Group 1 and 2. Group 1 + 2 are significantly less overweight compared to Group 3	No difference in height growth between the groups	High Wide range makes results difficult to interpret. On group basis no change between the 5- and 10-year followup
185/158	No difference between diet and diet + exercise groups. Significantly lower overweight in the groups receiving exercise advice vs group receiving advice on light exercise. 30 % of all children achieved normal weight (less than 20 % overweight)	No significant difference between those who had overweight parents and those who did not	High Not apparent whether other treatments were tested during the followup period
48/45	49 % maintained effect defined as reduction in relative weight by more than 10 %. No difference between groups		Medium
136/109	Cognitive behavior therapy groups together −15 %. Advice once −6 %. No difference between different cognitive behavior therapy groups. No difference between genders. 18 % acheived normal weight	No development of anorexia nervosa. No increase of eating disorders compared to expected rate in the normal population	Medium Uncertain comparability between groups
32/18	Group 1+2 have statistically significant lower percentage of overweight than control group after 3 years		Low High dropout. Wide range in age makes results uncertain

Table 5.3 Observations not fulfilling the minimum criteria.

Author Year Reference Country	Study design	Inclusion criteria (Recruitment)	Intervention method Study groups	Treatment/ Followup period
Spieth LE et al. 2000 [40] USA	CT	Children aged 7–16 y, received surgery at obesity clinic and placed in 2 programs based on possibility (time) to participate in program	Child and family counseling with problem-focused behavior therapy once/month for first 4 months. 1. Dietary advice for usual balanced low-energy–low-fat diet 2. Recommended food with low-glycemic index	4.3 months/0

CT = Controlled Trial, not randomized

5.2.3
Pharmacotherapy

Current drugs for treating obesity have been tested to only a limited extent in children and adolescents. The only controlled study, by Molnar et al., investigated 32 patients (Table 5.4) [31]. The study does not meet the minimum criteria established for this report. The combined caffeine/ephedrine mixture (for more information concerning the mode of action of this agent, see Chapter 4.5, Pharmacotherapy) was compared with placebo in combination with calorie restrictions for 20 weeks in adolescents aged 14–18 years of age. After 20 weeks of treatment, the average weight loss was significantly better in the caffeine/ephedrine group than in the placebo group. In the group receiving active substance, 81 % of the adolescents had more than 5 % weight loss compared to 31 % in the placebo group. The side effects were mild and did not vary between the placebo group and the group receiving active substance. This isolated study had a followup period of less than 1 year, and therefore the quality is low.

The observations reported here are intended to provide information about areas of potential interest, although none of the studies meet the inclusion criteria or are acceptable. These observations have not been used in formulating the conclusions drawn in this chapter.

5.2.4
Surgery

Only a few studies have addressed surgery for obesity in children and adolescents. Jejunoileal bypass (Chapter 4.6) is a surgical procedure that has been discontinued because of severe side effects. Hence, these studies have not been reported. The studies described below involve methods currently in use (Table 5.5).

No. of patients/ No. followed up	Results Weight change	Results/Other	Study quality Comments
107/107	BMI 1. −0.1 2. −1.5* Body weight, kg 1. +1.3 2. −2.1*	The study indicates that food with a low-glycemic index may be more effective than common low-energy diet in treating child obesity	Did not meet the minimum criteria

One patient series reports on 39 children and adolescents (aged 11–19 years) who underwent obesity surgery. Of these 39 children, 34 were available for followup, i. e., a 30-minute telephone interview [35]. The followup period varied between 1 and 13 years (mean followup time was 6 years). Thirty adolescents had received gastric bypass surgery and four had received vertical gastric banding. All were extremely overweight (mean BMI 47), and their quality of life prior to surgery was poor. At followup, the mean BMI was 32. Reoperation due to unsatisfactory weight increase had been undertaken or was planned in 5 cases (15%). Most of the respondents were satisfied with surgery. The side effects reported included gall bladder disorders in 5 cases, which is considered to be a general side effect of weight loss, low blood values (1 case), nausea, and vomiting (1 case).

Strauss et al. conducted a re-followup of 10 adolescents (15–17 years of age) who had received surgery within a 17-year period [41]. The surgical method used was the Roux-en-Y gastric bypass, and followup time was nine months to 12 years. The subjects were extremely overweight, with a BMI between 40 and 70 prior to surgery. At followup, 9 of 10 had lost more than 30 kg. Seven patients had another serious disease secondary to obesity that disappeared in all cases. Three of the young women who received surgery had undergone a normal pregnancy during the followup period. No serious complications were reported. Two patients had received surgery for gallstones, a common side effect from pronounced weight loss.

A study by Breaux re-checked 20 of 22 children and adolescents aged 8–18 years who had received vertical gastric banding, Roux-en-Y gastric bypass, or bilieopancreatic diversion [4]. Followup times varied between 6 and 131 months. Many of the children were extremely obese. The percentage of overweight varied between 84% and 537%, and BMI ranged between 41 and 105. Different surgical procedures were used with these children and adolescents, depending mainly on when the procedure was done and the technology available at the hospital. Eleven

Table 5.4 Pharmacotherapy

Author Year Reference Country	Study design	Inclusion criteria (Recruitment)	Intervention method Study groups	Treatment/ Followup period
Molnar D et al. 2000 [31] Hungary	RCT	Adolescents aged 14–18 years. Relative weight above 140 %	Group 1: Ephedrine/caffeine tablets Group 2: Placebo Both groups receive diet and exercise advice	20 weeks/ 1–2 weeks

RCT = Randomized Controlled Trial

Table 5.5 Surgical.

Author Year Reference Country	Study design	Inclusion criteria (Recruitment)	Intervention method Study groups	Followup time
Rand SC et al. 1994 [35] USA	Retrospective review of consecutive data	Children 11–19 years Mean weight 131 kg. Mean BMI 47 (38–66)	Roux-en-Y gastric bypass or vertical gastric banding	Mean 6 years (1–13 years)
Strauss RS et al. 2001 [41] USA	Retrospective review of patient data	Identification of adolescents under 17 years who received obesity surgery at one center since 1983. 10 adolescents aged 15–17 years at time of surgery	Roux-en-Y gastric bypass	9 months/ 12 years
Breaux CW 1995 [4] USA	Retrospective review of patient data	Identification of children and adolescents receiving obesity surgery at one center since 1983. 22 adolescents with extreme obesity aged 8–18 years at time of surgery (% overweight 84–537)	Vertical gastric banding, 5 procedures. Roux-en-Y gastric bypass, 14 procedures. Bileopancreatic diversion, 4 procedures (patients with severe sleep apnea and extreme obesity)	6 months/ 131 months

No. of patients/ No. followed up	Results Weight change	Results/Other	Study quality Comments
32/29	Group 1: −7.9* kg Group 2: −0.5 kg Share with ≥5 % weight loss Group 1: 81 % Group 2: 31 % (significance not specified)	No difference in side effects between placebo group and intervention group	Did not meet the minimum criteria. Short followup time and small number of patients

No. of patients/ No. followed up	Results Weight change	Results/Other	Study quality Comments
39/34 of whom 30 operated by Roux-en-Y gastric bypass	At followup: Mean BMI 32 Mean weight 89 kg Weight reduction 66 % 80 % of the patients >20 kg weight gain from lowest value	Views on operation: Clear acceptance 85 % Some acceptance 9 % No acceptance 6 % 3 patients re-operated 4 patients operated for gallstones	Did not meet the minimum criteria. Growth data not satisfactorily reported. Psyhcological reaction only evaluated by 30- minute phone interview
10/10	BMI before operation: 40–70. BMI after opera- tion: Major reduction in all cases, although 1 had increased BMI 70 at long-term followup. 9 of 10 had decreased >30 kg in weight. Mean weight loss 54 kg	7 of 10 serious secondary disease which disappeared in all cases. 2 operated for gallstones, 5 had mild iron deficiency anemia, and 3 developed folate deficiency. No serious side effects reported. 3 adolescents underwent normal pregnancy	Did not meet the minimum criteria. Deficient study design, but promising results as regards obesity surgery in adoles- cents.
22/20	All patients lost weight after surgery. One patient returned to original weight. Mean change for patients with sleep apnea from BMI 56 to BMI 35 after mean followup of 50 months	Strongly improved oxygen- ation in sleep apnea patients. Side effects: gallstones (2), protein deficiency (3), vitamin deficiency (2). Two deaths, 3.5 y and 15 mo after surgery, respectively. Probable associ- ation with surgery in one case	Did not meet the minimum criteria. Surgery may be a possible inter- vention for extreme obesity in younger children

Table continues on next page

Table 5.5 Surgical treatment.

Author Year Reference Country	Study design	Inclusion criteria (Recruitment)	Intervention method Study groups	Followup time
Greenstein RJ et al. 1995 [25] USA	Retrospective review of patient data	Identification of adolescents, 14–21 years of age between 1982–1984	Vertical gastric banding	5 months/ 9 years
Mason EE et al. 1995 [29] USA	Retrospective review of patient data	Children and adolescents receiving obesity surgery at one center since 1966. Aged 8–20 years. Focus on adolescents aged 14–20 years	Gastric bypass or horizontal gastroplasty in the first 70 patients. Vertical gastric banding (VBG) in the next 47 patients	5–10 years

of the children had sleep apnea and 9 of them were followed up. All patients initially lost weight following surgery, but returned to their original weights. Most, however, were helped by the procedure, even though most remained obese with a BMI above 30. Two of the adolescents died during the followup period, one of whom was a girl who died 3.5 years after surgery. It appears that this death was due to complications from morbid obesity rather than from the surgical procedure itself. The second patient had a brain tumor and hydrocephalus, and general organ failure developed.

A followup by Greenstein and Rabner investigated 14 patients who had received surgery at ages between 14 and 21 years between 1982 and 1984 [25]. The surgical procedure was vertical gastric banding. Followup was conducted either via personal interview or by telephone. The subjects consisted of 3 male and 11 female patients. One patient weighted more at followup than at surgery, while the others had lost weight. The mean BMI had fallen from 59 to 35 in the males and from 45 to 33 in the females. All were positive toward the operation. Quality of life was also assessed to some extent. At the time of followup, all of the adolescents were employed or attended school, and 69% reported that their relationships with the opposite sex had improved. Over 80% reported that their self-confidence had improved, and they perceived a better future following the surgery.

A followup by Mason et al. investigated 117 patients since 1966 who were between 8 and 20 years of age at the time of surgery [29]. The first 70 patients had received either gastric bypass surgery or horizontal gastroplasty. Following 1980, only adolescents aged 14 years and older received surgery, and the procedure was vertical gastric banding. Followup was based mainly on these 47 adolescents.

No. of patients/ No. followed up	Results Weight change	Results/Other	Study quality Comments
18/14 (3 men)	Preop BMI Men 59 Women 45 BMI at followup Men 35 Women 30	Positive to operation: 100 % In school or work: 100 % Improved relations with opposite sex: 69 %	Did not meet the minimum criteria. Promising results as regards obesity surgery in adolescents below 21 years of age
5 years: 35/25 10 years: 19/14	5 years Men (10): BMI 53 to 38.7 Women (15): BMI 45 to 35 10 years Men (5): BMI 56 to 46 Women (9): BMI 42 to 37	After 5 years 74 % had lost more than 25 % of surplus weight, after 10 years 61 %. Tendency for better results in men than in women	Did not meet the minimum criteria. Quality of life not reported, unclear whether all patients were asked

Some of the reporting is incomplete; however, approximately 25 of 35 adolescents were followed up, with observation times exceeding 5 years. Approximately 14 of 19 adolescents with observation times exceeding 10 years were also presented. One patient died, but the death was not attributed to obesity or the surgery. The subjects were extremely overweight, with a mean BMI above 50 prior to surgery. At 5-year followup, 74 % had lost more than 25 % of their overweight. This figure declined to 61 % at the later followup. Three of the patients were re-operated because of increasing weight. After more than 6 years of followup, 5 of 6 men were below their original weight and under 175 % of ideal weight. The results were somewhat worse in the young women, where 5 of 10 were below 175 % of ideal weight while most of the others had returned to their original weights. This study did not assess quality of life.

5.2.5
Very Low Calorie Diet (VLCD)

The use of very low calorie diets can be one way to lose weight rapidly. These diets can increase motivation and enhance the sense that weight problems can be managed. Consequently, several studies involving children and adolescents have tested VLCD (Table 5.6).

A study by Figueroa-Colon et al. compared children aged 7–17 years who had received either protein-enhanced VLCD or hypocaloric balanced diet for 10 weeks, after which both groups received a hypocaloric diet that was continually strengthened [20]. After 10 weeks, the VLCD group had reduced their overweight by 30 %

Table 5.6 Effects of VLCD (Very Low Calorie Diet).

Author Year Reference Country	Study design	Inclusion criteria (Recruitment)	Intervention method Study groups	Treatment/ Followup period
Figueroa-Colon R et al. 1993 [20] USA	CT	Children with severe overweight (45–131% of normal weight for age, sex, height). Aged 7–17 years	1. VLCD with high protein content for 10 weeks 2. Balanced low-energy diet for 10 weeks. Both groups then balanced diet for 10 weeks	10 weeks/ 1 year
Figueroa-Colon R et al. 1996 [21] USA	CT	Children with severe overweight (more than 40% above normal weight for age, sex, height). Identified in school screening in 2 schools. 12 av 44 in treatment school participated and 7 of 19 in control school. Mean age 10.5 years. (Range 8.8–12.9 y)	1. VLCD-group Protein-saving VLCD (600–800 kcal/day) for 10 weeks, then increased to 1200 kcal/day during the rest of study period. Increased physical activity + parental participation 2. Control group no treatment	6 months/ 0 month
Caroli M et al. 1992 [7] Italy	CT	Children and adolescents with at least 30% weight above normal weight for age, sex, height. 2 groups: Children 6–11 years Adolescents 12–19 y	Protein-enhanced VLCD, 10.5 kcal/kg body weight	8 weeks

[2] IGF-1 = Insulin-like growth factor 1, growth factor important for, e.g., height growth

and the hypocaloric group by 14%. The differences remained after 6 months, but not at followup 14.5 months later. Although both groups had returned to the baseline levels in terms of weight, an approximate 20% reduction in overweight remained because the children had grown during the study period. No significant differences were found in height growth between the groups, but both grew significantly more slowly during the first 6 months when the diet regimen was stricter than it was during the later 6 months of the study. Side effects such as muscle cramps, tiredness, dizziness, and appetite problems were noted in both groups. The number of children studied was small, and even fewer could be followed up after 1 year. Hence, the findings are unreliable.

Figueroa-Colon et al. also studied VLCD in school health services, and compared the results with a control school [21]. The study design was similar, with 10 weeks of VLCD and thereafter a successive increase in calorie intake. Nine of 11 children

No. of patients/ No. followed up	Results Weight change	Results/Other	Study quality Comments
9/11	VLCD-group: −30% Hypocaloric group: −14% after 10 weeks (sign difference). After 14.5 mo VLCD: −23%, Hypocaloric group: −20% (no difference between the groups)	No difference between groups in growth retardation. Both groups had significant growth retardation during first 6 months	Did not meet the minimum criteria
. 12/11 . 7/7	1. Relative overweight −24.3% 2. Weight gain 2.8 kg	No significant difference in blood pressure and blood lipids. Hunger, muscle cramps, tiredness, abdominal pain, and headache reported at a higher rate during VLCD-period	Did not meet the minimum criteria
0/26	Weight loss in child group 7.8 kg. Weight loss in adolescents 9.8 kg (mean values). Values of the groups are not significantly different	IGF-1[2] decreases significantly in the younger group and a trend toward decrease in the older group. Total cholesterol and LDL cholesterol decrease significantly during treatment in both groups. No substantial side effects were noted	Did not meet the minimum criteria

lost more than 5 kg in 10 weeks of VLCD, and 6 of these had a sustained weight loss of 5 kg or more after 6 months. The percent of overweight had declined on average 24% compared to −0.3% in the control group. However, the study was too short to justify claiming any permanent effects in the children who had a lower weight after 6 months.

Caroli et al. tested a protein-enhanced VLCD in children aged 6–11 years and in adolescents aged 12–19 years [17]. After 8 weeks, the younger group had lost on average 7 to 8 kg, and the adolescents had lost 9.8 kg. No particular side effects were noted. However, this is a short-term study, rendering the findings unreliable.

Table 5.7 Summer camp.

Author Year Reference Country	Study design	Inclusion criteria (Recruitment)	Intervention method Study groups	Treatment/ Followup period
Gately PJ et al. 2000 [23] Great Britain	Prospective	Children aged 9–15 y who participated in summer camp aimed at weight loss	Summer camp focused on energy restriction (1400 kcal/day), behavior modification and physical activity	8 weeks/ 1 year

5.2.6
Other Types of Treatment

5.2.6.1 Residential
Long-term residential treatment. is offered in several countries. This treatment combines reduced-energy diet, physical activity, and behavior modification. therapy (Table 5.7). Treatment time varies between 1 and 10 months. Risk factors were studied in a scientific study from these residential programs [42]. No controlled studies of this type were identified, although one followup study was found.

Gately et al. studied the effects of an 8-week camp in children aged between 9 and 15 years in the U.S.A. [23]. The study included 194 children, 102 of whom were followed up 1 year later when they returned for another camp. Since the parents paid for the camp themselves, the children are a selected sample with a good socioeconomic standard. The children lost, on average, 10.8 kg during the 8 weeks of camp. The children who returned 1 year later had a significantly lower mean BMI. The study did not report whether or not the children had any further treatment for their overweight during the year, and therefore it is not possible to determine whether the camp *per se* was responsible for the long-term effects on weight.

5.2.6.2 Weight Watcher Treatment. in Children
Although treatment based on the weight watchers' concept has been used in children, there are no published followups concerning the effects.

5.2.6.3 Physical Exercise.
Physical exercise as an isolated form of treatment has also been tested, but not in any controlled trials [10].

No. of patients/ No. followed up	Results Weight change	Results/Other	Study quality Comments
190/102	BMI decreased from 32.9 to 29.1 after 8 wk of treatment. After 1 year BMI increased to 30.1, still significantly below original BMI		Did not meet the minimum criteria

5.2.6.4 Alternative Medicine

Hypnosis and acupuncture have been attempted. Studies that include adolescents have been reported in the chapter addressing treatment methods in alternative medicine (Chapter 4.7). However, positive effects have not been reported.

5.3
Effects of Treatment on Risk Factors and Mental Health

There is a tendency for overweight children, primarily during their teenage years, to experience a lower quality of life. The effects of treatment on quality of life in children have been insufficiently studied. One study found a correlation between successful weight loss treatment and higher self-esteem [30]. Another study reported reduced behavioral disturbances in children who had received family-based treatment focused on long-term behavioral change [13].

Another goal in treating obesity is to reduce the long-term risks of diabetes and cardiovascular disease. These diseases mainly affect overweight adults, but risk markers are found already in childhood, e.g., elevated blood pressure, blood lipid disorders, high serum insulin levels, cardiac dysrhythmia. Several studies have shown that weight loss improves the markers.

A reduction in blood pressure has been reported after 10 weeks of VLCD (low energy diet) [20] and after 20 weeks of treatment with diet and exercise, mainly in combination [36]. Furthermore, several studies have shown a more favorable blood lipid profile after weight loss [7, 20]. Both weight loss and exercise have positive effects on heart activity expressed as lowered heart rate and favorable changes in the ECG pattern [26, 34]. Physical exercise and weight loss also have positive effects on insulin resistance in children and adolescents [19, 37].

Table 5.8 Side effects from obesity treatment in children and adolescents.

Author Year Reference Country	Study design	Inclusion criteria (Recruitment)	Intervention method Study groups	Treatment/ Followup period
Amador L et al. 1990 [1] Cuba	RCT	Children aged 10–13 y. Triceps skin fold >90th percentile. Relative weight boys more than 25%. Girls more than 30%	Diet, physical exercise, and behavior modification. 1. 0.25 MJ/kg 2. 0.15 MJ/kg	12 months/0
Dietz WHJ et al. 1985 [9] USA	Retro-spective	Children who lost >10% of their re-lative overweight in 8–11 months	Dietary treatment, approx. 60% of previous daily intake	Mean 9.7 months
Epstein LH et al. 1990 [11] USA	Analysis of 4 earlier CT	Families with complete growth data on children and height-weight data on parents. Aged 6–12 years	Traffic-light diet and behavior modification	6–12 months/ 5 years
Cameron JW 1999 [6] USA	CT	Adolescents aged 10–15 years without specific health prob-lems. Had not parti-cipated in previous weight programs	90-minute meetings once/week in group. Dietary advice, general nutrition, advice on exercise, and one physical exercise session. Control group: No treatment	12 weeks

RCT = Randomized Controlled Trial
CT = Controlled Trial, not randomized
SD = Standard Deviation

5.4
Side Effects of Treatment

Treating overweight in children and adolescents involves greater risks of undesir-able effects than corresponding treatment later in life. Height growth, puberty, bone mineralization, and muscle mass can be unfavorably affected by weight re-duction. Other potential risks for children and adolescents involve body awareness, which is undeveloped, as well as personality in a broader context. Furthermore, one cannot exclude the possibility that hunger-inhibiting drugs that act via the central nervous system may have types of side effects in children and adolescents that dif-fer from the side effects found in adults.

Three studies focus particularly on the effects that weight loss treatment have on height growth [1, 9, 11]. Amador et al. presented a well-designed study that ana-

No. of patients/ No. followed up	Results Weight change	Results/Other	Study quality Comments
94/78	6 months 1. −4.5 kg 2. −7.5 kg* 12 months 1. +2 kg 2. +2 kg	Puberty development slower in Group 2. Height growth lower during 6 months in Group 2	High
19/19	Weight loss 4.5 kg ± 5.3 kg Corresponding to 29% of ideal weight	High correlation between change in growth velocity and weight loss	High
158	Relative overweight −3.2%	Change in percentage of overweight did not influence height	Medium
114/109	No difference in mean BMI, either between groups or before and after 12 weeks	No difference between groups in self-esteem at study start. No decrease in self-esteem in the control group. Intervention group had significantly lower self-esteem after 12 weeks and was significantly below the control group at that time	Medium

lyzed the extent to which growth and puberty were affected by a strict versus a moderate reduced-energy diet in combination with an exercise program for 6 months (Table 5.8) [1]. They found that an average weight loss of 7.5 kg in the group receiving stricter dietary advice was associated with less growth and a slower development of puberty than occurred in the group with less stringent calorie reduction and a weight loss averaging 4.5 kg.

Dietz et al. found a very clear correlation between weight loss and reduced growth rate [9]. Findings in the third study, by Epstein, however, showed contrary results. After 5 to 10 years, no correlation could be found between changes in height growth and weight reduction [11]. This may suggest that the effects of weight loss are short-term, but the level of detail in this study is insufficient to exclude the possibility that children who lose weight rapidly remain of short stature.

Surgical treatment which compels a reduced intake/uptake of food is a major intervention. It may lead to anxiety in individuals who are not mentally prepared for the procedure, and such risks are probably greater in children and adolescents than in adults. The question which needs to be answered is whether the effects of weight loss, and thereby the possible gains in quality of life and future health, are reasonably proportional to the risks and injury associated with and following surgery. Patients who cannot resist overeating following surgery are also at risk of serious injury to the stomach and esophagus.

Side effects from behavior modification in obesity treatment are seldom reported in treatment studies. In a long-term followup, Braet et al. did not find an increased rate of eating disorders among the children treated [2] (Table 5.2). The findings from the studies presented above suggest that the effects of behavior modification therapy, dietary advice, and exercise advice are limited. Some of the children and adolescents were probably not helped by this treatment. The capacity for self-control is decisive for a successful result. Treatment that has no effect can lead to lower self-esteem and self-control. Hence, there is an obvious risk that ineffective treatment could have negative consequences and could lead to even greater weight gain. In part, this is shown to be the case in a study by Cameron, who investigated self-esteem in 54 children aged 10–15 years who participated in a 12-week weight loss program focusing on general dietary knowledge, physical exercise, and selection of food products [6]. No difference in weight was achieved, but the treatment group developed a significantly lower self-esteem than did the control group. The greatest decline concerned perceptions about one's own body. The study was short, and one cannot exclude the possibility that the loss in self-esteem might not have persisted if treatment had been continued.

5.5
Discussion

In assessing the results of obesity treatment in children, a key question concerns what should one compare the results with. Using an untreated control group in randomized trials is both unethical and unpractical, since dropout in the control group would be high. Patients who are waiting for treatment are also a dubious control group since such studies would be necessarily short, as it would be unreasonable to allow children and adolescents to wait more than a year for treatment. Given that obesity is a chronic disease, it takes several years before one can judge whether or not behavioral change is permanent. A followup period of 3 to 5 years is probably required before the results can reveal anything about future prognosis. Hence, usually two treatment strategies must be compared. In other cases, the treatment results must be compared with epidemiological data concerning the development of obesity in children from the same cultural and socioeconomic area. Many sources of uncertainty exist in either case. Consequently, all long-term results must be interpreted with caution.

5.5.1
Behavior Modification, Diet, and Exercise

All treatment for obesity must include advice on behavior modification as regards diet, exercise, and general lifestyle. Otherwise, the effects of treatment are temporary, and the weight soon returns. In most of the studies presented, behavior modification treatment was tested for a shorter period – from six weeks to 12 months. In most cases, this resulted in a significant reduction in obesity at followup, where the effectiveness measure was the mean weight in the treatment groups. There are no significant differences between the results of the different treatment strategies, but several studies show a correlation between the frequency of visits and the outcome. In most of the studies it is not possible to identify the share of the patients who experienced any effects from the intervention.

An initial weight loss may be followed by weight gain. This could be attributed either to a treatment period that is too short or to a return to the children's previous lifestyle, regardless of intervention.

Two studies provided children with longer treatment, 18 months and 2 years respectively. In both studies, significant changes remained 18 months and 3 years respectively after the start of treatment. This could suggest that longer treatment periods yield better long-term results.

Many of the studies involved children within a wide age range, often between 7 and 16 years of age. Epidemiological data suggest that the risk of remaining overweight is substantially greater in older children than in younger children. It is also probable that treatment should have different orientations for children prior to puberty compared with teenagers, for example, regarding the design of support for the parents. One study showed substantially better results when teenagers and parents received help separately than when they formed joint groups. However, no studies have attempted to reproduce these results, and no data indicate the ages at which interventions have the best chance for success.

It is possible that meal scheduling may play a role in the ability to maintain a planned diet. Meal frequency and content, e. g., concerning the glycemic index and fat content, may be important factors. No studies met the minimum criteria on this topic.

In two 10-year followups of 1-year treatment, significant differences remained between different approaches to family-based treatment. Direct support for behavior modification treatment was more successful than treatment that encouraged only group participation. The group that received exercise advice also had a significantly lower percentage of overweight after 10 years than that of the group that received advice aimed at light gymnastic exercises. These results suggest that long-term influence can be achieved through advice and support for families with overweight and can yield good results. On the other hand, only 30 % had normal weight at followup. It is doubtful whether these results are better than would be expected even among untreated obese children, based on available epidemiological studies (Chapter 1.2). In a 4-year followup from Finland, 18 % became of normal weight and in a Belgian 5-year study 30 % became of normal weight. Together, these results suggest that the long-term effects of intervention for six weeks to 1 year have been limited.

The side effects of behavior modification therapy have rarely been studied. One study found better self-esteem in the treatment group after 1 year of treatment than that in a control group who waited for treatment. A long-term followup found no increase in eating disorders in the treatment group. A short-term study found reduced self-esteem in the treatment group compared to the control group. Since there is some tendency for "spontaneous cure", mainly in children below 10 years of age, and since it is rare to find life-threatening health problems secondary to obesity during childhood and adolescence, demands on the effectiveness and safety of treatment should be extremely high. Hence, treatment should not involve excessive intervention in the psychosocial situation of the family and child.

5.5.2
Surgical Intervention

Several case series address surgical treatment of extremely obese children and adolescents. These studies have reported weight loss that lasted for 5–10 years. All of the case studies included very obese adolescents. The studies differed from those presented above where more moderately overweight and obese individuals were treated. Studies on surgical intervention for obesity deal with adolescents who have a very poor quality of life and are at great medical risk. In some cases, it was possible to report that quality of life had improved. Followup methods and selection of patients make these assessments somewhat uncertain. However, the results suggest that surgery may be an important intervention in extreme cases. More thorough investigation of both the advantages and risks is necessary before it is possible to identify which children and adolescents are appropriate for surgical treatment.

5.5.3
VLCD

Several studies have tested low-energy diets in children and adolescents. This treatment has not revealed any serious side effects. Often, VLCD is tested in severely obese children and adolescents. Hence, the results cannot be directly compared with those achieved by behavior modification therapy. It is not possible to show whether VLCD has a long-term effect which is superior to behavior modification therapy. Several studies involving VLCD reported reduced height growth and delayed puberty during treatment. Since there are no systematic long-term followups, it is not possible to assess whether VLCD negatively affects the individual's final height.

References

1. Amador L, Ramos LT, Morono M, Hermelo P. Growth rate reduction during energy restriction in obese adolescents. Clin Endocrinol 1990;96:73-82.

2. Braet C. Long-term follow-up of a cognitive behavioral treatment program for obese children. Behavior Therapy 2000;31:55-74.

3. Braet C, Van Winckel M, Van Leeuwen K. Follow-up results of different treatment programs for obese children. Acta Paediatrica 1997;86(4):397-402.

4. Breaux CW. Obesity Surgery in Children. Obes Surg 1995;5(3): 279-84.

5. Brownell KD, Kelman JH, Stunkard AJ. Treatment of obese children with and without their mothers: changes in weight and blood pressure. Pediatrics 1983;71(4):515-23.

6. Cameron JW. Self-esteem changes in children enrolled in weight management programs. Issues Compr Pediatr Nurs 1999;22(2-3):75-85.

7. Caroli M, Chiarappa S, Borelli R, Martinelli R. Efficiency and safety of using protein sparing modified fast in pediatric and adolescent obesity treatment. Nutr Res 1992;12:1325-34.

8. Christakis G, Sajecki S, Hillman RW, Miller E, Blumenthal S, Archer M. Effect of a combined nutrition education and physical fitness program on the weight status of obese high school boys. Fed Proc 1966;25(1):15-9.

9. Dietz WHJ, Hartung R. Changes in height velocity of obese preadolescents during weight reduction. Am J Dis Child 1985;139(7):705-7.

10. Epstein LH. Exercise in the treatment of childhood obesity. Int J Obes 1995;19(Suppl 4):S117-S21.

11. Epstein LH, McCurley J, Valoski A, Wing RR. Growth in obese children treated for obesity. Am J Dis Child 1990;144(12):1360-4.

12. Epstein LH, McKenzie SJ, Valoski S, Klein KR, Wing RR. Effects of mastery criteria and contingent reinforcement for family-based child weight control. Addict Behav 1994;19(2):135-45.

13. Epstein LH, Paluch RA, Gordy CC, Dorn J. Decreasing sedentary behaviors in treating pediatric obesity. Arch Pediatr Adolesc Med 2000; 154(3):220-6.

14. Epstein LH, Paluch RA, Gordy CC, Saelens BE, Ernst MM. Problem solving in the treatment of childhood obesity. J Consult Clin Psychol 2000;68(4):717-21.

15. Epstein LH, Valoski A, McCurley J. Effect of weight loss by obese children on long-term growth. Am J Dis Child 1993;147(10):1076-80.

16. Epstein LH, Valoski A, Wing RR, McCurley J. Ten-year follow-up of behavioral, family-based treatment for obese children. JAMA 1990;264(19):2519-23.

17. Epstein LH, Valoski A, Wing RR, McCurley J. Ten-year outcomes of behavioural family-based treatment for childhood obesity. Health Psychol 1994;13(5):373-83.

18. Epstein LH, Valoski AM, Vara LS, McCurley J, Wisniewski L, Kalarchian MA, et al. Effects of decreasing sedentary behaviour and increasing activity

on weight change in obese children. Health Psychol 1995;14(2):109-15.

19. Ferguson MA, Gutin B, Le NA, Karp W, Litaker M, Humphries M, et al. Effects of exercise training and its cessation on components of the insulin resistance syndrome in obese children. Int J Obes Relat Metab Disord 1999;23(8):889-95.

20. Figueroa-Colon R, von Almen TK, Franklin FA, Schuftan C, Suskind RM. Comparison of two hypocaloric diets in obese children. Am J Dis Child 1993;147(2):160-6.

21. Figueroa-Colon R, Franklin FA, Lee JY, von Almen TK, Suskind RM. Feasibility of a clinic-based hypocaloric dietary intervention implemented in a school setting for obese children. Obes Res 1996;4(5):419-29.

22. Flodmark CE, Ohlsson T, Ryden O, Sveger T. Prevention of progression to severe obesity in a group of obese schoolchildren treated with family therapy. Pediatrics 1993;91(5):880-4.

23. Gately PJ, Cooke CB, Butterly RJ, Mackreth P, Carroll S. The effects of a children's summer camp programme on weight loss, with a 10 month follow-up. Int J Obes Relat Metab Disord 2000;24(11):1445-52.

24. Golan M, Weizman A, Apter A, Fainaru M. Parents as the exclusive agents of change in the treatment of childhood obesity. Am J Clin Nutr 1998;67:1130-5.

25. Greenstein RJ, Rabner JG. Is adolescent gastric-restrictive antiobesity surgery warranted? Obes Surg 1995;5(2):138-44.

26. Gutin B, Owens S, Slavens G, Riggs S, Treiber F. Effect of physical training on heart-period variability in obese children. J Pediatr 1997;130(6):938-43.

27. Israel AC, Guile CA, Baker JE, Silverman WK. An evaluation of enhanced self-regulation training in the treatment of childhood obesity. J Pediatr Psychol 1994;19(6):737-49.

28. Johnson WG, Hinkle LK, Carr RE, Anderson DA, Lemmon CR, Engler LB, et al. Dietary and exercise interventions for juvenile obesity: long-term

effect of behavioral and public health models. Obes Res 1997;5(3):257-61.

29. Mason EE, Scott DH, Doherty C, Cullen JJ, Rodriguez EM, Maher JW, et al. Vertical banded gastroplasty in the severely obese under age twenty-one. Obes Surg 1995;5(1):23-33.

30. Mellin LM, Slinkard LA, E Irwin C. Adolescent obesity intervention: validation of the SHAPEDOWN program. J Am Diet Assoc 1987;87(3):333-8.

31. Molnar D, Torok K, Erhardt E, Jeges S. Safety and efficacy of treatment with an ephedrine/caffeine mixture. The first doubleblind placebo-controlled pilot study in adolescents. Int J Obes Relat Metab Disord 2000;24(12):1573-8.

32. Nuutinen O, Knip M. Long-term weight control in obese children: persistence of treatment outcome and metabolic changes. Int J Obes Relat Metab Disord 1992;16(4):279-87.

33. Nuutinen O, Knip M. Weight loss, body composition and risk factors for cardiovascular disease in obese children: long-term effects of two treatment strategies. J Am Coll Nutr 1992;11(6):707-14.

34. Pidlich J, Pfeffel F, Zwiauer K, Schneider B, Schmidinger H. The effect of weight reduction on the surface electrocardiogram: a prospective trial in obese children and adolescents. Int J Obes Relat Metab Disord 1997;21(11):1018-23.

35. Rand SC, Macgregor AMC, Gainesville F. Adolescents having obesity surgery: a 6-year follow-up. South Med J 1994;87(12):1208-13.

36. Rocchini AP, Katch V, Anderson J, Hinderliter J, Becque D, Martin M, et al. Blood pressure in obese adolescents: effect of weight loss. Pediatrics 1988;82(1):16-23.

37. Rocchini AP, Katch V, Schork A, Kelch RP. Insulin and blood pressure during weight loss in obese adolescents. Hypertension 1987;10(3):267-73.

38. Schwingshandl J, Sudi K, Eibl B, Wallner S, Borkenstein M. Effect of an individualised training programme during weight reduction on body

composition: a randomised trial. Arch Dis Child 1999;81(5):426-8.

39. Sothern MS, Loftin JM, Udall JN, Suskind RM, Ewing TL, Tang SC, et al. Safety, feasibility, and efficacy of a resistance training program in pre-adolescent obese children. Am J Med Sci 2000;319(6):370-5.

40. Spieth LE, Harnish JD, Lenders CM, Raezer LB, Pereira MA, Hangen SJ, et al. A low-glycemic index diet in the treatment of pediatric obesity. Arch Pediatr Adolesc Med 2000;154(9): 947-51.

41. Strauss RS, Bradley LJ, Brolin RE. Gastric bypass surgery in adolescents with morbid obesity. J Pediatr 2001;138(4):499-504.

42. Wabitsch M, Hauner H, Bockmann A, Parthon W, Mayer H, Teller W. The relationship between body fat distribution and weight loss in obese adolescent girls. Int J Obes Relat Metab Disord 1992;16(11):905-11.

43 Ylitalo VM. Treatment of obese schoolchildren. Klin Padiatr 1982;194(5):310-4.

6
Quality of Life

Summary

The primary reasons why obese people attempt to lose weight probably relate to the negative impact that obesity has on their quality of life, i. e., how they feel and function, and the perceived benefits of weight loss treatment. Research on quality of life and obesity is a relatively new field, but the knowledge gained already suggests that measuring the quality of life of obese people can provide new, valuable clinical information.

Results: Ten population studies were found in the scientific literature. They used the same instrument for obese individuals and normal weight individuals. Six studies addressed quality of life in people who had visited health services for obesity, and four studies compared quality of life with that in patients having other diseases. One large study investigated the effects of weight loss from surgery, and weight loss from nonsurgical methods was addressed in six studies.

Quality of life among obese people was clearly lower than that in the general population as regards physical function, general health status, and vitality (Evidence Grade 1). The situation was worse for women than for men, and was also worse in those with more pronounced obesity, in those with other concurrent disease, and in those who sought treatment (Evidence Grade 2). In many subjects, quality of life was lower in patients with severe obesity than in patients with other severe chronic diseases (Evidence Grade 3).

Quality of life improved with weight loss. The more pronounced the weight loss, the better was the quality of life (Evidence Grade 2). With pronounced weight loss (20–25 %), well-being and psychosocial functioning reached a level similar to the remainder of the population (Evidence Grade 2). This degree of improvement could be measured after surgical intervention only where dramatic and permanent weight loss was achieved. Uncertain short-term effects (less than 1 year) on quality of life have been documented with modest weight loss, but the data are insufficient for grading the evidence.

Conclusion: Obese people have a lower quality of life than do people of normal weight. With permanent weight loss, such as that achieved by surgical intervention for severe obesity, quality of life improves with the degree of weight loss.

Treating and Preventing Obesity. Edited by J. Östman, M. Britton, E. Jonsson
Copyright © 2004 WILEY-VCH Verlag GmbH & Co. KGaA, Weinheim
ISBN 3-527-30818-0

6.1
Introduction

The term "quality of life", like "health", is multifaceted and cannot be specifically defined. Although both concepts reflect different aspects of well-being, quality of life has a substantially broader context. The concept of health-related quality of life involves a pragmatic distinction and applies mainly to function and well-being during sickness, ill health, and treatment. The models for concepts and measures range from disease-specific to general aspects, from physical to psychological health, and from functional impairment to well-being (Table 6.1).

Measuring and evaluating aspects of quality of life and obesity were initially discussed by the research community in the late 1980s [26]. Physical, psychological, and psychosocial aspects were addressed. Among other issues, attention was given to problems involving prejudice and discrimination against obese people. One approach discussed was that research on quality of life should contribute toward changing public attitudes toward obesity, e.g., moving away from placing guilt on patients and moving toward effective health service interventions.

The previous, rather unilateral focus on weight, BMI, and the risks of obesity did not provide sufficient understanding of how an individual's quality of life is affected or of the benefits and limitations associated with medical treatment in a patient's life. The things that obese people perceive to be the most important are, on the one hand, avoiding severe symptoms, hospitalization, and heavy medication, and on the other hand surviving, feeling good, and being able to function in daily life.

In recent decades, reliable methods for measuring quality of life have been developed and tested via international collaboration between physicians and methodology experts. Standardized questionnaires are now sophisticated enough to measure experiences and draw international comparisons. These questionnaires can be self-administered by patients, following brief instructions, and cover important, well-defined areas such as symptom severity, functional impairment, and physical, psychological, and social well-being. The methods have been sufficiently assessed to permit the development of guidelines for their application and interpretation. To be used as an outcome measure, e.g., for obesity, the concept of quality of life should:

- rest on a foundation of patient-based information
- be multidimensional and health related
- have the capacity to confirm changes in how patients feel and function in daily life.

6.2
Methods

This chapter is based on a systematic literature review of studies addressing the quality of life of obese people and the effect that treating obesity has on the quality of life in adults. All available databases, including PsycInfo, were used to identify relevant studies. The search terms used, alone and in combination, were: "obesity and quality of life, and questionnaire", "SF-36", "mental health", and "BMI and quality of life". (SF-36 is an established method for measuring quality of life.) The final search was performed in December 2001. Only studies that had used standardized methods, described the process used, and reported adequate data were selected for the final review.

6.3
Results

6.3.1
Quality of Life in Overweight and Obese People

Table 6.2 presents the 10 population studies that were found in this subject area. The studies were conducted in Europe, Australia, and the United States. The same instrument, the SF-36 health questionnaire, was used to measure function and well-being (Table 6.1). Although the studies reveal differences in design, material, dropout, etc., they do provide an overview of the situation.

Obese people generally report impaired function and a lower level of well-being, more in a physical than in a psychological sense, than overweight and normal weight groups. Quality of life deteriorates as weight increases. Significant differences are found throughout the "physical function" scale, and mainly reflect impaired movement and mobility functions in obese people.

Even the "general health" and "vitality" scales, which include physical and psychological health, are consistently lower in obese people. Furthermore, the pain scale indicates that obese people often have more pain than others. Estimating the effect size confirms that these aspects in quality of life are the most impaired [6, 19, 20, 28]. In extreme obesity (BMI $\geq$ 40), both physical and psychological parameters are greatly impaired and differ significantly from all other groups. In comparisons between extremely obese and normal weight people, the greatest effect is on "physical function", 1.14 [6], 1.18 [19], and 1.06 [22] (BMI $\geq$ 35). Other scales such as " role function/physical causes", "pain", "general health", "vitality", and "social function" show major to moderate effects.

One study found that the greatest deterioration in quality of life was among obese women aged 35 through 64 years [19]. Other morbidity and physical inactivity were contributing factors. Each of these factors had a significant impact on impairing the quality of life, mainly as regards physical health. Several of the studies confirmed this, depending to some extent on the method of analysis and adjust-

Table 6.1 Health-related quality of life and obesity in population studies (SF-36 Health Questionnaire).

Author Year Reference	Country	Number, Response rate %	Age range, mean age years	Women %
Brown WJ et al. 1998 [2]	Australia	13 431 54	45–49 dm	100
Brown WJ et al. 2000 [3]	Australia	14 779 43	18–23 20	100
Burns CM et al. 2001 [4]	The Netherlands	4 601 44	20–59 42	53
Doll HA et al. 2000 [6]	Great Britain	8 889 64	18–64 41	56
Fine JT et al. 1999 [7]	USA	40 098 69	46–71 58	100
Han TS et al. 1998 [10]	The Netherlands	4 041 50	20–59 42	53
Larsson U et al. 2002 [19]	Sweden	5 633 72	16–64 dm	51
Le Pen C et al. 1998 [20]	France	853 85	18+ dm	45
Richards MM et al. 2000 [22]	USA	290 dm	43 dm	65
Sullivan M et al. 2001 [28]	Sweden	1 694 68	18+	51

dm = data missing; HRQL = Health-Related Quality of Life
[1] PF: Physical Functioning; RP: Role – Physical; BP: Bodily Pain; GH: General Health;
   VT: Vitality; SF: Social Functioning; RE: Role – Emotional; MH: Mental Health;
   (–) = significantly poorer quality of life; (+) = significantly better quality of life

Results Test of differences in SF-36[1] between weight groups	Study quality Comments
Comp: BMI <20 versus 30<BMI ≤40 PF, RP, BP, GH, VT (–)	Medium Part of Australian Longitudinal Study on Women's Health
Comp: 20 ≤BMI <25 versus BMI 25+ PF, GH, VT (–)	Medium Part of Australian Longitudinal Study on Women's Health
Comp: BMI <25 versus BMI 25+ Men: no difference Women: PF, RP, BP, GH, SF (–)	Medium BMI adjusted for age, education, and perceived weight status. Poorer HRQL for overweight people who perceive themselves as too fat
Comp: 18.5 ≤BMI <25 versus 30 ≤BMI <40 PF, RP, BP, GH, VT (–)	High Poorer HRQL for obese people with other chronic illness
Prospective cohort study over 4 years Weight gain: PF, BP, VT (–) Weight loss: PF, BP, VT (+)	High Nurses' Health Study
Comp: tertials of BMI (T1 versus T3) Men: PF, BP (–) Women: PF, BP, GH (–)	Medium Part of MORGEN (Monitoring Risk Factors and Health in the Netherlands)
Comp: 18.5 ≤BMI <25 versus 30 ≤BMI <40 Age group: 16–34 years Men: PF, RP, GH, VT, SF (–)/Women: PF, BP, GH (–) Age group: 35–64 years Men: PF (–)/Women: PF, RP, BP, GH, VT, SF, MH (–)	High
Comp: BMI <27 versus BMI 30+ PF, RP, BP, GH, VT (–)	Medium
Comp: BMI <27 versus BMI 35+ PF, RP, BP, GH, VT, SF, RE, MH (–)	Medium Comparison between adult sibling pairs reared in the same family where one is normal weight and one is severely obese
Comp: age- and gender-matched population norm versus BMI 30+ PF, RP, BP, GH, VT, SF, RE, MH (–)	Medium Based on Swedish population norm for SF-36, n=8930

Table 6.2 Health related quality of life and obesity. Differences in the SF-36 scales are expressed in effect sizes: trivial (0 to <0.2), small (0.2 to <0.5), moderate (0.5 to <0.8) and great (0.8+).

	Effect sizes		
SF-36	*Overweight and obese patients n=312 versus Normal weight population (USA) n=2474*	*Extremely obese patients n=80 versus Normal weight population (USA) n=2474*	*Overweight and obese patients n=312 versus Overweight and obese patients who did not seek treatment n=89*
Physical Functioning (PF)	Moderate	Great	Small
Role – Physical (RP)	Small	Great	Small
Bodily Pain (BP)	Great	Great	Moderate
General Health (GH)	Small	Great	Small
Vitality (VT)	Great	Great	Moderate
Social Functioning (SF)	Small	Moderate	Trivial
Role – Emotional (RE)	Trivial	Small	Trivial
Mental Health (MH)	Small	Moderate	Trivial

ment for the influence of various factors. Doll documented the impact of other morbidity on lowering the quality of life in both a physical and a psychological context [6].

Burns reports on other factors that contribute toward reduction of the quality of life due to overweight (BMI ≥ 25) [4]. Perceived overweight had a more negative influence on some aspects of quality of life than BMI, adjusted for age and education. The "general health" and "vitality" scales in both genders and the "physical function" scale in women were significantly lower for those who perceived themselves as obese. Frequent attempts at dieting during the past 5 years also showed a correlation with impaired quality of life. Among men, the "physical function" and "role function/emotional causes" scales had an impact, and in women a decline in 6 of 8 scales was documented, e. g., "physical well-being" and "role function/emotional causes". Middle-aged women (40–50 years) with 10 % or more weight gain showed significantly worse values in the "physical function", "general health", and "vitality" scales than groups with less weight gain or weight loss. The findings with regard to weight gain and diminished health status are comparable with Fine's documentation from a large cohort of women aged 46–71 years, who were followed prospectively for 4 years [7]. Weight gain correlated significantly to lower levels of "physical function", "vitality", and "pain". Weight loss over the 4-year period was significantly associated with improved levels in these three scales.

The "psychological well-being" scale surprisingly showed similar values among countries and degree of overweight, with the exception of extreme obesity. The results indicate that psychological stress levels do increase in a linear trend with increasing weight in the general population, up to the cutoff point for severe obesity. The low level of psychological health status in the extremely obese group suggests that there is a BMI level at which psychological well-being begins to deteriorate radically. However, it is uncertain whether the "psychological well-being" scale (in SF-36) is sufficiently sensitive to detect mood problems such as mild and more severe depression. One of the population studies used a study-specific measure in addition to SF-36 [20], but it did not improve the results.

6.3.2
Studies of Obese People who Seek Treatment

A few studies have reported data to highlight possible differences between obese people who seek treatment and population groups. The results point in the same direction. Fontaine presented data from a well-designed study of 312 patients who sought treatment for various levels of overweight in comparison with a normal American population (Table 6.3) [8]. The results agree with the pattern described in the population studies, i.e., the greater the obesity the lower the quality of life. However, the patients' values are substantially lower with regard to the physical aspects of quality of life than those presented in corresponding BMI groups in the population studies. The analyses controlled for other morbidity and sociodemographic variables. A comparison between people seeking treatment for obesity and those not seeking treatment showed that the non-seekers had lower values on the "pain", "vitality", and "general health" scales [9]. Obese patients who reported pain clearly had worse quality-of-life profiles, even in the other 7 scales, than other patients did [1].

The Swedish Obese Subjects (SOS) study (Chapter 4.6) investigated men with BMI >34 and women with BMI >38, aged 37–57 years, using an extensive battery of general and obesity-specific instruments that covered all important aspects of quality of life (Table 6.1). Comparison with a gender- and age-matched population group without obesity (58 % normal weight, 41.5 % overweight, 0.5 % underweight) shows that seekers of care within the framework of the SOS study (11 % obese, 43 % severely obese, 46 % extremely obese) clearly had a worse quality-of-life profile than the normal weight population. This applied to both men and women (Table 6.4). Obese women showed greater variations than the normal population as regards all physical and psychological aspects except "general health perception", where the differences for men and women were similar [14]. The general negative impact of obesity on quality of life confirms earlier comparisons in the SOS study. Functional health (based on the Sickness Impact Profile, which measures functional impairment in 12 areas) was found to be significantly worse in terms of both physical and psychological aspects than that of the normal weight population [28]. Cognitive

Table 6.3 Health-related quality of life and obesity. Comparison between obese patients (SOS) and normal weight people in the population. Differences expressed in effect sizes: trivial (0 to <0.2), small (0.2 to <0.5), moderate (0.5 to <0.8) and great (0.8+).

Area	Effect sizes Obesity versus non-obesity[1]	
	Men[2]	Women[2]
Eating behavior		
Restrained eating	Trivial	Trivial
Uncontrolled eating	Great	Great
Sense of hunger	Great	Great
Psychosocial function		
Psychosocial problems	Great	Great
Function		
Functional status, total	Great	Great
Gait	Moderate	Great
Housework	Moderate	Moderate
Employment	Moderate	Moderate
Free-time/recreation	Great	Great
Social interaction	Moderate	Moderate
General health perception		
Current health	Great	Great
Mental well-being		
Mood, total	Moderate	Great
Anxiety	Moderate	Moderate
Depression	Moderate	Great
Self-rating	Small	Great
Quality of life, total		
Global rating	Moderate	Great

[1] All tests of differences between obesity and non-obesity are significant,
 except tests for "restrained eating" in men (non-significant)
[2] Obesity: men=2601, women=4262
 Non-obesity: men=468, women=549

function, attention, memory, and communication were, however, not worse in obese people. The results agree with earlier data from the first 1743 SOS patients [27].

6.3.3
Comparisons with People having other Chronic Disease and Disability

The SOS study also drew comparisons with other groups in health care to better describe the type and extent of problems with obesity. Psychological well-being was worse among patients who sought treatment for severe obesity than among most other patient groups with chronic conditions, e. g., rheumatoid arthritis, cancer (2–3 years after diagnosis), or paralysis following spinal cord injury [27]. Mood was worse among obese people than in people who had survived cancer and was

Figure 6.1 Health-related quality of life – terms and instruments in SOS Quality of Life Survey. (Modified from Sullivan et al, 2001).

Term: **Disease-related/ general**	Instruments: **Obesity-related/ general**		

Condition-specific
Symptoms/problems/
consequences
	TFEQ
	– Restrained eating
	– Uncontrolled eating
	– Hunger
		OP
		– Obesity-specific
		  psychosocial
		  problems
			OD[1]
			– Intrusion
			– Helplessness

General			
Physical/movement- oriented consequences	SIP – Gait – Housework – Employment – Free-time/recreation	SF-36[2] – Physical functioning – Role – physical – Pain	
Health in general	GHRI – Current health	SF-36 – General health – Vitality	
Social/emotional consequences	SIP – Social interaction	SF-36 – Social functioning – Role – emotional	

Mental health/ill health	HAD
	– Depression
	– Anxiety
	
	MACL
	– Mood, total
	– Positive/Negative
	  basic mood
	– Mental activation/
	  Passivity
	– Relaxation/Tension
	
	SE
	– Self-esteem
		SF-36
		– Mental well-being	

Quality of life totally	Global rating		

TFEQ: Three-Factor Eating Questionnaire; OP: Obesity-related Problem scale;
OD: Obesity mental Distress scale; SIP: Sickness Impact Profile (5/12 categories);
SF-36: Short-Form Health Survey; GHRI: General Health Rating Index;
HAD: Hospital Anxiety and Depression scale; MACL: Mood Adjective Check List;
SE: Self-Esteem scale

[1] OD included at 0, 2, and 10 years
[2] SF-36 included at 10 years

approximately the same as that among patients who had relapsed to cancer [28]. Obese people had the same degree of psychological distress as individuals with spinal cord injury at an early stage (< 2 years after injury). Comparisons of the level of mental illness among patients with obesity and other chronic diseases support the conclusion that those who seek treatment for obesity have a markedly diminished level of psychological well-being [27].

Functional capacity among the earliest patients in the SOS study was compared to that of cancer survivors [28]. Functional health was found to be significantly worse when one considered both physical and psychosocial aspects in obese people. Further analyses show that the functional profile in obesity was comparable to that in subgroups with one or more relapses of cancer, except that mobility was better in obese patients. Function was also better than that in patients with permanently impaired mobility, e.g., that resulting from rheumatoid arthritis and healed spinal cord injury.

Two other studies addressing similar issues have been published. Fontaine compared the influence of pain in obese subjects with data published earlier from American studies of depression, heart failure, symptomatic HIV, and migraine [8]. Obese people reported significantly more pain than other patient groups, except for patients with migraine, where the values were similar, even though researchers adjusted for other morbidity that might explain the pain problem. However, these results have not been replicated/verified.

Katz presents cross-sectional data concerning the influence of overweight and obesity on quality of life in patients with various chronic diseases [15]. The results are from SF-36, which was applied in the largest American primary care study, the Medical Outcomes Study. Of 2931 patients, a little over one third were not overweight (BMI < 25), a similar number were overweight, while 18 % were obese and 12 % were severely obese (BMI ≥ 35). A subgroup of non-overweight patients with mild hypertension was used as a reference group in the analysis. A group of heart failure patients was also compared. The analyses were controlled for numerous demographic and lifestyle variables along with other mental and physical morbidity. The findings showed that both overweight and obese individuals had significantly lower values on physical scales in SF-36 than those of the reference group, mainly impaired physical function but also reduced role function on physical scales and elevated values on the pain scale. Obese patients also had significantly worse general health and vitality. In severe obesity, role function was impaired for emotional reasons. No differences could be documented in social function or psychological well-being. Severely obese people were close to the level of heart failure patients as regards physical function and vitality, but had higher pain scores. Compared to men, women in all overweight groups demonstrated lower values on most of the scales.

6.3.4
Specific Psychosocial Problems in Obese Patients

Obese people commonly face prejudicial attitudes in Western cultures, even in health services. Discrimination against obese people in working life and in several other social contexts has been documented [29]. This problem has not received sufficient attention and has not been evaluated by standardized measurement methods.

The SOS study integrated psychosocial function in the quality-of-life measurements (Figure 6.1). Obesity-related psychosocial problems are related, to different degrees, to the level of overweight in men and women [28]. Women report more problems in all areas regardless of level of obesity, while men report more problems with increasing obesity. Regardless of gender, social activities in public places, e.g., trying on and purchasing clothing, swimming, etc., present the greatest problems. Even participating in group activities and outdoor life are perceived as problems by many obese people. Background variables found to have an independent relationship with the measurement scale were, in declining order of importance, previous psychiatric symptomatology, female gender, perceived obesity, joint problems, many dieting attempts, physical inactivity, and angina. These variables, in combination, explained 28 % of the variance in the OP scale (see Chapter 4.6 on surgical treatment) [13, 27].

Obesity-related psychosocial problems – OP

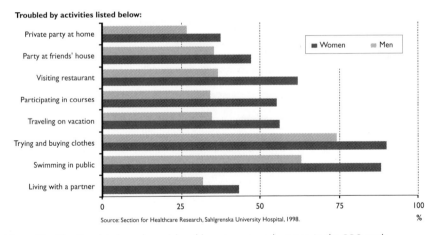

Source: Section for Healthcare Research, Sahlgrenska University Hospital, 1998.

Figure 6.1 Obesity-related psychosocial problems in men and women in the SOS study (n=5187). Share troubled (very or somehwat troubled) shown for each item on the OP scale.

6.3.5
Effects of Surgery on Quality of Life

A study on quality of life from the SOS intervention study showed dramatic improvements in quality of life after 6 months for the group receiving surgery, while the control group improved to a minor degree [13]. The positive results applied to both obesity-specific psychosocial problems and eating behavior as a function of general health perception and psychological well-being. However, the early improvements had subsided to some extent at 1 and 2 years after surgery. Nevertheless, long-term improvement in the surgically treated group is noticeable, with statistically significant differences in relation to the outset and to the values of the control groups. Most obvious was the influence on obesity-specific problems, eating behavior, and general health and depression. The effects on the health-related quality of life are probably related to the degree of weight loss, i.e., greater weight loss yields greater positive effects on quality of life, to the same degree in both men and women.

Treatment effects after 4 years

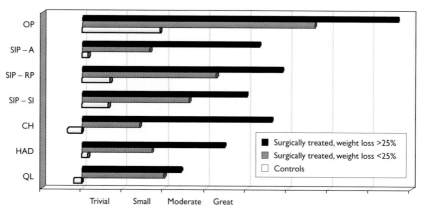

Source: Section for Healthcare Research, Sahlgrenska University Hospital, 1998.

Figure 6.2 Health-related quality of life and obesity.
Treatment effects after 4 years in the two groups of the SOS study (n=1088): surgical and conventional treatment (controls). Those treated by surgery have been grouped according to the size of the weight loss at 4 years. The effect have been expressed in "standardized response mean" (SRM) calculated as change in mean from baseline to 4 years divided by the standard deviation for the change:
– trivial (0 to <0.2)
– small (0.2 to <0.5)
– moderate (0.5 to <0.8)
– great (0.8+).
Obesity-related psychosocial problems (OP)
Function: gait, free-time recreation, social interaction (SIP-A; SIP-RP; SIP-SI)
Current Health (CH)
Depression (HAD)
Quality of life, global rating (QL)

Sullivan reported quality-of-life data up to 4 years after surgery [28]. The positive effects demonstrated the same patterns as in 2-year followup. A high retention of effects on quality of life requires a high retention of weight loss (20–25 %, Figure 6.2). Moderate weight loss, less than 10 %, did not cause a relapse to the original weight in the major obesity-specific scales (e. g., OP, Figure 6.3). The results are similar in men and women. Continued, unchanged values concerning quality of life were noted in the control groups. Improvements in psychosocial function and well-being showed that patients with major weight loss approached the levels of normal weight individuals. Even the high prevalence of suspected depression prior to treatment was nearly normalized in the group with major (20–25 %) weight loss.

Obesity-related psychosocial problems – OP

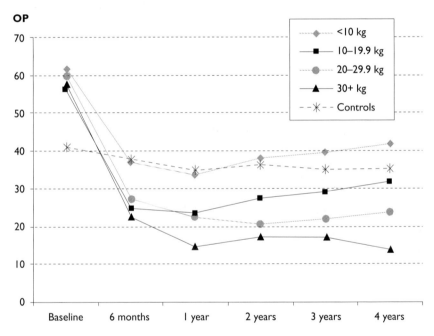

Source: Section for Healthcare Research, Sahlgrenska University Hospital, 1998.

Figure 6.3 Obesity-related psychosocial problems (OP scale).
Treatment effects over time in the two groups of the SOS study (n=1088): surgical and conventional treatment (controls). The effect in those treated by surgery is shown in relation to the size of the weight loss at 4 years.

6.3.6
Effects of Non-Surgical Treatment on Quality of Life

A 2-year followup of 60 moderately overweight women who were treated with either vegetarian or non-vegetarian diets reported an average weight reduction of 3.9 kg among those who complied with the vegetarian diet program [12]. The others increased in weight by 1.8 kg. The study documented health-related quality of life and eating behavior prior to the study and after 3, 8, and 24 months (75 % followup rate at 2 years). The study shows that overweight women who lost weight generally experienced greater self-esteem and well-being during weight loss, but their mood afterward returned to, or became worse than, the level at the outset due to difficulty in maintaining the diet and the lower weight. Functional status also improved in conjunction with weight loss, and the women who complied with the study reported a significant improvement in physical function after 2 years. Self-rated eating behavior prior to treatment correlated with later weight increase. This study demonstrates the importance that long-term followup of conventional dietary treatment effects has on health-related quality of life.

Two large randomized multicenter trials addressed the measurement of quality of life. One study focused on dietary treatment (comparative study for 1 year, no controls [21]). The second focused on pharmacotherapy (placebo-controlled, double-blind, orlistat study for 2 years) [23].

Both studies report significant effects on quality of life, but without thorough reporting of data. Also, both studies measure quality of life by general and nutritional- and obesity-related measures, probably study-specific, but unknown outside of these studies. The quality-of-life effect in the orlistat study is limited to differences in satisfaction with the treatment attempt, weight loss, medication, and the total dieting program between placebo and high- and low-dose groups of patients receiving medication. These assessments comprise an important part of the umbrella concept, Patient Reported Outcome (PRO), but do not belong to the conceptual model for quality-of-life measurement [5]. The second study reports p-values, statistical significance, for effects in all tested scales in the hypertension/dyslipidemia and type-2 diabetes disease groups. The study includes both overweight and obese people. The methods section describes a procedure for calculating effect size and a selected threshold at 0.3 points for the lowest meaningful clinical change for reporting results. Neither of these studies can be assessed based on the criteria for assessing quality of life.

A randomized comparative study investigated the influence of weight loss on asthma in 38 patients with obesity and asthma [25]. The experimental group completed a treatment program as a group, including VLCD (very low calorie diet), while the control group conducted a discussion program as a group during the same period. The primary outcome measures included a well-established health/quality-of-life measure used in pulmonary medicine to assess the impact of disease as regards symptoms, activities, and social/psychological consequences [11]. After 1 year, the treatment group had improved more than the control group in all respects. Weight loss averaged 11 % in the treatment group versus 2 % weight gain in the control group.

Several smaller studies have used an obesity-specific IWQOL (Impact of Weight on Quality of Life Questionnaire) developed in the United States following interviews with obese individuals [16]. Psychometric and clinical assessment and inclusion of instruments in the pharmacological testing resulted in a short form, IWQOL-Lite, with improved psychometric characteristics [17, 18].

Two studies are particularly noteworthy. The first concerns effects of moderate weight loss on quality of life, combining data from 4 randomized, double-blind, controlled multicenter trials of sibutramine versus placebo [24]. The study focused on responsiveness in quality-of-life measures, i. e., whether it follows a dose-response pattern after 8 to 12 weeks, 24 to 28 weeks, and 1 year. Mainly at 24 to 28 weeks, significant effects were achieved in several variables, e. g., physical function, general health, and vitality. Regarding a total quality-of-life index, a minor effect was reported in patients with weight loss of 5–10 %. At 1 year, the dose-response pattern was substantially weaker. The study, however, involves a short time frame, and concluded after 1 year.

The second study is a descriptive, 1-year followup of 141 women and 20 men using a combined diet and medication program (combination phentermine-fenfluramine) to determine the effects on physical function, self-esteem, sex life, public distress, and work [17, 18]. A significant correlation was found between the degree of weight loss (approximately 18 %) and improvement in quality of life. Approximately 14 % of the 1-year change in total points was explained by weight change. The threshold value, based on the criteria for meaningful change, was approximately a 10-point difference. Hence, the greater the weight loss the greater the percentage of patients who passed this threshold. In the group with the least weight loss (< 10 %) 44 % were above the threshold value, and in the group with the greatest weight loss (20 %) the rate was 76 %. This pattern was significant for physical function, sex life, and self-esteem, but not for work and public distress. The study needs to be replicated in controlled trials over a longer period, in larger groups, and with a higher percentage of men. Alternative methods for the least clinically meaningful difference should also be tested.

6.4

Appendix: Conclusions and Need for Research

6.4.1

Quality of Life[1] and Obesity: Population Studies

Obese people differ from overweight and normal weight people in the population. They report lower scores on function and well-being, more in a physical than in a psychological sense. The greatest differences concern physical function, general health, and vitality.

Generally, the greater the obesity the lower is the quality of life, mainly in regard to physical aspects. Overweight individuals, however, differ only marginally from normal weight individuals.

In extremely obese individuals, both physical and psychological aspects are substantially impaired, mainly physical function, role function – physical causes, pain, general health, vitality, and social function.

The greater the comorbidity, the lower is the quality of life.

Weight change (gain negative and loss positive) influences physical health more than psychological health in women.

6.4.2

Quality of Life and Obesity: Clinical Studies

Obese people differ from overweight and normal weight people in the population with greater margins than in corresponding comparisons of population samples.

Psychological well-being in severely obese patients is worse than that in the general public. Affective disorders are most common.

Psychosocial problems caused by obesity are common. Women are more affected than men.

Obese, especially severely obese, patients report lower function and well-being compared to many groups of chronically ill patients.

6.4.3

Quality of Life after Surgery for Severe Obesity

Surgical treatment represents the only long-term, effective method for substantial and maintained weight loss and, subsequently, for effects on quality of life. Improvements in quality of life can be assessed and related to weight loss. The greater the weight loss, the greater are the effects on quality of life in both men and women.

If weight loss is very substantial (20–25 %), psychosocial function and well-being are nearly restored, i. e., to a level similar to that of the general public.

---

1) "Quality of life" as a measure in the field of
   medicine is synonymous with the concept of
   "health-related quality of life".

Also, with very substantial weight loss (20–25 %), the high prevalence figures for suspected depression are nearly normalized.

6.4.4
Quality of Life after Nonsurgical Treatment for Obesity

Short-term effects on quality of life (less than 1 year) have been documented with moderate weight loss.

6.4.5
Need for Further Research

Further research should document the following, insufficiently addressed, areas:

Obese people in the population and obese patients who are physically inactive report a lower quality of life. The causal relationship is, however, unclear. The impact of lifestyle factors on quality of life in obese people should be studied in greater detail.

"Yo-yo" dieting, i. e., numerous dieting attempts, is thought to have a negative impact on quality of life in overweight/obese men and women alike. However, the influence of yo-yo dieting on quality of life has been insufficiently assessed.

Some studies have shown that weight loss has promising effects on quality of life in obese people with another specific chronic diagnosis, e. g., asthma, type 2 diabetes, and hypertension. Further research is needed regarding quality of life benefits for obese people with comorbidities. This requires the use/development of diagnosis-specific quality-of-life instruments (e. g., SGRQ for respiratory conditions) to cover disease-specific functional impairments and symptoms/problems.

References

1. Barofsky I, Fontaine KR, Cheskin LJ. Pain in the obese: impact on health-related quality of life. Ann Behav Med 1997;19:408-10.

2. Brown WJ, Dobson AJ, Mishra G. What is a healthy weight for middle aged women? Int J Obes 1998;22:520-8.

3. Brown WJ, Mishra G, Kenardy J, Dobson A. Relationships between body mass index and well-being in young Australian women. Int J Obes 2000;24:1360-8.

4. Burns CM, Tijhuis MAR, Seidell JC. The relationship between quality of life and perceived body weight and dieting history in Dutch men and women. Int J Obes 2001;25:1386-92.

5. Chassany O, Sagnier P, Marquis P, Fullerton S, Aaronson NK, for the European Regulatory Issues on Health-Related Quality of Life Assessment (ERIQA) Group. Patient-reported outcomes and regulatory issues: the example of health-related quality of life. DIA Journal 2002;36:209-38.

6. Doll HA, Petersen SEK, Stewart-Brown SL. Obesity and physical and emotional well-being: Associations between body mass index, chronic illness, and the physical and mental components of the SF-36 questionnaire. Obes Res 2000;8:160-70.

7. Fine JT, Colditz GA, Coakley EH, Moseley G, Manson JAE, Willett WC, et al. A prospective study of weight change and health-related quality of life in women. JAMA 1999;282:2136-42.

8. Fontaine KR, Cheskin LJ, Barofsky I. Health-related quality of life in obese persons seeking treatment. J Fam Pract 1996;43:265-70.

9. Fontaine KR, Bartlett SJ, Barofsky I. Health-related quality of life among obese persons seeking and not currently seeking treatment. Int J Eat Disord 2000;27:101-5.

10. Han TS, Tijhuis MAR, Lean MEJ, Seidell JC. Quality of life in relation to overweight and body fat distribution. Am J Public Health 1998;88:1814-20.

11. Jones PW, Quirk FH, Baveystock CM. The St George's Respiratory Questionnaire. Respir Med 1991;85:25-35.

12. Karlsson J, Hallgren P, Kral J, Lindroos AK, Sjöström L, Sullivan M. Predictors and effects of long-term dieting on mental well-being and weight loss in obese women. Appetite 1994;23:15-26.

13. Karlsson J, Sjöström L, Sullivan M. Swedish obese subjects (SOS) – an intervention study of obesity. Two-year followup of health-related quality of life (HRQL) and eating behavior after gastric surgery for severe obesity. Int J Obes 1998;22;113-26.

14. Karlsson J, Sjöström L, Sullivan M. Quality of life (HRQL) in obese seeking treatment compared to non-obese reference subjects. Qual Life Res 2001;10:273.

15. Katz DA, McHorney CA, Atkinson RL. Impact of obesity on health-related quality of life in patients with chronic illness. J Gen Intern Med 2000; 15:789-96.

16. Kolotkin RL, Head S, Hamilton M, Tse C J. Assessing impact of weight on quality of life. Obes Res 1995;3:49-56.

17. Kolotkin RL, Crosby RD, Kosloski KD, Williams GR. Development of a brief measure to assess quality of life in obesity. Obes Res 2001;9:102-11.

18. Kolotkin RL, Crosby RD, Williams GR, Hartley GG, Nicol S. The relationship between health-related quality of life and weight loss. Obes Res 2001;9: 564-71.

19. Larsson U, Karlsson J, Sullivan M. Impact of overweight and obesity on health-related quality of life – a Swedish population study. Int J Obes 2002;26:417-24.

20. Le Pen C, Levy E, Loos F, Banzet MN, Basdevant A. "Specific" scale compared with "generic" scale: a double measurement of the quality of life in a French community sample of obese subjects. J Epidemiol Community Health 1998;52:445-50.

21. Metz JA, Stern JS, Kris-Etherton P, Reusser ME, Morris CD, Hatton DC, et al. A randomized trial of improved weight loss with a prepared meal plan in overweight and obese patients. Impact on cardiovascular risk reduction. Arch Intern Med 2000;160:2150-8.

22. Richards MM, Adams TD, Hunt SC. Functional status and emotional well-being, dietary intake, and physical activity of severely obese subjects. J Am Diet Assoc 2000;100:67-75.

23. Rössner S, Sjöström L, Noack R, Meinders E, Nosedal G on behalf of the European Orlistat Obesity Study Group. Weight loss, weight maintenance, and improved cardiovascular risk factors after 2 years treatment with orlistat for obesity. Obes Res 2000;8: 49-61.

24. Samsa GP, Kolotkin RL, Williams GR, Nguyen MH, Mendel CM. Effect of moderate weight loss on health-related quality of life: an analysis of combined data from 4 randomized trials of sibutramine vs placebo. Am J Manag Care 2001;7:875-83.

25. Stenius-Aarniala B, Poussa T, Kvarnström J, Grönlund EL, Ylikahri M, Mustajoki P. Immediate and long term effects of weight reduction in obese people with asthma: randomised controlled study. BMJ 2000;320:827-32.

26. Sullivan M, Sullivan L, Kral J. Quality of life assessment in obesity: physical, psychological, and social function. Gastroenterol Clin North Am 1987;16:433-42.

27. Sullivan M, Karlsson J, Sjöström L, Backman L, Bengtsson C, Bouchard C, et al. Swedish obese subjects (SOS) – an intervention study of obesity. Baseline evaluation of health and psychosocial functioning in the first 1743 subjects examined. Int J Obes 1993;17:503-12.

28. Sullivan M, Karlsson J, Sjöström L, Taft C. Why quality-of-life measures should be used in the treatment of patients with obesity. In: P Björntorp (ed), International textbook of obesity, Chichester: Wiley, 2001;485-510.

29. Wadden TA, Sarwer DB, Womble LG, Foster GD, McGuckin BG, Schimmel A. Psychosocial aspects of obesity and obesity surgery. Surg Clin North Am 2001;81:1001-24.

7
Effects of Obesity Treatment on Diseases and Special Conditions

7.1
Diabetes Mellitus (Type 2)

Summary

Accompanying the global increase in obesity is a dramatic increase in type 2 diabetes. To examine this situation, this Section assesses the effect that obesity treatment has on

1. glucose control in type 2 diabetes
2. prevention of type 2 diabetes in people at risk.

Results: Ten treatment studies showed substantial differences regarding patient selection and obesity treatments including energy reduced diet, VLCD, physical activity, and medication (orlistat and sibutramine). An important finding is that a weight loss of 5–10 kg is a precondition for achieving clinically meaningful effects on glucose control during a 6- to 12-month period. Glucose control in these studies has been judged by determining glycated hemoglobin, a method that reflects mean blood glucose over the previous 1–2 months. The effects, therefore, are modest, since weight loss is usually not permanent, and the severity of diabetes increases. All studies present medium quality (Evidence Grade 2).

Most severely obese people who have lost substantial weight after stomach surgery have fully normalized blood glucose and no longer need to be treated for diabetes.

The incidence of type 2 diabetes can be markedly reduced in people with a high level of obesity who lose substantial weight following surgery.

One North American and one Finnish prevention study have shown that changing to a lifestyle that includes an energy-restricted diet and more exercise for 2 years can reduce by half the onset of type 2 diabetes in individuals in the risk zone because of overweight/obesity and impaired glucose tolerance (Evidence Grade 1).

Conclusions: Through various types of treatment that achieve a weight loss of at least 5 %, glucose control can be improved for 6 months to 1 year. Surgical treatment of high-level obesity results in more pronounced and permanent effects, and largely prevents new onset of type 2 diabetes. The onset of type 2 diabetes

Treating and Preventing Obesity. Edited by J. Östman, M. Britton, E. Jonsson
Copyright © 2004 WILEY-VCH Verlag GmbH & Co. KGaA, Weinheim
ISBN 3-527-30818-0

has been prevented in overweight/obese people by improved lifestyle, i. e., suitable diet and more exercise.

7.1.1
Introduction

An estimated 80 % of patients with type 2 diabetes are obese or overweight. Obesity represents the largest non-hereditary factor for type 2 diabetes. Studies from various countries and ethnic groups have shown a causal relationship between obesity/overweight and type 2 diabetes [31]. The Nurses' Health Study shows that the relative risk of onset of diabetes is ca. 20 times higher at BMI > 30 and ca. 40 times higher at BMI > 35 [12]. Risk factors for developing type 2 diabetes include obesity during childhood, substantial weight gain after age 18, and an increased volume of abdominal fat. This has been demonstrated in prospective studies of the waist-hip ratio [3, 4, 13, 21, 25]. Both reduced glucose tolerance and reduced insulin sensitivity (insulin resistance) are related to the level of abdominal fat.

The increasing prevalence of obesity is viewed to be the main cause behind the global increase in type 2 diabetes, particularly in developing countries [15]. This trend, however, is not the same in all countries. A large study from Nord-Tröndelag has shown that, despite the rapid increase in the prevalence of obesity during the periods 1984–1986 and 1994–1996, the prevalence of type 2 diabetes generally increased only moderately, from 2.9 % to 3.2 %, and applied only to men, mainly in the group aged 50–59 years [23].

According to the Framingham study, if weight loss is maintained for many years, the onset of type 2 diabetes declines by nearly 40 % in people aged 30–50 years with BMI > 27 [24].

7.1.2
Methods

The literature review also includes articles presented in Chapter 4. In addition, a followup was conducted throughout October 1, 2001. The review covers nonsurgical treatment studies that were randomized and have been under way at least 24 weeks and surgical studies with control groups. Only drug studies that involved orlistat and sibutramine were included. Prevention studies were randomized controlled trials except when surgical methods were assessed.

7.1.3
Results

7.1.3.1 **Effects of Obesity Treatment on Type 2 Diabetes**
Ten studies were reviewed (Table 7.1). A 2-year study with minor dropout compared conventional dietary treatment with an expanded treatment program involving behavior modification and advice on exercise training [2]. A common feature of

the programs was an energy reduction of 500 kcal/day. After 6 months, the average weight loss was greater in the group with the expanded program (2.9 kg) compared to the conventional program (1.2 kg). A greater decline in HbA_1 was reported in the experiment group (1.0 %) than in the control group (0.1 %). After 2 years, no differences were observed between the study groups.

Another study compared VLCD (400 kcal/day for 8 weeks) with conventional weight loss programs. VLCD resulted in substantially greater weight loss (18.6 kg) after 20 weeks than did the conventional diet regimen (10.1 kg), but no difference was found at followup after 72 weeks [36]. On both followup occasions, however, HbA_1 was lower in the group treated by VLCD. The strength of the evidence in this study is weakened by variations in the treatment of diabetes (diet, tablets, and insulin) and the small number of patients.

A similar study compared the effects of two 12-week periods of VLCD (400–500 kcal/day) with a conventional, balanced, and energy-balanced diet (1000–1200 kcal/day) [32]. After 1 year, weight losses were similar in the study groups, 14.2 kg and 10.5 kg respectively. A substantial part of the weight loss noted already after 12 weeks remained, but not the improvement in glucose control.

A Finnish study was carried out on patients with newly diagnosed type 2 diabetes and a mean BMI of ca. 34. They first received 3 months of basic dietary instruction [17], and were randomized during the following year to conventional diet treatment or to an intensive educational program aimed at reducing the content of energy and fat in the diet. These effects were achieved, but not weight loss or improved glucose control (HbA_{1c}). However, a decrease in triglycerides and an increase in HDL cholesterol were reported.

The value of exercise in addition to dietary programs has been studied [34]. A moderately intensive exercise program involving at least three 5-kilometer walks per week led to greater weight loss after 62 weeks than did the diet regimen alone. The study groups, however, reported no difference in glucose control or self-reported energy intake.

A multicenter study of nearly 400 individuals treated with tablet medication for type 2 diabetes and obesity/overweight showed greater weight loss (6.2 kg) after 1 year of treatment with orlistat (120 mg $\times$ 3) than with placebo (4.3 kg weight loss) [11]. HbA_{1c} dropped from the initial value, ca. 7.5 % corresponding to 0.28 percentage points in the orlistat group, but increased by 0.18 percentage points in the control group. Tablet medication (sulfonylurea) could be reduced in the orlistat group. Dropout was 30 % in this group and 12 % in the control group, which somewhat weakens the value of the evidence.

A multicenter study from Sweden was aimed at investigating the effects of weight loss with orlistat on the risk factors for cardiovascular disease, type 2 diabetes, hypertension, and high cholesterol in patients with high BMI (28–38). After 8 weeks of treatment with a reduced-energy intake, 376 patients were randomized to treatment with orlistat (120 mg $\times$ 3) or placebo (1 $\times$ 3) for 1 year. Of the patients with type 2 diabetes, 54 were treated with orlistat and 44 were treated with placebo. The average weight loss after 1 year was greater in the orlistat group (5.4 %) than in the placebo group (3.5 %), which corresponds to a difference of

Table 7.1 Randomized trials on the effect of obesity treatment on body weight and glycated hemoglobin in type 2 diabetes.

Author Year Reference	Intervention method	Starting data Mean BMI Mean weight, kg	Other diabetic treatment (n=no. of patients)

Blonk MC
et al.
1994
[2]
	1. Extended program
	  (behavior therapy,
	  physical activity)
	2. Conventional
	  program
		1. 31.3/92.3
		
		2. 32.3/89.8
			Diet (15)
			Sulfonylurea (45)

Wing RR et al. 1991 [36]	1. VLCD (8 weeks) 2. Conventional weight reduction program	1. 37.3/102.1 2. 38.1/104.5	Diet (6) Tablets (20) Insulin (7)

Wing RR
et al.
1994
[32]
	1. VLCD
	  (400–500 kcal/day)
	  2 × 12 weeks
	  + low-energy diet 24 weeks
	2. Low-energy diet
	  (1000–1200 kcal/day)
	  48 weeks
		1. 37.4/105.8
		
		2. 38.3/107.7
			Diet (15)
			Tablets (52)
			Insulin (23)

Laitinen JH
et al.
1993
[17]
	1. Intensive diet program
	2. Conventional diet program.
	  Preceded by 3 months
	  basic diet education
		1. Men=32.6
		  Women=35.3
		2. Men=32.1
		  Women=35.1	

Wing RR
et al.
1988
[34]
	1. Physical activity
	  (walking >5 km × 3/week
	  + diet program
	2. Diet program for 10 weeks
		1. 37.5/104.1
		
		2. 37.9/102.0
			Diet (3)
			Tablets (19)
			Insulin (8)

Hollander PA
et al.
1998
[11]
	1. Orlistat (120 mg × 3)
	2. Placebo (1 × 3)
	  Low-energy diet in both
	  groups. DB
		1. 34.5/99.6
		2. 34.0/99.7
			Tablets
			(Sulfonylurea)

Lindgärde F
2000
[19]
	1. Orlistat (120 mg × 3)
	2. Placebo (1 × 3)
	  Energy-reduced diet
	  for 2 weeks and after
	  6 months. DB
		u	u

Fujioka K
et al.
2000
[6]
	1. Sibutramine
	  (5 mg × 1 → 20 mg × 1)
	2. Placebo (1 × 1)
	  Five weeks run-in
	  period with energy-
	  reduced diet. DB
		1. 34.1/99.3
		
		2. 33.8/98.2
			Diet (30)
			Sulfonylurea (118)
			Metformin (27)

See legend on page 286

No. of patients/ No. followed up	Result Weight, kg	Results a) HbA$_1$ b) HbA$_{1C}$ %	Results/Other	Study quality Comments
1. 30/27	6 months 1. −2.9 kg* 2. −1.2 kg	a) 6 months 1. −1.0* 2. −0.1		Medium
2. 30/26 Women approx. 65 %	2 years 1. −3.5 kg 2. −2.1 kg	2 years 1. 0 2. +0.4		
1. 17/16 2. 19/19 Women approx. 75 %	20 weeks 1. −18.6 kg* 2. −10.4 kg 72 weeks 1. −8.6 kg 2. −6.8 kg	a) 20 weeks 1. −3.1* 2. −1.6 72 weeks 1. −1.2* 2. 1.4		Medium Non-uniform medication makes comparison between groups difficult
1. 45/38	12 weeks 1. −16.0 kg* 2. −11.1 kg 1 year	a) 12 weeks 1. −2.5 2. −1.4 1 year	Reduced anti-diabetic medication in Group 1. Effect of VLCD on	Medium
2. 48/41 Women 65 %	1. −14.2 kg 2. −10.5 kg	1. 0.1 2. 0.2	weight loss. Loss was greater after 1 year in women	
1.40/40	Between month 3–15 1. −1.8 kg* 2. +1.0 kg	b) 1. −0.6 2. 0.3	HDL cholesterol increased and TG decreased in Group 1	Medium
2.46/40 Women approx. 45 %				
1. 15/13	10 weeks 1. −9.3 kg* 2. −5.6 kg 62 weeks	a) 10 weeks 1. −2.4 2. −1.9 62 weeks	Weight loss correlated to level of self-reported physical activity	Medium
2. 15/15 Women approx. 70 %	1. −7.9 kg* 2. −3.8 kg	1. −1.4 2. −0.8		
1. 163/139 2. 159/115 Women approx. 50 %	1 year 1. −6.2 kg* 2. −4.3 kg	b) 1 year 1. −0.28* 2. 0.18	Reduced anti-diabetic medication in Group 1	Medium
1. 54/u 2. 44/u	52 weeks 1. −5.4 %* 2. −3.5 %	b) 52 weeks 1. −0.65* 2. −0.14	Reduced anti-diabetic medication in Group 1	Low
1. 89/60 2. 86/61 Women 55 %	24 weeks 1. −4.3 kg* 2. −0.3 kg	b) 1. 0.06 2. 0.25	TG decreased in Group 1	Medium

Table continues on next page

Table 7.1 continued.

Author Year Reference	Intervention method	Starting data Mean BMI Mean weight, kg	Other diabetic treatment (n=no. of patients)
Gokcel A et al. 2001 [7]	1. Sibutramine (10 mg × 2) 2. Placebo (1 × 2) Low-energy diet (25 kcal/kg ideal weight and day) Fat <30%	1. HbA$_{1C}$ 10.0% 2. HbA$_{1C}$ 9.8% BP <160/<100. No participation in weight program	Oral anti- diabetics, maximum dose
Lee A et al. 1998 [18]	1. Metformin (850 mg × 2) 2. Placebo (1 × 2) DB	1. 39.6/112.3 2. 40.0/109.8	Diet (48)

IGT = Impaired Glucose Tolerance
* = Statistically significant difference between groups
u = no data on patients in subgroup with type 2 diabetes
VLCD = Very Low Calorie Diet
TG = Triglycerides
DB = Double-Blind
BP = Blood Pressure

ca. 2 kg. HbA$_{1c}$ declined more in the orlistat group (0.65 percentage points) than in the placebo group (0.14 percentage points). The clinical relevance is difficult to assess, since the HbA$_{1c}$ values are not given in absolute numbers but only as changes over time. Furthermore, dropout was not reported.

In a randomized, placebo-controlled and double-blind multicenter study, Fujioka et al. assessed the effects of sibutramine in patients with BMI 27–40 and with type 2 diabetes who did not respond satisfactorily to tablet treatment or diet alone [6]. After a 5-week introductory period, 89 patients were randomized to sibutramine treatment using an initial dose of 5 mg/day which, if needed, was increased to a maximum of 20 mg/day, or to treatment with placebo. After 24 weeks, weight loss was greater (4.3 kg) in the sibutramine group than in the placebo group (0.3 kg). In both study groups, HbA$_{1c}$ increased marginally. In 5 patients with at least 10% weight loss, HbA$_{1c}$ declined noticeably (1.40 percentage points), but it did not decline in the 19 patients with only 5–10% weight loss.

The effect of sibutramine (10 mg × 2) along with reduced energy intake was assessed in a randomized control study in patients with unsatisfactory control (HbA$_{1c}$ > 8%) of type 2 diabetes despite a maximum dose of sulfonylurea in combination with metformin [7]. After 6 months, weight loss was greater in the sibutramine group (9.6 kg) than after placebo (0.9 kg). Furthermore, HbA$_{1c}$ declined more in the sibutramine group, 2.7 percentage points, compared to 0.5 percentage points in those treated with placebo.

The effects of a well-established agent for treating diabetes (metformin, 1700 mg/day) were investigated in obese subjects with type 2 diabetes who were not sa-

No. of patients/ No. followed up	Result Weight, kg	Results a) HbA$_1$ b) HbA$_{1c}$ %	Results/Other	Study quality Comments
1. 30/29 2. 30/25 Women 100%	Weight 1. −9.6 kg* 2. 0.9 kg BMI 1. −3.9* 2. −0.4	b) 6 months 1. −2.7* 2. −0.5	Cholesterol, TG, blood pressure, and heart rate decreased and HDL cholesterol increased in Group 1	Medium
1. 24/24 2. 24/24 Women 100%	24 weeks 1. −8.8 kg* 2. −1.0 kg	b) 24 weeks 1. −1.0 2. −0.1	In part of the study appetite reduction was higher with 1700 mg compared to 850 mg of metformin	Medium

tisfactorily controlled by diet alone [18]. Compared to placebo, metformin resulted in both greater weight loss (8.8 kg compared to 1.0 kg) and improved glucose control (HbA$_{1c}$ 7.4% compared to 8.3%).

Two studies investigated the magnitude of weight loss required to achieve a certain level of glucose control, HbA$_{1c}$ or HbA$_1$, and fasting blood glucose [1, 35]. Using group information about diet and exercise, after one year only 6 of 114 patients reached a satisfactory fasting blood glucose level (< 6.1 mmol/L) [35]. Reaching this goal required a weight loss of at least 13.6 kg. In the 20 patients who had lost 6.9–13.6 kg, the treatment results were acceptable, with a fasting blood glucose of 6.1–9.0 mmol/L.

Results of a comprehensive study in Great Britain (UKPDS) provided a more thorough analysis of the correlation between weight loss and the effects on glucose levels [1]. The study was designed in such a way that the 482 patients with newly diagnosed type 2 diabetes who, after 3 months of energy-restricted diet, met the treatment goal (fasting plasma glucose < 6.0 mmol/L) were allowed to stay with this diet regimen for another year. Furthermore, 341 diabetics with fasting plasma glucose > 6.0 mmol/L were treated with this regimen based on a randomization protocol. The correlation between weight loss and the effects on fasting glucose were analyzed in all of the patients. From this, it was estimated that a hypothetical average patient with a fasting plasma glucose of 12.0 mmol/L on diagnosis would need a weight loss of ca. 30% (20 kg) to achieve fully satisfactory glucose control (fasting plasma glucose < 6.0 mmol/L). In fact the variation was wide, and it was not unusual to observe substantial improvements in blood glucose even in patients with marginal weight loss.

A followup of patients with type 2 diabetes (n = 146) and reduced glucose tolerance (n = 152) was carried out ca. 14 years after obesity surgery (gastric bypass) [27]. Approximately 90 % of all patients showed completely normal values in fasting glucose and HbA_{1c}. Mean BMI had declined from ca. 50 to ca. 35.

Another followup involved 154 individuals with type 2 diabetes who, 9 years earlier (average), had undergone surgery (Roux-en-Y gastric bypass) for high-level obesity (not included in Table 7.1) [22]. The control group (n = 74), composed of individuals who declined surgery, was followed for ca. 6 years (average). The share of patients who were initially treated with insulin or tablets decreased from 39 % to 9 % in the surgery group, while in the control group it increased from 56 % to 88 %.

7.1.3.2 Prevention of Type 2 Diabetes

Eight studies have reported on the effects of various methods to prevent type 2 diabetes in special risk groups [10, 16, 20, 26, 28–30, 37] (See Table 7.2).

A randomized study from China assessed three different intervention programs (energy-restricted diet, increased exercise, and combination of the two) in patients with impaired glucose tolerance who were identified by comprehensive screening [26]. In overweight individuals (mean BMI 28), the aim was to achieve a reduction to BMI 23. After 6 years, BMI had, on average, declined by 1.6 units in the combination group, and by ca. 1 unit in the other two intervention groups and in the control group. No significant change in diet composition or energy intake was shown, but the combination group self-reported greater physical activity. Everyone without known diabetes received an oral glucose tolerance test every second year, whereupon the incidence of diabetes was found to be ca. one third lower in three intervention groups (11 per 100 person years) than in the control group (17 per 100 person years). The strength of the study was somewhat diminished since the subjects were randomized on a clinic basis and not an individual basis. Furthermore, dropout was not reported.

One of the studies addresses individuals at high risk of type 2 diabetes based on one or both of the biological parents having type 2 diabetes and a body weight exceeding the ideal body weight by 30 % to 100 % [37]. The participants (n = 154) were aged 40–55 years and were randomized to four intervention groups:

1. Low energy diet, initially 800–1000 kcal and later 1200–1500 kcal/day
2. Exercise corresponding to 1500 kcal/week
3. Exercise and low energy diet
4. Written information including advice on diet and exercise.

The two groups treated by energy-restricted diets achieved greater weight loss than other groups after 6 and 12 months, but no significant differences were found among the groups after 24 months. In total, 21 people contracted diabetes, with no differences among the groups. The authors estimated that a weight loss of 4.5 kg carried a 30 % lower risk for the onset of type 2 diabetes.

The effects of reduced energy intake through limiting the amount of fat have been studied in individuals with impaired glucose tolerance or mildly elevated fasting glucose and a mean BMI of 29 [29]. Weight loss was greater in the intervention group after both 1 and 2 years, on average 3.3 kg and 3.2 kg respectively, but the difference was not sustained after 5 years. The initial favorable effects on glucose intolerance diminished at the same rate. Dropout was high, ca. 40 %.

A review of findings from numerous American and European multicenter studies of orlistat in combination with low energy diets has been reported [10]. The studies included individuals with a BMI of ca. 36, most of whom had normal glucose tolerance. After ca. 580 days, the average weight loss was 6.7 kg in the orlistat group and 3.8 kg in the placebo group. The incidence of type 2 diabetes after 1 year was lower (2 of 303 patients) after treatment with orlistat (120 mg $\times$ 3) than with placebo (7 of 245 patients). Dropout was ca. 30 % in both of the study groups, which diminishes the strength of the evidence.

The ongoing Swedish obese subject study (SOS) reported 8-year results following surgery, mainly vertical banded gastroplasty (VBG) [28]. The average weight loss was 20.1 kg (16.3 %) in the 483 patients (70 %) followed up, who initially had a mean BMI of 41.7. The incidence of diabetes was markedly lower in the surgery group, (3.6 %) than in the matched and conventionally treated control group (18.5 %).

Similar results were found in a North American study [20]. Patients with high-level obesity (> 45 kg overweight) who received gastric bypass (n = 109) and patients who, lacking medical reasons, did not receive surgery (n = 27) were followed up for 5.8 years (average). Type 2 diabetes was diagnosed in 1 patient (incidence 0.15 per 100 person years) in the experiment group and in 6 patients (incidence 4.72 per 100 person years) in the control group, which shows a substantial preventive effect. Weight loss was somewhat above 50 % of overweight.

Only relatively recently have studies been initiated that are sufficiently large to provide a foundation for guidelines on diabetes prevention by nonpharmacological and pharmacological methods. In Finland, a comprehensive Diabetes Prevention Study (DPS) was started in 1993 that included 522 overweight (BMI > 25) individuals (mean age 55 years) with impaired glucose tolerance [5, 30]. The participants were randomized to programs with lifestyle improvement interventions, weight loss, and increased exercise, or to no preventive intervention. An interim report shows that after 2 years the intervention groups had lost 3.5 kg (average) and the control group had lost 0.8 kg [30]. The incidence of diabetes in the control group (6 %) was twice as high as that in the intervention groups (3 %).

A similar, more comprehensive prevention study involving 3234 people was carried out in the United States. The mean age of the subjects was 51 years, mean BMI was 34, average waist circumference was 105 cm, and they had impaired glucose tolerance and a genetic predisposition to diabetes [16]. The participants were randomized to three groups: lifestyle-improving interventions, metformin, or placebo. The treatment goals, which included 7 % weight loss and 2.5 hours of walking per week, were achieved in 38 % and 58 %, respectively, of the subjects in the lifestyle group. After 2 years, weight loss was greater in this group (5.6 kg) than in other groups (metformin 2.1 kg, placebo 0.1 kg). The incidence of type 2 diabetes in

Table 7.2 Effects of weight reduction by various methods on the prevention of type 2 diabetes.

Author Year Reference	Study design	Inclusion criteria	Intervention method	Starting data Mean BMI/ Mean weight, kg
Pan XR et al. 1997 [26]	RCT (with regard to clinic)	IGT BMI ≥25 >25 years	1. Energy-reduced diet 2. Physical activity 3. Energy-reduced diet + physical activity 4. Control group	BMI 1. 28.3 2. 27.9 3. 28.6 4. 28.5
Wing RR et al. 1998 [37]	RCT	One or both biological parents with type 2 diabetes. 30%–100% overweight 40–55 years	1. Energy reduced diet 2. Physical activity 3. Energy-reduced diet + physical activity 4. Control group	
Swinburn BA et al. 2001 [29]	RCT	IGT (n=162) or high normal blood glucose (n=114) at screening. >40 years	1. Fat-reduced diet + repeated education 2. Ordinary diet	1. 29/86 2. 29/84

Heymsfield SB
et al.
2000
[10]
	RCT	Studied by OGTT
		BMI 30–43
			1. Orlistat 120 mg × 3
			2. Placebo 1 × 3 + energy-
			   reduced (500–800 kcal) and
			   energy-reduced
			   4 weeks before
			   randomization
				BMI kg
				1. 35.6/ 29.6
				2. 36.0/ 29.8

Sjöström CD et al. 2000 SOS [28]	Match	BMI >38 (Women) >34 (Men) 37–60 years	1. Stomach surgery (mainly VBG) 2. Control group	1. 42.2/121.6 2. 40.2/115.2
Long SD et al. 1994 [20]	CT	IGT >45 kg overweight	1. Stomach surgery 2. Conventional treatment	1. BMI 48 2. BMI 51
Tuomilehto J et al. 2001 [30]	RCT	IGT BMI >25 40–65 years	1. Multifactorial 2. No measures	1. BMI 31.3 2. BMI 31.0

See legend on page 292

Followup period	No. of pat/ No. followed up	Results Weight/kg	Results Diabetes incidence	Study quality Comments
6 years	1. nr/75 2. nr/84 3. nr/80 4. nr/83	BMI: 1. −1.2 2. −0.9 3. −1.6* 4. −1.0	1. 36 (48%)* 2. 43 (51%)* 3. 42 (53%)* 4. 60 (72%)	Medium
2 years	1. 37/35 2. 37/31 3. 40/32 4. 40/31 Women approx. 80%	<u>6 months</u> 1. −9.1 kg 2. −2.1 kg 3. −10.3 kg* 4. −1.5 kg <u>2 years</u> 1. −2.1 kg 2. 1.0 kg 3. −2.5 kg 4. −0.3 kg	<u>2 years</u> 1. 10 (30%) 2. 4 (14%) 3. 5 (16%) 4. 2 (7%)	Medium
5 years	<u>1 y</u> 1. 66 fu 2. 70 fu <u>2 y</u> 1. 47 fu 2. 57 fu <u>3 y</u> 1. 48 fu 2. 51 fu <u>5 y</u> 1. 51 fu 2. 52 fu Women approx. 25%	<u>1 y</u> 1.−3.3 kg* 2. 0.6 kg <u>2 y</u> 1. −3.2 kg* 2. 1.1 kg <u>3 y</u> 1. −1.6 kg 2. 2.1 kg <u>5 y</u> 1. 1.1 kg 2. 1.3 kg	Diabetes or IGT after 1 year: 1. 47%* 2. 67% Following year no difference	Low
580 days	1. 359/246 2. 316/217 Women approx. 80%	1. −6.7 kg* 2. −3.8 kg	<u>IGT → DM</u> 1. 3%* 2. 8% <u>IGT → normal</u> <u>blood glucose</u> 1. 72%* 2. 49%	Medium
8 years	1. 346/251 2. 346/232 Women approx. 65%	1. −20.1 kg* 2. −0.7 kg <u>BMI</u> 1. −6.8* 2. −0.5*	1. 3.6% 2. 18.5%	High
5.8 years (2–10 y)	1. 109 2. 27 Women approx. 80%		1. 1/109 2. 6/27	Medium
2 years	1. 256 2. 250 Women approx. 65% (After 2 years 471 remained)	<u>1 year</u> 1. −4.2 kg (5%)* 2. −0.8 kg (16%) <u>2 years</u> 1. −3.5 kg (15%)* 2. −0.8 kg (37%)	<u>1 year</u> 1. 5 2. 16 <u>2 years</u> 1. 15 2. 37	High

Table continues on next page

Table 7.2 continued.

Author Year Reference	Study design	Inclusion criteria	Intervention method	Starting data Mean BMI/ Mean weight, kg
Knowler WC et al. 2002 [16]	RCT	IGT BMI ≥24 >25 years Women 70%	1. Energy reduction + physical activity 2. Metformin 3. Placebo	BMI 30–35 (n=995) BMI >35 (n=1194)

RCT = Randomized Controlled Trial
CT = Controlled Trial, not randomized
VBG = Vertical Banded Gastroplasty
IGT = Impaired Glucose Tolerance
DM = Diabetes Mellitus
OGTT = Oral Glucose Tolerance Test
* = Statistical significance
nr = not reported
fu = followed up

obese people (BMI 30–35) was substantially lower, four cases per 100 person years, than in the metformin and placebo groups, 8 cases and 9 cases per 100 person years respectively. In people with high-level obesity, BMI > 35, the incidence was 14 cases per 100 person years in the placebo group and in the other groups 7 cases per 100 person years. As a consequence of the results, the study was discontinued 1 year prematurely.

7.1.4
Discussion

The strength of the treatment studies lies in the fact that they are randomized and that, with the exception of the pharmaceutical studies, dropout was noticeably small. Seven studies reported a treatment period of at least 1 year, which is a followup time necessary for evaluating clinical relevance, but none of the studies exceeded 2 years. The degree of glucose control was measured by HbA_{1c} or HbA_1, which shows glucose values for the past 6-week period. Nine of the ten studies presented moderate-grade evidence and one study presented poor-grade evidence (Table 7.1).

The treatment studies show substantial heterogeneity as regards intervention methods, patient numbers, and diabetes treatments. Some studies included patients with newly diagnosed type 2 diabetes that was treated by energy-restricted diet alone. Other studies included patients with long-term disease in which diabetes treatment was discontinued or reduced during the study. This approach is clinically motivated, but uncertain as an outcome variable if guidelines for adjusting dosage are not used and carefully described.

Followup period	No. of pat/ No. followed up	Results Weight/kg	Results Diabetes incidence	Study quality Comments
Approx. 2.5 years	1. 1079 2. 1073 3. 1082 (Total drop-out 8%)	1. −5.6 kg* 2. −2.1 kg* 3. −0.1 kg	BMI 30–35 reported per 100 person years 1. 3.7 2. 7.6 3. 11 BMI >35 1. 7.3 2. 7.0 3. 14.3	High

Although the variations in design render interpretation of the results more difficult, there are several important and concordant findings. Both marked and lasting, preferably progressive, weight loss is a condition for clinically important effects on glucose control. The correlation between weight loss and effects on glucose is, however, weak because of the wide variation in the severity of disease and its course in different individuals.

Improvements in glucose control achieved through weight loss are explained by increased insulin sensitivity. This effect is related to a reduction in the amount of fat in the abdomen, but is also due to changes in metabolism. Clinical and experimental clinical studies have shown that even before weight is lost, marked energy restriction can lead to greater insulin sensitivity and thereby improved glucose metabolism [8, 9, 14, 33].

The eight individual-based prevention studies show substantial heterogeneity as regards both intervention methods and inclusion criteria above overweight/obesity, i.e., glucose intolerance, slightly elevated blood glucose, or hereditary diabetes alone. Of the 8 studies, 3 present high quality [16, 28, 30], 4 present medium quality, and 1 presents low quality. A recurring finding is that weight loss of ca. 3 kg for 1 to 2 years, regardless of intervention method, somewhat lowers the incidence of diabetes. This applies to the ongoing Finnish, individual-based study in which the intervention group, after 2 years, had lost 3 kg more than the control group, and had a ca. 50% lower incidence of diabetes. The more comprehensive North American study achieved, during 3 years, a 58% reduction in the incidence of diabetes.

References Section 7.1

1. UK Prospective Diabetes Study 7: response of fasting plasma glucose to diet therapy in newly presenting type II diabetic patients, UKPDS Group. Metabolism 1990;39(9):905-12.
2. Blonk MC, Jacobs MA, Biesheuvel EH, Weeda-Mannak WL, Heine RJ. Influences on weight loss in type 2 diabetic patients: little long-term benefit from group behaviour therapy and exercise training. Diabet Med 1994;11(5):449-57.
3. Carey VJ, Walters EE, Colditz GA, Solomon CG, Willett WC, Rosner BA, et al. Body fat distribution and risk of non-insulin-dependent diabetes mellitus in women. The Nurses' Health Study. Am J Epidemiol 1997;145(7):614-9.
4. Colditz GA, Willett WC, Rotnitzky A, Manson JE. Weight gain as a risk factor for clinical diabetes mellitus in women. Ann Intern Med 1995;122(7):481-6.
5. Eriksson J, Lindström J, Valle T, Aunola S, Hamalainen H, Ilanne-Parikka P, et al. Prevention of Type II diabetes in subjects with impaired glucose tolerance: the Diabetes Prevention Study (DPS) in Finland. Study design and 1-year interim report on the feasibility of the lifestyle intervention programme. Diabetologia 1999;42(7):793-801.
6. Fujioka K, Seaton TB, Rowe E, Jelinek CA, Raskin P, Lebovitz HE, et al. Weight loss with sibutramine improves glycaemic control and other metabolic parameters in obese patients with type 2 diabetes mellitus. Diabetes Obes Metab 2000;2(3):175-87.
7. Gokcel A, Karakose H, Ertorer EM, Tanaci N, Tutuncu NB, Guvener N. Effects of sibutramine in obese female subjects with type 2 diabetes and poor blood glucose control. Diabetes Care 2001;24(11):1957-60.
8. Goodpaster BH, Kelley DE, Wing RR, Meier A, Thaete FL. Effects of weight loss on regional fat distribution and insulin sensitivity in obesity. Diabetes 1999;48(4):839-47.
9. Henry RR, Scheaffer L, Olefsky JM. Glycemic effects of intensive caloric restriction and isocaloric refeeding in noninsulin-dependent diabetes mellitus. J Clin Endocrinol Metab 1985;61(5):917-25.
10. Heymsfield SB, Segal KR, Hauptman J, Lucas CP, Boldrin MN, Rissanen A, et al. Effects of weight loss with orlistat on glucose tolerance and progression to type 2 diabetes in obese adults. Arch Intern Med 2000;160(9):1321-6.
11. Hollander PA, Elbein SC, Hirsch IB, Kelley D, McGill J, Taylor T, et al. Role of orlistat in the treatment of obese patients with type 2 diabetes. A 1-year randomized double-blind study. Diabetes Care 1998;21(8):1288-94.
12. Hu FB, Manson JE, Stampfer MJ, Colditz G, Liu S, Solomon CG, et al. Diet, lifestyle, and the risk of type 2 diabetes mellitus in women. N Engl J Med 2001;345(11):790-7.
13. Kaye SA, Folsom AR, Sprafka JM, Prineas RJ, Wallace RB. Increased incidence of diabetes mellitus in relation to abdominal adiposity in older women. J Clin Epidemiol 1991;44(3):329-34.

14. Kelley DE, Wing R, Buonocore C, Sturis J, Polonsky K, Fitzsimmons M. Relative effects of calorie restriction and weight loss in noninsulin-dependent diabetes mellitus. J Clin Endocrinol Metab 1993;77(5):1287-93.

15. King H, Rewers M. Global estimates for prevalence of diabetes mellitus and impaired glucose tolerance in adults. WHO Ad Hoc Diabetes Reporting Group. Diabetes Care 1993;16(1):157-77.

16. Knowler WC, Barrett-Connor E, Fowler SE, Hamman RF, Lachin JM, Walker EA, et al. Reduction in the incidence of type 2 diabetes with lifestyle intervention or metformin. N Engl J Med 2002;346(6):393-403.

17. Laitinen JH, Ahola IE, Sarkkinen ES, Winberg RL, Harmaakorpi-Iivonen PA, Uusitupa MI. Impact of intensified dietary therapy on energy and nutrient intakes and fatty acid composition of serum lipids in patients with recently diagnosed noninsulin-dependent diabetes mellitus. J Am Diet Assoc 1993;93(3):276-83.

18. Lee A, Morley JE. Metformin decreases food consumption and induces weight loss in subjects with obesity with type II noninsulin-dependent diabetes. Obes Res 1998;6(1):47-53.

19. Lindgärde F. The effect of orlistat on body weight and coronary heart disease risk profile in obese patients: the Swedish Multimorbidity Study. J Intern Med 2000;248(3):245-54.

20. Long SD, O'Brien K, MacDonald KG, Jr, Leggett-Frazier N, Swanson MS, Pories WJ, et al. Weight loss in severely obese subjects prevents the progression of impaired glucose tolerance to type II diabetes. A longitudinal interventional study. Diabetes Care 1994;17(5):372-5.

21. Lundgren H, Bengtsson C, Blohme G, Lapidus L, Sjöstrom L. Adiposity and adipose tissue distribution in relation to incidence of diabetes in women: results from a prospective population study in Gothenburg, Sweden. Int J Obes 1989;13(4):413-23.

22. MacDonald KG, Jr, Long SD, Swanson MS, Brown BM, Morris P, Dohm GL, et al. The gastric bypass operation reduces the progression and mortality of non-insulin-dependent diabetes mellitus. J Gastrointest Surg 1997;1(3): 213-20.

23. Midthjell K, Kruger O, Holmen J, Tverdal A, Claudi T, Bjorndal A, et al. Rapid changes in the prevalence of obesity and known diabetes in an adult Norwegian population. The Nord-Trondelag Health Surveys: 1984–1986 and 1995–1997. Diabetes Care 1999;22(11):1813-20.

24. Moore LL, Visioni AJ, Wilson PW, D'Agostino RB, Finkle WD, Ellison RC. Can sustained weight loss in overweight individuals reduce the risk of diabetes mellitus? Epidemiology 2000;11(3):269-73.

25. Ohlson LO, Larsson B, Svärdsudd K, Welin L, Eriksson H, Wilhelmsen L, et al. The influence of body fat distribution on the incidence of diabetes mellitus. 13.5 years of follow-up of the participants in the study of men born in 1913. Diabetes 1985;34(10):1055-8.

26. Pan XR, Li GW, Hu YH, Wang JX, Yang WY, An ZX, et al. Effects of diet and exercise in preventing NIDDM in people with impaired glucose tolerance. The Da Qing IGT and Diabetes Study. Diabetes Care 1997;20(4): 537-44.

27. Pories WJ, Swanson MS, MacDonald KG, Long SB, Morris PG, Brown BM, et al. Who would have thought it? An operation proves to be the most effective therapy for adult-onset diabetes mellitus. Ann Surg 1995;222(3):339-50; discussion 50-2.

28. Sjöström CD, Peltonen M, Wedel H, Sjöström L. Differentiated long-term effects of intentional weight loss on diabetes and hypertension. Hypertension 2000;36(1):20-5.

29. Swinburn BA, Metcalf PA, Ley SJ. Long-term (5-year) effects of a reduced-fat diet intervention in individuals with glucose intolerance. Diabetes Care 2001;24(4):619-24.

30. Tuomilehto J, Lindström J, Eriksson JG, Valle TT, Hamalainen H, Ilanne-Parikka P, et al. Prevention of type 2 diabetes mellitus by changes in lifestyle among subjects with impaired

glucose tolerance. N Engl J Med 2001;344(18):1343-50.

31. West KM, Kalbfleisch JM. Influence of nutritional factors on prevalence of diabetes. Diabetes 1971;20(2):99-108.

32. Wing RR, Blair E, Marcus M, Epstein LH, Harvey J. Year-long weight loss treatment for obese patients with type II diabetes: does including an intermittent very-low-calorie diet improve outcome? Am J Med 1994;97(4):354-62.

33. Wing RR, Blair EH, Bononi P, Marcus MD, Watanabe R, Bergman RN. Caloric restriction per se is a significant factor in improvements in glycemic control and insulin sensitivity during weight loss in obese NIDDM patients. Diabetes Care 1994;17(1):30-6.

34. Wing RR, Epstein LH, Paternostro-Bayles M, Kriska A, Nowalk MP, Gooding W. Exercise in a behavioural weight control programme for obese patients with Type 2 (non-insulin-dependent) diabetes. Diabetologia 1988;31(12):902-9.

35. Wing RR, Koeske R, Epstein LH, Nowalk MP, Gooding W, Becker D. Long-term effects of modest weight loss in type II diabetic patients. Arch Intern Med 1987;147(10):1749-53.

36. Wing RR, Marcus MD, Salata R, Epstein LH, Miaskiewicz S, Blair EH. Effects of a very-low-calorie diet on longterm glycemic control in obese type 2 diabetic subjects. Arch Intern Med 1991;151(7):1334-40.

37. Wing RR, Venditti E, Jakicic JM, Polley BA, Lang W. Lifestyle intervention in overweight individuals with a family history of diabetes. Diabetes Care 1998;21(3):350-9.

7.2
Hypertension

Summary

As overweight and obese people are at greater risk of hypertension and cardiovascular disease, studies on the long-term effects of weight loss in people with elevated blood pressure and overweight/obesity were reviewed.

Results: Four studies show that blood pressure decreases with an energy-reduced diet resulting in significant weight loss (5–8 kg) for 6 months (Evidence Grade 2). A Swedish study presenting high quality shows that lifestyle improvements resulted in substantial weight loss after 1 year. Nevertheless, the reduction in blood pressure was markedly poorer than that following conventional pharmacological treatment.

Prevention studies of 2–5 years have shown that weight loss of ca. 2–3 kg prevents, to some degree, hypertension and blood-pressure-related cardiovascular diseases (Evidence Grade 2).

The Swedish Obese Subjects (SOS) study noted a favorable effect on blood pressure during the first years after gastric surgery in people with high-grade obesity. However, despite sustained weight loss after 8 years, no difference in blood pressure was noted at that time compared to the control group which did not lose weight.

Conclusions: In overweight/obese persons, weight loss of at least 5 % can result in lowered blood pressure. However, the magnitude of this reduction decreases with time even in cases where weight loss is sustained. Weight loss can also prevent the onset of elevated blood pressure.

7.2.1
Introduction

Hypertension is found in more than half of the overweight population, and the blood pressure is closely correlated with BMI. Weight loss, mainly in overweight/obese people, can reduce blood pressure and is a feasible component in nonpharmacological treatment of hypertension.

A critical review of the scientific literature was undertaken to determine the extent to which weight loss can reduce and prevent elevated blood pressure in overweight/obese people. This review included only randomized controlled trials of at least 6 months duration and with at least 30 persons in each study group.

7.2.2
Results

7.2.2.1 Effect of Obesity Treatment on Hypertension

Antihypertensive effects were analyzed in 5 studies of nonsurgical treatment (Table 7.3) and in 2 studies of surgical treatment for obesity.

Table 7.3 Randomized studies addressing the effects of weight loss on blood pressure in overweight persons with hypertension.

Author Year Reference	Inclusion criteria Weight, BMI, DBP mmHg	Intervention method	Treatment period
Reisin E et al. 1978 [8]	>120 % ideal weight 106–118 mmHg	1. Energy-reduced diet 2. Energy-reduced diet + blood pressure medication 3. Control	6 months
Haynes RB et al. 1984 [7]	>110 % ideal weight 85–104 mmHg 21–61 years	1. Energy-reduced diet 2. Controls	6 months
Croft PR et al. 1986 [4]	BMI >25 >140/>90 mmHg untreated 35–60 years	1. Energy-reduced diet 2. Controls	6 months
Berglund A et al. 1989 [2]	BMI >30 90–104 mmHg Men 40–69 years	1. Multifactorial 2. Blood pressure therapy (stepped)	1 year

Wassertheil-
Smoller S
et al.
TAIM
1992
[13]
	110 %–160 % ideal weight
	90–100 mmHg
	21–65 years
		1. Energy-reduced diet
		   a) thiazide
		   b) beta-adrenergic
		      blocker
		   c) placebo
		2. Controls
		   a) thiazide
		   b) beta-adrenergic
		      blocker
		   c) placebo
			6 months

LS = Low-Sodium diet
DBP = Diastolic Blood Pressure
SBP = Systolic Blood Pressure
TG = Triglycerides
* = Statistical significance

No. of patients/ No. followed up	Results Weight change	Results SBP/DBP, DBP with DBP < 90 mmHg		Study quality Comments
1. 24 (24) 2. 57 (57) 3. 26 (26)	1. −8.8 kg* 2. −9.8 kg* 3. −0.5 kg	1. −26/−17 2. −33/−21 3. 7/23	75 % 61 % 0	Low Unclear randomization
1. 30 (27) 2. 30 (24)	1. −4.1 kg 2. −0.1 kg	Difference between groups 4/1		Medium Analysis only of patients who did not receive blood pressure treatment
1. 66 (47) 2. 64 (50)	1. −8.0 kg* 2. −0.5 kg	1. −13/−9* 2. −3/0		Medium Analysis of patients who did not receive blood pressure medication and who did not try to lose weight in Group 2
1. 31 (31) 2. 30 (30)	1. −7.6 kg* 2. 0.9 kg	1. −4/−3 2. −16/−11*	29 % 73 %	High TG dropped, HDL Cholesterol increased in Group 1
1. a) 87 b) 88 c) 90 2. a) 87 b) 87 c) 90	1. −4.7 kg* a) −6.9 kg b) −3.0 kg c) −4.4 kg 2. −0.9 kg	1. a) −15* b) −15 c) −9 2. a) −11 b) −12 c) −11		Low High transfer of patients between treatment groups

A substantial energy reduction has been shown to markedly reduce both weight (ca. 9 kg) and blood pressure (ca. 30 mm Hg systolic and 20 mm Hg diastolic) in moderately overweight patients [8]. In one experimental group, the patients did not receive blood pressure lowering medication, and in the other the patients maintained previous medication. In the control group, which was not treated with energy-reduced diet, the blood pressure did not change. The patient groups were not comparable, but differed in size, age, and initial blood pressure because of a non-stringent randomization process.

In a study of overweight patients with untreated, moderately elevated blood pressure, an energy-reduced diet for 6 months resulted in an average weight loss of ca. 4 kg [7]. The effect on the blood pressure was insignificant. Dropout was relatively low (15 %), in part because patients treated with antihypertensive medication were excluded in the analysis.

Another study of 6 months reported on the effects of weight loss in overweight patients with untreated moderate hypertension ($>$ 140 mm Hg systolic and/or $>$ 90 mm Hg diastolic) [4]. Patients whose blood pressure exceeded certain limits received pharmacological treatment and were excluded from the final analysis. Furthermore, a not insignificant number of control patients were excluded when it was found that they had attempted to lose weight. Although some criticism can be directed toward this procedure, the finding is well supported, namely that both weight (around 8 kg) and blood pressure (13/9 mm Hg) dropped in the treatment group.

Berglund et al. randomized 61 men (BMI $>$ 30) with moderately elevated blood pressure to lifestyle-altering intervention alone (reduced intake of energy, sodium, and alcohol) or to antihypertensive medication involving one or more agents [2]. Weight loss averaged 7.6 kg in the intervention group after 1 year. The effect on the blood pressure was, however, substantially less pronounced than in the group treated with medication. However, favorable effects were observed in the blood lipid profile. The study is relatively small, but presents high quality because of its design and absence of dropout.

An extensive study, "Trials of Antihypertensive Intervention Management", compared effects of energy restriction combined with antihypertensive medication [13]. Treatment in the six study groups was with and without energy-reduced diet in combination with placebo or drugs (diuretic agents and beta-adrenergic blockers). After 6 months, the average weight loss was nearly 5 kg in the three intervention groups and was, as with the effect on the blood pressure, most pronounced in the group treated with diuretic agents. A large share of patients were transferred from their original groups to one of the treatment groups if the effect on blood pressure was unsatisfactory or if side effects appeared. Hence, it is considerably more difficult to interpret the data. In patients who lost at least 4.5 kg, diastolic blood pressure dropped by ca. 12 mm Hg, i.e., comparable to the effect of a low dose of diuretic agents or beta-adrenergic blockers. At followup after 4 to 5 years, diastolic blood pressure had increased over the established treatment limit, 90 mm Hg, as frequently in the control group (57 %) as in the intervention group (50 %) [5].

Two studies including ca. 120 hypertensive patients (total) who received gastric bypass (Roux-en-Y) showed a normalization in blood pressure and that the medication could be discontinued in at least half of the patients [3, 6].

7.2.2.2 Prevention of Hypertension

A change in diet was included in a program of lifestyle-improving interventions in moderately overweight subjects aged 30–44 years with an insignificant and untreated elevation in diastolic blood pressure (Table 7.4) [11]. After 5 years, weight had decreased by 2 kg in the intervention group and increased by almost 1 kg in the control group. At that time, hypertension that required treatment (diastolic blood pressure > 90 mm Hg) was twice as common in the control group (19%) as in the intervention group (9%). In this study, increased physical activity and decreased alcohol consumption in the intervention group was self-reported, which may have contributed to the positive effect.

An extensive study randomized overweight subjects (mean BMI 29) with mild, untreated hypertension to four study groups: diet change with restriction of energy and sodium, separately, or in combination, and a control group [1]. In the group treated by energy reduction alone, weight decreased after 3 years by almost 2 kg and diastolic blood pressure decreased by ca. 4 mm Hg. In the control group, weight had increased by almost 2 kg and diastolic blood pressure by 2 mm Hg. In other experimental groups with a reduced sodium and energy intake, the effects were even more modest. After three years, the presence of hypertension that required treatment was about the same (10%) in all study groups.

The effects from reduced intake of energy or sodium, alone or in combination, have been illustrated in a controlled study of elderly persons (60–80 years) whose blood pressure was well-regulated by medication [14]. This medication was terminated so that the study's endpoint was the need for renewed blood pressure treatment (limit = 150/90 mm Hg). In obese patients, weight had decreased after 3 years by nearly 5 kg in groups that were recommended a reduced energy intake and by around 1 kg in the other groups. Compared to the control group, the three intervention groups showed a lower relative risk (0.47–0.64) for the onset of hypertension (> 150/> 90 mm Hg) or cardiovascular disease. Changes in blood pressure in the separate study groups were not reported.

Energy restriction in combination with increased physical activity was evaluated after 3 years in an extensive study "Trial of Hypertension Prevention" (TOHP II) which included 595 overweight persons (110–165%) [12]. Weight increased only in the control group, and the relative risk of the onset of hypertension (> 140/> 90 mm Hg) was higher than in the intervention group. These differences between the groups were significantly higher during the first years.

An 8-year followup in the SOS study showed that an average weight loss of 20.1 kg after surgery did not prevent hypertension (> 160/≥ 95 mm Hg) any more effectively than traditional obesity treatment in the control group where the weight remained unchanged [10].

Table 7.4 Randomized studies addressing the prevention of hypertension in overweight patients.

Author Year Reference	Inclusion criteria Weight, BMI, SBP/DBP DBP	Intervention method	Treatment period
Stamler R et al. 1989 [11]	30–44 years 110%–140% ideal weight 80–89 mmHg Women=approx. 15%	1. Multifactorial 2. Controls	5 years
HPTR-group 1990 [1]	25–45 years <u>BMI</u> Men=25–35 Women=23–35 78–89 mmHg Women=35%	1a. Energy-reduced diet 1b. Sodium-reduced diet 1c. Energy- and sodium-reduced diet 2. Controls	3 years
Whelton PK et al. 1998 TONE [14]	60–80 years <u>BMI</u> Men ≥25.8 Women ≥27.3 <145/<85 mmHg Women=approx. 55%	1a. Energy-reduced diet 1b. Sodium-reduced diet 1c. Energy- and sodium-reduced diet 2. Controls	30 months
Stevens VJ et al. 2001 TOHP II [12]	30–54 years 110%–165% ideal weight 83–89 mmHg Women=35%	1. Energy-reduced diet + physical activity 2. Controls	3 years

* = Statistical significance
TG = Triglycerides
DBP = Diastolic Blood Pressure
SBP = Systolic Blood Pressure
nr = not reported

7.2.3
Discussion

Five randomized studies evaluated the effect of weight loss on blood pressure. Treatment time was usually only 6 months. The study designs differ in many respects. Initial blood pressures varied, from insignificantly elevated levels to levels that require treatment according to current guidelines. Some studies combined dietary counseling aimed at weight loss with recommendations of increased physical activity and reduced alcohol consumption. It was difficult to interpret the findings in some of the studies since blood pressure was high and medication was initiated or the drug dose or type was changed.

Even with these reservations, all of the studies presented medium quality, and the findings are generally in agreement. Weight loss of less than 5 kg at 6 months has not been shown to lower the diastolic blood pressure more than placebo or no

No. of patients/ No. followed up	Results Weight change	Results DBP Share (%) with DBP >90 mmHg or SBP >140 mmHg	Study quality Comments
1. 102/99 2. 99/95	1. −2.0 kg* 2. 0.8 kg	1. −0.7 mmHg 2. 1.2 mmHg 1. 9%* 2. 19%	Medium
1a. 125/117 1b. 126/113 1c. 129/115 2. 126/113	1a. −1.6 kg* 1b. 0.7 kg 1c. 0.4 kg 2. 1.9 kg	1a. −4 mmHg* 1b. −2 mmHg 1c. 4 mmHg 2. 2 mmHg No difference in no. of patients who developed hypertension requiring treatment	Medium
1a. 147/145 1b. 144/nr 1c. 147/141 2. 147/nr	1a + 1c= −4.7 kg* 1b + 2 = 0.9 kg	Small risk (0.64*) of developing hyper- tension or cardiovascular disease	Medium
1. 595/547 2. 596/554	1. −0.2 kg* 2. 1.8 kg	Small risk (0.81) of developing hypertension	High

treatment [7, 13]. However, following greater weight loss, ca. 8–9 kg, a substantial decrease in blood pressure was reported [4, 8].

Interventions to improve lifestyle, including an energy-reduced diet, resulted in substantial weight loss after 1 year, but in poorer blood pressure reduction than that achieved by conventional medication [2].

Four long-term, randomized controlled prevention studies (3–5 years) involved a large number (200–1200) of patients. Three of these studies present medium quality and one study presents high quality [12]. A couple of study groups received counseling on energy restriction only, but usually other interventions, e. g., sodium restriction, were included [1, 14]. After 3 years, average body weight decreased by 2 kg and nearly 5 kg, respectively, while it increased by ca. 1 kg in the two control groups. Some favorable effects on blood pressure were achieved. In the study of elderly persons, aged 60–80 years, hypertension or hypertension-related cardiovascular complications requiring treatment developed in several patient groups that received advice on energy restriction [14].

From these four studies, it is not apparent how physical activity affects body weight and blood pressure. In these studies, diets with reduced sodium and/or increased potassium have not shown any effects on blood pressure, which deviates from the findings in the large DASH study (Dietary Approaches to Stop Hypertension) where the diet contained, e. g., increased fiber and fish and reduced sodium [9]. The difference in results may be explained, in part, by unsatisfactory compliance regarding sodium intake in the earlier prevention studies.

References Section 7.2

1. The Hypertension Prevention Trial: three-year effects of dietary changes on blood pressure. Hypertension Prevention Trial Research Group. Arch Intern Med 1990;150(1):153-62.

2. Berglund A, Andersson OK, Berglund G, Fagerberg B. Antihypertensive effect of diet compared with drug treatment in obese men with mild hypertension. BMJ 1989;299(6697):480-5.

3. Carson JL, Ruddy ME, Duff AE, Holmes NJ, Cody RP, Brolin RE. The effect of gastric bypass surgery on hypertension in morbidly obese patients. Arch Intern Med 1994;154(2):193-200.

4. Croft PR, Brigg D, Smith S, Harrison CB, Branthwaite A, Collins MF. How useful is weight reduction in the management of hypertension? J R Coll Gen Pract 1986;36(291):445-8.

5. Davis BR, Blaufox MD, Oberman A, Wassertheil-Smoller S, Zimbaldi N, Cutler JA, et al. Reduction in long-term antihypertensive medication requirements. Effects of weight reduction by dietary intervention in overweight persons with mild hypertension. Arch Intern Med 1993;153(15):1773-82.

6. Foley EF, Benotti PN, Borlase BC, Hollingshead J, Blackburn GL. Impact of gastric restrictive surgery on hypertension in the morbidly obese. Am J Surg 1992;163(3):294-7.

7. Haynes RB, Harper AC, Costley SR, Johnston M, Logan AG, Flanagan PT, et al. Failure of weight reduction to reduce mildly elevated blood pressure: a randomized trial. J Hypertens 1984;2(5): 535-9.

8. Reisin E, Abel R, Modan M, Silverberg DS, Eliahou HE, Modan B. Effect of weight loss without salt restriction on the reduction of blood pressure in overweight hypertensive patients. N Engl J Med 1978;298(1):1-6.

9. Sacks FM, Svetkey LP, Vollmer WM, Appel LJ, Bray GA, Harsha D, et al. Effects on blood pressure of reduced dietary sodium and the Dietary Approaches to Stop Hypertension (DASH) diet. DASH Sodium Collaborative Research Group. N Engl J Med 2001;344(1):3-10.

10. Sjöström CD, Peltonen M, Wedel H, Sjöström L. Differentiated long-term effects of intentional weight loss on diabetes and hypertension. Hypertension 2000;36(1):20-5.

11. Stamler R, Stamler J, Gosch FC, Civinelli J, Fishman J, McKeever P, et al. Primary prevention of hypertension by nutritional-hygienic means. Final report of a randomized, controlled trial. JAMA 1989;262(13):1801-7.

12. Stevens VJ, Obarzanek E, Cook NR, Lee IM, Appel LJ, Smith West D, et al. Long-term weight loss and changes in blood pressure: results of the Trials of Hypertension Prevention, phase II. Ann Intern Med 2001;134(1):1-11.

13. Wassertheil-Smoller S, Blaufox MD, Oberman AS, Langford HG, Davis BR, Wylie-Rosett J. The Trial of Antihypertensive Interventions and Management (TAIM) study. Adequate weight loss, alone and combined with drug therapy in the treatment of mild hypertension. Arch Intern Med 1992;152(1):131-6.

14. Whelton PK, Appel LJ, Espeland MA, Applegate WB, Ettinger WH, Jr, Kostis JB, et al. Sodium reduction and weight loss in the treatment of hypertension in older persons: a randomized controlled trial of nonpharmacologic interventions in the elderly (TONE). TONE Collaborative Research Group. JAMA 1998;279(11):839-46.

7.3
Blood Lipid Disorders

Summary

Disturbances of blood lipids, i.e., total cholesterol, LDL cholesterol, HDL cholesterol, and triglycerides, are of importance for the risk of developing cardiovascular
disease. Hence, it is of interest to assess the degree to which treatment of obesity
may counteract these problems in the long run. Short-term changes in blood lipids
probably have little or no impact on the development of cardiovascular disease.

Results: Five studies of adults (where dietary treatments were based on varying
degrees of energy restriction) found that HDL cholesterol increases somewhat during weight loss that is sustained for more than 1 year (Evidence Grade 3). Other
blood lipids did not show any long-term change. Likewise, two studies of children
did not find any distinct differences, compared to the original values, for any blood
lipids other than HDL cholesterol.

In weight loss achieved by pharmacotherapy, two studies of orlistat have shown a
significant decrease in total cholesterol and LDL cholesterol, but no change in
either triglycerides or HDL cholesterol (Evidence Grade 3). A study of sibutramine,
however, showed that triglycerides decreased and HDL cholesterol/LDL cholesterol
increased more than would have been expected from the weight change.

Seven studies where weight loss was achieved by surgical treatment have shown
that substantial weight loss (20–30 kg) is required for cholesterol to decrease, while
decreased triglycerides and increased HDL cholesterol values are often observed already at a weight loss of around 10 % (Evidence Grade 2). The changes achieved in
major and sustained weight loss for several years after surgery include an increase in
HDL cholesterol (ca. 0.3 mmol/L) and a decrease in triglycerides (ca. 0.7 mmol/L).

Conclusions: Weight loss can lead to changes in blood lipids in a manner which
lowers the risk of cardiovascular disease. These effects, which correlate with the
level and duration of weight loss, are achieved independently of the method
used (diet treatment, drugs, surgery). Insufficient data are available to illustrate
the extent to which these results affect morbidity and mortality in cardiovascular
disease.

7.3.1
Background

Changes in blood lipids (total cholesterol, LDL cholesterol, HDL cholesterol, and
triglycerides) affect the risk of cardiovascular disease. Primary and secondary prevention studies have shown that a reduction in LDL cholesterol (around 25 %),
achieved with the drugs pravastatin and simvastatin, yields a substantial reduction
in the incidence of cardiovascular disease. Secondary prevention studies have reported increased survival with this type of treatment.

7.3.2
Method

A literature search was conducted in MEDLINE (1966–2001). Sixty-eight references were found on obesity treatment and its effects on total cholesterol, triglycerides, HDL cholesterol, and LDL cholesterol, blood pressure, blood glucose, and body weight. Of these, 16 studies reported a followup of at least 1 year, and 13 of these are presented in Table 7.5. The main purpose in most of these studies was to investigate something other than changes in blood lipids.

7.3.3
Results

7.3.3.1 **Diet Treatment Including VLCD**
The "Oslo Diet and Exercise" study is often referenced in this context. This study randomized over 200 persons to either dietary treatment (55 persons), physical activity (54 persons), diet and physical activity (65 persons), or to a control group without intervention (43 persons) [4]. After 1 year, waist circumference was the only measure which could independently predict changes in HDL cholesterol and triglycerides.

In a followup study of 24 women (who initially weighed 120–150 % of ideal body weight and who were treated by an energy-reduced diet of 800 kcal/day), blood lipids were studied in those who lost at least 10 kg or achieved normal weight [12]. Total cholesterol and LDL cholesterol decreased by 8 % and triglycerides by 13 %. HDL cholesterol and LDL/HDL ratios did not change. After 4 years of followup, when ca. 90 % of the weight loss had been regained, the levels of total cholesterol, LDL cholesterol, and triglycerides had approached the original values, and blood pressure had increased to a level that exceeded the level at the outset of the study. However, a substantial decrease in triglycerides and a strong increase in HDL were noted.

In a Finnish randomized controlled trial, a weight loss of 11 kg in men and 6 kg in women yielded a significant increase in HDL cholesterol compared to the control group [15].

A study of 80 adult women and men with a BMI > 40 found linear associations between a BMI decrease of 10 % and a decrease in total cholesterol (5.6 %), LDL cholesterol (6.9 %), and triglycerides (14.2 %), and an increase in HDL cholesterol (4.8 %) [3]. The study noted that after a substantial initial weight loss (35 kg) during 26 weeks of VLCD treatment, including education and behavioral treatment, HDL cholesterol had decreased by 15 % in women but increased by 5 % in men. This corresponds to 0.15 mmol/L and 0.04 mmol/L, respectively. After 2 years, the average sustained weight loss was around 20 kg.

From data on 4026 persons with severe obesity who had been treated by VLCD, 362 medical records were selected for review. Before treatment, 41 % had elevated total cholesterol (> 6.5 mmol/L) and elevated blood pressure, and 29 % had elevated triglycerides (> 1.9 mmol/L) [16]. VLCD treatment for 13 weeks resulted

Table 7.5 Blood Lipid Disorders.

Author Year Reference	Study design	Inclusion criteria (Recruitment)	Intervention method Study groups	Treatment/ followup period
Anderssen SA et al. 1998 [4]	RCT	BMI >24, T chol 5.20–7.74 mmol/l, HDL <1.20, TG >1.4. Age 40–50 years, men and women	1. Diet (n=55) 2. Physical activity (n=56) 3. Diet + physical activity (n=65) 4. Controls (n=43)	1 year
Hensrud DD et al. 1995 [12]	Followup of 24 in treatment group and 24 in control group	Women after menopause. 120%–150% of ideal body weight. 49–67 years	800 kcal diet until at least 10 kg weight reduction or return to normal body weight (<120% of the ideal body weight)	Followup after 4 years
Karvetti RL et al. 1992 [15]	RCT	17–65 years BMI >27	Weight loss program education, no drugs	6 weeks treatment and 1 year followup for lipids
Anderson JW et al. 1994 [3]	Followup study	80 patients with BMI >40 and mean age 55 women 42 years 25 men 44 years	Education, physical activity, behavior in group	14 weeks intensive minimum, and 18 months monthly. Followed up after 2 years
Kirschner MA et al. 1988 [16]	Reviewed 362 medical records of 4026 patients	Between 16–70 years, no type 2 diabetes	VLCD for 13 weeks	Uncertain
Nuutinen O et al. 1992 [18]	Invitation to study (48 patients) and control group (32)	Relative body weight (>120%), 6–16 years, 33 girls, 12 boys	16 individually 16 in group 16 in school health care	1 year/ 5 years

See legend on page 310

No. of patents/ No. followed up	Results Weight change/ Lipid change	Results/Other	Study quality Comments
219/209	Expressed in regression analysis and correlation coefficient	Change of waist circumference is only independent significant predictor of 1-year change in HDL and TG. Change in weight significantly correlated (positive) to T chol, LDL and TG, and (negative) to HDL	Medium
24/21	90% of lost weight regained during follow up. Lipids de-creased TG −13%, T chol −8%, LDL −8%, HDL −3% during weight loss and increased +7%, +10%, +3%, and +37%, respectively during re-gain	Strong HDL increase probably due to initiated estrogen treatment in 6 patients. Those who exercised during followup had better sustained weight	Medium No absolute numbers reported
93 in treatment group and 96 in control group, all followed up	Weight reduction 11 kg for men and 6 kg for women in treatment group. Controls increased 0.9 kg. T chol increased significantly in women in treatment group. HDL increased in men and women also compared to controls		Medium Well executed study, but meas-ured only T chol and HDL
80/69 (86%)	After 26 weeks −35 kg average. T chol −16%, HDL −8%, LDL −16%, TG −26%	Linear association lipid changes with weight reduction and 10% dropout in BMI considered to yield T chol −5.6%, LDL −6.9%, HDL +4.8%, TG −14.2%	Medium
Dropout 18%	All had lower lipid values, none stated. 73% normalized lipid values	Descriptive followup study, no values stated	Low Difficult to inter-pret. Claims that 70% would have hyperlipidemia. No results
90% followed up	22 patients lost 10% weight, no differences in T chol, LDL, HDL or TG	Lipids on normal levels initially	Medium

Table continues on next page

Table 7.5 continued.

Author Year Reference	Study design	Inclusion criteria (Recruitment)	Intervention method Study groups	Treatment/ followup period
Epstein LH et al. 1989 [11]	RCT	8–12 years of age, child + 1 biological parent <20% ideal weight, triceps sub-cutaneous fat >95 percentile	1. Diet 2. Diet + lifestyle + physical exercise 3. Controls (19 patients)	Treatment 6 months. Some were followed up after 5 years
Davidson MH et al. 1999 [10]	Randomized, double-blind, placebo-controlled 2-year trial with orlistat	Over 18 years, BMI 30–43, no weight loss past 3 months. No diabetes (19% men)	Diet + placebo or orlistat	2 years
Sjöström L et al. 1998 [22]	Randomized controlled treatment study	>18 years, BMI 28–47	1. Orlistat 2. Placebo	2 years
James WP et al. 2000 [13]	RCT	17–65 years BMI 30–45	1. Sibutramine 2. Placebo	2 years treatment 18 months followup
Karason K et al. 1999 [14]	Controlled 4-year inter-vention study	56 men and 18 women, 28–63 y in two groups: 1. 39 patients with BMI 30–40 2. 35 patients with BMI 20–28	1. Stomach surgery 2. Conventional treatment	Followup 4 years (study on carotid artery)
Sjöström CD et al. 1999 [21]	Followup after surgery and conventional treatment. Matched controls	BMI 35–40	Surgery and conventional primary care. No drugs	2-year followup
Sjöström CD et al. 1997 [20]	Observation study	37–60 years From SOS study	50% surgery. 50% conventional treatment	2-year followup

RCT = Randomized Controlled Trial   TG = Triglycerides
HDL = HDL cholesterol   LDL = LDL cholesterol
VLCD = Very Low Calorie Diet   T chol = Total cholesterol
* = Statistical significance

No. of patents/ No. followed up	Results Weight change/ Lipid change	Results/Other	Study quality Comments
91 % followed for 6 months	Weight loss 6 % in treatment groups. T chol decreased, HDL increased, TG decreased but after 5 years only sustained HDL increase (0.99–1.23 mmol/l), no controls	Only 16 patients in treatment groups checked at 5 years, ie, 43 %. T chol, HDL, TG related to weight change. Only HDL increase sustained after 5 years	Medium Good study at 6 months, uncertain at 5 years
892 patients, 403 followed up	Weight loss ca. 6 kg, based on intention to treat, T chol −0.15* mmol/l, LDL −0.08* versus placebo. No change in TG and HDL	T chol and LDL increased since day 1 of study, which is calculated on "lead-in"day	Medium
743 at start, 133 in treatment group and 123 in control group followed up	Weight loss 10 kg in treatment group (3,9 kg more than placebo). T chol increased significantly in women in treatment group. HDL and TG no signifi-cant change. T chol and LDL decreased		Medium High dropout
605 patients at start, 467 randomized, 42 %–50 % followed up	Weight loss 10 kg for sibutramine and 4.7 kg for placebo. T chol unchanged. TG decreased 1.87–1.40 in treatment group and 1.73–1.62 in placebo. HDL increase of 0,24 mmol/l in treatment group and 0.11 in placbo.		Medium High dropout
19/17	Operated patients reduced 22 kg in weight, 0 kg for control. T chol and LDL no change, HDL +0.3*, TG −0.7*	20 kg weight loss after 4 years yielded TG −0.7 mmol/l and HDL +0.3 mmol/l but no change in T chol or LDL	Medium
845 in surgery group and 845 in control group, 9.2 % and 16 % drop-out, respectively	Weight loss 28 (±15 kg in surgery group). Weight loss of 9 % reduced incidence of hyper-TG and hypo-HDL. TG −0.7, T chol −0.25, and HDL +0.18 in weight loss		Medium
842 patients with dropout 7 %–15 %	Weight change −95 kg to +30 kg. T chol change requires 20–30 kg weight loss. TG and HDL follows proportional and best weight change		Medium

in marked weight reduction, and the blood lipid values in 73 % of the subjects were normalized. However, the study presents low quality concerning sustained changes in blood lipids.

Potential blood lipid problems in children during weight loss are poorly studied. A controlled study from Finland included 48 children who were monitored for 5 years after having received diet education for 1 year – individually, in a group, or from the school health services [18]. Favorable changes in blood lipids were found after initial weight loss of about 25 %. However, compared to the original values, after 5 years no significant differences were found in HDL cholesterol, the HDL cholesterol/total cholesterol ratio, or triglycerides. This also applied for a small group of children who maintained their weight loss of 10 %.

In a study of children aged 8–12 years, 6 months of treatment (with diet alone or a combination of diet treatment and increased physical activity) yielded a mean weight loss of 6 % [11]. Total cholesterol and triglycerides decreased, while HDL cholesterol increased. These changes covaried with the level of weight loss. At followup after 5 years, when dropout was high and there was no control group, HDL cholesterol had increased significantly (from 0.99 to 1.23 mmol/L) in the group of children with sustained weight loss.

7.3.3.2 Pharmacotherapy

A randomized, controlled trial involving the use of orlistat for 2 years found that cholesterol decreased by 0.15 mmol/L and LDL cholesterol by 0.08 mmol/L [10]. Triglycerides and HDL cholesterol did not change compared to the control group. The results in the study might possibly have been different had the authors chosen day 1 of the study as the calculation point instead of the first day of a 4-week run-in period. Judging from the study data, both total cholesterol and LDL cholesterol seem to have increased from day 1 to the final evaluation. Dropout from the study was very high.

Another randomized controlled trial involving orlistat for 2 years reported an average of 10 kg decrease in body weight, which was ca. 4 kg more than that in the group receiving placebo [22]. Both total cholesterol and LDL cholesterol decreased, while triglycerides and HDL cholesterol did not change. Dropout was relatively high.

A randomized placebo-controlled trial involving the use of sibutramine for 2 years reported an average weight decrease of 10 kg with pharmacotherapy and ca. 5 kg with placebo [13]. Triglycerides decreased from 1.87 to 1.40 mmol/L and HDL cholesterol increased from 1.24 to 1.48 mmol/L, which was higher than in the placebo group. The increase in HDL cholesterol noted in the sibutramine group was around 2 to 3 times greater than what could be expected from the weight loss alone. The increase in HDL cholesterol was more pronounced in women.

7.3.3.3 Surgical Treatment

A study in which the primary aim was to evaluate the effects of weight loss on atherosclerosis in the carotid artery noted a slight increase in HDL cholesterol of 0.3 mmol/L and a decrease in triglycerides of 0.7 mmol/L. However, total cholesterol and LDL cholesterol did not change. These effects were measured 4 years after surgical intervention that yielded a weight loss of ca. 20 kg [14].

Studies in the SOS project have analyzed changes in risk factors [20, 21]. Weight loss of 9 % yielded an average decrease in triglycerides of 0.7 mmol/L and an increase in HDL cholesterol of 0.18 mmol/L, while total cholesterol did not decrease significantly [21]. These results are in agreement with other findings in the SOS study, namely that a reduction in total cholesterol is achieved only with substantial weight loss (20–30 kg) and that changes in triglycerides and HDL cholesterol correlate well with the degree of weight loss [20].

A study involving a large number of patients who were examined prior to possible surgery for high-grade obesity shows a low rate of hypercholesterolemia (severely elevated cholesterol level) [6]. In this study, blood lipids were also analyzed in 6 patients who lost considerable weight (40 kg) after surgical treatment. In these 6 patients, with an initial BMI > 40, total cholesterol decreased by 73 % and triglycerides by 95 %.

A hypothesis-generating study involving 7 overweight persons illustrates the association between weight loss, insulin resistance, and blood lipid changes [17]. After surgery, blood lipids decreased and insulin resistance also decreased (measured by the clamp method) even before weight loss became pronounced.

A non-obesity-related project randomized (from 1975 to 1983) patients to surgical treatment (partial ileal bypass operation, i. e., bypass of the lower segment of the small intestine) with the intent of seriously reducing elevated blood lipid levels [5]. Total cholesterol decreased by 34 %, LDL cholesterol by 38 %, and HDL cholesterol increased by 4 % [8]. However, no significant differences could be found at the 5-year followup. Only after a mean observation time of 14.7 years was a significant reduction shown in morbidity and mortality from coronary artery disease [7].

7.3.3.4 Other Studies on Lowering Blood Lipids

Studies that are recognized for demonstrating the effects of lowering blood lipids with drugs (statins) have not focused on obese subjects, the mean BMI having been only slightly elevated.

In a secondary prevention study (the 4S study) involving simvastatin, the mean BMI was 26.0 in both the placebo and treatment groups [1]. In studies of pravastatin, which showed decreased morbidity and mortality from pharmacotherapy, the mean BMI was 26 in the WOSCOPS study (primary prevention), 28 in the CARE study (secondary prevention), and 27 in the LIPID study (secondary prevention). The CARE study (2078 individuals in the placebo group and 2081 in the treatment group) and the LIPID studies monitored (on average 5 years) 13 173 individuals with a mean BMI of 27 ± 4. No changes in BMI during the study were reported. There are no subgroup analyses of individuals with a BMI of > 30, probably because there were few obese subjects. Hence, there are no studies of obese patients to demonstrate whether or not simvastatin and pravastatin have similar effects in normal-weight and overweight people.

Several studies have shown that blood lipid disorders in obesity, mainly elevated triglycerides and low HDL cholesterol, can be expected to normalize after moderate weight loss [9]. A meta-analysis of 70 studies shows that for each kg of weight lost, LDL is estimated to decrease by 1% (around 0.02 mmol/L) and triglycerides by 0.05 mmol/L [9]. A published guideline suggests that weight loss of 10 kg yields a 10% reduction in total cholesterol, a 15% reduction in LDL cholesterol, a 30% reduction in the triglyceride level, and an 8% increase in HDL cholesterol [2].

7.3.4
Discussion

Different interventions aimed at weight reduction (surgery, drugs, various dietary treatments) have demonstrated similar effects as regards changes in blood lipids. These changes are related to the degree of weight loss. In people with a high waist/hip ratio, mainly serum triglycerides and HDL cholesterol have been favorably influenced by weight loss.

Obesity in children appears to be associated with an increase in total cholesterol and a decrease in HDL cholesterol, although these changes have not been noted in physically active obese children. Rather, these children tend to have lower triglyceride levels. In adults, physical exercise, compared to weight loss, seems to yield a greater increase in the level of HDL cholesterol. Weight loss seems to have a greater impact on blood lipids than physical exercise.

References Section 7.3

1. Randomised trial of cholesterol lowering in 4444 patients with coronary heart disease: the Scandinavian Simvastatin Survival Study (4S). Lancet 1994;344(8934):1383-9.

2. Obesity in Scotland. Integrating prevention with weight management. A national clinical guideline recommended for use in Scotland. Edinburgh, Scottish Intercollegiate Guidelines Network; 1996.

3. Anderson JW, Brinkman-Kaplan VL, Lee H, Wood CL. Relationship of weight loss to cardiovascular risk factors in morbidly obese individuals. J Am Coll Nutr 1994;13(3):256-61.

4. Anderssen SA, Holme I, Urdal P, Hjermann I. Associations between central obesity and indexes of hemostatic, carbohydrate and lipid metabolism. Results of a 1-year intervention from the Oslo Diet and Exercise Study. Scand J Med Sci Sports 1998;8(2):109-15.

5. Buchwald H, Matts JP, Fitch LL, Varco RL, Campbell GS, Pearce M, et al. Program on the Surgical Control of the Hyperlipidemias (POSCH): design and methodology. POSCH Group. J Clin Epidemiol 1989;42(12):1111-27.

6. Buchwald H, Schone JL. Gastric obesity surgery combined with partial ileal bypass for hypercholesterolemia. Obes Surg 1997;7(4):313-6.

7. Buchwald H, Varco RL, Boen JR, Williams SE, Hansen BJ, Campos CT, et al. Effective lipid modification by partial ileal bypass reduced long-term coronary heart disease mortality and morbidity: five-year post-trial follow-up report from the POSCH. Program on

the Surgical Control of the Hyperlipidemias. Arch Intern Med 1998;158(11):1253-61.

8. Buchwald H, Varco RL, Matts JP, Long JM, Fitch LL, Campbell GS, et al. Effect of partial ileal bypass surgery on mortality and morbidity from coronary heart disease in patients with hypercholesterolemia. Report of the Program on the Surgical Control of the Hyperlipidemias (POSCH). N Engl J Med 1990;323(14):946-55.

9. Dattilo AM, Kris-Etherton PM. Effects of weight reduction on blood lipids and lipoproteins: a meta-analysis. Am J Clin Nutr 1992;56(2):320-8.

10. Davidson MH, Hauptman J, DiGirolamo M, Foreyt JP, Halsted CH, Heber D, et al. Weight control and risk factor reduction in obese subjects treated for 2 years with orlistat: a randomized controlled trial. JAMA 1999;281(3):235-42.

11. Epstein LH, Kuller LH, Wing RR, Valoski A, McCurley J. The effect of weight control on lipid changes in obese children. Am J Dis Child 1989;143(4):454-7.

12. Hensrud DD, Weinsier RL, Darnell BE, Hunter GR. Relationship of co-morbidities of obesity to weight loss and four-year weight maintenance/rebound. Obes Res 1995;3(Suppl 2):217S-222S.

13. James WP, Astrup A, Finer N, Hilsted J, Kopelman P, Rössner S, et al. Effect of sibutramine on weight maintenance after weight loss: a randomised trial. STORM Study Group. Sibutramine Trial of Obesity Reduction and Maintenance. Lancet 2000;356(9248):2119-25.

14. Karason K, Wikstrand J, Sjöstrom L, Wendelhag I. Weight loss and progression of early atherosclerosis in the carotid artery: a four-year controlled study of obese subjects. Int J Obes Relat Metab Disord 1999;23(9):948-56.

15. Karvetti RL, Hakala P. A seven-year follow-up of a weight reduction programme in Finnish primary health care. Eur J Clin Nutr 1992;46(10): 743-52.

16. Kirschner MA, Schneider G, Ertel NH, Gorman J. An eight-year experience with a very-low-calorie formula diet for control of major obesity. Int J Obes 1988;12(1):69-80.

17. Mingrone G, DeGaetano A, Greco AV, Capristo E, Benedetti G, Castagneto M, et al. Reversibility of insulin resistance in obese diabetic patients: role of plasma lipids. Diabetologia 1997;40(5):599-605.

18. Nuutinen O, Knip M. Long-term weight control in obese children: persistence of treatment outcome and metabolic changes. Int J Obes Relat Metab Disord 1992;16(4):279-87.

19. Scott HW, Jr, Dean RH, Shull HJ, Gluck F. Results of jejunoileal bypass in two hundred patients with morbid obesity. Surg Gynecol Obstet 1977;145(5):661-73.

20. Sjöstrom CD, Lissner L, Sjöstrom L. Relationships between changes in body composition and changes in cardiovascular risk factors: the SOS Intervention Study. Swedish Obese Subjects. Obes Res 1997;5(6):519-30.

21. Sjöstrom CD, Lissner L, Wedel H, Sjöstrom L. Reduction in incidence of diabetes, hypertension and lipid disturbances after intentional weight loss induced by bariatric surgery: the SOS Intervention Study. Obes Res 1999;7(5):477-84.

22. Sjöstrom L, Rissanen A, Andersen T, Boldrin M, Golay A, Koppeschaar HP, et al. Randomised placebo-controlled trial of orlistat for weight loss and prevention of weight regain in obese patients. European Multicentre Orlistat Study Group. Lancet 1998;352(9123): 167-72.

7.4
Sleep Apnea

Summary and Conclusion

Few well-executed studies address the question of whether non-surgical weight loss has favorable effects on sleep apnea. Despite weight loss, patients with sleep apnea are seldom weaned from continuous positive airway pressure (CPAP) treatment. Surgical treatment for obesity helps diminish various problems associated with sleep apnea.

7.4.1
Introduction

A characteristic of sleep apnea is that, during sleep, at least five breathing cessation events occur per hour. Obesity is one of the greatest risk factors, along with high alcohol consumption and male gender. Most people with sleep apnea have a BMI > 30.

7.4.2
Method

A search using the words "obesity", "sleep apnea", and "weight loss" identified 19 studies. Most of the articles address methodological aspects and registration methods, while clinical treatment results generally consist of case descriptions or very small patient groups. The effect variables usually reported are pulmonary function and sleep quality. Some articles address specific subgroups of individuals with weight problems, e.g., patients with spinal cord injuries. Five studies, of which only one is controlled, are presented, since they give an indication of the potential effects of weight loss on sleep apnea.

7.4.3
Results

A prospective, controlled, but non-randomized, study of 13 patients with sleep apnea (mean BMI 42) showed that after a weight loss of ca. 17%, the number of apneic events decreased from 83 episodes to 33 episodes per hour. In the control group which had been matched for age and BMI, no change was noted. In patients with the greatest weight loss, nearly all episodes of sleep apnea were eliminated.

The effect of treatment combining weight loss and Continuous Positive Airway Pressure (CPAP) via a mini-ventilator has been studied [4]. The study included 95 persons receiving CPAP treatment at home. Weight loss was achieved by simple dietary advice in 36 persons and by surgery (vertical gastroplasty) in 3 patients with BMI > 40. After 1 year, an average weight decrease from 108.3 to 99.7 kg was achieved in the 36 persons receiving dietary treatment. The apnea frequency improved from 66.5 to 50.3 attacks per hour and the breathing cessation events became shorter. The reduction correlated well with the decrease in BMI. Four patients, three of whom had lost weight, could be weaned from CPAP. The study is methodologically weak in that a control group is lacking and dropout is high.

Weight loss as a complement to ongoing treatment for snoring (involving side position and nasal spray) has been evaluated by one study [1]. Nineteen men affected by severe snoring were treated for 6 months in a conventional weight program. Among the nine individuals who lost at least 3 kg, the number of snores per hour decreased from 320 to 176.

A followup examination was performed in 14 patients with sleep apnea who had received gastric bypass or vertical banded gastroplasty for high-level obesity [5]. BMI had decreased from 45 to 35 after 7.5 years (average). The apnea index, estimated as the number of episodes of apnea ≥ 10 seconds per hour, decreased from 40 to 24.

A study investigated the effect of a simple but ambitious weight loss program as primary treatment for newly diagnosed sleep apnea [3]. Twenty-four patients with a mean BMI of 36 were treated for the first 6 weeks with a Very Low Calorie Diet (VLCD), i. e., 500 kcal/day, and then a balanced low-energy diet. Conventional support intervention was given at monthly meetings. In the 22 patients who completed 1 year of treatment, the mean BMI decreased to 31 and weight decreased from 110 kg to 99 kg. The degree of sleep apnea, measured as the number of occasions with deficient oxygen, decreased considerably. Also, the need of sleep (daytime somnolence) as judged by a visual rating scale decreased. Comparing to the previous study from the same clinic, weight loss was as effective as CPAP. The total cost of the weight loss program (which could be managed by specially trained nurses) was 1600 USD, and the cost of CPAP was 3000 USD. An association between reduced BMI and improved quality of sleep was not reported.

The SOS study used questionnaires and sleep apnea registration in subgroups to survey the effect of weight loss on cardiorespiratory symptoms. Data from 1210 surgical cases were compared to 1099 controls after the surgery patients had lost 23 % (average) in weight [2]. Although smoking habits, for example, did not change, the sleep apnea problems improved significantly after weight loss. Concurrently, chest pain and breathing problems decreased.

References Section 7.4

1. Braver HM, Block AJ, Perri MG. Treatment for snoring. Combined weight loss, sleeping on side, and nasal spray. Chest 1995;107(5):1283-8.
2. Karason K, Lindroos AK, Stenlof K, Sjöstrom L. Relief of cardiorespiratory symptoms and increased physical activity after surgically induced weight loss: results from the Swedish Obese Subjects study. Arch Intern Med 2000;160(12):1797-802.
3. Lojander J, Mustajoki P, Ronka S, Mecklin P, Maasilta P. A nurse-managed weight reduction programme for obstructive sleep apnoea syndrome. J Intern Med 1998;244(3):251-5.
4. Noseda A, Kempenaers C, Kerkhofs M, Houben JJ, Linkowski P. Sleep apnea after 1 year domiciliary nasal-continuous positive airway pressure and attempted weight reduction. Potential for weaning from continuous positive airway pressure. Chest 1996;109(1):138-43.
5. Pillar G, Peled R, Lavie P. Recurrence of sleep apnea without concomitant weight increase 7.5 years after weight reduction surgery. Chest 1994;106(6):1702-4.

7.5
Infertility and Pregnancy Outcome

Summary and Conclusions

Weight loss appears to be an effective treatment to normalize the hormonal situation, increase fertility, and improve pregnancy outcome in obese women with menstrual disorders. However, the studies reviewed involve few patients and few are controlled. The strength of the evidence is attributed to consistency in the results of the studies.

7.5.1
Introduction

Obese women often experience fertility problems, and there is an association between obesity and polycystic ovaries, menstrual disorders, and masculine hair growth. However, no studies have used established scientific methods to evaluate the treatment effects of weight loss. The literature is limited mainly to isolated reports where the scientific design was insufficient to classify the studies and grade the evidence according to the protocol used in this report.

7.5.2
Results

Kiddy et al. studied 24 women with obesity and polycystic ovaries. The original weight was 91.5 kg [3]. The participants were treated for 6 months with an energy-reduced diet, ca. 1000 kcal/day. Each of the 24 participants had menstrual disorders, 12 were infertile, and 5 had masculine hair growth. Around half of the women (13 participants) reduced their weight by ca. 5 %. In this group, hormonal changes were noted, with an increased concentration of sex hormone binding globulin (SHBG) and a relative decrease in free testosterone. Concurrently, fasting insulin decreased significantly. These changes were not noted in women who had lost less weight. Of the 13 women, 5 became pregnant, and all had a more normal menstrual pattern, previously having had menstrual disorders. The prevalence of masculine hair growth decreased by 40 % in this group. No such changes were observed in the group that did not lose 5 % of the original weight.

Pasquali et al. monitored women with overweight/obesity and signs of masculinity and menstrual disorders (initial mean BMI 32.1) [5]. The women were treated with an energy-reduced diet, 1000–1500 kcal/day, which yielded a mean weight loss of 9.7 ± 3.1 kg. Concurrently, the waist/hip ratio decreased from 0.86 to 0.81. The weight reduction led to normalized menstrual periods in 8 of 20, to periods of ovulation in 33 % of the entire group, and to four pregnancies. Masculine hair growth decreased in more than half of the group. The improvements occurred regardless of the prevalence of polycystic ovaries, the degree of masculinity, and the distribution of adipose tissue.

Guzick et al. performed one of the few available, controlled, prospective, randomized trials, unfortunately with only 6 women in each group [1]. The women were randomized to 12 weeks of weight reduction or to a waiting list. During a 12-week program, the women were first treated by VLCD formula, then a low-energy diet and standard behavior modification. Compared to the control group, where no changes could be noted, the 6 treated women lost 16.2 kg (mean) which increased SHBG and decreased testosterone and fasting insulin. Four of six women showed signs of ovulation. These changes occurred even if secretion patterns for FSH and LH (superior pituitary hormones) did not change.

Another study treated 35 women in a conventional program with an energy-reduced diet [2]. Initial BMI was 35, and the women lost 10.2 kg (mean) during treatment. A decrease in blood sugar, insulin, and male sex hormones followed weight loss. Ten of the women became pregnant, and menstruation improved in 80% of the group.

Kiddy et al., in their initial study, described the effect of weight loss on endocrine variables in women of normal weight and in overweight /obese (BMI 36.1) women with polycystic ovaries [4]. Both groups were treated for up to 4 weeks with VLCD, 330 kcal/day. Hormone determinations were performed before and after a weight loss of ca. 5 kg in the control group and 7 kg in the group with polycystic ovaries. SHBG increased, while free testosterone and serum insulin decreased. The study shows that even short-term weight loss can lead to clinically significant hormonal changes.

An extensive case-control study from Sweden found a higher rate of fetal mortality in overweight or obese women [6].

In summary, the referenced studies indicate that weight loss is an effective treatment method to normalize the hormonal situation, increase fertility, and improve the outcome of pregnancy in obese women with menstrual disorders.

References Section 7.5

1. Guzick DS, Wing R, Smith D, Berga SL, Winters SJ. Endocrine consequences of weight loss in obese, hyperandrogenic, anovulatory women. Fertil Steril 1994;61(4): 598-604.

2. Hollmann M, Runnebaum B, Gerhard I. Effects of weight loss on the hormonal profile in obese, infertile women. Hum Reprod 1996;11(9):1884-91.

3. Kiddy DS, Hamilton-Fairley D, Bush A, Short F, Anyaoku V, Reed MJ, et al. Improvement in endocrine and ovarian function during dietary treatment of obese women with polycystic ovary syndrome. Clin Endocrinol (Oxf) 1992;36(1):105-11.

4. Kiddy DS, Hamilton-Fairley D, Seppala M, Koistinen R, James VH, Reed MJ, et al. Diet-induced changes in sex hormone binding globulin and free testosterone in women with normal or polycystic ovaries: correlation with serum insulin and insulin-like growth factor-I. Clin Endocrinol (Oxf) 1989;31(6):757-63.

5. Pasquali R, Antenucci D, Casimirri F, Venturoli S, Paradisi R, Fabbri R, et al. Clinical and hormonal characteristics of obese amenorrheic hyperandrogenic women before and after weight loss. J Clin Endocrinol Metab 1989;68(1): 173-9.

6. Stephansson O, Dickman PW, Johansson A, Cnattingius S. Maternal weight, pregnancy weight gain, and the risk of antepartum stillbirth. Am J Obstet Gynecol 2001;184(3):463-9.

8
Economic Evaluation of Treatment Methods

Summary

This Section presents the economic assessments found in database searches of the medical and economic scientific literature. Few economic studies have assessed interventions to prevent and treat obesity.

Results: Five studies on diet, behavior therapy, and VLCD (Very Low Calorie Diet) were reviewed that met the established quality criteria. One of these studies shows that dietary counseling by a dietician alone or a dietician and a physician together resulted in weight loss at a low cost. The finding is based on one year of followup. Another study shows that behavior therapy can lead to weight loss at a low cost. The cost of VLCD, or a combination of behavior therapy and VLCD, was somewhat higher. However, the overall evidence grade is so low that reliable conclusions cannot be drawn regarding the cost effectiveness of dietary counseling and VLCD.

Several health-economic model analyses show that surgical treatment yields a significant weight loss at a relatively low cost. These studies, which generally present low quality, are based on small numbers of subjects and short followup periods. Three Swedish studies (high quality) compared surgical intervention to management in primary care. These studies show no difference in the costs for drugs and sick leave, but the cost of other hospital care was higher in the surgical group. Overall, these three studies show that total costs, 4 to 6 years after surgery, are approximately 70 000 Swedish Kronor (SEK) higher than those for traditional management in primary care. Related to the 16 % weight loss reported after 6 years in the SOS study, the cost is slightly more than 4000 SEK per percentage point of weight loss in 1996 monetary value.

A producer-independent economic assessment of pharmacotherapy using orlistat in obesity has been published. The manufacturer has presented an unpublished study. Both of these studies use models to calculate the cost per quality-adjusted life-year (period of decreased health is converted to years of full health) related to orlistat treatment. The independent study estimated the cost per quality-adjusted life-year to be just over 600 000 SEK, while the manufacturer estimated the cost at approximately 150 000 SEK. The assessment agency in England (NICE) found the independent model analysis to be most compatible with the available scientific evidence.

Treating and Preventing Obesity. Edited by J. Östman, M. Britton, E. Jonsson
Copyright © 2004 WILEY-VCH Verlag GmbH & Co. KGaA, Weinheim
ISBN 3-527-30818-0

Conclusion: The information available on the cost effectiveness of different methods is limited. The cost effectiveness of the preventive methods cannot be calculated because of the prevailing uncertainty about their effects. In treating obesity, the cost is relatively low for the weight loss achieved by dietary counseling, behavior therapy, VLCD, diet replacement agents with a low energy content, and surgical intervention, but far higher for pharmacological treatment. No studies were found that estimated cost effectiveness based on observed reduction in morbidity or mortality or based on improved quality of life.

8.1
Method

The databases searched were Cinahl, MEDLINE, HEED, and NHS (Centre for Reviews and Dissemination). HEED and NHS were searched using the term "obesity". In addition to the term "obesity", the search in Cinahl and MEDLINE used the MeSH term "costs and cost analysis".

The most recent literature search was performed in early January 2002, yielding 309 articles. After review of titles and abstracts, a large number of studies of little or no relevance were excluded. Over 70 articles were retrieved and reviewed for relevance. Furthermore, reference lists in the articles reviewed, and other sources, were searched. In total, 12 studies were found based on economic assessment of interventions to prevent or treat obesity.

The literature has been reviewed for quality and rated according to the established criteria for health economic assessment [4]. The assessment manual used is presented at the end of this chapter.

The studies presented below were classified into the following three groups:

- Low quality
- Medium quality
- High quality

8.2
Results

8.2.1
Counseling and VLCD (see Table 8.1)

A study from Australia examined the effects of different types of dietary counseling in treating obesity [11]. The study population included 273 persons, 198 of whom were women, with one or more of the following risk factors: overweight (BMI > 25), hypertension, and type 2 diabetes. The patients were randomized to one of three alternatives: counseling by a dietician only (n = 88), counseling by a dietician and a general practitioner (n = 92), or traditional management only (n = 90). The dietician group was offered six individual counseling sessions during a 12-month period. The program in the dietician/physician group was designed in the same manner, but with the addition that a general practitioner invited the patient to discuss the treatment twice during the study period. After 12 months, weight increased on average 0.58 kg in the control group, while it decreased by 5.05 kg in the group meeting a dietician and by 6.13 kg in the dietician/physician group. In the two counseling groups, the additional cost per kg weight loss was lower compared to the control group.

Similar results were found in a study that investigated the effects of VLCD, behavioral therapy, and a combination of the two [14, 16]. After completion of the treatment, the average weight loss for the individuals in the different groups ranged between 14 kg and 19 kg. The cost to decrease body weight by 1 % was around 200 to 300 SEK. After 1 year, the cost to decrease body weight by 1 % was higher because of weight gain after completed treatment. This was particularly obvious in the group receiving VLCD only. The cost calculations have not been thoroughly reported, so the results must be interpreted with caution. The study presents poor-grade evidence.

The effects of a VLCD program in overweight diabetic patients (BMI 30–40) were studied to examine changes in pharmaceutical costs [3]. Forty people were randomized to treatment with only liquid meal replacement five times per day or liquid meal replacement twice per day and an evening meal. However, the results are reported only for the study population as a whole. In the 30 subjects who completed the study, mean weight decreased from 103.7 kg to 88.4 kg after 12 weeks of treatment. One year after completed treatment, mean weight had increased to 94.7 kg, but the patients' costs for prescribed drugs had decreased, on average, by 50 %, corresponding to just over 200 SEK per month. Deficiencies in the reporting make the results difficult to interpret, but the study gives an indication that treatment with VLCD may lead to savings in pharmaceutical costs.

A Danish study investigated the effects of a work site-based counseling program [13]. After being given information about the study, the participants could decide for themselves whether to participate in the control or the intervention group. The participants in the control group (16 persons) were instructed to continue their current diet, but received no other instructions. Those in the intervention group (50 persons) were informed about nutrition and a diet rich in carbohydrates but low in fat. The results after 12 weeks showed that overweight subjects in the intervention group (BMI > 25) had an average weight loss of just over 5 kg. In the control group the corresponding weight loss was 0.8 kg. Considering the cost of implementing the program, the cost for a 1 % reduction in overweight was estimated to be 80 SEK. The results are uncertain because of deficiencies in the study design. However, these results confirm other study results, namely that counseling and treatment with VLCD appear in the short term to lead to weight loss at low cost.

Another study at work sites in the United States investigated the effects of a weight loss competition [15]. In total, 1177 employees from 15 different work sites participated. They were divided into teams, and all the teams were given the same weight loss goal. The competition lasted for 12 weeks. Among partici-

Table 8.1 Studies on advice/counseling and VLCD[1].

Author Year Reference	Design	Recruitment	Inclusion criteria	Study groups	Followup period
Pritchard et al. 1999 [11]	RCT	Screening	Overweight, high blood pressure or type 2 diabetes	1. Dietician n = 88 2. Dietician + physician n = 92 3. Control n = 90	12 months
Wadden & Stunkard 1986 [16] Stunkard 1987 [14]	RCT	Advertisement	25 kg overweight	1. VLCD n = 18 2. Behavior therapy n = 18 3. Combination n = 23	12 months after completed treatment
Collins & Anderson 1995 [3]	RCT (stratification)	Advertisement	Type 2 diabetes 40–70 years, BMI 30–40, fasting serum C peptides >1.4 nm/loch serum creatinine <176 µmol/L Mean BMI 35.2	1. Only liquid meal replacement n = 20 2. Liquid meal replacement and evening meal n = 20	12 months after completed treatment
Siggaard et al. 1996 [13]	Prospective Controlled	Voluntary recruitment after information	Employed at worksite 1. Mean BMI 30.9 Mean age 45.3 2. Mean BMI 23.8 Mean age 34.7 3. Mean BMI 27 Mean age 36.3	1. Diet information BMI >25 2. Diet information BMI <25 n 1+2 = 69 3. Control n = 17	3 months
Stunkard et al. 1989 [15]	Prospective Not controlled	Voluntary participation after information	Employed at worksite	n = 1177	3 months

[1] VLCD = Very Low Calorie Diet
RCT = Randomized Controlled Trial
ITT = Intention to Treat

No. patients followed up	Results Body weight	Other effects	Cost Cost/kg or %	Study quality Comments
1. n = 64 2. n = 65 3. n = 48	1. −5.05 kg 2. −6.13 kg 3. +0.58 kg ITT analysis		40 SEK/kg 50 SEK/kg (1993 price level)	Low
	1. −4.6 kg 2. −9.5 kg 3. −12.9 kg Statistical significance		280 SEK/ 1 % reduction 200 SEK/ 1 % reduction 260 SEK/ 1 % reduction (Price level unknown)	Low
n = 30 total, no reporting by group	−9 kg	210 SEK/ month saved drug costs (Price level unknown)		Low
1. n = 32 2. n = 18 3. n = 16	1. −5.2 kg 2. −2.5 kg 3. −0.8 kg		80 SEK/ 1 % reduction in overweight (Price level unknown)	Low
n = 1151	−6.3 kg for men −4.4 kg for women		<10 SEK/ 1 % reduction of body weight (Price level unknown)	Low

pants who were initially above 10% overweight, weight loss after 12 weeks was 9.1% of the overweight in men and 8% in women. The costs for administering the competition and lost work time were included in the total costs. The cost to reduce 1% of the body weight was very low. Since the results are based on relatively old data (probably prior to 1984) and are not thoroughly reported, they should be interpreted with great caution. Furthermore, the study did not include a control group.

8.2.2
Surgical intervention

One study compared the costs of surgical intervention with the costs of counseling in combination with VLCD [6]. The patients in the study were allowed to choose between the two treatment options. The costs for the respective programs were calculated retrospectively by means of receipts and medical bills. The costs were nearly 10 times higher for surgical intervention than those for the counseling program. The cost per lost kg was lower for the counseling program during the first 5 years, but after 6 years of followup the surgery cost was lower. The study has many weaknesses, e. g., the patients themselves chose the treatment option and dropout was high in the last years of followup. No conclusions can be drawn from this study.

A report from the NHS Development and Evaluation Committee from 1997 presents a model calculation on the cost effectiveness of surgery for severe obesity (BMI > 40) [2]. A successful surgical procedure is defined as a 50% reduction in overweight, or a BMI below 35. The literature showed that approximately 40% of treated patients fulfilled these criteria after 3 years and approximately 16% did so after 5 years. The improvement in quality of life that could be attributed to a successful procedure was estimated by the authors by means of a three-dimensional classification, Index of Health-Related Quality of Life (IHQL), to be 0.16–0.29. Hence, between 0.16 and 0.29 quality-adjusted life-years (QALYs) are received for each year that the treatment effect is maintained. The treatment effect after 5 years was considered to be uncertain, which is the reason why the analysis did not reach beyond that point in time. Based on the above assumptions, it was estimated that 100 patients received between 24 and 44 QALYs. The cost estimates covered the procedure itself and followup visits for 5 years, which included any re-operation costs. Making different assumptions about the rate of reoperation, the cost per patient was estimated to be approximately 80 000 to 90 000 SEK. The cost per quality-adjusted life-year gained was 180 000 to 380 000 SEK. Only direct medical costs are included in the estimate.

In a review on surgery in obesity, the Scottish Health Purchasing Information Centre (SHPIC) applied costs from a clinic in Scotland on the basis of the above study. The cost per QALY ranged between 37 000 and 75 000 SEK [12]. The calculations are not fully reported, and the value of the evidence presented in the study cannot be assessed.

An analysis concerning how surgery influences the indirect costs of sick leave and early retirement pension has been reported based on data from the Swedish Obese Subjects (SOS) study [8]. Indirect costs for those undergoing surgical treatment (369 persons) were compared to those for a control group (371 persons). The control group received no extra intervention beyond standard health care. For each person in the surgery group, a matched control was selected on the basis of 18 different variables. Mean BMI before treatment was above 40 in both groups. The costs were calculated as the mean sickness benefit cost and the mean early retirement pension 1 year before treatment and 5 years after inclusion in the study. The results clearly show a greater weight loss in the surgery group than that in the control group. The number of absent days due to sick leave and sick pension was considerably higher in the surgery group for the first year after treatment. From the second year onward, sick leave was higher in the control group (significant difference year 2 and 3, not a significant difference year 4). Figure-based data indicate that total sick leave was somewhat higher in the surgery group than in the control group.

Another study investigated the costs for inpatient care after surgical intervention for obesity [17]. Within the framework of the SOS study, 962 patients were consecutively recruited from 1987 to 1991. Half were treated by surgery while the others received conventional treatment. Information on the number of days in inpatient care from the year prior to inclusion in the study and the following six years was collected from the national care registry of the National Board of Health and Welfare. The length of stay was based on the care delivered as a direct consequence of obesity surgery or care resulting from complications of surgery. After excluding the length of stay for the original operation, the accumulated length of stay in the surgical group was 14 days compared to 6.9 days in the control group. After excluding the length of stay attributed to interventions that are common after obesity surgery, no difference could be observed between the two groups. The accumulated cost of inpatient care in the surgical group was 99 000 SEK compared to 27 000 SEK in the conventional treatment group. There were no indications that the improvements achieved in risk factors for cardiovascular disease reduced the need of inpatient care during the first 6 years after surgery. The conclusion is that surgery which reduces weight by 16% or less does not lead to lower costs for inpatient care during the subsequent 6 years. Future cost reductions cannot, however, be ruled out. Although the study is not a comprehensive cost analysis, it presents high quality.

Another sub-analysis of SOS data addressing the economic effects of obesity surgery investigated the consumption of medication for 6 years after surgery [9]. A comparison was drawn between the intervention group and a matched control group treated by conservative therapy. Each group included 647 patients. When the costs during the first year after surgery had been excluded, the annual mean cost of drugs was 1950 SEK in the surgery group and 2048 SEK in the control group. The difference after adjusting for differences between the groups was 43 SEK. Although the study is not a comprehensive cost analysis, it presents high quality.

Table 8.2 Studies of surgery and pharmacotherapy.

Author Year Reference	Design	Recruitment	Inclusion criteria Mean BMI Mean age	Study groups	Followup period

Martin et al. 1995 [6]	Prospective non-controlled	Patients seeking care	1. Mean BMI 49.3
			  Mean age 38.9
			2. Mean BMI 41.2
			  Mean age 42.7
				1. Surgery
				  n = 201
				2. VLCD +
				  advice
				  n = 161
					6 years
					2 years
					6 years
					2 years

Bryant et al. NHS DEC-report 1997 [2]	Model analysis			1. Surgery
				2. No
				  treatment
				  – model
					5 years

Narbro et al. 1999 [8]	Prospective controlled (matching)	Advertisement	37–60 years,
			BMI ≥34 for men and
			BMI ≥38 for women
			1. Mean BMI 41.6
			  Mean age 47
			2. Mean BMI 41.0
			  Mean age 48
				1. Surgery
				  n = 369
				2. Control
				  n = 371
					5 years
					(1 year before
					4 years after
					surgery)

Ågren et al. 2001 [17]	Prospective controlled (matching)	Advertisement	37–60 years,
			BMI ≥34 for men and
			BMI ≥38 for women
			1. Mean BMI 41.9
			  Mean age 47
			2. Mean BMI 40.1
			  Mean age 48.2
				1. Surgery
				  n = 481
				2. Conventional
				  treatment
				  n = 481
					6 years

Narbro et al. 2001 [9]	Prospective controlled (matching)	Advertisement	37–60 years,
			BMI ≥34 for men and
			BMI ≥38 for women
			1. Mean BMI 41.8
			  Mean age 47.1
			2. Mean BMI 39.9
			  Mean age 48.6
				1. Surgery
				  n = 647
				2. Conventional
				  treatment
				  n = 647
					6 years

Nguyen et al. 2001 [10]	RCT	Consecutive	21–60 years, BMI = 40–60
			Previous failed non-surgical intervention
			1. Mean BMI 48.4
			  Mean age 42
			2. Mean BMI 47.6
			  Mean age 40
				1. Open bypass
				  n = 76
				2. Laparoscopic
				  bypass
				  n = 79
					1 year

NHS Executive 1999 [1]	Model Analysis		1. Orlistat 2. No treatment – model		

RCT = Randomized Controlled Trial

No. patients followed up	Results Body weight	Other effects	Cost Cost/kg	Study quality Comments
1. n = 30 1. n = 153 2. n = 14 2. n = 97			3940 SEK/kg 3620 SEK/kg 4720 SEK/kg 950 SEK/kg (Price level unknown)	Low
			181 000– 379 000 SEK/ QALY (1997 price level)	Medium
1. n = 339 (weight) n = 369 (sick leave) 2. n = 296 (weight) n = 371 (sick leave)	1. –23.5 kg (4 years after surgery) 2. +0.8 kg (5 years after inclusion)	Total number of sick leave/early retirement days equal among the groups during the entire study period (figure data)		High
1. n = 401 (weight) n = 466 (inpatient care) 2. n = 344 (weight) n = 467 (inpatient care)	1. –16.7% of body weight 2. +0.9% of body weight	Total cost for inpatient care from intervention until year 6 1. 99 080 SEK 2. 27 450 SEK (Statistical significance) (1996 price level)		High
1. n = 510 2. n = 455		Average annual cost for drugs during study period 1. 1849 SEK 2. 1905 SEK Not significant Year 2–6 1. 1950 SEK 2. 2048 SEK Not significant (1997 price level)		High
1. n = 25 2. n = 28	1. –62% of initial overweight 2. –68% of initial overweight		Cost for treatment 1. 145 630 SEK 2. 145 520 SEK Not significant (Price level unknown) 615 000 SEK/ QALY (1999 price level)	Medium Medium

One study compared the costs and effects of laparoscopic surgery and open surgery [10]. In this study, 79 patients were randomized to laparoscopic surgery and 76 to open surgery. The cost estimates involved direct and indirect costs. SF-36 was used to measure quality of life. The results after 3 months showed that patients in both treatment groups lost just over 30 % of their excess weight. At a 1-year followup the corresponding weight loss was just over 60 % for the two groups. A high dropout rate at 1-year followup makes it difficult to draw any conclusions on the effects after one year.

No significant differences were found in the direct or indirect costs between the groups. The total mean cost for the respective treatment group was just over 140 000 SEK. After 1 month, the laparoscopic surgery group had a higher quality of life than the open surgery group. The differences in quality of life between the groups were smaller and not significant after 3 and 6 months. The study presents medium quality.

8.2.3
Pharmacotherapy

A report from the DEC-NHS Executive in England presents a cost-benefit analysis of orlistat [1]. Three clinical studies of orlistat form the basis for this model calculation. The point of departure in the model is that orlistat yields a weight loss for 2 years, but the long-term effects cannot be determined because of insufficient data. Hence, it is not included in the analysis. The Index for Health Related Quality of Life was used to calculate the expected increase in quality of life resulting from reduced weight. A calculation including 100 persons showed that pharmacotherapy for 2 years with orlistat yields an overall gain in quality of life for the entire group of 1601 quality-adjusted life years (QALYs). The average total direct cost of treating 100 persons with orlistat for 1 year is reported to be approximately one million SEK. The costs included, e. g., physician visits, consultations, and drug costs. Cost per QALY gained by orlistat treatment was estimated to be just over 600 000 SEK. It should be emphasized that the cost estimates do not cover, e. g., travel expenses and the cost for any specially required diet for the patient. Likewise, decreased sick leave and reduced consumption of care after treatment with orlistat is not included in the estimates.

References

1. NHS Executive, Orlistat for the treatment of obesity: Development and Evaluation Committe; 1999. Report No 10.

2. Bryant J, Best L, Milne R. Gastroplasty for severe obesity. Southampton: Wessex Institute for Health Research and Development. Development and Evalutation Committee Report; 1997. Report No 68.

3. Collins RW, Anderson JW. Medication cost savings associated with weight loss for obese non-insulin-dependent diabetic men and women. Prev Med 1995;24(4):369-74.

4. Drummond MF, et al. Methods for the economic evaluation of health care programmes, 2nd edn. Oxford University Press 1997.

5. Foxcroft D, Ludders J. Orlistat for the treatment of obesity. Southampton: Wessex Institute for Health Research and Development. Development and Evaluation Committee Report; 1999. Report No 101.

6. Martin LF, Tan TL, Horn JR, Bixler EO, Kauffman GL, Becker DA, et al. Comparison of the costs associated with medical and surgical treatment of obesity. Surgery 1995;118(4): 599-606.

7. Narbro K. Sick leave and disability pension before and after treatment of obesity. 1997.

8. Narbro K, Ågren G, Jonsson E, Larsson B, Näslund I, Wedel H, et al. Sick leave and disability pension before and after treatment for obesity: a report from the Swedish Obese Subjects (SOS) study. Int J Obes Relat Metab Disord 1999;23(6):619-24.

9. Narbro K, Ågren G, Jonsson E, Näslund I, Sjöström L, Peltonen M. Pharmaceutical costs in obesity: A comparison with randomly selected population sample, and long-term changes after conventional and surgical treatment. The SOS intervention study. I: Narbro K, Economic aspects on obesity, Göteborgs universitet (dissertation); 2001.

10. Nguyen NT, Goldman C, Rosenquist CJ, Arango A, Cole CJ, Lee SJ, et al. Laparoscopic versus open gastric bypass: a randomized study of outcomes, quality of life, and costs. Ann Surg 2001;234(3):279-89; discussion 89-91.

11. Pritchard DA, Hyndman J, Taba F. Nutritional counselling in general practice: a cost effective analysis. J Epidemiol Community Health 1999;53(5):311-6.

12. SHPIC Report. Gastric Surgery for Obesity: Scottish Health Purchasing Information Center; 1998.

13. Siggaard R, Raben A, Astrup A. Weight loss during 12 week's ad libitum carbohydrate-rich diet in overweight and normal-weight subjects at a Danish work site. Obes Res 1996;4(4):347-56.

14. Stunkard AJ. Conservative treatments for obesity. Am J Clin Nutr 1987;45 (5 Suppl):1142-54.

15. Stunkard AJ, Cohen RY, Felix MR. Weight loss competitions at the worksite: how they work and how well. Prev Med 1989;18(4):460-74.

16. Wadden TA, Stunkard AJ. Controlled trial of very low calorie diet, behavior therapy, and their combination in the treatment of obesity. J Consult Clin Psychol 1986;54(4):482-8.

17. Ågren G, Narbro K, Jonsson E, Näslund I, Sjöström L, Peltonen M. Cost of in-patient care among the obese. A prospective study of surgically and conventionally treated patients in the Swedish Obese Subjects intervention study. I: Narbro K, Economic aspects on obesity, Göteborgs universitet (dissertation); 2001.

9
Ethical Aspects

Ethics refers to a discipline or a systematic discussion concerning what is morally right and wrong. Medical ethics addresses the moral aspects of diagnosis, treatment, care, and prevention. Obviously, the general principles of medical ethics also apply in the treatment of obesity. *The principle of beneficence* means that medical intervention shall benefit the patient in some way. For diagnostic and therapeutic interventions to be justified they must be able to improve health or quality of life. *The principle of nonmalficence*, the principle to do no harm, means that the patients shall not be exposed to injury or the risk for injury that exceeds the potential benefits of the intervention. *The principle of justice* means, e. g., that patients who find themselves in the same medical situation shall be given equal access to treatment. *The principle of autonomy* means that the patient's integrity and right to self-determination shall be respected and that treatment shall, to the extent possible, be designed and carried out in consultation with the patient [2].

Many diseases give rise to ethical issues that lie beyond the actual boundaries of medical ethics. Examples include questions on lifestyles that lead to obesity, how we approach obese people in both private and public contexts, and how the weak position of patients due to their vulnerability could possibly be exploited in trying various untested treatments.

Further moral aspects may arise when it comes to prioritizing patients and interventions within and among various disease groups [1]. The overriding principles here concern human equality; the strongest needs should receive the highest priority. Cost effectiveness may also be an important aspect.

Hence, it is essential to aim to consider all of the different ethical aspects related to interventions for obesity. Individual patient's rights need to be highlighted and protected. Concurrently, society has a strong interest in preventing obesity and obesity-related disorders, and in using available resources effectively.

Treating and Preventing Obesity. Edited by J. Östman, M. Britton, E. Jonsson
Copyright © 2004 WILEY-VCH Verlag GmbH & Co. KGaA, Weinheim
ISBN 3-527-30818-0

9.1
Patients' Problems

In many situations, obese people face practical problems that generate a sense of not belonging. Examples of practical problems include narrow seats on buses, trains, airplanes, movie theatres, etc., and difficulties in finding suitable clothes. The experience of negative attitudes from the environment is, however, even more serious for an obese person. At the same time that obesity has become more common in society, there has also been a trend toward greater fixation on appearance and an ideal body image, thus reinforcing negative attitudes toward obesity. Obese people face discrimination in employment and have a lower average income than others [7, 10, 11]. Also, obese children are often exposed to negative attitudes from their environment [3, 5]. Many studies show an association between obesity in children and psychosocial ill health. Experience also shows that the social consequences of obesity may be challenging even for the family members of obese patients.

Many obese people perceive that their situation is dominated by a sense of guilt. Few other diseases are so often portrayed as the "person's own fault". This is an obsolete view [9]. Knowledge is growing about the impact of the changes in diet and exercise that have taken place across western society, and about the role of the genetic factors in the development of obesity. Attitudes that focus on "guilt", from health services and from society at large, are mentally stressful. They may counteract the will to try to keep weight under control or to make new attempts. Because of the attitudes and actions of others, many obese people stay at home so that they do not have to show themselves. This is unfortunate since exercise is an important component of treatment.

9.2
Treatment

Many patients have unrealistic expectations about how to lose weight, and require counseling to change diet and exercise habits and set realistic goals. It is essential that advice to lose weight be followed by adequate support, counseling, and long-term followup.

The question of whether or not to start intensive treatment must take into account the fact that treatment may be stressful and demanding, and that failure may have negative psychological consequences as a result of frustration and self-blame. Therefore, it is not ethically defensible to initiate an intensive treatment program if the prospects for success are small [8]. Rather, patients should be offered basic support regarding diet and exercise. This applies particularly to patients who, for various reasons, cannot participate in the more demanding treatment programs (e. g., patients with dementia and mental disorders), since active participation is a necessary condition for success in such interventions. Special ethical problems also exist in the case of patients who have a severely increased appetite resulting from genetic conditions [6]. Since the elderly have a substantially lower risk of obesity-related disease, intensive treatment for obesity in this group should also be limited. Many failed attempts at weight loss represent another contraindication. Unless the odds for success have changed, it is doubtful from both a medical and ethical standpoint whether further similar attempts should be made.

Since obesity is common, the issue of treatment may arise in many health care situations where the patient seeks care for some other illness. If the patient seeks care for an obesity-related disease or asks for general advice during a health check-up, the caregiver should discuss the value of weight loss and offer counseling on appropriate treatment alternatives. The caregiver is often justified in providing health advice that is not directly related to the reason for the patient's visit, particularly in primary care, where there is a holistic responsibility for care. When discussing obesity in such a context it is particularly important to be sensitive to the patient's point of view and to avoid expressions that may be perceived as patronizing.

The treatment effects of current methods are often limited. An inevitable question is whether it may do more harm than good for the patient to make repeated attempts at weight loss that do not succeed. The patient's self-esteem may be further damaged by such failures. Given this situation, among others, it is essential that long-term followup and patient support are included in the treatment of obesity.

Obviously, treatments having a low level of effectiveness also have a low level of cost-effectiveness. Consequently, these treatments are not prioritized very highly. However, obese people may have higher morbidity and a substantially lower quality of life, and thereby have a greater need for health services and psychosocial support. It is therefore essential to develop effective methods of care, treatment, and prevention. To achieve this, specific forms of care and research groups may be needed.

Very severely obese patients should be offered the opportunity to discuss and consider surgical interventions, since these methods have both substantial and lasting effects, but also important side effects. These patients need long-term, professional and human support along with expert advice on treatment alternatives.

9.3
Interaction with Health Services

Obese patients often report negative experiences from their interaction with health services. Providers need to give serious consideration to these perspectives. For example, the physical environment is often perceived as unwelcoming, scales may be inadequate, and beds, operating tables, X-ray machines, and blood pressure cuffs are often too small. Even more serious are the complaints that patients often do not receive the understanding and the attention they need. Obviously, this must be viewed in relation to the limited options for effective treatment. An important medical-ethical principle is, nevertheless, that the quality of interaction with health services should not be poorer even if there are few treatment options. Health care plays a key role in these issues. A professional, i. e., expert and compassionate, approach in health care may have a major psychological and social impact. It is important for health services to set a good example in caring for obese and overweight individuals in a welcoming, understanding, and secure way.

9.4
Quackery

Obese people are constantly in a weak position due to their vulnerability, their resignation, and their desperation to see a lasting result from their attempts to take control over their weight. Most obese people have tried, in one way or another, to lose weight, often many times and generally with temporary results and relapses. The strong desire for access to more effective methods for weight reduction opens the market for dubious, untested products and fraud. With dramatic headlines and unrealistic promises, these products represent a last resort, even though the user is often aware of the unrealistic claims.

From an ethical standpoint, there is reason to be critical of those who exploit the weak position of obese people by offering expensive, untested, in many cases harmful methods for weight loss. Primarily, this criticism concerns those who sell medically inappropriate products and treatments. To use false claims to offer cures that do not improve (and in the worst cases harm) the patient's health is unethical.

The media also play a role in the launching of unverified diet cures, thus contributing toward exposing individual patients to costly and frustrating treatment failures. At the same time, the media can contribute toward giving the public inaccurate and prejudicial attitudes about the disease and the opportunities for cure.

9.5
Obesity as a Social Problem

The increasing prevalence of obesity and the high costs arising from obesity-related disease push ethics and economics in the same direction. It is urgent to develop and offer effective programs for prevention and treatment. This requires an increased effort in research, both in basic and clinical research.

Preventing obesity and improving the situation for obese people also requires a change in attitudes. This is not only an issue for health care. Some ethical problems must be managed outside of the health care sector. The fashion and entertainment industries have a major impact on body image, fixation on appearance, and the general attitude toward obese people. The food and restaurant industries have a major impact on our dietary habits, often not in a way that promotes the treatment and prevention of obesity. Patients can actively contribute, e. g., via patient associations, toward increasing the understanding of obesity, and can thereby improve the attitudes of society.

The often-used term "lifestyle disease" may be justified at the societal level, since publicly conditioned living conditions contribute toward an increased rate of obesity. The word "style" may, however, lead people to believe that fairly simple measures are required from the individual for treatment to be successful. Hence, the term may contribute toward negative attitudes about the problems faced by obese persons. An improved understanding of the situation is an important condition for society to better prevent and take action against the serious threat to public health presented by the obesity trend.

9.6
General Prevention

As is apparent from the material in this book, treating obesity is very difficult, and long-term results are generally discouraging. These facts reinforce the importance of preventing obesity.

Citizens of all ages need positive stimulus to achieve a healthy lifestyle involving a nutritious and varied diet and ample opportunity to exercise. This can be achieved through general information via the media, in school, at workplaces, via associations, and not least in sports programs. All levels of education should allocate adequate space for physical activity and the development of practical skills related to diet and health, including cooking. This is especially important to avoid obesity-promoting lifestyles.

The public needs objective information about obesity and how it can be prevented, and high standards should established for such information. A patronizing attitude must be avoided, and the message should be designed to counteract rather than reinforce prejudice and anorectic body image. Here, the media also has an important responsibility for reporting reliable information and not fuel false hopes for "miracle cures".

It is also essential to give the correct message about the relationship between smoking and overweight as regards health risks. Smoking cessation often leads to weight gain. However, this weight gain does not result in health risks that are greater than the risk of continued smoking [4].

Informational interventions are important, but direct interventions to improve dietary and exercise habits are also needed. Potential measures to influence the food supply include higher standards for labeling and information about the fat content in products (not least in ready-cooked meals), taxes adjusted to nutritional content, and certain restrictions in food advertising.

Structural measures to form a society that stimulates greater physical activity appear to be increasingly urgent. Examples would include safe and well-lit walking and bicycle pathways, and playgrounds and exercise facilities that are easily accessible to citizens. Other feasible examples include walkways and planning schemes that make it convenient and natural to walk, even to somewhat remote parking areas and bus stops, and also stairs and stairwells that offer attractive alternatives to escalators and elevators.

References

1. Prioriteringsutredningens slutrapport, Vårdens svåra val. SOU;1995. Rapport Nr 5.

2. Beauchamp T, Childress J. Principles of biomedical ethics. Oxford University Press 5th edn., New York. 2001.

3. Braet C, Mervielde I, Vandereycken W. Psychological aspects of childhood obesity: a controlled study in a clinical and nonclinical sample. J Pediatr Psychol 1997;22(1):59-71.

4. Danielsson T, Rössner S, Westin A. Open randomised trial of intermittent very low energy diet together with nicotine gum for stopping smoking in women who gained weight in previous attempts to quit. BMJ 1999;319 (7208): 490-3; discussion 494.

5. Gortmaker SL, Must A, Perrin JM, Sobol AM, Dietz WH. Social and economic consequences of overweight in adolescence and young adulthood. N Engl J Med 1993;329(14): 1008-12.

6. Holland AJ, Wong J. Genetically determined obesity in Prader-Willi syndrome: the ethics and legality of treatment. J Med Ethics 1999;25(3):230-6.

7. Klesges RC, Klem ML, Hanson CL, Eck LH, Ernst J, O'Laughlin D, et al. The effects of applicant's health status and qualifications on simulated hiring decisions. Int J Obes 1990;14(6):527-35.

8. Lustig A. Weight loss programs: failing to meet ethical standards? J Am Diet Assoc 1991;91(10):1252-4.

9. Proietto J. Why staying lean is not a matter of ethics. Med J Aust 1999;171(11-12):611-3.

10. Rothblum E, Brand P, Miller C, Oetien H. The relationship between obesity, employment discrimination and employment-related victimization. J Vocat Behav 1990;37(3):251-66.

11. Rothblum E, Miller C, Garbutt B. Stereotypes of obese female job applicants. Int J Eat Disord 1988;7(2): 277-83.

Glossary and Definitions (see also Section 4.6.6)

Androgens
Male sex hormones.

Atherosclerosis
A type of arteriosclerosis, i. e., thickening of the walls of the arteries.

Blinding
Measures to keep certain central conditions in a study confidential until the study is complete and the results are to be analyzed. The most important example: in a blinded clinical treatment trial it is not known which of the participants receive which of the forms of treatment being tested. An important piece of information is from whom the information has been kept secret – the subjects, the investigator, and/or statistician.

Double-blind: Neither the patient nor the doctor knows whether or not an agent contains an active substance.

Single-blind: The doctor, but not the patient, knows whether or not an agent contains an active substance.

BMI
Body Mass Index – weight (kg)/[height (m)]^2.

Cohort study
A study concerning a group of persons who form a cohort, i. e. have certain defined qualities in common (e. g., everyone who was treated for a certain disease during a particular period). Usually, the study concerns two or more different subgroups in the cohort which are to be compared in the long-term, e. g., as regards survival or the origin of obesity. This approach has the disadvantage that the groups were not formed by *randomization*, and therefore may not be fully comparable.

Treating and Preventing Obesity. Edited by J. Östman, M. Britton, E. Jonsson
Copyright © 2004 WILEY-VCH Verlag GmbH & Co. KGaA, Weinheim
ISBN 3-527-30818-0

Comorbidity
Concurrent disease. The presence of a disease in the participants of the study other than the one being investigated. Comorbidity may be disadvantageous, since the groups are less uniform. However, in many cases, it has the advantage of reflecting the actual condition in the population (e. g., that people with high blood pressure often have another cardiovascular disease).

Completers
Those who completed a study.

Compliance
Complying with the prescribed treatment.

Controlled trial
A trial that is comparative, i. e., the participants are divided into two or more groups. The most common example is a controlled *clinical trial*, but also *case-control trial* and *cohort trial* are under this classification.

Control group
The group in a clinical trial that receives inactive treatment, e. g., placebo or the current standard treatment. The results of the group are compared to those in a group receiving new treatment, e. g., a new drug. The term also indicates the control group in *case-control trial*.

Cost effectiveness analysis
Health-economic analysis calculating the cost per achieved effect for a given treatment, e. g., cost per kg weight reduction or per QALY. Enables comparisons to be made between treatment methods.

CPAP (Continuous Positive Airway Pressure)
Spontaneous breathing against continuous positive pressure via a breathing mask.

Cross-sectional study
A study of the relationship between diseases and other variables in a defined population at a given time. Example: The subjects are interviewed about their diet and exercise habits, and are examined for body weight, blood sugar, and blood cholesterol.

Dropout
Those (patients or healthy test subjects) who agreed to participate in a study, but who quit before it was completed.

Evidence
Information found to indicate that a certain condition prevails (from the Latin evidentia or "clarity"). In the phrase *evidence-based medicine*, the term "evidence" refers to systematic observations that meet scientifically reliable criteria in such a manner that they are considered to constitute the "best available evidence". Evidence is often generally available as published facts or possibly in systematic reviews or meta-analyses based on scientific methods for summarizing and commenting on all available publications on such facts.

Evidence grade
The strength of a conclusion, whereby Evidence Grade 1 refers to the best-supported conclusions and Evidence Grade 3 refers to the least-supported, but yet scientific, conclusions (Chapter 2).

Exclusion criteria
Circumstances that would prevent someone from participating in a study. These criteria should be specified in the study protocol. Example: a condition, in addition to the one studied, which can be expected to interfere with the assessment. Pregnancy is an exclusion criterion in nearly all drug trials.

Followup
Regular studies, during a given time period, of the participants in an intervention or cohort study.

Frequency
How often something occurs, or how many individuals belong to a particular category.

Gastric bypass
A surgical method used to treat obesity, being the best-documented method in terms of weight loss, long-term results, and complications (Chapter 4.6).

Glucose tolerance test
Test to study the body's ability to metabolize glucose. Decreased capacity = risk of developing diabetes.

HbA$_1$, HbA$_{1C}$ (Hemoglobin A$_{1C}$)
The part of the protein hemoglobin (in red blood cells) which contains glucose. The content reflects the blood glucose level during the preceding 1- to 2-month period. Previously HbA$_1$ was measured by a nonspecific method. Currently, the more specific HbA$_{1C}$ is measured.

HDL cholesterol (HDL)
Cholesterol bound to high-density lipoproteins (HDL), "good cholesterol".

Hyperlipidemia
Elevated blood lipids.

Hypertension
Elevated blood pressure.

Incitement
Stimulus, releasing impulse.

Inclusion criteria
The conditions which need to prevail for a person to be eligible to participate in a study. The criteria, which should be specified in the project plan, may concern a particular diagnosis, age group, etc.

Insulin resistance
Decreased effect of insulin.

Intention-to-treat analysis, ITT
Analysis of results (in a clinical trial) by applying the "intention to treat" principle. This means that results from all participating patients are included, even results from patients who did not comply with the treatment (e. g., stopped taking test drugs after a time). Intention-to-treat analysis is desirable, since the results of some participants might otherwise be excluded on insufficient or incorrect grounds.

Intervention study
A study where the participants are exposed to an intervention, usually treatments (drug, operation, etc.) for a disease or measures to prevent disease.

Investigation
In a medical context, this term may refer to a physical examination of a patient in routine health care, or a scientific investigation, i. e. a study.

KAL
Energy-reduced diet.

Ketones
A group of organic substances (e. g., beta-hydroxybutyric acid and others) which are formed in an increased amount, e. g., during starvation as end products of fat metabolism.

LDL cholesterol (LDL)
Cholesterol bound to low-density lipoproteins (LDL), "bad cholesterol".

Leptin
A hormone which is secreted from fat cells and signals the brain when to stop eating.

Liquid protein diet
Protein-rich drinks that are used to replace ordinary food.

Mean value (Mv)
Mean, arithmetic mean value, average. The sum of all observation numbers divided by the number of observations.

Morbid obesity
Also referred to as extreme obesity, usually of patients with a BMI of > 40.

Morbidity
Ill health, i. e., any departure from a state of well-being.

Mortality
The term may be used in two different ways. It may refer either to
(a) the number of deaths per year in a given number of people (usually 100 000), or
(b) all deaths in an entire population (country, gender, age group, etc.) or from a given cause of death.

Mortality rate
A rate that expresses the proportion of a population that die from a disease or from all causes.

Moxibustion
Method used in traditional Chinese medicine where mugwort is placed on an acupuncture point and burned.

Multicenter study
A study in which several different health care centers participate.

Nadir
Lowest or deepest point (the point diametrically opposite to the zenith).

Nihilism
Negative attitude, aversion, complete denial, disbelief in the value of treatment.

Normal weight
The weight at which the risk of mortality and morbidity is not increased. The WHO definition is BMI 20–25.

Peristalsis
Wavelike contraction and relaxation of the muscles in the gastrointestinal tract that force the contents onward.

Placebo
Pharmacologically inactive treatment used to compare effects and side effects with those of active treatment. The most common forms of placebo are inactive pharmacological agents (e. g., sugar pills or "blind pills"). In some situations, placebo measures may be used in trials of surgery, physical therapy, etc.

Polycystic ovaries (PCO)
Ovarian disease composed of many cysts – often associated with insulin resistance, indicating risk of type 2 diabetes.

Ponderal index
Weight (kg)/[height (m)]^3.

Population
A group of persons who share common characteristics, e. g., all citizens of a certain country with a specific disease. Clinical trials are usually based on a sample of the population, e. g., those with a specific diagnosis who are known at a certain clinic, live in the immediate area, agree to participate in the trial, and fulfill the inclusion and exclusion criteria. Such a sample can also be called a study population.

Pound (unit of weight)
1 lb (pound) = Approx. 0.45 kg.

Prevalence
Occurrence, expressed as, e. g., number of people with a given disease per 100 000 inhabitants.

Prevention
Prophylaxis, preventive medical intervention, e. g., vaccination or intervention to keep people from becoming overweight or obese.

Primary prevention
Interventions aimed at preventing disease, e. g., obesity, from occurring in the general population.

Publication bias
In published results of studies, bias resulting from the preference of investigators, and even journal editors, to publish trials that report good results, i. e., showing that treatment makes a difference, usually a positive difference favoring treatment. Studies often remain unpublished if treatment is not shown to make a difference. Hence, treatment is often portrayed as having a favorable value although this may not necessarily be justified.

Quality-Adjusted Life-Year (QALY)
Time with decreased health converted to year with full health.

Quality of life
A person's view of his/her life value, as reflected in systematic interviews based on an instrument constructed to evaluate the quality of life. An estimate of quality of life is one of the outcome measures used in many clinical trials.

Randomization
Random distribution of trial participants to treatment and control groups. This reduces the risk of systematic differences arising between the groups. Randomization also makes it possible to assess the probability that the results of the study have arisen by random chance.

Relative risk (RR)
The result in the treatment group in relation to the result in the control group.

RCT
Randomized controlled trial.

Risk factor
A quality or condition that indicates an elevated risk of a person having one or more diseases. Example: prevalence of genetic disease in a family or tobacco smoking.

Sagittal diameter, abdomen
The distance from the base to the highest point of the abdomen in a supine position.

Sample
The units in a population selected for study. In a medical context, a sample consists of the patients (among healthy persons) who have been selected for a study from a larger population. Ideally, the sample would be random, i. e., each person in the population (e. g., everyone in a geographic area with a certain disease) should have had an equal probability of being included in the study. In practice this is seldom fulfilled.

Secondary prevention
Preventive measures aiming at preventing a disease, e. g., recurrence of obesity in people already treated.

SHBG (Sex Hormone Binding Globulin)
A protein in blood plasma which binds and transports sex hormones.

Sleep apnea
Breathing cessation lasting > 10 seconds during sleep.

SOS
Swedish Obese Subjects. Extensive intervention study including a surgical treatment group of more than 2000 patients compared to an equally large control group followed up in primary care. Mentioned in several chapters.

Standard deviation (SD)
A statistical measure of the dispersion of observations around the mean value.

Statistical significance
Statistical significance shows the probability that the results achieved occurred by chance, or a more extreme result even if no difference was present. The level of significance is expressed as a p value, where p stands for probability. The highest risk accepted is often $p = 0.05$. Different significance levels may also be indicated by asterisks: * for $p < 0.05$, ** for $p < 0.01$, and *** for $p < 0.001$.

Study
General term for a scientific trial. The terms "study" and "trial" are used synonymously here. Different types of studies/trials are specified in this glossary.

TG
Triglycerides. A type of fat consisting of glycerol with all three hydroxyl groups esterified with a fatty acid. The fat in food consists mainly of TG.

Thermogenesis
Heat production. The energy that is lost in the form of heat and is influenced by what we eat.

VLCD
Very Low Calorie Diet, defined as products, usually from protein sources such as milk and soy products, giving a balanced, adequate diet, but only between 400 and 800 kcal per day.

WHR
Waist/Hip circumference Ratio = The circumference of the waist divided by the circumference of the body at the hip.

Index

Treating and Preventing Obesity. Edited by J. Östman, M. Britton, E. Jonsson
Copyright © 2004 WILEY-VCH Verlag GmbH & Co. KGaA, Weinheim
ISBN 3-527-30818-0